HULL

CULTURE, HISTORY, PLACE

Edited by

David J. Starkey, David Atkinson,
Briony McDonagh, Sarah McKeon
and Elisabeth Salter

LIVERPOOL UNIVERSITY PRESS

First published 2017 by
Liverpool University Press
4 Cambridge Street
Liverpool
L69 7ZU

British Library Cataloguing-in-Publication data
A British Library CIP record is available

Front cover image: The Deep aquarium and tidal barrier on the River Humber
seen from Corporation Pier, Hull. Mark Buckle/Alamy Stock Photo.

Back cover image: 'Trawler – Made in Hull' © Mike Bartlett
(www.mikebartlettphotography.com).

Front endpaper: 'Bird's-eye view' of Hull, 1880. Image courtesy of Guildhall,
Hull: Hull Museums.

Back endpaper: 'General Development', from Lutyens and Abercrombie,
Plan for Hull (1945).

ISBN 978-1-78138-419-0 HB
ISBN 978-1-78138-420-6 PB
ISBN 978-1-78138-421-3 special edition in slipcase

Typeset by Carnegie Publishing Ltd, Lancaster

Printed and bound by Gomer Press, Llandysul, Wales

HULL
CULTURE, HISTORY, PLACE

Contents

Acknowledgements

Hull: Culture, History, Place had its origins in the wave of creative energy unleashed by the announcement on 20 November 2013 that Hull was to be the UK City of Culture in 2017. In thanking those who contributed to the production of this book, we (the editorial team of David Atkinson, Briony McDonagh, Sarah McKeon, Elisabeth Salter and David J. Starkey) therefore acknowledge with pleasure the part played by the people from all walks of Hull life who not only conceived of their city as a place worthy of this award, but then converted their vision into a reality.

Responding positively to this opportunity, and to an expression of interest from Liverpool University Press, we decided to initiate a scheme to produce in 2017 a new perspective on Hull's historical and cultural development. In executing this design, we greatly benefited from the investment of time, skill and resource by various groups of collaborators. Without funding, this project would not have progressed, and so we were very fortunate in acquiring financial support from the Ferens Education Trust, largely through the skilful agency of two of our colleagues at the University of Hull – Professor Glenn Burgess (Deputy Vice Chancellor) and Dr John McLoughlin (Director of Development, Alumni and External Affairs) – to whom we owe a great debt of gratitude. On this secure basis, the volume was crafted by the authors of the chapters and vignettes that comprise the book, and we are delighted to salute the research and writing efforts of the 22 experts who contributed knowledge and insight into our collective interpretation of the character and significance of Hull. Support for the work of these contributors was generously provided by and gratefully received from the staff at the British Library, the Victoria and Albert Museum, the National Trust, Ferens Art Gallery, Hull Maritime Museum, Hull City Council Archaeology, the Hepworth Wakefield, the National Fairground Archive at the University of Sheffield, the Borthwick Institute for Archives at the University of York, and various other museums and heritage organisations. We owe special thanks to our colleagues at Hull History Centre, notably to Simon Wilson (University of Hull Archivist) and Martin Taylor (Hull City Council Archivist), whose informed and enthusiastic help proved invaluable. Moreover, in the conception, planning and production of the book, we profited strongly from the exceptional editorial and publishing professionalism (and patience) of staff at Liverpool University Press, especially Alison Welsby (Editorial Director), Patrick Brereton, Andrew Kirk and Heather Gallagher.

In drawing upon this stock of expertise, we hope to have captured the essence of the distinctive, inspiring and mundane histories and cultures of the people who over many centuries have lived, worked, loved, fought and died in a very particular place on the Yorkshire bank of the River Humber in eastern central England. Evolving from settlement to city, this place has never become the heart of a conurbation. Yet, as the pages that follow make clear, Hullensians, Hullness and Hull – properly known, perhaps, as the King's Town on the River Hull – have played many a significant role in the human dramas that have unfolded on local, national and global stages since the earliest times.

The Editorial Team
Hull, 2017

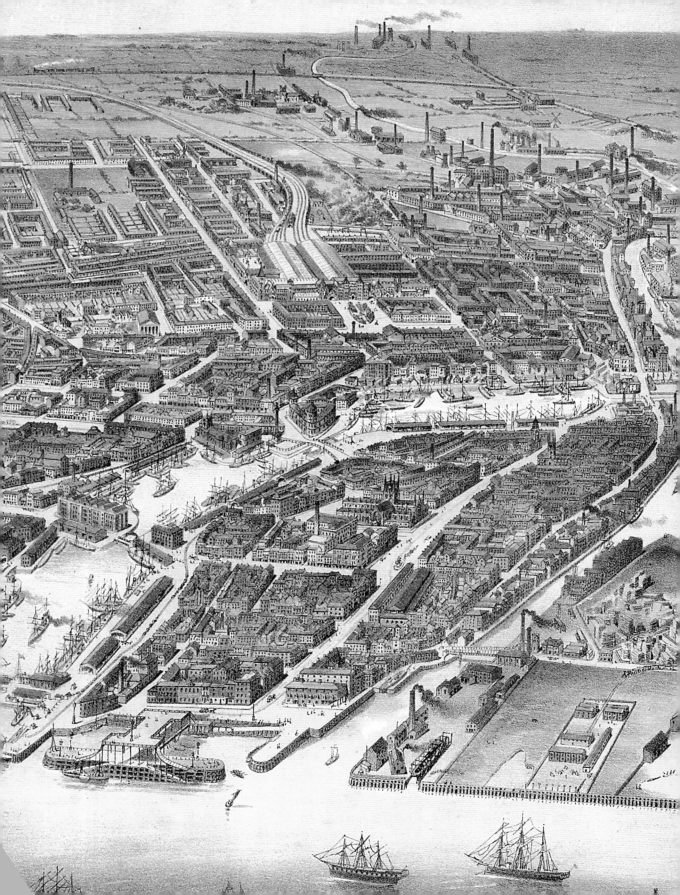

Introduction

DAVID ATKINSON, BRIONY McDONAGH,
SARAH McKEON, ELISABETH SALTER,
DAVID J. STARKEY and MARTIN WILCOX

When your train comes to rest in Paragon Station against a row of docile buffers, you alight with an end-of-the-line sense of freedom. Signs in foreign languages welcome you. Outside is a working city, yet one neither clenched in the blackened grip of the industrial revolution nor hiding behind a cathedral to pretend it is York or Canterbury. Unpretentious, recent, full of shops and special offers like a television commercial, it might be Australia or America, until you come upon Trinity House or the Dock Offices. For Hull has its own sudden elegancies.

People are slow to leave it, quick to return. And there are others who come, as they think, for a year or two, and stay a lifetime, sensing that they have found a city that is in the world, yet sufficiently on the edge of it to have a different resonance. Behind Hull is the plain of Holderness, lonelier and lonelier, and after that the birds and lights of Spurn Head, and then the sea. One can go ten years without seeing these things, yet they are always there, giving Hull the air of having its face half-turned towards distance and silence, and what lies beyond them.[1]

For over 700 years Kingston upon Hull has played unique and crucial roles in the histories of Britain and northern Europe. Throughout this period Hull has been a port of central importance to trade and exchange. It was a place where the peoples, commodities and finances of the northern European world connected, it has been the third port of Britain by trade at various times, and it was a town of great wealth and social significance as a result. Hull has also been a city of major political and military importance. This place was pivotal to the abolition of slavery in the British Empire in 1833, to prompting the English Civil War in 1642, and to resisting the

Hull in its region, from the Land Utilisation Survey of Great Britain, carried out during the 1930s.
© L. Dudley Stamp/Geographical Publications Ltd, Audrey N. Clark, Environment Agency/DEFRA and Great Britain Historical GIS

blitz on British cities in the 1940s. Hull also played major roles in the success of the 1688 Glorious Revolution and the defeat of the 1536 Pilgrimage of Grace uprising. These episodes changed British history and shaped global affairs – and Hull was central to them all.

Hull has also been a vibrant city of industry, commerce and business across a series of trades and manufacturing sectors. It was a world-leading whaling port in the early nineteenth century, and was central to the commodity culture that grew up around highly lucrative whale oil and other products. Hull subsequently became home to the world's largest distant-water fishing fleet, and when landed for processing and transportation, the fish transformed British food cultures. Hull also carved out prominent manufacturing and processing roles in the industrial revolution and, subsequently, in shipbuilding, pharmaceuticals, chemical products and oil processing. These roles likewise saw Hull transform aspects of modern consumer cultures and catalyse industrial progress in Britain and further afield.

Hull has also been a location of marked cultural creativity, producing leading writers, poets, dramatists, actors and musicians – many of whom benefited from a distinctive, independent voice and perspective forged in this different, inimitable place. Philip Larkin, one of the most famous local writers, lived in the city from 1955 and wrote the lines that preface this introduction in 1982 as the foreword for an anthology of work by other Hull poets. For one recent commentator they are 'a model of graceful and unemotional praise for his adoptive city'.[2] Thirty-one years later, Tom Courtenay, one of Hull's most celebrated actors, spoke some of Larkin's words over the well-received film that promoted Hull's bid to be UK City of Culture, 2017. Once again, words about 'sudden elegancies' and a 'different resonance' conveyed a sense of Hull and its idiosyncratic character to wider audiences. These creative people, and their original voices, helped to shape how Britons understood their world and, in turn, how the world made sense of Britain. Some of them, like Larkin and Courtenay, also help us to think about the character of twentieth-century Hull.[3]

For the planning and architectural commentator Adrian Jones, 'Kingston upon Hull is a great city, one of the most distinctive and unusual places in England.'[4] In all the ways mentioned above, Hull has played significant roles in British and global history. The pages that follow outline these themes in more detail and set the scene for the subsequent chapters.

The making of cities

Cities are produced by the flows of economic, social, cultural and political actors and processes (like those outlined above) that coincide and collide in particular places over time. Through this incremental process, these flows and collisions produce distinctive, unique cities. Thus, Hull has been produced by trade, cargoes, shipping, sailors and dockers; by commodities such as whales, fish, wood and oil; by politics, ideas, abolitionists and campaigners; by migrants and different ethnic groups; and by the cultural figures whom the city has produced and the audiences they forged. Further, these activities generated great wealth and prestige that established Hull as a significant city in Britain and Europe. This wealth and importance also informed local civic pride and a positive sense of Hull's identity and role during much of its history.

In 1354 the wealthy merchant William de la Pole founded a hospital for poor people to the north of the walled town. The hospital was incorporated into the Carthusian priory, or Charterhouse, that was founded by Michael de la Pole, Earl of Suffolk, on the same site in 1379. Five years later the hospital was separated from the priory, which ensured its survival when the priory was dissolved in 1538. The patronage of the hospital was taken over by Hull Corporation in 1552. Destroyed at the start of the English Civil War in 1643, the hospital and master's house were rebuilt in 1649–50, with further additions, including a chapel, in the 1660s–1670s. The northern section of the hospital, with a handsome Georgian chapel, was rebuilt in its present form in 1778–80.
David and Susan Neave

All these factors collided and enmeshed at the confluence of the rivers Humber and Hull to create the town, then later (from 1897) the city of Kingston upon Hull, more commonly known as Hull. This book focuses on the histories, development and geographies of this proud city and on various key episodes and processes that have brought Hull into being over the centuries.[5] How did Hull come to be so distinctive? How did it develop into this singular place? How were its cultures and characteristics and its marked sense of place shaped by the many actors that, collectively and over the years, generated this great city? And how can we make sense of these histories and their legacies in the twenty-first century? This book tackles these questions, and opens by briefly considering three elements that help to make Hull a specific place: water, commodities and the people of Hull.

Top left Maister House, High Street. A particular feature of this elegant eighteenth-century merchant's house, now owned by the National Trust, is its impressive staircase with Robert Bakewell's wrought-iron balustrade, while the walls feature decorated stucco panels by Joseph Page and a fine statue of Ceres by Sir Henry Cheere. Portraits on the staircase depict members of the historically significant Maister family.
David and Susan Neave

Water

Hull has been shaped by the water that girdles it and by the various hinterlands that this water connects. Hull's origins and growth were prompted by the confluence of the Humber estuary and the River Hull's safe harbour which enabled the town's port functions to become established in the medieval period (see Chapter 1). Its subsequent growth as a regional and international port was enabled by the Humber, which connected Hull to the river systems of most of central and northern England.[6] These rivers, and later canals, funnelled trade through Hull to the rest of the world. In turn, the Humber served as an entry point for goods from around the globe which made their way into Britain along these watery routes (the Humber drains about 20% of England). Hull thus became a strategic, hugely successful and wealthy transhipment point, where smaller rivercraft transferred cargoes and people travelling to and from the heart of England on to larger, seagoing vessels that sailed out across the ocean.[7] Some grew wealthy from this trading, and the town, and its sense of community and civic identity, developed (see Chapter 4).

Maritime trade continued to flourish over the centuries. To facilitate trade and transhipment further, the docks grew around the historic centre, surrounding Hull's Old Town with water until the 1930s. As industrialisation developed in the nineteenth century, docks were built along the Humber foreshore too, extending stretches of enclosed, industrialised water seven miles along the estuary banks (see Chapter 5). The parallel flow of other commodities through the port accelerated as the industrial revolution transformed the economies and exports of the English north and Midlands. The water that surrounded Hull enabled its success and wealth; this same water sometimes flooded its streets too.

Hull was shaped by its hinterlands, ashore and at sea, which were connected by these waterways. The town was moulded in turn by the politics, traditions and cultures of these surrounding and connected regions. Hull's long-standing maritime hinterland included traditional trading partners in northern Europe, and the cities of the Hanseatic League that stretched across the North Sea and into the Baltic. This sustained engagement with the Hansa ports left traces in the medieval and early modern town's commercial growth, its architecture, and its crafts and decorative cultures.[8] Hull merchants often had family representatives based elsewhere around northern Europe, and in turn, northern Europeans made Hull their home and helped to make their adopted base a more multicultural place (see Chapter 6). These ties were all enabled by the shuttling of ships, people and goods across the seas and along estuaries and rivers. In these respects, too, water moulded Hull.

In addition, in the eighteenth and nineteenth centuries, as maritime technologies advanced, the town developed new hinterlands in distant Arctic waters as its seafarers pursued the 'right whales' that fuelled Hull's world-leading whaling industry.[9] This was a business initially transacted afloat, as whales were pursued, caught, killed and then partially processed while the ships returned to port. Once the carcasses reached Hull, they were shipped up the River Hull to a district that had evolved just north of the Old Town on the river banks. Here, the whales came ashore to be processed in the so-called 'Greenland yards' (named after the seas around Greenland where the right whales were hunted). The whale oil and whalebone that were produced became central to Britain's expanding consumer capitalism of the late eighteenth century. Their many commercial applications made these commodities highly valuable, and Hull was a centre of this pivotal maritime industry.[10]

From the mid-nineteenth century whaling declined, but attention turned to the expanding fishing opportunities of the North Sea. In the later nineteenth and twentieth centuries, Hull's trawling fleet sailed out to forge a lucrative, and particularly dangerous, distant-water fishing industry in the North Atlantic and Arctic regions.[11] The fish were partially processed on the journey home, but the town was reshaped once more by the infrastructure of docks and transport, and the support and processing industries that enabled the fishing industry and that were driven by the growing demand for this marine resource (see Chapter 8). The particular rhythms of trawling, and the absence of the trawlermen (who lived most of their working lives afloat and were far from their families for weeks at a time), also created a very particular community and culture around Hessle Road and St Andrew's Dock (the 'fish dock').[12] The mutual support and community that developed among the women and children of the district was a response to the way that this crucial 'local' industry was stretched across the North Atlantic Ocean (see Chapter 10). Hence the city, and its major business for a century, were shaped by a relationship with, and across, water.

The third home of the Dock Company was built at the junction of Queen's Dock (formerly the Old Dock) and Prince's Dock (1868–71). Hull Maritime Museum has occupied the building, with its splendid domes, since the mid-1970s.
David and Susan Neave

Thos. Wilson Sons & Co. Ltd was a large-scale shipping firm that dominated Hull's maritime interests from the 1860s to the First World War. Reputed to be the world's largest privately owned shipping company, the Wilson Line and its many subsidiaries were administered from the offices shown here, which lie at the junction of Commercial Road and Kingston Street.
David and Susan Neave

Commodities

Hull's distinctive nature was also shaped by the commodities and produce that were shipped back and forth through the growing port. The production of wool, leather and bricks in medieval Yorkshire saw these materials shipped out of the region through Hull (in return for the timber, wine, various foodstuffs and building materials that were imported from the continent). The town centre was full of quays and warehouses to store and transfer these commodities. These buildings were financed by the craft guilds and the merchant families that flourished on the back of this commerce. In the nineteenth and twentieth centuries the port handled the coal, iron and steel produced by its industrialising hinterland and exported them to markets in the British Isles and further afield. The shipping and financial services that enabled these exports also grew apace: Hull's Wilson Line became the largest privately owned shipping line in the world.[13] These commodities and their associated services generated riches and influence for their local owners and commercial sectors; they likewise produced dockland, transport and storage infrastructure across swathes of the growing town – helping to shape its particular nature.

The flows of commodities also reshaped the social and community structure of the growing town. The people who moved to work in the expanding docks and their connected industries forged working-class districts, communities and cultures which became entrenched as the years passed. The dockworkers of East Hull and the fishing community of Hessle Road are two obvious examples. In turn, the families who controlled the growing industries, the commodities they produced, and their trade and transport first built impressive town houses on and around High Street (see Chapter 4), and later moved to elite suburbs (such as the Avenues). As this modern, industrial society emerged, its component communities, and the increasingly separate locations where they lived, each shaped Hull's growth in particular ways.

Hull's industrial and commercial success in the Victorian and Edwardian period was fuelled by other commodities and their associated industries that reshaped the city. Grain mills, oil-seed mills and oil-processing plants developed alongside the River Hull (often adapting sites vacated by the declining whale-processing trade). Other associated industries such as paint manufacturing evolved in this corridor, while chemicals, pharmaceuticals and medical industries developed a little further from the river. Shipbuilders and ancillary businesses (such as chandlery and maritime engineering) located on the Humber shore to the east and west of the centre, and the long-standing Scandinavian and eastern European timber trade became increasingly focused around Victoria Dock. As the port continued to grow, the railways, roads and wharfs that served it reworked Hull's singular geography still further.

In sum, the import and export of commodities, the processing of these commodities, and the production and distribution of manufactured goods helped to forge the specific contours of Hull's economy. Equally, the money, wealth and prestige that all this business generated reworked Hull's social structures and its geographical form, rendering it a distinctive city in additional ways.

This 'bird's-eye view' from 1880 clearly shows Hull Town Docks, with Queen's Dock, Prince's Dock and Humber Dock following the line of the walls that protected the medieval town from attack. With the River Hull flowing north, what is now the Old Town of Hull was virtually an island in the middle of a ring of navigable water.
Guildhall, Hull: Hull Museums

People

One further element that affected the particular form, growth and nature of Hull over the centuries were the groups, communities and individuals that constituted the town and influenced how it, and its particular civic consciousness, developed. Hull can trace its origins to the initial settlement of Wyke, which was founded by Cistercian monks from nearby Meaux Abbey in the late twelfth century. The Church, the clergy and religious fraternities played roles in the area subsequently. The town was granted a charter by Edward I in 1299 and signs of a civic awareness developed from this point onwards.[14] In a growing medieval settlement, with an outward-looking focus on trade and commodities, civic consciousness derived in part from the rules and customs of its medieval guilds. In Hull these included the wealthy Hull Trinity House, which was associated with maritime business and controlled navigation in the Humber. Further afield, the trading privileges granted by the Hanseatic League also shaped Hull's outlook, perspectives and sense of its particular international role. The flows of people from Europe and other parts of the British Isles likewise date from the earliest years of Hull.[15] As with all ports, many different groups passed through or worked in the town as part of its trading and transhipment business. Some groups and individuals moved to Hull deliberately; others were transmigrants passing through who decided to stay; others were escaping persecution or displaced by wars.[16] Hence, since its origins, migrants have contributed to Hull's social and cultural profile.

Hull's sense of identity as a trading town was reinforced subsequently by the merchant families and other traders of the seventeenth and eighteenth centuries who nurtured a growing pride in Hull as its profile and reputation grew.[17] This civic sense was promoted further by various Victorian industrialists, shipowners and philanthropists who donated funds to improve the town. Local industrialists such as Thomas Ferens and James Reckitt inaugurated parks, libraries, arts infrastructure and a university through their philanthropy. This was needed. The nineteenth century was a period of significant growth in Hull as the expansion of British industrial and mercantile capitalism continued to generate great development and, for some, considerable wealth. But this growth also entailed social and health problems for the poor. The slums that emerged in nineteenth-century Hull contributed to the cholera epidemic of 1849 which killed over 1,800 people.[18] In partial response, alliances of churches, guilds and local authorities prompted the gradual appearance of schools, healthcare and public services throughout the nineteenth century. By the time Hull had been granted city status in 1897, elegant and leafy suburbs were shaped by, and for, the middle and upper classes – some of whom also commissioned architects to realise further parks and public institutions for their city. The council also created additional sites for the arts and learning, and new civic structures such as the Guildhall and City Hall, in a city that demonstrated a 'fin de siècle confidence and … civic pomp [that was] breathtaking'.[19] Space was also made for popular leisure pursuits and sports, especially rugby league, which became embedded in local cultures and helped to distinguish Hull (see Chapter 7). Significant

Corporation Pier and the Minerva public house, c. 1900. The movement of goods has always gone hand in hand with the movement of people. In the late Victorian and Edwardian periods, distinct areas of Hull dealt with different commodities and trade processes. Small businesses, such as hotels and lodging houses, were vital for welcoming and accommodating those coming to Hull for business and pleasure, while cab services were important for transporting traders and business people across the city, joining the dots between the different trade, commerce and produce sectors.
Nick Cox: http://www.disused-stations.org.uk/h/hull_corporation_pier/hull_corporation(c1900_nick_cox)pier_old6.jpg

slum clearance and new housing policies to benefit the working classes were also initiated in the twentieth century, and this process was accelerated by the bomb damage of the Second World War (see Chapter 9).[20]

Hull enjoys an often-stated reputation as an independent, free-thinking place – and this, too, contributes to its self-perception as a different kind of city. As mentioned above, this was the town where the local elite closed Beverley Gate to King Charles I and accelerated the onset of the English Civil War (see Chapter 3). Hull survived two sieges in 1642 and 1643 as a rare parliamentarian outpost in the English North. Hull was the town where William Wilberforce grew up, which he represented in Parliament, and from which he felt able to campaign against slavery. Hull was the home city of Amy Johnson, who defied gender expectations to fly to Australia in 1930. It was the place where anti-fascists battled Oswald Mosley's Blackshirts in the 1930s, where Lil Bilocca led the struggle for safer conditions on trawlers, and it was a centre of activity for suffragists, strikers and protesters challenging established norms. During the same period, Hull refused to subsume its telephone system into the national post office structure, keeping its own telephone exchange. It was the home of original voices in the arts such as Andrew Marvell, Winifred Holtby and Philip Larkin. Most recently, Hull earned its status as UK City of Culture for 2017 partially thanks to the specific and distinct 'Hullness' of the city's culture.

Finally, Hull is also seen as being different and unique by visitors from elsewhere. For some, such as writer and social commentator J. B. Priestley on his 1934 *English Journey*, it is the city's geographical location that makes it different.[21] Seen from the rest of England, Hull appears to be peripheral: a port tight against the east coast, detached from the heartland of Yorkshire and England more generally, with only Holderness between it and the sea. For much of its history the broad Humber estuary fostered the impression that Hull was divided from the lands to the south too. In recent years, this sense of remoteness from everywhere else has been articulated by various media voices. In turn, local communities sometimes reproduce these sentiments, expressing alienation from London or other distant centres of power and authority. But as the preceding pages have suggested, Hull's history is one of centrality to various trading routes. Indeed, ships registered in Hull, and carrying commodities and manufactured goods to and from the city, displayed the name 'Hull' on their sterns in ports around the world. This was a place with a global presence, and one that functioned as a hub for the flows of people, ideas, wealth and influence in and out of England, and throughout the wider world. In all these ways Hull is different.

Celebrating Hull

Hull was shaped over the centuries by this collision of people, commodities, ideas and trade, and the flow of these elements across and through various hinterlands and regions elsewhere. The result is a distinctive city with a long-standing, varied,

Hull is the only city in Britain to have its own independently operated telephone system. It was wholly owned by Hull City Council from 1902 to 1999, when over 50 per cent of the enterprise was sold to Kingston Communications (now KCOM). The council sold its remaining 157,499,999 shares in 2007. Hull's distinctive 'white' telephone boxes – 'cream' would be a more accurate description – are the same design (K6) as those of the General Post Office, designed by Sir Giles Gilbert Scott in 1935. Hull's K6s, however, did not include the Royal Crown emblem. The white phone boxes were largely redundant by the early twenty-first century, but their removal sparked a local public outcry and a number were therefore left as a reminder of one of Hull's many successful independent local businesses.
David and Susan Neave

proud and often remarkable history. This is a place that has enjoyed long periods of significance, influence and wealth. This dense, entwined heritage is perhaps too deep and too extensive to be captured and encompassed wholly within one book, but in the following chapters various episodes that illuminate the city and its historical roles and significance over several centuries are brought to light and life.

It is too simplistic to read Hull and its history from our contemporary perspectives. Unfortunately, over recent years too many reports about Hull have focused primarily upon current problems. These include the sudden, virtually terminal contraction of the fishing industry, the decline of dock labour (due to containerisation), the relative decline of other traditional industries, and poor school results and social indicators. In part these representations have persisted because of Hull's apparently peripheral location within Britain. The city has struggled to shake off this reputation because, until recently, few people visited and had their assumptions challenged. Furthermore, poor social indicators are in part a reflection of how the city boundaries divide Hull from its natural, wealthier hinterland in the East Riding of Yorkshire. However, the local pride prompted by Hull's status as UK City of Culture is not new. As outlined in the chapters that follow, Hull has often enjoyed wealth and significance through previous centuries. A longer historical perspective undermines more recent partial and problematic representations of Hull and highlights instead its rich, varied and important past. This longer perspective on the city's success is worth celebrating.

By incorporating some of the communities that have been marginalised in previous writing on the city, this book gives voice to these groups and individuals. Formal histories have traditionally been written by privileged groups in society: the learned, the wealthy and the powerful. Too often these people were male and white, and the voices of other social groups were seldom heard. The last few decades have witnessed overdue efforts to include the voices of those previously excluded from history and there have been welcome shifts to include women's voices, the histories of working-class people and ordinary lives, and the voices of the old, the young, and those of different ethnicities, abilities and sexualities. Articulated in this book are the voices of medieval women that survive in their written wills; the essays detailing schoolgirls' experiences of the 1940s blitz; a trawler skipper's life; and the families of the Hessle Road fishing community and the dockers of East Hull. These voices have seldom been heard, but

Andrew Motion, Douglas Dunn and Philip Larkin, 6 November 1979. Philip Larkin was Librarian at the University of Hull's Brynmor Jones library for thirty years. During this time he became something of a mentor to both Andrew Motion and Douglas Dunn. Motion worked as a lecturer at the university during the 1970s, publishing his first volume of poetry at the age of 24 while teaching in Hull. He later became one of Larkin's literary executors and biographer. Dunn took on part-time work in the university's library in 1966 in order to fund his English degree. In 1969 he passed his degree with first class honours, publishing his debut collection of poetry the same year to great critical acclaim.
Hull History Centre, University Photographer Collection (U PHO A4634)

they illuminate our history of the city in fascinating ways: they allow us to retrieve neglected groups and their stories, and to retell more familiar histories in a more comprehensive fashion. This shift towards including additional voices from Hull's history is worth celebrating too.

Across 2017, and through the legacies of the UK City of Culture process, Hull will be visited, researched, reported on and assessed to an unprecedented degree. Much will be said and written about this place: some people will reproduce predictable, long-established narratives, others will look at the city anew. This book will add depth and breadth to these debates. The depth will demonstrate that Hull has been a place of importance, pride and success, of trade, commerce and industry, and of ideas, creativity and vision throughout its history. The breadth will show how Hull has been an innovative, successful city in a range of different activities that encompass industry, trade, commerce, politics, culture and sport. Together, this depth and breadth demonstrate that Hull has made important contributions to Britain and the world in the past. A better understanding of Hull's history helps us to understand Hull's situation today, and the possibilities for Hull's future.

Hull's stance against apartheid is now largely forgotten, but the Museum Gardens were renamed Nelson Mandela Gardens in 1983 as a sign of solidarity with those campaigning against racism in South Africa. Mandela was one of three anti-apartheid activists to be made Honorary Freemen of the City of Kingston upon Hull on 2 July 1987. The other two were Dame Helen Suzman and Archbishop Desmond Tutu. The Freedom Festival, founded in 2007, was one of the events that marked the bicentenary of the Abolition of the Slave Trade Act. It promotes the legacy of Wilberforce and the ongoing campaigns for human rights. The piece of artwork shown here was part of a series marking the life of the post-apartheid president of South Africa, Nelson Mandela, who died in 2013.
Nicholas J. Evans

Notes

1   Philip Larkin, 'Foreword', in Douglas Dunn (ed.), *A Rumoured City: New Poets from Hull* (Newcastle upon Tyne, 1982), p. 9.

2   David Wheatley, 'Dafter than We Care to Own: The Poetry of Place in Some Poets of the North of England', in P. Robinson (ed.), *The Oxford Handbook of Contemporary British and Irish Poetry* (Oxford, 2013), pp. 407–23 (p. 409).

3   Tom Courtenay, *Dear Tom: Letters from Home* (London, 2000).

4   Adrian Jones and Chris Matthews, *Cities of the North* (Nottingham, 2016), p. 131.

5   For general histories of the city, see Keith Allison (ed.), *A History of the County of York East Riding: Volume 1, the City of Kingston upon Hull* (Oxford, 1969); Edward Gillett and Kenneth MacMahon, *A History of Hull* (Hull, 2nd edn, 1989). For the architecture, see David Neave and Susan Neave, *Hull* (London and New Haven, 2010).

6   Susan Neave and Stephen Ellis (eds), *An Historical Atlas of East Yorkshire* (Hull, 1996); Gillett and MacMahon, *A History of Hull*; M. T. Wild, 'The Geographical Shaping of Hull from Pre-industrial to Modern Times', in Stephen Ellis and David Crowther (eds), *Humber Perspectives: A Region through the Ages* (Hull, 1989), pp. 10–19.

7   Jenny Kermode, *Medieval Merchants: York, Beverley and Hull in the Later Middle Ages* (Cambridge, 2002).

8   Gordon Jackson, *Hull in the 18th Century* (London, 1972).

9   Arthur Credland, *The Hull Whaling Trade: An Arctic Enterprise* (Beverley, 1995).

10 Bernard Stonehouse, 'Accounts and Balance Sheet of Hull Whale Fishery Company, 1754–1757', *Polar Record*, 51.3 (2015), pp. 318–29.

11 Jeremy Tunstall, *The Fishermen: The Sociology of an Extreme Occupation* (Hull, 1969).

12 Tunstall, *The Fishermen*.

13 Michaela Barnard and David J. Starkey, 'Private Companies, Culture and Place in the Development of Hull's Maritime Business Sector, c.1860–1914', in G. Harlaftis, S. Tenold and J. M. Valdalaiso (eds), *The World's Key Industry: History and Economics of International Shipping* (Basingstoke, 2012), pp. 200–19.

14 Gillett and MacMahon, *A History of Hull*; Rosemary Horrox, *The Changing Plan of Hull, 1290–1650: A Guide to Documentary Sources for the Early Topography of Hull* (Hull, 1978).

15 Gillett and MacMahon, *A History of Hull*.

16 Nick Evans, 'Indirect Passage from Europe. European Transmigration via the UK, 1836–1914', *Journal for Maritime Research*, 3.1 (2001), pp. 70–84; Nick Evans and Fred Woods, 'Latter-day Saint Scandinavian Migration through Hull, England, 1852–1894', *BYU Studies*, 41.4 (2002), pp. 75–102.

17 Jackson, *Hull in the 18th Century*.

18 Gillett and MacMahon, *A History of Hull*.

19 Jones and Matthews, *Cities of the North*, p. 131.

20 Edwin Lutyens and Patrick Abercrombie, *A Plan for the City & County of Kingston-upon-Hull* (London and Hull, 1945).

21 J. B. Priestley, *English Journey* (London, 1934).

CHAPTER ONE

The Origins and Early Development of Kingston upon Hull:

An Archaeological Perspective

D. H. EVANS

Hull was to develop as a deep-sea port at the confluence of two of Yorkshire's great water systems: the River Hull and the Humber estuary. The physical relief of this area is of relatively recent origin in geological terms, as both the Hull valley and the lower half of the estuary (from about the Humber Bridge to the mouth of the Humber) were formed at the end of the last Ice Age (approximately 16000 to 8000 BC). Hence, it will come as little surprise that the earliest archaeological remains within the confines of the modern city are barely 7,000 years old (a Later Mesolithic stone object from Sutton, dating to perhaps *c.* 4900–4000 BC). This is also a low-lying wetland landscape, something that has not only influenced land-use and the ways in which settlement has subsequently developed, but has also greatly contributed to the quality of survival of buried archaeological remains, particularly those which were made of organic materials. Some parts of the modern city are only about 2 metres above sea level; in the past, they were even lower, as the ground level within the Old Town has been raised substantially since the mid-thirteenth century. In the northern part of the city, ground level is a couple of metres higher, particularly where raised outcrops of till, sands or gravels have formed within the floor of the Hull valley. Those raised outcrops proved to be a very attractive location for early settlement.

This chapter considers the prehistoric origins and the Romano-British settlement of this part of the lower Hull valley. It then discusses evidence for the early medieval settlement of Wyke (Hull's predecessor) before examining the development of the Old Town and the growth of Hull as a major port and town during the Middle Ages.

Prehistoric origins: Mesolithic to Bronze Age

The lower Hull valley, in common with neighbouring parts of the Hull valley (now the East Riding of Yorkshire), was a very different landscape during the Middle and New Stone Age (respectively, the Mesolithic and the Neolithic), the Bronze Age and the Iron Age from the one we encounter today, and this section covers what happened in those parts of the lower Hull valley that now lie within the city limits. The Humber shoreline lay much further inland throughout the prehistoric era than it does now. While its precise position will have fluctuated somewhat as the climate deteriorated between the Bronze and Iron Ages, the shoreline would have lain at least half a mile (0.8 km) further to the north than the current line of the Humber – and, at times, considerably further inland. Activity begins with nomadic hunter-gatherers living off the rich food resources represented by the fish, birds and animals occupying the wetlands of the river valley. This was superseded by the introduction of agriculture during the Neolithic and Bronze Ages, and followed by the development of permanent settlements during the Iron Age. Finds of Early Bronze Age boats from the foreshore near North Ferriby (to the west of Hull) show that ocean-going boats were being used on the Humber as early as about 1800 BC. Hence, the local peoples of this area may well have had contacts not only with those living in other parts of the Humber region, but also with Europe, even at this early date. Later finds of imported European metalwork and pottery show clearly that cultural exchanges of goods were taking place in this area during the later Bronze Age and the Iron Age.

During the Later Mesolithic era, at the beginning of the fifth millennium BC, the area of the modern city occupied the floor of the valley, and would have been wet and marshy. The River Hull, particularly near its mouth, may have fanned out into a number of streams rather than forming just one deep cutting as it does today; and there are likely to have been alder and willow trees close to its banks, and stretches of salt-marsh with clumps of reeds and other plants typical of those environments. Towards the better-drained sides of the valley would have been small woods and groves of oak, birch and hazel, along with bushes and scrub. This varied environment would have provided rich grazing and nesting possibilities for the local wildlife, and these, in turn, would have attracted hunter-gatherers.

The study of geological bore-hole data suggests that parts of the central area were covered with a thick layer of peat and bog oak *c.* 4900 BC. Peat deposits have also been found in the suburbs (for example at Kingswood) – though of much younger date, radiocarbon samples have demonstrated that peat formation was taking place *c.* 3290 BC at Stoneferry, and at 2355–2280 cal BC at Saltshouse Road – that is, both during the Early and the Late Neolithic period (*c.* 4400 –*c.* 2300 BC), and probably extending into the Early Bronze Age (*c.* 2300–*c.* 1500 BC). These appear to have been natural peats forming in woodland ponds or in fen *carrs* (the local term for marshy ground). Antiquarian observations record the discovery of parts of a submerged forest during the deepening of the Alexandra Dock in 1884, and similar remains were also observed on the foreshore near Earle's Yard. This is probably all part of a Holocene forest environment which was present in a number of areas in the city, as also attested by periodic finds of 'bog oaks' in north Hull. It is into this context that early finds of red deer antlers, buried deep within the central area (such as at Clarence Street and Salthouse Lane), would best be placed. Similarly, casual finds of polished stone axes and Neolithic flints – both in the suburbs and on the periphery of the city – demonstrate not only Neolithic activity (*c.* 4400–*c.* 2300 BC), but also suggest that some forest clearance was already taking place in this part of the valley.

The published evidence for Bronze Age activity (*c.* 2300–*c.* 750 BC) is so far relatively sparse, but as in the Neolithic, the wetlands of the lower Hull valley would have provided a rich food resource for hunting, fishing and fowling, while a certain amount of forest clearance may have been taking place. A Middle Bronze Age axe is recorded from the Humber, while a Late Bronze Age continental winged axe was found at Alexandra Dock – apparently with a nearby boat – and two sherds of Bronze Age pottery were found at the Tesco site on Hall Road, near Orchard Park. Aerial photographs have identified the crop-marks of a probable earthwork, which could be either a triple dyke or a droveway, in north-east Hull, and while undated, its form is characteristic of the Bronze Age.[1] In addition to this modest sum of Bronze Age records, it is likely that far more material of this date once existed, for recent work on the north-western boundary of the city, as part of flood alleviation works, has apparently revealed a much more intensive pattern of early prehistoric activity (both Late Neolithic and Bronze Age in date, and including burials) in this part of the Hull valley than previously identified. As yet, no details of that work are publicly available.

Iron Age Hull

The introduction of iron-working technology into Britain after *c.* 750 BC led to the more widespread use of metal tools and weapons, as it would have been a cheaper commodity to produce than bronze, and would have used native sources of ore. Throughout eastern Yorkshire there is clear evidence for permanent settlement sites, burial sites, and for the practice of agriculture (marked by the appearance of both clusters of stock enclosures and our first recognisable field systems). There is also evidence of early industrial activity: salt was made at numerous *salterns* across the region (including a possible site off Preston Road in Hull), and iron ore was extracted and smelted at numerous sites adjoining both sides of the Wallingfen (to the west of Hull). Large boats were used to trade goods across the Humber (like the Hasholme Boat in the Hull and East Riding Museum), and over 65 of these have been found in and around the Humber estuary.

This was a warrior society, for which there is extensive evidence of the ownership of prized weapons, and where the elite members of society were sometimes buried with dismantled carts or chariots. Moreover, the scars of past conflicts are sometimes visible on bodies excavated in some of the region's Iron Age cemeteries (for example, as sword cuts). The onset of this era is marked by the appearance of defended hill-top or hill-slope enclosures (as we see at Castle Hill, on the north-eastern edges of Hull).

This period sees the first clear evidence for settlement within the future city boundaries. On the north-eastern limits, the Early Iron Age (*c.* 750–500 BC) is represented by pottery of Hallstatt-type found at the foot of Castle Hill, Swine.[2] Castle Hill itself has never been archaeologically excavated, but may well have its origins as a defended hill-top enclosure of Late Bronze Age or Early Iron Age date. The Middle Iron Age is represented by the upper part of a La Tène II sword from Hymers Avenue,[3] while there is also pottery from various sites in the city (including National Avenue, Shakespeare Road, Princess Royal Hospital, the Kingswood development and Marfleet). The most significant site of this period is a complex ditched settlement with roundhouses at Saltshouse Road. This is a multi-period site, located on a raised island of till, the occupation of which would appear to have begun in the Late Iron Age (probably first century BC or early first century AD), and continued into the Roman period. It was first investigated in 1964, but further excavations took place in 2007–08, 2010 and 2011. Its plan includes at least two ditched enclosures, at least five roundhouses and a number of linking enclosure ditches.[4] The pattern of enclosures suggests that this was a small farming community that kept livestock. Settlements of this nature have been found in several parts of east Yorkshire in the Middle and Later Iron Age, and were probably more common than the number of excavated sites suggests.

Out of Place, Out of Time: Peter Didsbury's Hull

Born in Lancashire in 1946, Peter Didsbury moved to Hull at the age of six. After studying English and Hebrew at Oxford, he returned to the city, teaching English for eight years before becoming a professional archaeologist. Didsbury's poetry is deeply informed by his archaeology, by Hull, by characters from the past, and by the hidden and not-so-hidden presence of past places. In his art, Didsbury instinctively perceives the past within the present; to read his work is to be taken on a tour of Hull and Holderness, with the region's local colour, contexts and lived experiences.

Didsbury's poems are multi-layered and multi-textured. In 'The Drainage', a modern man awakens one morning in a prehistoric age, but the 'flat wet landscape' is still recognisably that of the East Riding, with its 'Sluices. Ditches. Drains. Frozen mud and leafcake. Dykes.'[1] As in the poetry of Philip Larkin, the soggy, estuarine and maritime quality of Hull is a key feature of Didsbury's work: drains and wide skies abound; 'fluvial' and 'pluvial' are two favourite words.

CULTURE
HISTORY
PLACE

Drains and drainage are a key feature of Peter Didsbury's Hull, as 'The Drainage', one of his more celebrated poems, suggests. The weed screen depicted here is situated close to the point where the Beverley and Barmston drain joins the River Hull, with the Driffield Navigation serving as its other terminus. The public house in the background is The Whalebone, a name befitting and explaining its location in the former 'blubber-boiling' district of Hull.

Larkin's image of 'The river's level drifting breadth' in 'The Whitsun Weddings'[2] is reworked by Didsbury in 'A Daft Place', which heads 'south from here to the river' – though 'Even the river mud is dafter than we care to own./ There are more gulls on the dustbins than on the estuary now.'[3] The poet, like the water, reforms and reinvents.

Reality and physical place may inspire much of his work, but they certainly do not constrain or contain the poet. 'I'm the cause of all this. Of all I see', writes the narrator of one of Didsbury's poems, self-conscious about his poetic practice; another wonders whether 'the truth of the world/ mightn't be the best way/ of getting some things down'.[4] Lines like these get to the heart of Didsbury's attitude to geography: paradoxically irreverent and yet fascinated by the local and the particular, he uses reality as a springboard to transform and transfigure environments. A number of Didsbury's poems undergo sudden moments of vision: swans on the park lake fly 'out of the Stone Age', Byron swims across the Humber rather than the Hellespont, and the shops of the 'butchers of Hull' are 'like Catholic shrines, like Walsingham'.[5]

The past frequently provides a creative space, one full of possibilities, even if only imagined. In 'Queen Victoria's Chaffinch', Didsbury describes the statues of Queen Victoria and Prince Albert in Pearson Park, positioned awkwardly away from one another.

> They do not even face each other.
> The Consort has his back towards the Queen,
> and she in turn is seated upfield of him,
> compelled to watch what she does not care to observe.
> They have been like this for one hundred and forty years,
> and no one round here is quite sure that they understand why.[6]

This peculiarity leads Didsbury to imagine the statues 'invested with the right/ to leave their plinths on the stroke of midnight,/ and house souls again for the durance of the chimes'. 'Surely,' his poem speculates, 'there will be time, just once,/ for them to find each other, for fingertips to touch.'

Hull is the 'lodestar' of Didsbury's 'extremely various work',[7] according to his fellow Hull poet, Sean O'Brien. Numerous communities of poets have blossomed in the city since Larkin moved there in 1955, and Didsbury's work often references those who have helped to construct a 'literary Hull'. Sometimes implicitly, sometimes explicitly, his poems map the places where Hull's poets meet, think and drink. Hull's vernacular pubs, for instance, appear a number of times: Didsbury's description of 'A long saloon with mirrors' brings to mind the Polar Bear on Spring Bank, while his even more oblique reference to a pub with 'The name of the goddess of arts and trades' suggests the Minerva, established on Hull's riverfront in 1829, and containing the smallest pub room in Britain.[8] Andrew Marvell is mentioned in Didsbury's poem 'Back of the House'. Said to be addressed to O'Brien, the narrator takes refuge in 'your garden,/ this hot afternoon, your English garden', where 'Language, fat and prone beneath her fountain, idly dispenses curling parchment notes'.[9] 'A Civil Garden' is dedicated to another Hull poet, Tony Petch,[10] while 'Cat Nights', this time explicitly dedicated to O'Brien, takes place outside Hull's 'terraces' and 'corner shops', where a comradely cigarette can be smoked among the gathering nocturnal felines.[11] 'The Web' is dedicated to Douglas Dunn,[12] whose 1982 anthology of new Hull poets, *A Rumoured City*, brought Didsbury and O'Brien to national attention; the poem's central image reinforces the idea of a bardic community conversing within and across the city.

Sean O'Brien suggests that Peter Didsbury is a poet far more rooted in the city of Hull than his forebears, Douglas Dunn and Philip Larkin.[13] Didsbury still lives in Hull, and continues to write poetry that, like the city and the land it is built on, can surprise us with historical curios and sudden moments of transformation.

James Underwood

Notes

1   Peter Didsbury, 'The Drainage', in *Scenes from a Long Sleep: New & Collected Poems* (Tarset, 2003), pp. 194–95. All subsequent quotations from Didsbury's poetry are taken from this edition.

2   Philip Larkin, 'The Whitsun Weddings', in *Collected Poems* (London, 2003), pp. 92–94.

3   'A Daft Place', p. 199

4   'During a Storm', p. 172; 'The Flowers of Finland', pp. 196–97.

5   'The Library Steps', p. 207; 'The Pierhead', p. 129; 'The Butchers of Hull', p. 178.

6   'Queen Victoria's Chaffinch', p. 46.

7   Sean O'Brien, 'The Unknown City: Larkin, Dunn and Didsbury', in Katharine Cockin (ed.), *The Literary North* (Basingstoke, 2012), pp. 145–56 (p. 151).

8   'The Library Steps', p. 207; 'The Pierhead', p. 129.

9   'Back of the House', p. 175.

10   'A Civil Garden', p. 205.

11   'Cat Nights', p. 198.

12   'The Web', p. 204.

13   O'Brien, 'The Unknown City', p. 155.

The arrival of the Romans and their impact

The Roman army crossed the Humber in about AD 71, and advanced north-westwards from Brough, first to Malton and then York. Much of the East Riding is thought to have been occupied by the *Parisi* – a local tribe who appear to have had cordial relations with their new rulers. Accordingly, this area was not subject to either military occupation or intensive Romanisation. Instead, most of the local inhabitants appear to have been allowed to continue as a largely Iron Age society, but with at least occasional access to a certain amount of Roman goods and foodstuffs. Their settlements and culture are best described as being Romano-British, rather than Roman.

Some of the existing settlements (such as that at Saltshouse Road) continued in use in the Romano-British period, but they were soon joined by a range of newly founded settlements, possibly by the end of the first century AD, and certainly by the early second century. Many of these new settlements took the form of rows of rectangular enclosures arranged along one or both sides of a trackway, so-called 'ladder' settlements. Several were associated with a pastoral farming regime; many were sited in bends of the River Hull, and spaced perhaps half to three-quarters of a mile (0.8–1.1 km) apart. The Roman foreshore lay about half a mile (0.8 km) inland from the modern foreshore, and these new settlements alongside the River Hull began at about Stoneferry and extended northwards.[5] They are also present in east Hull. The character of these sites – particularly those along the river – is quasi-urban. Their frequency and separation are consistent with that of an extended dispersed settlement, rather like ribbon-development along a major road. These Hull sites, once founded, tended to be long-lived, with most continuing into the fourth or even the fifth centuries AD. Roman goods found on these sites included fully Romanised wares and glass, and part of a stamped legionary tile. Casual finds from the city and its environs have helped to map the pattern of settlement and land-use throughout the lower Hull valley,[6] and are best understood when seen in the wider context of crop-marks and finds from the adjoining areas of the East Riding, rather than being viewed in isolation.[7] Exploitation of the heavier alluvial carr lands surrounding the Sutton clays had begun by at least the first half of the fourth century, as evidenced by a coin hoard dated to AD 330–35.

Anglo-Saxon and Viking Hull

Occupation of the Romano-British sites did not continue long into the fifth century, and thereafter there is a dearth of activity until the late ninth or early tenth centuries, when place-name evidence suggests that fresh colonisation had begun to exploit the heavy clay tills and alluvial soils of north and east Hull.

The east Yorkshire coast and the Humber estuary offered numerous locations for invaders to land, and, as a result, this was an area that was extensively colonised by successive groups of settlers. There is abundant evidence for Saxon

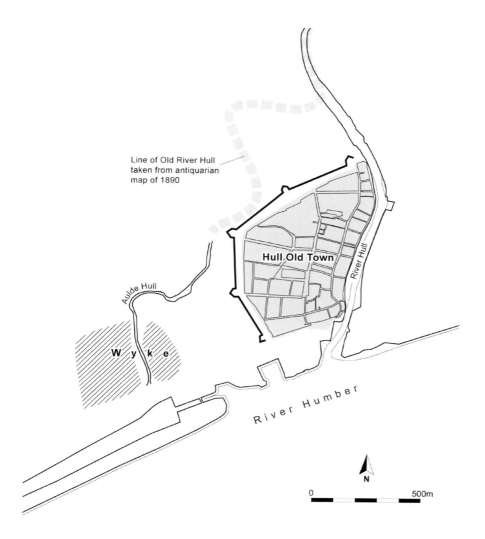

Line of Old River Hull
taken from antiquarian
map of 1890

Hull Old Town

River Hull

Aulde Hull

W y k e

River Humber

0   500m

N

1.1 The suggested course
of the Old Hull (based
on historic maps), and a
suggested location for the
later twelfth-century port
of Wyke, about 1 km to the
west of the modern course
of the River Hull and the later
site of the Old Town.
Illustration by Dave Watt © D. H.
Evans and Dave Watt, 2015

burial sites throughout the East Riding, along with occasional monastic sites; the surviving place names attest that there would once also have been widespread settlement, but the archaeological evidence for actual settlement sites has been harder to identify. From the later ninth century this area was part of the Danelaw and was ruled from the Viking centre at York. Once again, we have extensive place-name evidence to attest to the Anglo-Scandinavian influence throughout the area, but a dearth of rural settlement evidence. Most of our evidence for Viking influences in east Yorkshire consists of casual finds of metalwork or carved bone and antler objects.

The only possible evidence for any activity in this era consists of a single Northumbrian coin (a so-called *styca*), a possible re-deposited copper alloy pin from Sewer Lane – which might be of seventh- or eighth-century type – and one or two re-deposited sherds of Ipswich-type ware. However, there were major documented

Anglo-Saxon estates in Hessle to the west and in the –*Ella* settlements to the north-west (including Kirk Ella and West Ella), and this meagre amount of material may have been brought into the medieval town at a later date with construction materials.

However, this does not mean that we are left with no traces of Viking-age settlement in the area. Surviving place names hint at the Old Scandinavian impact on Hull, place names such as Inglemire, Owstmarsk, Sculcoates, Southcoates, Stoneferry and Summergangs. In contrast, Marfleet, Myton, Sutton and perhaps Drypool are deemed to derive from Old English. Their etymology would be consistent with many of these places having been founded between the later ninth and the eleventh centuries. Thus, place names can reveal a patchwork of cultures settling and integrating in this region over this period of history.

Medieval Hull (Wyke)

At the time of the Norman Conquest, the only settlements within the limits of the future city comprised the village of Sutton and a handful of hamlets. However, by the time of Domesday Book (1086), not only was the raised till island of Sutton being used once again for permanent settlement, but a number of apparently new hamlets (such as Drypool, Marfleet, Myton and Southcoates) had been established, slightly further downstream than their Romano-British counterparts. As a result of monastic activity, drainage and land reclamation, the development of a major port, and, finally, royal intervention and patronage, the landscape and the ways in which people interacted with the land (and waterways) began to change.

The estuary has been one of the busiest routes for shipping on the east coast of England for the last 5,000 years. Because the Humber estuary is fed by a number of major river systems, it serves as the natural inlet and outlet for a very large area of northern and central England – including such major inland medieval towns as York, Lincoln and Nottingham – and reaches a hinterland almost as far to the south-west as Tamworth (in the West Midlands). Some of these other towns were ports in their own right during the period from the ninth to the mid-twelfth centuries – when they could be comfortably reached by the shallow-draught vessels of the Anglo-Scandinavian era – but the development of the Hanseatic *cogs* (a type of deeper-draught ocean-going ship, originating in the Baltic) was to change all that. These vessels were revolutionary in their impact, both in terms of the volume of goods that could be traded over long distances, and on the development of harbours and waterfronts. Because they sat much deeper in the water, they needed deep-water anchorages. This provided the stimulus for the development of deep-water ports such as Hull, and it also led to the construction of vertically faced waterfront revetments set in deeper water, further out into rivers and harbours. Hence, the arrival of such ships on the northern European trading routes in the mid-twelfth century meant that a new deep-water port would have to be built on the Humber. There were a number of early candidates for such a port, but Hull's strategic position and safe deep-water anchorages were to ensure that it emerged as the clear winner.

Wyke

Today, the River Hull flows along the eastern side of the Old Town to join the Humber at the town's south-eastern corner, but this is a very different course from its original route in the twelfth century and before. The old course of the river formerly turned to the west – probably at High Flags, on Wincolmlee just to the north of the northern limits of what is now the Old Town – and followed a meandering course in a broadly south-westerly direction for some distance before once again turning southwards to exit into the Humber almost 1 km to the west of its modern course (Figure 1.1). This course is referred to in 1298 and 1303 as *Veilhull*, or the Old Hull.[8] Later entries in the town's Bench Books refer to it by names such as the *Oldehull*, *Alde Hull* or *Auld Hull*.[9] Although badly silted up, its course was still recognisable in places as late as *c.* 1860, and it is shown on a number of historic maps. Its outlet into the Humber was known as Limekiln Creek in 1552, or Limehouse Creek on some later maps.[10]

This was clearly the route of the River Hull during the later Saxon period, when a settlement called Myton was established close to its mouth: the name Myton derives from the Old English for a farm at the mouth or confluence of the two rivers.[11] The settlement was already in existence in 1086, when it was recorded in Domesday Book as a *berewick*, consisting of one and a half carucates, forming part of the manor of Ferriby, held by Ralph de Mortemer.[12] The precise site of the settlement of Myton is lost, but it clearly lay to the west of the future Old Town, as one of the latter's main east–west streets was later called Mytongate, that is, the street leading towards Myton. Moreover, as it lay outside of the future town, its lands continued to be mentioned in medieval documents for several centuries, and its memory is still preserved in several more recent street names and in the name of a modern council ward.

By about 1160 Myton had become a lordship, and it is mentioned as such in a grant of lands by Matilda, the daughter of Hugh Camin, to the newly founded Cistercian Abbey of Meaux in the period 1160–82.[13] This is a key document, as it also contains the first record of the port of Wyke, within the lordship of Myton:

> Know ye that I have demised and sold to the Monks of Melsa, the entire two parts of the land of my patrimony of Wyc of Mitune, and also the entire two parts of my patrimony of seven stangs and four oxgangs of land in the territory of the aforesaid Vill of Mitune…

The wording of this charter makes it clear that the place names Myton and Wyke were not synonymous, but that Wyke formed a discrete part of the lordship of Myton – quite separate from the *vill* of Myton. The meaning of a *vill* was actually an administrative unit of taxation, rather than a settlement *per se*. Hence, it is possible that, at this stage, Myton comprised a large block of demesne land and a severalty holding, rather than a nucleated settlement. The name *Wyke*, or *Wyk'*, probably derives from the Old Scandinavian for a creek or inlet and probably relates specifically to a settlement that had developed alongside the Old Hull.[14]

Subsequent documents clearly show that Wyke upon Hull was soon to emerge as a major port on the estuary. In 1193 wool for the ransom of King Richard I was being collected at 'the port of Hull',[15] while in 1197–99 the Pipe Rolls record the sale of 45 sacks of wool at Hull.[16] In the taxation of the ports of the south and east coasts of England by King John in 1203–05, 'Hull' was listed as already making the sixth largest contribution.[17] At this date, the settlement was usually called Wyke or Wyke upon Hull; however, royal customs records increasingly used the shortened form of 'Hull' in their returns. During the thirteenth century, it continually appeared among the ports to which royal mandates were sent, concerning wool exports, detention of alien masters, the discovery of clipped money and piracy, and by the 1220s a number of royal bailiffs were stationed there.

The next major step in the development of the port was brought about by a change in the course of the river. According to the *Chronicles of Melsa* (the Latin name for Meaux Abbey), the powerful lord of a neighbouring manor to the north – Saer (or Sayer) de Sutton – cut a new channel to the east, both to drain the marshes around Sutton and to give him direct access to the Humber.[18] Whether this attribution to Saer is based on fact or is simply fanciful is uncertain, but the new

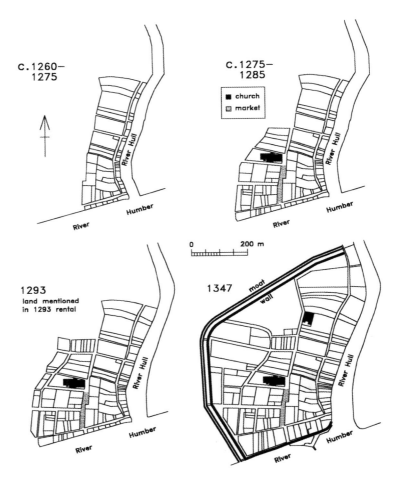

1.2 A suggested model for the development of the later site of Wyke and its successor, the Old Town, *c.* 1260–*c.* 1350. The final plan shows the street layout as recorded in the 1347 Town Rental. The town defences shown here had been completed as an earth and timber circuit by this date, and were being gradually replaced in brick, though the latter work would not be completed until the early fifteenth century.
Illustration by Mike Frankland
© D. H. Evans and the Humber Archaeology Partnership, 2004

channel became known as Sayer's Creek, and ran directly southwards from High Flags to the Humber (a much shorter route, and probably faster-flowing). Although described by the chronicler and in later accounts as being a new channel, it is likely that it would have taken advantage of any pre-existing natural watercourses through these marshes, and widened and deepened them to form the new cut. Drainage of neighbouring marshes around Cottingham (to the west) had begun in the period between 1160 and 1182, and it is possible that the cutting of Sayer's Creek was simply an attempt to emulate this process.[19] However, if the attribution to Saer de Sutton is correct, then this would suggest that the new cut was excavated in the first three decades of the thirteenth century.

Although a new channel had been created, water continued to flow down the old course of the river, and for a while both channels appear to have been in use. Eventually, however, the old course of the river began to silt up, and, according to the chronicle, it barely merited being described as more than a drain. The same account goes on to record that, as a result, the Hull changed its course and ran into the new channel of Sayer's Creek; a similar account was offered at a judicial inquiry in the later fourteenth century. The nineteenth-century historian Charles Frost suggested that it was likely that such a dramatic change of course would have been associated with a major natural calamity such as a disastrous episode of flooding. Britain enjoyed a Little Climatic Optimum in the eleventh and twelfth centuries, with summer temperatures of perhaps 1°C higher than those of today, but with the advent of the thirteenth century climatic deterioration began to set in,[20] introducing a less stable period characterised by more dramatic fluctuations in weather patterns. From about 1250 onwards, there are more frequent documentary records of storminess and episodes of flooding.[21] Much of the east coast of England was particularly badly affected by disastrous floods in 1253.[22] Locally, the flood waters swept inland as far as the fisheries and woods at Cottingham (perhaps 3 km from the Humber), and the monastic chronicles record that several people and large numbers of cattle were swept away by the flood waters; in addition, a considerable quantity of land which the monastery had held in Myton was washed away into the Humber, and could never afterwards be regained.[23] It is this major environmental disaster that is thought to have been a key factor in the River Hull changing its course and shifting eastwards to flow into Sayer's Creek. It would also have produced the conditions necessary for the development of the Old Town in its current position. The port's business represented the economic life of Wyke; thus, once the Old Hull had silted up so badly that it could no longer be used for shipping, the port had to move. The focus of the settlement was relocated to the banks of Sayer's Creek and it is here that the Old Town of Hull would later develop. On the basis of what is currently known,[24] one might tentatively suggest that any settlement on the east bank of the Old Hull watercourse might lie to the south-west of the disused Holy Trinity burial ground near Commercial Road.[25]

Study of the layout of the tenements and the documentary history of individual plots within the Old Town suggests that the earliest focus for settlement after *c.* 1260 lay alongside the west bank of the River Hull, with the new High Street and its adjoining tenements mirroring the course of the river (Figure 1.2). The new port flourished and quickly grew, both in importance and size. In 1275 it was made a customs head port for the north of England (Figure 1.3). Four years later it was granted weekly markets and an annual fair – effectively gaining the status of a borough, in all but name – and in the period 1285–91 there occurs the first mention of a chapel having been built there. By that date, the settlement had expanded to include the area around the market and the church; at this stage, its western limits may have been marked by a natural watercourse running along the lines of the later Dagger Lane and Sewer Lane. By 1290 the thriving port had become the third highest source of customs revenue on England's east and south coasts.

The abbey which owned the land on which the settlement now stood badly needed cash, while the king was looking for a suitable northern base from which to supply a planned invasion of Scotland. This combination of high revenues and a

1.4 The Old Town of Hull, seen from the south, in 1989; the River Hull is on the right-hand side of the photograph. Much of the medieval street pattern is still recognisable today, for example the way that High Street (on the right of the photo) closely mirrors the course of the River Hull, just to its right. The former lines of the medieval town ditch around the western and northern sides of the town are preserved in a series of late eighteenth- and nineteenth-century docks which replaced much of that defensive circuit.
Dr John Dent © Humberside Archaeological Unit

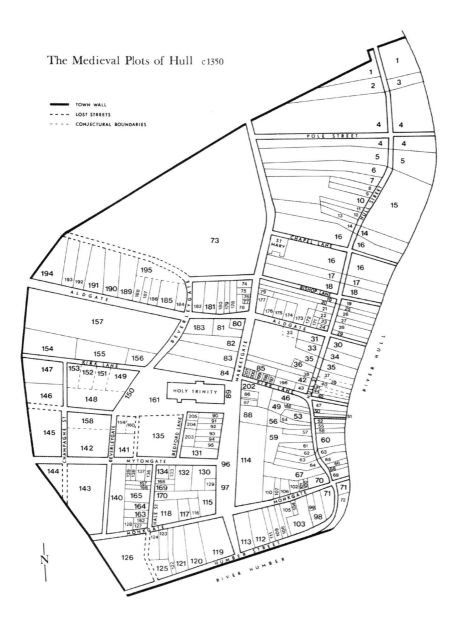

The Medieval Plots of Hull c1350

TOWN WALL
LOST STREETS
CONJECTURAL BOUNDARIES

1.5 The main street plan and topography of Hull in the mid-fourteenth century, as suggested by the 1347 Town Rental.

Map used in R. E. Horrox, *The Changing Plan of Hull, 1290–1650: A Guide to Documentary Sources for the Early Topography of Hull* (Hull: Hull City Council, 1978), and loosely based on an original prepared for J. Bilson, 'Wyke upon Hull in 1293', *Transactions of the East Riding Antiquarian Society*, 26 (1926–28), pp. 37–105 © the former Hull City Record Office

strategic port proved a great temptation for him, and an ideal opportunity, with the result that he decided to purchase the whole of the lands on which the town stood in 1293. A Crown Survey of that year records that Wyke then consisted of a mere 61 households; the details of the accompanying rental allow us to identify those plots.[26]

The archaeology of the King's Town

In March 1293 Edward I took possession of both Wyke and Myton – an act that was quickly followed by a valuation (first of those settlements, and then of the grange belonging to Myton) and subsequently by a royal rental. A bailiff was appointed to govern the town and the grange. Following the acquisition, Edward renamed his new town Kingston upon Hull (that is, 'the King's Town on the River Hull'). He also decided to create a substantial number of new tenements in the areas to the west and north-west, laying out the newer parts of the town with more of a grid pattern of streets (Figure 1.2). At first many of these new tenements lay undeveloped, as the rents were too high; it was not until 1317, when his son dropped the rents to one-third of their former level, that they were to attract new tenants.

The new town, created in 1293, was significantly larger than Wyke, and was made into a royal borough in 1299. Thanks to a series of very detailed royal rentals, and a valuable collection of surviving deeds, we can recreate the tenement pattern with some confidence, and thus date many of the plot boundaries and some of the buildings.[27] Much of the medieval street plan still survives within the Old Town, and the lines of its town ditches are preserved in the layout of the later docks (Figures 1.4 and 1.5).

The earliest surviving parts of the main medieval church, Holy Trinity, date from the period 1302–20, with the brickwork in the transepts being among the earliest known in the region. The bricks almost certainly came from a new corporation brickyard[28] established at this time. As well as Holy Trinity, there were also two friaries founded in the late thirteenth and early fourteenth centuries: a Carmelite friary and an Augustinian friary. The Carmelite friary (founded 1289) is known mainly from documentary sources, but the Augustinian friary, founded in 1316–17, has been extensively excavated in one of the largest programmes of excavation carried out on any mendicant house in Britain (Figure 1.6).[29] An early phase of timber buildings was replaced in the mid-fourteenth century by more permanent brick buildings set on stone footings. The southern part of the precinct was taken up with a large formal monastic garden, excavation of which has enabled the reconstruction of its full layout. This was the last Augustinian friary in the country to surrender to the Crown in March 1539. In addition to the details of its various buildings and formal areas, excavation enabled the recovery of over 250 articulated burials which were associated with the friary. While some of these were monks,

1.6 The remains of the main claustral complex of the Augustinian friary under excavation in the summer of 1994, viewed from the north-east. The friary church can be seen on the right-hand side of the photograph; the east range occupies the left centre-ground, with the cloister beyond. The west range is in the far background. The A63 now overlies part of its monastic gardens.
Bill Marsden © BM Photographic Services and the Humberside Archaeological Unit, 1994

1.7 Part of a fourteenth-century timber waterfront revetment at Chapel Lane Staith, excavated in 1978; this probably dates to *c.* 1330, on the basis of the stoneware found in the associated dumps behind the revetment.
© Humberside Archaeological Unit, 1978

many were townspeople who had chosen to be buried within the friary, and study of these burials has given us a very detailed picture of the health and diet of this community, as well as a great deal of information about their costumes and dress accessories. Among the more interesting aspects is the fact that 43 of the burials were contained in coffins made of Baltic oak, demonstrating the strong links with the Hanseatic area, while isotope analysis of some of the skeletons has revealed the presence of a number of immigrants into the port both from other parts of Britain, and from Scandinavia and the eastern Baltic (see Chapters 2 and 4).

Later religious buildings in and around the Old Town included the church of St Mary Lowgate, a Carthusian priory just to the north of the town, and seven hospitals, nine *maisons dieu* and one bedehouse. All of the above-listed smaller religious houses had been documented by *c.* 1700, but not all of these were in contemporary use, and some were early post-medieval foundations. The first mention of St Mary's is as a chapel of ease, dependent on the mother church at North Ferriby in 1327, and it is described as being newly built in 1333. The stone-faced building which we see today is a result of a major 'restoration' – effectively almost a rebuilding – in 1861–63 by Sir George Gilbert Scott. The original later medieval building would, like Holy Trinity, have been built largely of brick, with stone being used sparingly for details such as door and window jambs, quoins and finials. A major rebuilding began in *c.* 1400 at its east end, and continued throughout the fifteenth century, finishing with its west tower. In 1423–24 some 10,000 bricks were purchased from the corporation brickyard for use at St Mary's. Its tower apparently collapsed in the early sixteenth century, demolishing part of the west end of the church. The present west tower was erected in 1697.

Medieval public works and infrastructure included the development of major waterfronts,[30] the creation of a defensive circuit (see Chapter 3)[31] and the construction of a new Guildhall and town gaol.[32] There was also a short-lived mint in the town in 1300, which is thought to have produced over a million silver pennies to pay the soldiers fighting in Edward I's Scottish wars.[33] The waterfronts lay along the west bank of the River Hull, and included both public and private wharves. Several of these have now been investigated, and parts of their timber revetments have been found to survive in excellent condition, up to 3.47 m in height (Figure 1.7). A small section of part of a late medieval revetment from Chapel Lane Staith (incorporating a reused section of planking from a ship built in *c.* 1421), and part of a large timber vat of *c.* 1490 from Blaydes Staith, are now on display at the Hull and East Riding Museum.

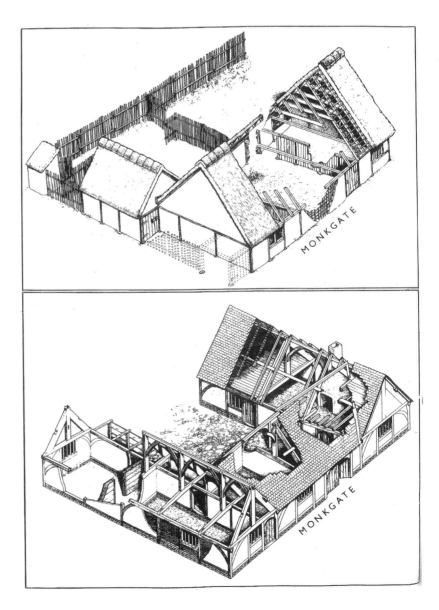

1.8 The evolution of the Wytelard property on Blackfriargate during the fourteenth century; this was excavated as site MG76A. A late thirteenth-century padstone-based structure, which was aligned lengthways to the road (top) was replaced in the mid-fourteenth century by a framed house, with a front range and two wings.
Illustration by Rob Gillam © Humberside Archaeological Unit, 1987

Domestic buildings in the medieval town took a variety of forms.[34] Some of the smaller houses and outbuildings had clay walls, moulded into large blocks which were held together with a wet clay slip, and often incorporated timber uprights to support the weight of the roof. Many of the houses and larger buildings had their principal timbers supported on padstones; this form of construction was widely used in Hull from the later thirteenth to the later sixteenth centuries, and occasional examples were still standing as late as the twentieth century (for example, at 85 Queen Street; part of the timber frame for this building is now on display in the Hull and East Riding Museum). There were also fourteenth-century examples of buildings with more complex plans, such as rear service wings at right-angles to the frontages, and carriage entrances (for example, the Wytelard property on Blackfriargate; Figure 1.8). A number of inns were in existence by the fifteenth century. One well-known example was the fifteenth-century, three-storied King's Head Inn on the High Street. Another was The George (Figure 1.9), again off High Street, while a third was The White Horse on the Market Place. Many of Hull's medieval buildings were demolished in the first half of the twentieth century, but detailed drawings and early photographs of several of the more celebrated examples do survive, and a tiny handful of buildings are still standing. One of the best of the latter is No. 5 Scale Lane (Figure 1.10), a small jettied building erected in the first half of the fifteenth century; there are other survivals at Nos. 153 and 153A High Street. As the Scale Lane property is now a public house, and parts of the High Street buildings are now used as a restaurant, the reader can not only see their exteriors but can gain access to some of their interiors.

The most prestigious building complex in the medieval town was the de la Pole manor, or Suffolk Palace. This was a large manorial complex of buildings belonging to the powerful de la Pole family, who would rise to become Earls of Suffolk, and it occupied a large triangular block in the north-western corner of the Old Town, extending from its western limits as far east as Lowgate. In 1388 Sir Michael de la Pole, who was then Chancellor of England and thus one of the most powerful politicians in the land, was impeached, and all of his property was seized. The Crown Survey describes his manor house in Hull as a capital messuage, with two dovecotes and three gardens with three ponds. The rooms within the manor house listed in that survey included the hall, the 'Somerhalle', at least seven chambers, a great chamber, a chapel with a chamber over it, a solar, a wine cellar, a pantry, a buttery in the Somerhalle, a kitchen, a bakehouse, a well-equipped granary and stables.[35] While there are no more details to explain what was meant by the 'Somerhalle', it was presumably another large reception room or hall, and may have been particularly well-lit in summer. An even more detailed description of the Suffolk Palace survives from 1538, giving details of the dimensions of individual rooms, the nature of their roof coverings, and the location of individual privies and chimneys.

Fortunately, the palace survived long enough into the seventeenth century to figure in two topographical views. An undated print in the Cottonian collection of manuscripts may depict it in the early 1540s, and offers quite a detailed view, while the *c.* 1640 Hollar map of Hull shows the palace in the formal setting of its grounds (see Chapter 3 for copies of the plans). Part of a fifteenth-century gilded and painted

1.9 Timber-framed buildings in High Street in 1941, including the entrance to George Yard, demolished in 1943. This building was probably of similar date and construction technique to the King's Head Inn. The upper storeys were both jettied, and there appear to be vestiges of close studding partly masked by later plaster rendering. A tunnel entry into George Yard (to the rear) was flanked by carved beams; projecting corbels can be glimpsed beneath the jettied upper storeys. This was a large complex of buildings, which began life as a Cloth Hall; parts of it dated back to at least the fifteenth century. Sir John Summerson, from collections held by the former Royal Commission on the Historical Monuments of England stone screen fragment was recovered from excavations within its former grounds in 2001. This is presumed to have come from the chapel, which is mentioned in the 1538 survey as lying on the north side of the main hall. The only other part of the former palace which has so far been located in any excavations or building work is a flight of stone stairs or steps which led down to a small creek, in which was found a complete sixteenth-century pine boat. These were discovered during the construction of the Guildhall in 1908, and the pine boat survives and is on display in the Maritime Museum. This discovery shows that the Earls of Suffolk were sufficiently important to be able to have their own private access by creek to the main waterways, and it also serves as a salutary reminder that a number of old waterways formerly flowed through the Old Town and were not culverted or covered over until about 1750; this creek was clearly one of these.

The long series of town rentals allow us to plot the distribution of wealth in 1347 (Figure 1.11).[36] Apart from the powerful de la Pole manor in the north-western quadrant of the town, many of the wealthier properties were concentrated around High Street, with one or two outliers near Market Place. What is perhaps more interesting is a large body of less prosperous properties clustered around the church and both sides of Market Place, and also extending westwards along Mytongate. The urban poor were distributed throughout the town, but had strong concentrations in the southern, western and northern suburbs. These rentals also tell us that several families owned multiple properties in the town, and that some of these must have been investment properties. Yet when we come to plot the homes of the richer merchants,[37] we find that they were spread evenly through the town, rather than being clustered in any one area. Some of their houses were quite grand buildings: hence, a residence of Richard de la Pole off Grimsby Lane had a stone spiral staircase leading to the upper floor.[38] Surviving medieval deeds in the city archives show that there were many more buildings with elaborate features such as stone towers and cranes, while archaeological excavations attest occasional finds of cellars, louvres, architectural stonework, roof furniture, specially moulded bricks and painted window glass.[39] We also have occasional examples of merchant seals.[40]

1.10 Three-storied fifteenth-century timber-framed building at 5 Scale Lane, set at right angles to the street; surveyed in 1984, prior to renovation. Narrow gable-front to the street, with jetties to the first and second floors, upward curving braces at the corners of the second floor, and mid-rails on the first floor.
© D. H. Evans, 2016

The town's infrastructure

Some of the street pattern in the eastern half of the Old Town was inherited from the later years of Wyke, but that to its west and north-west was established following the foundation of the King's Town. Its subsequent evolution can be traced through a series of royal rentals. The records of

Rental per annum
- over £4
- £2 - £4
- £1 - £2
- 10s - £1
- under 10s

1.11 The distribution of wealth in 1347, as indicated by the amounts paid annually in rent within the town, taken from details of the fee farm rentals set out in R. E. Horrox (ed.), *Selected Rentals and Accounts of Medieval Hull 1293–1528*, Yorkshire Archaeological Society Record Series 141 (Leeds, 1983), based on PRO manuscript Exchequer T.R. Misc. 274 ff. 170v-171, 187–8. Illustration by Mike Frankland © D. H. Evans and the Humber Archaeology Partnership, 2006

paving grants survive from 1300 onwards, and record the purchase of stone (chalk) from Brough and Hessle, and 'small stones' (cobbles) and sand from the east Yorkshire coast, for repairing the roads. Excavations in the roadway at Blanket Row exposed a succession of medieval stone-paved surfaces.

The River Hull was initially crossed by a ferry at Drypool, and by a stone-paved ford at Stoneferry in the later thirteenth century; but the Drypool crossing was replaced by a bridge in 1538–41, and the Stoneferry ford was replaced by a ferry at the end of the fourteenth century. Passage across the Humber was via ferries from Barton and Barrow to Hessle (just to the west of Hull), and is attested by 1315. Once the town ditch was created in 1321–24, access across this to and from the Old Town was provided by wooden bridges outside three of the main gates; there were also planked bridges outside two of the posterns.

Markets were first established in Wyke in 1279 and then in the King's Town in 1293. The main market area was in and around what is now Market Place, with a number of individual commodity markets. A shambles was established in The Butchery (what is now Queen Street) in 1331–34. On the west side of Market Place was a collection of shops or stalls known as The Dings, which were let by the corporation from the mid-fourteenth to the mid-eighteenth centuries. Fish was initially sold at the staiths, but in 1515 a specialised fish shambles was built in what became Fish Street.

There were two mills actually within the Old Town (on High Street and on Beverley Street), and several windmills just outside to the north and west. There was also a watermill next to the Humber. By the sixteenth century, these mills had been augmented by a number of additional windmills, horse-mills and mills for crushing rapeseed to produce oil. These were particularly prevalent in Trippett, an industrial suburb to the north of the town.

Many of the properties within the town had their own wells, and there were also two ponds for watering animals. A freshwater supply was first created by cutting a dyke from Anlaby in 1282. This was replaced in 1401 by Julian's Dyke, which then fed into the main town ditch near the Beverley Gate, from where water was carried into the town in barrels. For a brief period between 1449 and 1461 Hull had a piped water supply, one of the very few towns in northern England to enjoy such a facility (see Chapter 2). Sadly, the town fell on hard times during the Wars of the Roses, and dug up its lead water pipes to sell off the lead (approximately 56 tons were recovered from the pipes and tanks).[41]

Education was to play an important part in the life of the town from an early stage. A school had clearly been established on the south side of Holy Trinity by 1347, presumably to educate clerks in the use of Latin, as there are references to School Lane and School Street. Thus, within sixty years of its foundation the borough already boasted a school. In 1431 the Chamberlains' Accounts show that the borough had appointed a schoolmaster and given him a schoolroom. In 1479 an endowment enabled the appointment of a chaplain to teach there. By the end of the Middle Ages the fortunes of the school were tied to a chantry, and so it could easily have closed under the reforms of Edward VI in the 1540s, but the corporation stepped in and took it over. The school was subsequently maintained by the corporation, and in 1548 was given a royal warrant. A new and bigger schoolroom was built to the west in 1583: this now forms part of the Old Grammar School in South Churchside. By the seventeenth century the town would be funding a small number of exhibitions to send pupils to Cambridge University.

By the close of the period covered by this chapter, Hull had emerged as the 21st largest town in England, and was attracting visitors from all over Europe. One of these was the antiquary William Camden, who wrote in 1586:

> The Town is of no great antiquity for King Edward the first … having observ'd the advantagious situation of the place (which was first call'd Wik) had it in exchange from the Abbot of Meaux, he built the Town call'd Kingston, signifying the King's Town, and there (as the words of the Record are) 'he made a harbour and a free burgh, making the inhabitants of it free burgesses, and granting them many liberties'. By degrees it has grown to that dignity, that for stately building, strong forts, rich fleets, resort of merchants, and plenty of all things, 'tis without doubt the most celebrated Town in these parts. All this increase is owing, partly to Michael de la Pole, who upon his advancement to the Earldom of Suffolk by King Richard the second, procur'd them their privileges, and partly to their trade of Iseland-fish dry'd and harden'd, term'd by them Stock-fish, which turns to great gain, and has strangely enrich'd the Town.[42]

Holy Trinity

The impressive church of Holy Trinity is one of the largest and greatest medieval churches in England. It rises to 46 metres, is 87 metres long and 22 metres wide. The church's stately and beautiful structure, which consists of a nave, chancel, transepts and a very fine tower with four arches, is a monument to the pious aspirations of Hull's medieval residents.

Holy Trinity was built on the site of the chapel of ease at Wyke, which was founded by James Helward and dedicated to the 'Holy Trinitie' c. 1285–91. The chapel was dependent on All Saints church at Hessle. However, around the time of the founding of the new town of Kingston upon Hull by Edward I, the chapel was replaced with the beginnings of Holy Trinity church. Despite the new church's impressive scale, it was not until 1661 that Holy Trinity was granted parish status by an Act of Parliament.

The transepts and the lower part of the tower form the earliest parts of the church, built c. 1300–20. The choir was rebuilt c. 1340–70, followed by the nave c. 1380–1420. A remarkable feature of the walls of the transepts and sections of the choir is that they are built of brick, making them one of the earliest examples of medieval brickwork in the region. It is likely that the bricks came from a new corporation brickyard.

From the outside, one of the most outstanding features is the church tower, which was built in three stages and completed during the sixteenth century. Money bequeathed by parishioners was used for the construction of the tower. Similarly, last will and testament evidence shows that bequests also funded the rebuilding of the nave from c. 1390 onwards. Indeed, the people of Hull invested heavily in the fabric of the church itself *and* in the life and activity of the church, mainly by leaving money for services, requiem masses, and for the general upkeep of the building.

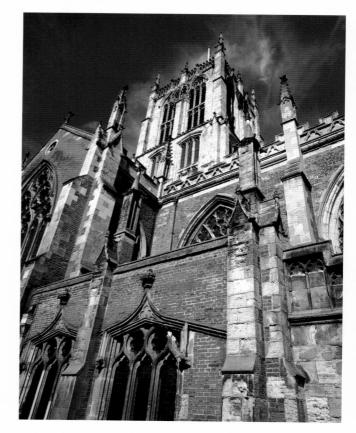

Holy Trinity church is one of the largest brick-built structures of the medieval era.
© Andy Beecroft, licensed under the Creative Commons Attribution-Share Alike 2.0 Generic Licence

The interior of the church reflects the vitality of its importance to Hull's residents over the centuries. It is anything but dull. The colour and light from the ornate stained glass windows – mostly dating from the nineteenth century – give the space vibrancy, while Thomas Binks of Hull's painted ceiling (1845) provides a colourful contrast to the rather heavy and dark woodwork of the Victorian pews, screens and organ case. Memorials to some of Hull's wealthiest inhabitants from the fourteenth century onwards decorate the floors and walls of the church and numerous other ornate furnishings honour the lives, successes and interests of Holy Trinity's parishioners. Some detailed woodwork from the fifteenth century remains: attached to the late nineteenth-century stalls are several fourteenth- and fifteenth-century bench ends with poppyheads. Two of these contain representations of the conflict between St George and the Dragon, while the remainder bear merchants' marks, demonstrating, once again, the close connection between prosperity and piety in the early life of the church.

Sarah McKeon

Hull: a county in its own right

In the space of barely 300 years Hull had gone from being a small fishing and trading community of less than 60 households to being one of the 25 largest towns in England; and it had supplanted its major rivals, Boston and King's Lynn, to become the second most important port on England's east and south coasts. Its extensive trading connections stretched from Spain and Portugal in the south, to Iceland in the north, and Russia and the Baltic states in the east. By the end of the Middle Ages the people who lived and worked in the town included immigrants and settlers from many different parts of Europe, as well as from other parts of Britain. It had developed a major deep-sea fishing industry which exploited the Icelandic and Greenland fishing areas; fish made up nearly 40 per cent of the recorded imports into Hull. By c. 1500 there were around 20 religious houses either within or immediately adjoining the town, yet it had developed so quickly that its main church was still officially classed as being only a chapel, and would not become a parish church until 1661. It had become a county in its own right and its corporation had established elaborate measures to pave and drain the streets, clean and remove rubbish, ensure a clean water supply, and keep the harbour and river free of obstructions. As a major strategic port, it now boasted an array of wharves and waterfronts, defended on the landward sides by an extensive walled circuit, while the entrance to the Hull could be closed off in times of threat. It had also endeavoured to ensure safe navigation on the dangerous waters of the Humber – one of the very first initiatives in English waters to provide safe passage for seafarers – and one which would later be copied by many other areas.

Notes

1 See S. Evans, Y. Boutwood, D. Knight and M. Oakey, *East Riding of Yorkshire: Chalk Lowland and the Hull Valley NMP. Aerial Investigations and Mapping Report*, English Heritage Research Report Series no. 39-2012 (Swindon, 2012), pp. 10–14.

2 Pers. comm. Peter Didsbury.

3 I. M. Stead, *British Iron Age Swords and Scabbards* (London: British Museum Press, 2006), p. 189, cat. no. 191, and fig. 96.

4 See D. H. Evans with K. A. Steedman, 'Archaeology in the Modern City of Kingston upon Hull, and Recent Research at Kingswood', in R. Van de Noort and S. Ellis (eds), *Wetland Heritage of the Hull Valley: An Archaeological Survey* (Humber Wetland Project, University of Hull, 2000), pp. 193–216, fig. 10.3.

5 Evans with Steedman, 'Archaeology in the Modern City', pp. 205–11, and fig. 10.7.

6 Evans with Steedman, 'Archaeology in the Modern City', figs 10.1–10.4, and pl. 15.

7 See M. P. T. Didsbury, 'Aspects of Late Iron Age and Romano-British Settlement in the Lower Hull Valley', unpublished MPhil thesis, University of Durham, 1990. Fig. 10.4 in Evans with Steedman, *Wetland Heritage*, is based on Didsbury's excellent and exhaustive gazetteer.

8 E. Gillett and K. A. MacMahon, *A History of Hull* (Hull: Hull University Press, 2nd edn, 1989), pp. 4 and 9; C. Frost, 'Of the change which took place in the course of the River Hull in the thirteenth century', in *Notices relating to the early history of the town and port of Hull, compiled from original records and unpublished manuscripts* (London, 1827), pp. 28–39, esp. p. 39.

9 See J. Travis-Cook, 'The Change in the Course of the River Hull', in J. Travis-Cook, *Notes relating to the Manor of Myton* (Hull and London: A. Brown and Sons, 1890), pp. 183–98, esp. p. 183; J. Travis-Cook, *Alde Hull* (Hull: Eastern Morning and News Co., 1905).

10 Travis-Cook, *Notes relating to the Manor of Myton*, pp. 133–34.

11 A. H. Smith, *The Place-Names of the East Riding of Yorkshire and York*, English Place-Name Society 14 (Cambridge, 1937), p. 213.

12 Travis-Cook, *Notes relating to the Manor of Myton*, p. 32.

13 Frost, *Notices relating to the early history*, pp. 7–8, and footnotes.

14 Smith, *The Place-Names of the East Riding*, p. 209.

15 K. J. Allison (ed.), *A History of the County of York East Riding: Volume 1, the City of Kingston upon Hull* (London: Victoria County History, 1969), p. 13 [hereafter *VCH*]. The reason that the wool for Richard's ransom was collected at Wyke is that the Humber was already developing as one of England's premier outlets for wool exports to mainland Europe – a reflection of the success of the Cistercians in turning large areas of upland waste into massive sheep-grazing areas on the Wolds, in the Dales or on the North York moors. By the end of the following century, the wool from some million and a half sheep would be exported through Hull every year, either as fleeces or as bales of finished cloth.

16 *The Great Roll of the Pipe for the tenth year of the Reign of King Richard I, Michaelmas 1198*, Pipe Roll Society, vol. 57 (New Series no. 9), p. 182.

17 N. S. B. Gras, 'The Early English Customs System', *Harvard Economic Studies*, 18 (1918), pp. 224–44; see also D. H. Evans, 'The Trade of Hull between 1200 and 1700', in M. Gläser (ed.), *Lübecker Kolloquium zur Stadtarchäologie im Hanseraum II: der Handel* (Lübeck, 1999), pp. 59–97, esp. Table 1.

18 E. A. Bond (ed.), *Chronica Monasterii de Melsa*, 3 vols, Rolls Series 43 (London, 1866–68), vol. I, p. 169.

19 *VCH*, p. 12.

20 As shown in raised bog sequences in both Britain and Scandinavia: J. G. Evans, *The Environment of Early Man in the British Isles* (London: Paul Elek, 1975), p. 175. See also C. Platt, *Medieval England: A Social History and Archaeology from the Conquest to 1600 AD* (London: Routledge and Kegan Paul, 1978), pp. 93–96.

21 See also R. Van de Noort, 'Medieval Wetland Exploitation', in R. Van de Noort, *The Humber Wetlands: The Archaeology of a Dynamic Landscape* (Macclesfield: Windgather Press, 2004), pp. 127–53 (p. 153); R. Van de Noort and P. Davies, 'Sea-level and Climatic Change', in R. Van de Noort and P. Davies, *Wetland Heritage: An Archaeological Assessment of the Humber Wetlands* (Humber Wetlands Project, University of Hull, 1993), pp. 38–40.

22 Gillett and MacMahon, *A History of Hull*, pp. 3–4. Charles Frost gave more detail, but dated these floods to 1256; Frost, *Notices relating to the early history*, p. 33.

23 Frost, *Notices relating to the early history*, p. 33; Bond, *Chronica Monasterii de Melsa*, vol. II, p. 91.

24 R. Gregory (ed.), *A63 Castle Street Improvements, Kingston upon Hull. Assessment, Mitigation and Deposit Modelling* (Lancaster: Oxford Archaeology North and Humber Field Archaeology, 2014).

25 Gregory, *A63 Castle Street Improvements*, fig. 34.

26 J. Bilson, 'Wyke upon Hull in 1293', *Transactions of the East Riding Antiquarian Society*, 26 (1926–28), pp. 37–105.

27 See Bilson, 'Wyke upon Hull in 1293'; R. E. Horrox, *The Changing Plan of Hull, 1290–1650: A Guide to Documentary Sources for the Early Topography of Hull* (Hull, 1978); R. E. Horrox (ed.), *Selected Rentals and Accounts of Medieval Hull 1293–1528*, Yorkshire Archaeological Society Record Series 141 (Leeds, 1983).

28 See F. W. Brooks, 'A Medieval Brick-Yard at Hull', *Journal of the British Archaeological Association*, (3rd ser.) 4 (1939), pp. 151–74.

29 See D. H. Evans, 'The Archaeology of Religious Houses in Beverley and Hull', in M. Gläser (ed.), *Lübecker Kolloquium zur Stadtarchäologie im Hanseraum IX: die Klöster* (Lübeck, 2014), pp. 47–62. For earlier publications, see D. H. Evans, 'Buried with the Friars', *British Archaeology*, 53 (2000), pp. 18–23; and D. H. Evans, 'Buried with the Friars', in P. Bahn (ed.), *Written in Bones:*

How Human Remains Unlock the Secrets of the Dead (Buffalo, NY, and London: Firefly Books, 2003), pp. 27–31.

30 B. S. Ayers, *Excavations at Chapel Lane Staith, 1978*, East Riding Archaeologist 5 (Hull Old Town Rep. Ser. no. 3) (Hull, 1979). See also D. H. Evans and J. Bradley, *An Archaeological Evaluation on Land at Blaydes Staith, Little High Street, Kingston upon Hull*, Humber Archaeological Reports 177 (Hull, 2004). Other waterfront structures have been examined at 54–58 and 60 High Street, while post-medieval waterfronts were investigated at 10–18 Wincolmlee.

31 D. H. Evans, 'The Fortifications of Hull between 1300 and 1700', in M. Gläser (ed.), *Lübecker Kolloquium zur Stadtarchäologie im Hanseraum VII: die Befestigungen* (Lübeck, 2010), pp. 47–70, fig. 1. See also D. H. Evans, *Excavations at the Beverley Gate, and Other Parts of the Town Defences of Kingston-upon-Hull*, archive report prepared for Historic England (Hull, 2015).

32 D. H. Evans, 'The Infrastructure of Hull between 1275 and 1700', in M. Gläser (ed.), *Lübecker Kolloquium zur Stadtarchäologie im Hanseraum IV: die Infrastruktur* (Lübeck, 2004), pp. 51–73, fig. 12.

33 P. Whitting, *Coins, Tokens and Medals of the East Riding of Yorkshire*, East Yorkshire Local History Series 23 (Beverley: East Yorkshire Local History Society, 1969), p. 7.

34 See also D. H. Evans, 'Urban Domestic Architecture in the Lower Hull Valley in the Medieval and Early Post-medieval Periods', in M. Gläser (ed.), *Lübecker Kolloquium zur Stadtarchäologie im Hanseraum, III: der Hausbau* (Lübeck, 2001), pp. 49–76, where this is discussed in more detail.

35 Horrox (ed.), *Selected Rentals*, p. 62.

36 Cf. D. H. Evans, 'Luxury in the Medieval Town? Reflections on the Evidence for Lifestyles and Wealth Distribution in Hull from 1300 to 1700', in M. Gläser (ed.), *Lübecker Kolloquium zur Stadtarchäologie im Hanseraum VI: Luxus und Lifestyle* (Lübeck, 2008), pp. 63–93, fig. 1.

37 Evans, 'Luxury', fig. 2.

38 Evans, 'Luxury', fig. 6.

39 Evans, 'Luxury', figs 7–8 and 13.

40 Evans, 'Luxury', fig. 12.

41 *VCH*, pp. 25 and 371. In all, 57 *fothers* of lead, worth £93, were recovered by digging up this water supply. A *fother* was an old measure of weight which in the later Middle Ages equated to 19½ hundredweight, but which in the post-medieval period could equate to 20 or even 22 hundredweight. See W. R. Childs (ed.), *The Customs Accounts of Hull 1453–1490*, Yorkshire Archaeological Society Record Series CXLIV (Leeds, 1986), Appendix III, p. 254.

42 For the full text, see D. Woodward (ed.), *Descriptions of East Yorkshire: Leland to Defoe*, East Yorkshire Local History Series 39 (Beverley: East Yorkshire Local History Society, 1985), pp. 22–23.

In dei nomine Amen Ego Agnes Bea[...]
corpore tamen sana mente quartodecimo [...]
Anno [...] nono meam ultimam voluntatem
[...] meam omnipotenti Deo bte mar[...]
meum sepeliendum in capella Sanct[...]
Sancte appe de pyte vocat mortuar[...]
penultatum capacie meie myta item Gill[...]
[...] et fabrice capelle pdict p sepultura
Summo Altar Summ brudcloith et [...]
meo dna mea pecia upient opt et coopt me[...]
cocliar meum optimum butt meum optim[...]
meum optimum pec deamyat Summ ulm pe[...]
men optimum Salt Cclar cum cooptoz vnum
byoche meum optimum onche de Auro Item
meie optime vnum par blankett de fust[...]
alios annulos Sumatoz ynozum vnum h[...]
Sperrett avtient Item Elizabeth spa em[...]
oznat Summ par ppicium de Auro cum Sm[...]
cozall cum Gullee de Gold meum optim[...]
de ppopr cosevo Item Agneti Olivan mea[...]
baper throtth onte et deamvat Sum de mer[...]
cum Akehornee Sum pmum maffy nonu vnu[...]
par cozall bedee lautfeft cum Sno byoche de
optime coseie meum optimum Cadell Harn[...]
ptuent ad eafom monm nonu jmapnm [...]
[...]una Sulton capellam meum fecundu[...]

CHAPTER TWO

Hull's Medieval Lives

ELISABETH SALTER

The medieval men and women of Hull had culturally vibrant lives. They developed the fabric of their town by building and renovating homes, commercial properties and civic buildings, and through the construction and repair of roads, causeways and wharfs. In so doing, they exhibited a sense of civic pride, a feature of which was manifest in the care and attention they lavished on religious buildings. Medieval Christianity was a vehicle for the expression of individual ideas and creativity, as well as comprising a set of beliefs and values imposed from above. It was therefore an important element in the cultural and social dimensions of Hull's development. The people of Hull also had interests and loyalties beyond the town through their connections with villages and towns in the surrounding area and across the Humber, and with places in more distant parts of the British Isles. Others forged significant links with the wider world. A number of Hull's inhabitants had lived elsewhere before settling in the town, while many townsfolk consumed goods and food that had been imported through their port, and others produced goods that were destined for overseas markets. Still more conveyed goods in and out of the haven in the River Hull, either as merchants or as seafarers charged with ensuring the safe passage of cargoes and people to and from Scandinavia, north-west Europe, Iberia and the Mediterranean, as well as numerous shipping places along Britain's coasts.

The documentary and archaeological fragments left by the men and women who dwelled in Hull during the late medieval era offer glimpses of the economy, society and cultural activity of a medieval town. The written record of the town's government demonstrates how Hull developed following its foundation in 1299, and provides insights into how the place was governed and the processes by which its ruling elite gained and retained power. The financial records of the borough identify the sources and fluctuating scale of the income streams that sustained Hull's civic authorities during the late medieval era. Key contributions included the entry fines paid by wealthy people who wished to be affiliated to the town, local taxes imposed for various town building and repair projects, and port dues exacted from the owners of coastal and foreign-going merchant vessels that utilised the facilities of the port to load and discharge cargoes. Surviving records also indicate the town's main outgoings, notably the money it paid annually to the Crown. The records of religious guilds and institutions reveal much about the role of the Church in the spiritual and cultural life of the town, while the archives of central government illuminate key developments in the town's constitutional and political evolution.

But how do we know about the lifestyles, cultures and beliefs of the people who made up the majority of the medieval population of Hull – the people whose lives and voices are otherwise lost to us because they were not part of a ruling elite? What can we discover about those who were not commemorated for their artistic, political or cultural contribution to the life of the city? One of the most useful sources of evidence about these people's lives is their last wills and testaments – documents drawn up, ironically, in anticipation of the end of those lives (Figure 2.1). Medieval wills are, in fact, vibrant sources of information about a person's hopes for the future. They demonstrate and define the testator's loyalty to places of current or past residence, and his or her devotion to religious and cultural groups. And they also specify bequests and other forms of support designed to contribute to the prosperity and health of surviving family members, friends and people of the same

2.1 The will of Agnes Bedford of Kingston upon Hull, proved October 1459. Last will and testament evidence can be used to trace the personal connections that were fundamental to people's lives and can be used to understand more about the interests, aspirations and constraints on individuals and communities. A selection of last will and testament documents can also help to build a picture of the ways in which Hull property owners interacted with their immediate vicinity as well as further afield. Wills are valuable documents for discovering more about the relationship between 'people' and 'place' over the course of history.
Reproduction from an original in the Borthwick Institute for Archives, University of York, Prob. Reg. 2, f.418

occupation, who, it was hoped, would continue to play a part in the remembrance of the deceased's life and the ongoing success of his or her family.[1]

Numerous last will and testament documents made by Hull people during the 1350–1500 period have survived and are now held in either the National Archives (Kew, London), the Borthwick Institute (University of York) or Hull History Centre. Most of the wills made before 1480 were written in Latin, with more in English thereafter. As legal instruments, the wills are formulaic, with each text reflecting a set of cultural norms, some of which were local and regional customs, while others were facets of the medieval world view. Although medieval people from quite far down the social scale made wills, the poorest people were not in a position to create a written document, partly due to cost, but largely because they had few items to bequeath. Their hopes for the future and any possessions they owned would have been transmitted informally to the next generation. Notwithstanding these limitations, wonderful nuggets of biographical information are contained in the last will and testament documents that have survived. The richest insights relate to the will-maker and his or her family, but light is also cast on the lives of beneficiaries who have otherwise left no traces of their existence. Such light by no means tells the whole story but it is sufficient to illuminate important aspects of the lives of Hull's medieval people.

Trade: the fount of Hull's medieval prosperity

Following its establishment as a town by Edward I in the charter of 1299, Kingston upon Hull grew in size and organisational complexity during the fourteenth and fifteenth centuries. A self-governing structure was established in 1440 when the town was 'incorporated'. This enabled Hull to form a governance structure of aldermen and burgesses, comprising members of the civic elite and incomers able to pay to assume the status of burgess. A mayor was elected from among the burgesses and aldermen. During the fifteenth century, merchants dominated the group of people serving as aldermen, which meant very strong connections between civic identity, decision-making and the town's commercial activities.[2]

Hull's economy was dependent to a significant extent on overseas trade in the fourteenth and fifteenth centuries.[3] Fishing vessels based in Hull extracted cod, ling and haddock from the waters off Norway and Iceland, curing their catches on the adjacent shores before sailing for markets in England and northern Europe. Merchant ships carried goods between Hull and an array of ports in Scandinavia, the eastern Baltic and the Low Countries. Vessels belonging to local and alien merchants frequently brought goods such as wine, salt, dye and cloth into Hull, and then conveyed outbound cargoes of wool, cloth and corn across the North Sea, and occasionally south through the Channel to Iberia and the Mediterranean.[4] Although there were fluctuations in the scale and direction of seaborne trade, Hull remained 'one of the busiest provincial ports in the whole of England, ranking second only to Boston in wool exports, second or third to Bristol and Southampton in cloth exports and wine imports up to the mid-fifteenth century'.[5] Relatively high traffic volumes in the port, however, did not necessarily mean that the town was proportionately prosperous, for the lay subsidy returns of 1334 and the 1377 poll tax accounts reveal that Hull was the least affluent of the six major east coast ports north of London – largely because many of the merchants who controlled the key trades were resident in Hull's hinterland, notably in York and Beverley.[6] Ship-owning was more closely geared to port traffic levels, and was therefore important in Hull, as witnessed by the fact that vessels, or shares in vessels, were identified as heirlooms in the last will and testament documents prepared for numerous Hull people. In 1437, for instance, when John Gregg, a prominent and wealthy merchant of Hull, died, Joan, his wife, became a wealthy widow and soon afterwards she bequeathed to Stephen Gildhouse and William Arnold a 32nd share in her vessel, the *George*.[7] In another instance, in 1455, John Herryson, a burgess of Hull, bequeathed to his wife, Agnes, all his shares in two vessels, the *Anne of Hull* and the *Julian*.[8]

The Hull people who traded as Merchants of the Staple during the late fourteenth and fifteenth centuries were often members of the town's civic elite. Like other medieval towns, Hull was required to pay a specific amount of money, known as 'the king's farm', to the Crown on an annual basis. This was gathered from property owners in the town as a form of taxation. Other taxes were imposed on the commons for particular purposes according to the needs of the town, with contributions to the repair of the staiths and jetties regularly required. Most of the town's income derived from payments by new burgesses and rents from town property, together with monies generated by Hull's status as a customs head port, which included the rent of the South Ferry, profits from the weigh house and various tolls. These incomes varied according to the prosperity of the town on a year-by-year basis, with a general decline evident in the income received by Kingston upon Hull during the mid-fifteenth century, a pattern observed in other port-towns in England. The contraction was perhaps due to the emergence of new towns, which may have diverted money away from older towns such as Hull.[9] However, by the fifteenth century, due to the prosperity of Hull's foreign commerce, the wills of local people rival those of London with respect to the ownership of valuable items such as silverware, fine textiles and fashionable styles of furniture (Figure 2.2). In 1459, for example, Agnes Bedford honoured and remembered her family and kinsfolk through the bequest of money, land and goods. Her son, John Dalton, was the main beneficiary, his mother's will listing a range of valuable items that he stood to inherit, including a set of silver best spoons, a silver salt cellar with a cover, unidentified pieces of gilted silverware, brooches, and other pieces of jewellery, notably three rings, one of which was a signet ring decorated with a cross, and a silver 'powderbox'. Agnes also willed to John an 'Arryswarke' (Arras) tapestry, together with her fine bed (Figure 2.3). John's wife, Elizabeth, was honoured in her mother-in-law's will through gifts of precious gold jewellery decorated with beryl, a pair of coral beads with various trinkets and her best decorated girdle. Further bequests were made to Agnes Swan, who was to receive 'a christenynge gyrdell' decorated with bars of silver-gilt, together with silver spoons decorated with acorns ('akehornes'), a new maser cup, the longest of her coral beads, one of her finest coffers, her best saddle and a harness made of worsted cloth.[10]

While these kinds of goods do not paint a full picture of the wealth and economic fortunes of a town, they are indicative of a level of prosperity among a group of people who represented the commonality and their servants. This group was not fixed, however, and it is possible that the balance of wealth may have been shifting within Hull during the fifteenth century, as once-wealthy families declined while new families emerged as leaders in the town's economy and society. This did not happen overnight and the close-knit nature of the ruling elite (especially the aldermen) protected against sudden shifts in the power structure. Fluctuations in the fortunes of families, as indicated by property ownership, are sometimes signalled in wills in which the distribution and inheritance of property is addressed. A reference by John Dalton, in the codicil to his will written in 1492, to property recently purchased from Thomas Lazenby, which had previously been owned by John Gregg, suggests how wealth might pass quickly between families.[11] As John and Joan Gregg died without living children, their family name failed to survive regardless of the wealth they generated and the success they enjoyed, through lack of direct heirs. Another influence on the shifting pattern of wealth may have been the arrival of new people in the town, either from other parts of England or from further afield.

As a significant port, Hull experienced population flows related to trading patterns. Foreigners, mainly from the Netherlands, Germany, the Hanse ports and Iceland, were known as 'aliens'. Some of the rules and restrictions over the trading rights of 'aliens' caused controversy and commotion. There were disputes, for instance, about the commercial obligations of Hanseatic merchants, which

2.2 This rosary box is the type of personal item that was sometimes bequeathed in medieval wills. As an heirloom, it suggests that the owner was concerned about his or her faith and wanted to be remembered as pious. It could also be viewed as an object intended to enable the deceased person to encourage devotion and religious practice after his or her death. The box was found in a sandpit at Sancton in the East Riding of Yorkshire in about 1858. A small linen label is attached to the rosary and inscribed with ink. The rosary is of 30 unglazed earthenware beads of red and black clay. The inscription in Latin reads: *IESU MV(?) HOMINUM SAVATOR* and *PAPCRRSS*. There is one larger lozenge-shaped bead incised with a cross. The box is made of leather-covered wood, decorated with stylised leaf motifs and bound with narrow iron strips with brass nails. The lining is blue velvet. The box was portable and could be locked.
© The Trustees of the British Museum. Paris, 1480–1520

occasionally generated rivalry with traders in neighbouring commercial centres such as York.[12] Hull's role as a port is reflected in the occupations of its medieval men and women, many of whom were described as merchants, with some being away from home, presumably on business, according to the testamentary record. A case in point is the ailing John Paynton of Hull, who was described in his will text of 1474 as 'lyeing in extremis' in the port-town of Sandwich in Kent.[13]

Alien merchants might only stay for a short time in Hull, where they were 'hosted' by families in the town, which generated valuable income for those who accommodated the visitors. Some stayed longer and became naturalised, with people from Germany, the Netherlands and Scotland prominent among the immigrants.[14] Twelve Icelanders paid an alien tax known as a subsidy in 1465–66, which implies that they had stayed for longer than the statutory visiting time. A significant number of Hull's brewers, moreover, were 'Dutchmen', including Brand Adryanson, a 'berebrewer' who was active in Hull in the second half of the fifteenth century.[15] In his will text, made in 1502, there are hints that he belonged to a community of brewers, many of whom had Netherlandish connections, judging by their names. Adryanson specified that his body be buried in St Mary's church in Hull 'under the stone where one Florien berebrewer was buryed'. Given the extent of his property ownership in the town and surrounding area, he had clearly become a full member of Hull's business community by the time of his death. Adryanson identified Alison Johnson, widow, late the wife of Cornelius Johnson 'berebrewer', as the person to assist in donating money to the church for mourning vestments.[16] Cornelius made his will in August 1502.[17] He also wished to be buried in St Mary's, before the image of St Salvator, suggesting that the Netherlandish brewers of Hull used this church, rather than the alternative, Holy Trinity, which was used by many merchants, as a key point in the formation and maintenance of their community (Figures 2.4–2.6).

In describing the alien visitors to medieval Hull – some of whom became residents like the Dutch brewers – it is difficult to define a stable native population of the town. In the fourteenth and fifteenth centuries, in-migration from outlying villages and further afield was common. The surnames of medieval Hull people offer

2.3 Entombment, from a tapestry with scenes of the Passion of Christ. Agnes Bedford describes a tapestry of 'Arryswarke' (tapestry work made in the Arras region of France), which was bequeathed to John alongside her best bed. The tapestry mentioned by Agnes could have been very similar to this one and would have been used to decorate the home. The possession of a beautiful object such as this is yet another indication that the Bedfords were wealthy people and that they lived in a thriving trading environment with access to a wide range of goods.
© Victoria and Albert Museum. Wool woven. Arras, France, c. 1400–25. Museum number: T.1-1921

2.4 St Mary's church, Lowgate. The churches in and around Hull were at the centre of people's lives and the people of Hull gave generously to support religious institutions and their communities in the region. The church underwent two significant restoration projects in the twentieth century – one in 1936–37 and a longer project lasting from 2000 to 2007. The project during the 1930s addressed issues resulting from weathered stonework and made repairs to the nave and chancel roofs. The more recent restoration project attended to the pinnacles on the tower and worn stone. During this period of restoration the clear clerestory glass was also replaced.
Courtesy of Hull History Centre

clues as to the recent origins of families, with numerous villages in Holderness, the Wolds and the Vale of York, as well as the towns and villages of the West Riding, represented in the roll call of the town's population. In 1377 approximately one-third of the adult population that was surveyed had names resonant of places both near to and far beyond Hull.[18] In the 1377 poll tax return for Hull, nearby place names used as surnames include, for example, Barton, Bainton, Beverley, Cottingham, Easingwold, Hedon, Hemingbrough, Hessle and Swinefleet. Slightly further afield, places are represented by names such as Alnwick, Chesterfield, Darlington, Derby,

2.5 St Mary's church now reflects the Gothic Revival restoration work carried out by Sir George Gilbert Scott during the nineteenth century. As this image of the churchyard and south aisle indicates, however, it still retains a sense of its authentic medieval past.
David and Susan Neave

2.6 One of St Mary's tall slender pillars with carved capitals, dating from the fifteenth century. Carved heads and winged angels sit between the large pillars and their arches, separating the nave from the single north aisle and double south aisle. David and Susan Neave

Gateshead, Nottingham, Spalding, Wetherby and Whitby. References from further afield include, for example, Bristol, Canterbury, Norfolk and also Ireland.[19]

The flow of people and cargoes from across the seas and around the coasts contributed to the diversity of goods consumed, and clothing worn, by medieval Hull townsfolk. The spruce chests mentioned in a number of fifteenth-century wills were almost certainly imported from the regions of northern Europe with which Hull had strong commercial links.[20] The 'oversea' work mentioned by Robert Herryson in 1520 in his request for a commemorative tablet to the honour of Corpus Christi is also, presumably, a reference to a fashion of craftsmanship associated with another country, possibly the Netherlands.[21] And the request by Brand Adryanson for a 'mass of Jesus' to be said every Friday in the almshouse he founded in Hull shows that it was not only new goods that passed through Hull, but also ideas about the new devotions (the *Devotio moderna*) associated with the development of Protestantism, which was more sustained from an earlier date in Adryanson's native Netherlands.[22]

Property ownership in medieval Hull and its vicinity

Testators generally perceived Kingston upon Hull as the centre of their lives. The town was divided into six wards from *c.* 1442 – Humber, Blackfriar (also called Austin Ward), Trinity, Whitefriar, St Mary and Trippett (called North Ward after 1459) – which functioned largely as administrative units, each deploying two constables and two aldermen for governance purposes.[23] Ward names, however, were rarely used in the wills of Hull people to describe the location of their property, most electing to cite street name and occupier, or the person from whom the property had recently been purchased. In 1459, for example, Agnes Bedford bequeathed to her son, John Dalton, her tenement with all its appurtenances called 'Hedon' lying in 'le hygate' within the town of Kingston upon Hull.[24] Nearly thirty years later, Dalton still had assets in central Hull, for in 1487 he requested that debts be settled using 'one of the houses on Lowgate'.[25] John Herryson (burgess) bequeathed to his wife Agnes his tenanted tenement in Hull Street, which was described in 1455 as being 'on the west side of the town'.[26] John and Joan Gregg also owned property on Hull Street, where Hugo Swynfleet was the tenant. John Gregg also owned a rented house in Whitefriargate.[27] In 1502 Brand Adryanson's portfolio of properties included a house that he had purchased from Jenet Copyndale 'next to the customhouse', a house in 'Kyrkelane' that he had bought from Hull merchant Robert Matthew, and a tenement annexed to his chapel and bede house (a type of almshouse).[28] In 1520 Robert Herryson identified two tenements in Salthouse Lane, which he left to his wife on condition that she used the funds to pay for prayers for his soul.[29] These Hull property owners invariably stated that their final resting place should be in their home town, most willing that they should be buried in the 'chapel' or 'kirk' of 'St Trinity' – Holy Trinity church (Figures 2.7–2.11) – or 'St Mary Chapel'.

The wills suggest how individuals perceived Hull in relation to the surrounding area. In 1474 John Paynton referred to Drypool – late at the heart of the town – as being 'beside' Hull.[30] In 1502 Brand Adryanson described properties that were near Kingston upon Hull, but not in a central location, as being situated in the 'lordship of Myton'. This included the 'wynd mille' that he purchased from Maude Ettan, who had remarried to become the wife of John Bowdon, a goldsmith.[31] Ties with places in the vicinity and further afield were often expressed in a last will and testament through a charitable or religious bequest. For example, in 1437 John Gregg left £4 for a window in the nearby church of Brantingham, as well as £10 towards the fabric

2.7 The church of Holy Trinity benefited greatly from the wealth and piety of the people of Hull. Money from bequests was used to construct the building and furnish it. People used the church as a site to memorialise their lives by paying for engravings and other decorative features that often referred to the individuals' personal religious interests.
London: J. H. Hinton, 1829; courtesy of Hull History Centre

TRINITY CHURCH, HULL.

London: Published by J.T.Hinton, N°4 Warwick Square, June 1829.

of the church at Ellerker.[32] In 1438 John's wife Joan gave 100s towards the mending of vestments at Weighton church.[33] No clues were given as to how the Greggs were associated with these three places. In 1487 John Dalton (d. 1502) left 6s 8d for the making of a rood loft at Patrington and other church works; his will suggests that he had family connections in this locality, as he also bequeathed money to members of the Gildhouse family of Patrington. Other members of the Dalton family referred to people of this surname, particularly Stephen Gildhouse of Hull.[34]

Connections to places in the near vicinity were made more explicit by other Hull testators. Robert Herryson (1520), for example, had various interests in the north Lincolnshire area: the supervisor of his will was John Cole, the vicar of Barton upon Humber; he bequeathed 20s to the Saint Katherine chapel in Saltfleet Haven, and 20s to the chapel's cross 'in the said town'; and he left his tenement in 'Saltflete' haven and a croft called 'sedyke croft' to his wife with the request that this property be given to the Our Lady guild at Skidbrooke – the parish that now incorporates Saltfleet Haven – on her death. The parish church of St Botulph in Skidbrooke was of particular significance for Robert Herryson because, as he narrated through his will text, 'there I was born'.[35] His gift of 20s for the repair of the causeway between Saltfleet Haven and the church implies that he had personal experience of living in this environment, where the land was prone to flooding from the sea.

Other individuals maintained connections with places beyond the immediate vicinity due to family ties, past and present. Agnes Bedford made several references to 'Novi Castri' (Newcastle) in her Latin will text of 1459. In particular, she requested

2.8 This view of Holy Trinity church from Trinity Square offers a sense of the continued importance of the church as an integral part of the town. Holy Trinity is a prime example of a place of worship founded on the prosperity of the local worshippers' success in business, trade and commerce.
David and Susan Neave

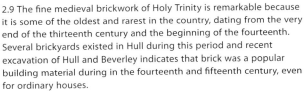

2.9 The fine medieval brickwork of Holy Trinity is remarkable because it is some of the oldest and rarest in the country, dating from the very end of the thirteenth century and the beginning of the fourteenth. Several brickyards existed in Hull during this period and recent excavation of Hull and Beverley indicates that brick was a popular building material during in the fourteenth and fifteenth century, even for ordinary houses.
David and Susan Neave

2.10 The Selby monument in Holy Trinity church features late fourteenth- or early fifteenth-century *gisants* (recumbent effigies) in local Ledsham alabaster. The effigies are of a wealthy husband and wife resting on a tomb chest, decorated with shields and quatrefoils. They are believed to depict Richard de Selby and his wife. Selby served at least six times as mayor of Hull and was an important merchant, trading with Gascony and the Low Countries. The Selby family gave generous amounts of money to support the church, most of which came through mercantile activities.
David and Susan Neave

2.11 Some of the detailed woodwork from the fifteenth century remains in Holy Trinity church. This image on a bench end in the choir shows St George standing triumphant over the slain dragon.
David and Susan Neave

that the Friars Minor of Newcastle say prayers for the souls of Richard Dalton and John Strother (her first two husbands before she married John Bedford), as well as herself, her deceased children and her parents. Rents to the value of 8s per annum from her properties in the 'Kirkstyle' part of the parish of St Nicholas, Newcastle, were to be used to fund this request. Another indication of Agnes Bedford's determination to maintain her connection commemoratively with Newcastle and the Strother family lay in gifts of fine clothing and bedding made to kinswoman Johanne Strother, and a small powderbox and some money to Johanne's son, John.[36]

Religious institutions in the vicinity of Hull were frequently cited in wills, suggesting that they constituted significant markers in the mental maps that medieval people sketched of their locality. As well as Beverley Minster and the Cathedral Church of St Peter in York, some testators were very specific, Joan Gregg, for instance, referring to 'each female anchorite of Beverley' to whom she gave a mantel with a hood, perhaps fearing for the cold conditions in which these people lived.[37] Occasionally, a testator gave a more particular sense of connectedness between places, using religious and charitable institutions to map the links. Both John and Joan Gregg (1437, 1438), for example, made bequests to the guild of St Mary in Hull, as well as the guild of St Mary in the Church of St Bridget in London. Joan's will text hinted at a particular spiritual or symbolic connection between London and Hull by including, in a single sentence, bequests of money to the guild of St Mary at both locations.[38]

Hull's medieval communities

The men and women of Hull tended to live, work and die in networks and communities that comprised interlocking and overlapping groupings of close and extended family members and people with common occupational interests and religious beliefs. These interpersonal associations, both formal and informal, were expressed, extended and confirmed through the giving of gifts as prescribed in an individual's last will and testament. The significance of family groups in medieval Hull is clearly evident in surviving wills. One such familial network can be perceived in the willed distribution of Agnes Bedford's property, which shows the ties that connected the Bedfords, Daltons and Swans. In passing to her son, John Dalton, all her land and tenements in the area of Hull known as Highgate, Agnes requested that should John die before he produced an heir all this property should revert to Agnes Swan, and that after Agnes's death it should pass to John Swan (junior), the son of John (senior) and Agnes. Sadly, we know from the will of John Swan that both his wife, Agnes, and their son, John, were already deceased by the time that he made his will in 1476. In that document, he requested specifically that all the goods that Agnes Bedford had left to his wife and son be passed to his daughter, Joanne.[39]

John and Joan Gregg have already been identified as a wealthy couple who had no surviving children when they came to make their wills in 1437 and 1438, respectively. As both gave to people from the same families, we can deduce that their wills were used to confirm and develop a network of kin, perhaps of extended family, in the absence of direct heirs. For example, both John and Joan employed Stephen Gildhouse to take responsibility for the execution of their wishes,[40] and both identified Radulph Forme, Christopher (and John) Wells and William Arnold as significant beneficiaries. Accordingly, Christopher and John Wells each received silver pots from Joan, while from John they were both given a piece of silver worth 66s 8d. John Gregg also identified Christopher Wells as a major beneficiary in lands and property after the death of Joan, with an estate that included rents in Whitefriargate, messuages in Hull and the main dwelling house, which would have been occupied by Joan in her widowhood. Like her husband, Joan gave 8lb of wax to all the saints' lights in Holy Trinity, with the exception of the light of St Anne. Given that St Anne is the patron saint of motherhood and childbirth, one wonders if that light had already received an excess of gifts from Joan, or whether the benefactor had little in the way of thanks to offer this saint.[41]

This was just one of many bequests made by the Greggs to religious institutions in the town. They remembered in their wills the Charterhouse a mile north of the city wall, as well as the Carmelite and Augustinian friars, with Joan making a bequest of lead to mend the roofs of the friars' houses to the value of £10 for each order.[42] Both John and Joan commemorated an extensive list of religious guilds in the church of Holy Trinity: St Trinity, Corpus Christi, the Resurrection, Blessed Mary, St John the Baptist, St George, St Anne, St Elias and St Katherine. The Greggs' identification of so many guilds was quite unusual, and probably indicated a desire to demonstrate their civic identity and pride as well as their religious commitments and activities. Another notable benefactor of such guilds was Cornelius Johnson, a brewer from the Netherlands, who may have valued the support offered by religious guilds to aliens and incomers, for in his 1452 will he referred extensively to Hull's religious guilds, especially those of St Salvator, St James the Apostle, St Anne, St George, the Resurrection, St Barbara and St Ninian (Figure 2.12).[43]

As well as religious guilds, there were guilds organised according to occupation. Medieval Hull seems to have been relatively poorly served by clearly defined occupational guilds, but it did have a number of religious guilds that provided support in matters of trade, finance and markets.[44] The St Mary Guild of Holy Trinity had a preponderance of members engaged in merchant activity. The customs accounts of the second half of the fifteenth century indicate that guild officers such as Thomas Calthorne were engaged in large-scale international trade, including the shipment of armour, cutlery, cloth, grain and metals. Some of Hull's religious guilds did change their identity to emphasise the specific occupations they increasingly represented. In 1456, for example, the Holy Trinity Guild – which was responsible for the performance of the Noah Play annually on Plough Monday – became a shipmen's guild exclusively for mariners skilled in navigation, while in 1499 the guild of St George evolved into a merchants' guild intent on supplying religious and civic support to that occupational community.[45] Institutions such as the St Mary Guild functioned as a sort of building society, providing loans for trading ventures,[46] while other guilds enabled people to belong to a group with shared interests, through which good practice could be disseminated and a level of protection might be afforded by common financial arrangements.[47] Such bodies catered for the needs and activities of mariners, merchants, brewers and other trades dominated by men. Whether guilds were concerned with the needs of women in commerce is unclear. But we can be sure that women were taking part in business activities and, judging from the ways that land and property were described in wills, that women engaged to a significant degree in the management of the rents, lands and properties that were passed to them when they became widows.

Another form of communal activity is apparent in the provision of aid for the needy by well-to-do benefactors. One of the ways that more wealthy testators could assist with providing support to the poor people of the town was the provision of housing or shelter, such as almshouses, hospitals and *maisons dieu*. In 1438 Joan Gregg's gift of the almshouse that she had had built in Aldkirk Lane (Posterngate) was intended to support thirteen poor people. Her bequest was designed to continue that provision long after her death and the death of its first custodian, Thomas Marflete, a local chaplain, as she proposed that the responsibility for the provision should revert to the mayor and corporation of the town after Marflete's death. Money from rents on other of her properties to the value of £5 4s was to pay for this provision in perpetuity, with the poor people themselves receiving 2s 7d twice per year.[48] In 1502 Brand Adryanson, the brewer, demonstrated his continued loyalty to what was probably his adopted home town by bequeathing a 'Beydhouse and Chappell with a garden thereto', to be paid for by his wife using money she would be receiving from various rents in the town. This was to provide a dwelling place for four old men with the provision of a quantity of coal twice per year, in return for their attendance at the weekly 'mass of Jesus' that was to be established through his will.[49] Gifts to *maisons dieu* are mentioned by a number of testators. Hull had a number of these institutions during the fifteenth century, including Holy Trinity *maison dieu*, which was located in Holy Trinity churchyard and housed twelve poor men and women in 1463, Kingston's *maison dieu*, which was active on Whitefriargate until about 1540, and others on Scale Lane, Chapel Lane (next to St Mary's church), and at Beverley Gate.[50]

There were other ways of supporting the poor members of Hull's medieval community through customary charitable bequests. A standard bequest was to provide mourning clothing and a small amount of money to enable and oblige poor people to serve as mourners at the burial service and offer prayers for the dead, a requirement that might last for several weeks. Other individuals embellished this custom by giving more substantial or complex gifts to the poor, with Joan Gregg (again) leaving money for the provision and repair of poor people's woollen clothes.[51] A number of testators provided gifts of money or goods to their servants. In 1520, for example, Robert Herryson gave 6s 8d to each of his male and female servants, as well as a coat of black cloth to another named servant, Robert Forth. Agnes Bedford bequeathed a blue coverlet, with a pair of gloves, to one of her woman servants,[52] while John Gregg left utensils worth 40 shillings to three women servants – Marie, Ellen Chesterton and Alice Wellam – together with sums of money to other individuals in the service of his kinsfolk, specifically Andrew, the servant of Elene Kirkton, and Robert Johnson, the servant of Radulph Form. John further charged his executors with ensuring that all of his servants were well looked after following his death.[53]

A further way for medieval townspeople to provide for the community as a whole, including the poor, in the places that mattered to them was to make bequests that sought to improve the living environment. In the Hull area, gifts of money to repair causeways were noticeably frequent, presumably due to the specific geographical features of the area. The Greggs did not miss this opportunity to undertake civic good works, and duly left money to improve the causeways from Newland to Beverley, and from Hull to Anlaby. Others chose to donate this element of their civic identity to places outside Hull, one example being Robert Herryson, who provided for the repair of the causeway between Saltfleet Haven and the church at Skidbrooke. Others gave money for the repair of roads and bridges, with Joan Gregg surpassing most by bequeathing £20 for the maintenance of the 'conduit of sweet water' that descended into Hull.[54]

Medieval Hull was also characterised by its literate culture – the diffusion of book learning and enjoyment through a community comprising many members who

2.13 The merchant mark of William Gee on Hull Grammar School, dated 1583, is a lasting reminder of the important role of merchants and their investments in the building of Hull and its social spaces. Financial support for the grammar school would have been a prudent investment strategy for the merchant families of Hull, since in this way they could help to ensure that future generations would have the skills and education to prosper in the wider world and to continue to build on the town's prosperity.
David and Susan Neave

could not necessarily read in the way we understand reading today (Figure 2.13). The gift of books, as itemised in wills, illustrates the literate activities of fifteenth-century Hull people. Agnes Bedford, for instance, bequeathed to Agnes Swan her new primer book, alongside a book with prayers which 'once belong[ed] to John Dalton'.[55] These two books are both associated with religion, the primer being a service book containing all the various liturgies for the year, and we might therefore consider them as providing less access to the cultural interests of these people than if they were recognisably works of literature. It is important to remember that for medieval people, books were less readily available than today, and that works of religious instruction and books associated with church services were a main source of literate activity for most. Furthermore, just because these are religious works does not mean that they were entirely governed by liturgy. The book 'with prayers' mentioned by Agnes Bedford may well have contained some of the very beautiful and moving lyrical verses that were circulating in English in the fifteenth century. These were designed to engage the reader's emotional focus on important themes in the Christian story, such as the crucifixion of Christ, and were highly wrought literary pieces rather than simply works of religious devotion. Agnes also gave another book to her kinswoman's son, 'John Junior', which was described as being 'for everyday use', implying that it was a less valuable item. Perhaps this gift to the young John was intended to encourage him in developing his reading.

This Bedford/Dalton family group provide some particularly good evidence of Hull people's involvement with literate culture and the ways that gifts passing through families might have enhanced literate activity. Both the brothers John and Thomas Dalton (1487 and 1502) refer specifically to their own work in writing their last will and testament documents: John notes that 'I knowledge all in the testament scraped or rased is done in my own hand', and Thomas states that his documents were 'raysed with my own hand'.[56] The successful brewer Brand Adryanson also signalled his involvement in the literate culture of doing business by referring to the arrangements he had made for preserving his Bedehouse 'as my wrytynge thereupon speciefyed'.[57]

Medieval Hull people had opportunities to engage in literate culture, but as is the case with other parts of England, this was not always evidenced with direct references to writing or reading. Agnes Bedford's husband, John (1450), and his near contemporary John Tutbury (1432), both included service books among their gifts of vestments and vessels to chantries.[58] John Bedford also itemised the gift of four books to his kin, two of which were service books bequeathed to his son, Richard. He gave the other two to his wife, Agnes, one being a best primer with a picture of the head of Saint John the Baptist, while the other was a book with seven psalms and various prayers.[59] Not everyone owned books themselves, but parish churches served as one of the earliest forms of libraries, with religious and service books made available for ordinary people to witness – the £5 left by John Burnham for a 'new antiphoner' to be purchased for Holy Trinity in 1448 is one indication of this sort of parish book culture.[60] This, together with the gifting of books within families, fostered literate activity and created communities of readers, either within the kin network or beyond it.

Hull Fair

The Fairs Act 1871 closed many fairs in England. It was enacted because certain local authorities saw their towns' fairs as disruptive, disorderly and the cause of nuisance behaviour. The Act enabled the Home Secretary to order the abolition of unwanted fairs. However, such was Hull people's love of what had become the annual October Fair that they maintained it and preserved the long tradition of fair-going in Hull.

On founding Kingston upon Hull in 1293, Edward I ordered that a yearly fair should be held to last six weeks from 25 May to 6 July. In 1299 the duration of the fair was reduced to 30 days, beginning on 26 May, and this fair was replaced in 1598 by one held over the last two weeks of September, the starting date of which was moved some time in the 1630s to 29 September. Following Britain's adoption of the Gregorian calendar to conform with the rest of Europe, which involved the loss of 11 days, the start of the fair was moved to 11 October in 1752. This calendar change caused widespread consternation and it is said to have infuriated the people of Hull, who, according to local legend, joined in the national chorus demanding: 'Give us back our eleven days!' The people's protest worked and from then on the start date of the fair was 11 October, or the Friday nearest to it.

Hull Fair c. 1904
William Keating Collection, with thanks to the National Fairground Archive, University of Sheffield

Just as the date of the fair has shifted slightly over time, so too has its location changed. Walton Street is the current home of the October Fair and has been since 1888, but from 1865 to 1888 it was held on the Corporation field on Park Street, while it had previously taken place in various locations, including the Market Place and Brown Cow field outside the town.

The fair has evolved markedly from its humble beginnings as an annual market. Theatrics, showmanship, puppet shows, jugglers, the famous Bostock and Wombwell's Menagerie and various other delights characterised the fair in the eighteenth and nineteenth centuries, while advances in mechanisation and engineering from the 1870s onwards ensured that novelty continued to be a strong feature of the event. Furthermore, the development of the railways meant that thousands flocked to Hull's yearly fair. It continues to attract visitors from near and far: in recent years, up to a million people have come to Hull to take part in and enjoy the fair.

Like all great traditions, Hull Fair includes an element of ceremony. Here, however, pomp is fused with the peculiar, capturing the carnivalesque element of fairground shenanigans. At 5 p.m. on the first evening of the fair, the enrobed Lord Mayor and councillors, and all the leaders of the guilds in their fabulously flamboyant chains of office and regalia, parade to the fair to take up their seats on one of the fairground rides, where they offer prayers. Once the Lord Mayor has rung the Hull Fair bell, the annual raucous merriments begin.

Sarah McKeon

The pride of medieval Hull

The word 'medieval' is often used in modern parlance to describe barbaric, backward or primitive events or practices that properly belong to one of our 'Horrible Histories'. Yet, in contrast to the stereotypes fabricated by film-makers and fiction-mongers, medieval lives were rich, varied, culturally sophisticated and aesthetically aware.[61] Of course, the world has changed between then and now. The ways in which people frame their lives is different, while the ways in which individuals perceive and experience life are as infinitely variable and kaleidoscopic as individual personalities. One of the single biggest differences between the more secularised society of 'now' and the medieval 'then' is that medieval people had a Catholic world view, and religious culture was very significant in shaping people's daily lives and their understanding of themselves (Figure 2.14). This conditioned the cultural vibrancy of medieval people's lives – they saw things through a lens of religious belief, although this was more of a dragon's eye which led to many possible interpretations of the truth.

2.14 Lay people gather to hear a medieval preacher. Religious ideas and religious practice played an important role in the lives of medieval people. Evidence from last will and testament material in Hull suggests that people referenced themselves and their interests in diverse ways, often through place and property. However, one of the most common ways that people chose to frame their lives in their wills was through bequests that were intended to confirm and celebrate their religious practice and beliefs over the course of their lives and beyond the grave.

Medieval Hull people were proud of their town. This is evident in the civic works in which people engaged during their lives and through their commemorative requests. The last will and testament evidence gives us a snapshot of the multifaceted communities of townspeople, families, servants, business allies and dependents that formed the living city. This medieval port was never static. It experienced and depended upon flows of people travelling near and far, and it was an important site for the inflow and outflow of commercial goods and prestige items. All of this activity made the medieval town of Hull a dynamic focal point for the exchange of ideas and the redistribution of wealth within the town, the region, the nation and the world. And the medieval people whose lives were influenced by Hull present to us a rich tapestry of individual commitments, personal hopes and fears, and a determination to create and maintain a city of culture.

Notes

1 Elisabeth Salter, *Cultural Creativity in the Early English Renaissance* (Basingstoke and New York: Palgrave Macmillan, 2006).

2 K. J. Allison (ed.), *A History of the County of York East Riding: Volume 1, the City of Kingston upon Hull* (London: Victoria County History, 1969), pp. 26–41 [hereafter *VCH*].

3 Jenny Kermode, *Medieval Merchants: York, Beverley and Hull in the Later Middle Ages* (Cambridge: Cambridge University Press, 1998), pp. 217–19, 254–75; *VCH*, pp. 59–61.

4 *VCH*, p. 65.

5 W. R. Childs, 'Concentration, Dependency and Maritime Activity at the Regional and Community Levels: The Case of Hull, Scarborough and their Yorkshire Hinterlands', in David J. Starkey and Morten Hahn-Pedersen (eds), *Concentration and Dependency: The Role of Maritime Activities in North Sea Communities, 1299–1999* (Esbjerg: Fisheries and Shipping Museum, 2002), pp. 25–26.

6 Childs, 'Concentration, Dependency', p. 26.

7 Will references for John Gregg (1437), Borthwick 3/507, and Joan Gregg (1438), Borthwick 3/555.

8 John Herryson (1455), Borthwick 2/325.

9 See, for example, John Hatcher, 'The Great Slump of the Mid-fifteenth Century', in Britnell and Hatcher (eds), *Progress and Problems in Medieval England. Essays in Honour of Edward Miller* (Cambridge: Cambridge University Press, 1996), pp. 237–72.

10 Agnes Bedford (1459), Borthwick 2/418.

11 John Dalton (begun 1487, codicil 1492, proved 1497), PRO 11/11/116r-117r.

12 *VCH*, pp. 51–52; Kermode, *Medieval Merchants*, pp. 248–52.

13 John Paynton (1474), PRO 11/6/91.

14 Kermode, *Medieval Merchants*, p. 74.

15 Brand Adryanson (1502), Borthwick 6/64

16 Brand Adryanson (1502), Borthwick 6/64

17 Cornelius Johnson (1502), Borthwick 6/49.

18 *VCH*, p. 80.

19 C. Fenwick, *The Poll Taxes of 1377, 1379 and 1381, Part 3 (Wiltshire to Yorkshire)*, Records of Social and Economic History, New Series, 37 (Oxford: Oxford University Press, 2005), pp. 190–93.

20 See, for example, Agnes Bedford (1459), Borthwick 2/418.

21 Robert Herryson (1520), PRO 11/19/250v-251r.

22 Brand Adryanson (1502), Borthwick 6/64; Peter Heath, 'Urban Piety in the Later Middle Ages: The Evidence of Hull Wills', in Barrie Dobson (ed.), *The Church, Politics and Patronage in the Fifteenth Century* (Gloucester/New York: Alan Sutton/St. Martin's Press, 1984), pp. 209–34 (p. 210).

23 *VCH*, p. 35.

24 Agnes Bedford (1459), Borthwick 2/418.

25 John Dalton (begun 1487, codicil 1492, proved 1497), PRO 11/11/116r-117r.

26 John Herryson (1455), Borthwick 2/325.

27 John Gregg (1437), Borthwick 3/507.

28 Brand Adryanson (1502), Borthwick 6/64.

29 Robert Herryson (1520), PRO 11/19/250v-251r.

30 John Paynton (1474), PRO 11/6/91.

31 Brand Adryanson (1502), Borthwick 6/64.

32 John Gregg (1437), Borthwick 3/507.

33 Joan Gregg (1438), Borthwick 3/555.

34 John Dalton (begun 1487, codicil 1492, proved 1497), PRO 11/11/116r-117r.

35 Robert Herryson (1520), PRO 11/19/250v-251r.

36 Agnes Bedford (1459), Borthwick 2/418; on Kirkstile, see H. Bourne, *The history of Newcastle upon Tyne: or, the ancient and present state of that town. By the late Henry Bourne, 1696–1733* (Newcastle upon Tyne: John White, 1736), p. 12.

37 Joan Gregg (1438), Borthwick 3/555.

38 Joan Gregg (1438), Borthwick 3/555; John Gregg (1437), Borthwick 3/507.

39 John Swan (1476), Borthwick 5/7r-v; Heath, 'Urban Piety', pp. 217, 220.

40 Agnes Bedford (d. 1459) also named Stephen Gildhouse as a witness, which indicates Gildhouse's wider involvement in testamentary matters in Hull.

41 Joan Gregg (1438), Borthwick 3/555; John Gregg (1437), Borthwick 3/507.

42 Joan Gregg (1438), Borthwick 3/555.

43 Cornelius Johnson (1452), Borthwick 6/49.

44 David F. Crouch, *Piety, Fraternity and Power: Religious Gilds in Late Medieval Yorkshire 1389–1547* (Woodbridge: York Medieval Press, 2000), p. 112.

45 Crouch, *Piety, Fraternity and Power*, p. 79.

46 Crouch, *Piety, Fraternity and Power*, p. 204.

47 Kermode, *Medieval Merchants*, p. 18.

48 Joan Gregg (1438), Borthwick 3/555.

49 Brand Adryanson (1502), Borthwick 6/64.

50 *VCH*, p. 335; see, for example, John Dalton (begun 1487, codicil 1492, proved 1497), PRO 11/11/116r-117r; Thomas Dalton (1502), Borthwick 6/51; and John Herryson (1550), PRO 11/33/211r/v for his *maison dieu* 'on the chapel land'.

51 Joan Gregg (1438), Borthwick 3/555.

52 Agnes Bedford (1459), Borthwick 2/418.

53 John Gregg (1437), Borthwick 3/507.

54 Joan Gregg (1438), Borthwick 3/555; John Gregg (1437), Borthwick 3/507; Robert Herryson (1520), PRO 11/19/250v-251r.

55 Agnes Bedford (1459), Borthwick 2/418.

56 John Dalton (begun 1487, codicil 1492, proved 1497), PRO 11/11/116r-117r; Thomas Dalton (1502), Borthwick 6/51; Heath, 'Urban Piety', p. 212.

57 Brand Adryanson (1502), Borthwick 6/64.

58 Heath, 'Urban Piety', p. 220.

59 John Bedford (1450), Borthwick 3/371-372.

60 Heath, 'Urban Piety', p. 216.

61 Terry Jones, *Terry Jones' Medieval Lives* (BBC Video, 2008).

CHAPTER THREE

Rebellious Hull

BRIONY McDONAGH

Writing in *The Guardian* in 2011, Paul Heaton – the former singer with Hull-based bands The Housemartins and The Beautiful South – argued that Hull today was a city with a strong current of anti-authority or even anti-royal feeling. For him, Kingston upon Hull was anything but a king's town.[1] Something of the same idea was also evident in the film produced for the UK City of Culture competition in 2013. For the bid team, Hull was a city with 'a different resonance', a place where the 'golden rules of Hull' hold firm.[2] Here then is a city imagined as a defiant, rebellious place, somewhere where things are done differently and without too much attention to the rules, or at least a place where the rules are locally constituted and distinctive.

Central within these narratives is Beverley Gate, the excavated remains of which lie at the east end of Whitefriargate just off Queen Victoria Square and close to the modern Princes Quay shopping centre (Figure 3.1). It was here that Sir John Hotham denied King Charles I access to the town in the months leading up to the English Civil War and where just over a hundred years earlier the rebels of the Pilgrimage of Grace were captured and hanged. Local identities have long been closely associated with these rebellious moments and specifically with Beverley Gate. Early twentieth-century newspaper columnists, for example, made much of the events of 1642 while the civic authorities went as far as to recreate the gate for the royal visit of 1903 (Figure 3.2).[3] Yet the excavation of the site in the 1980s provided an additional material focus for these processes of identity-making, and the remains of the gate have subsequently come to be closely bound up in the construction of local identities. As cultural and historical geographers have argued, historic buildings, monuments and heritage sites all provide material and imaginative spaces for the construction of local, regional and national identities. Moreover, the ideas and unspoken assumptions lying behind the production of such identities often come most clearly to the fore at moments of conflict or tension – as was the case in Hull in late 2015.[4]

Plans by the city council to fill in the Beverley Gate excavations – and thus safeguard the in situ medieval material at the same time as enhancing the appearance of the area and improving pedestrian access between Queen Victoria Square and Whitefriargate – sparked considerable controversy. A campaign to preserve the remains above ground quickly gathered local support, helped by an active social media profile and various print and broadcast media appearances by key figures in the group.[5] A public consultation was opened by the council in November 2015 and asked local residents to vote on the council's two preferred plans for the site, essentially a choice between filling in and landscaping the excavations or keeping them open but providing a new access point, illuminations, landscaping and seating. The consultation attracted almost 4,000 contributions, of whom 87 per cent wanted the site to remain open. As a result of the consultation, the council agreed to keep the site open and the archaeological remains visible, and in January 2016 the gate and adjacent archaeological remains were identified as a scheduled monument on advice from Historic England.[6]

Online forums buzzed with comments, many of which explicitly linked the site with historical events, including those of 1642. Contributors often recognised the importance of Beverley Gate within local historical imaginations and civic identities, even while some also felt that the current site was unattractive. Thus, for example, one contributor noted that the gate was 'the most underwhelming, disappointing piece of so called history I've ever set my eyes on … a horrible eyesore … [I] can't see these old foundations and pile of bricks ever doing the Beverley gate justice.'[7] The theme of doing the gate and its history 'justice' ran through many of the comments, with contributors arguing that 'the gate should be celebrated. Made into a feature for inhabitants of Hull to be once again proud of.' Many contributors acknowledged the archaeological remains of the gate to be worthy of preservation and that something had to be done to better present them to the public, though a wide range of different suggestions for dealing with the site were offered. Several advocated that the remains be removed and rebuilt above ground or that a replica of the gate be built at street level. One individual joked that the council should 'Fill it with water and fish [so that] a dismayed underwater King on his horse with his army looks up at passers-by as the mock underwater fort gates slowly close before him'. However outlandish some of the suggestions might have been – and as a result very unlikely to meet with approval from archaeologists, heritage officers or the city council – it is clear from them that Beverley Gate and the historical events played out atop and in front of it are an important focus for local popular and civic identities. Much the same idea was echoed by Historic

3.1 The partially excavated Beverley Gate in the 1980s.
© Humberside Archaeological Unit/ Humber Historic Environment Record

England when it submitted evidence to Hull City Council's Planning Committee in early March 2016: while not a wholly authentic structure – the medieval remains having been underpinned with concrete and modern brickwork added – in their view the site remained 'a key part of the identity of Hull', and sensitive redisplay provided the opportunity to 'raise the profile of the Gate' and its history.[8]

Yet beyond twenty-first-century mobilisations of earlier events – always necessarily written through with our own century's interests and concerns – what exactly is the history of the town's defences and just how rebellious a town was Kingston upon Hull in the early modern period? It is these questions that this chapter explores, presenting a historical geography of early modern Kingston upon Hull that focuses specifically on the walls, gates and other fortifications which surrounded the sixteenth- and seventeenth-century town. It maps out a now almost completely lost feature of the Hull townscape and uses the fortifications to frame the two key episodes of rebellion that took place in the early modern town – the fall of the town to the rebel army in 1536–37 and the infamous incident when the king was turned away from the town gates in April 1642, long claimed as the first act of the English Civil War. This allows us both to reassess the place of the town in each episode and to critically re-examine the idea of Hull as a rebellious town. In doing so, we also explore the fortifications and associated historical events as one example of the uses of the past in the present, thinking about some of the ways in which Hull's medieval and early modern past has come to be bound up in and constitutive of twenty-first-century identities within the city.

Town Taking Day

Hull has a reputation for independent thinking and, sometimes, political defiance. 'Town Taking Day' was a public holiday held locally to commemorate the events of 1688 when, for the second time in the seventeenth century, Hull defied a reigning monarch. Just as Hull people had refused to allow Charles I into their town in 1642, so James II was embarrassed as Hull citizens again declined to bend to royal will forty-six years later.

James had alienated the town and corporation by interfering in the appointment of officials and MPs, and by promoting Roman Catholics. Hull's governor, Lord Langdale, and high steward, Lord Dover, were both Catholics, as were Colonel Henry Gage and Lord Montgomery, who commanded the regiments sent to reinforce the garrison in the belief that William of Orange intended to lead an invasion force up the Humber. In fact, William's army landed in Torbay, Devon, on 5 November 1688, with the Earl of Danby securing York for William two weeks later and declaring that Hull would fall next. Langdale prepared for a siege by opening the dykes and flooding the land outside the walls, putting a chain across the entry to the River Hull, and planning to arrest Captain Lionel Copley, the deputy governor, and other Protestant officers and soldiers in the garrison. Learning of this on Monday 3 December, Copley met with the mayor, aldermen, chief inhabitants and fellow officers at his residence, now Ye Olde White Harte pub, where in the so-called 'Plotting Chamber' they planned a pre-emptive strike. At 10 o'clock that night Langdale and 400 Catholic soldiers advanced in the dark, presumably towards the deputy governor's house. At a pre-arranged signal, given by the beat of a drum, all the windows in the town were illuminated and the governor was confronted by Copley and armed soldiers in Market Place. Copley then walked up to Langdale, took him by the cravat and declared him a prisoner; there was no resistance. Lord Montgomery was also taken, but other Catholic officers fled to the Citadel where they were apprehended the next day. Once the town and garrison had been secured for William, the prisoners were set free.

Statue of William III, Market Place, by Peter Scheemakers, erected 1734.
David and Susan Neave

This bloodless coup, for which Copley was rewarded with the Royal Governorship of Maryland, was commemorated annually on 4 December – 'Town Taking Day' – until the late eighteenth century. Church bells were rung, merchants and tradesmen processed to Holy Trinity church to hear a sermon, and schoolchildren were given a holiday. Protestant Hull took pride in its role in the 'Glorious Revolution' and when offered a statue of William III, by the sculptor Peter Scheemakers, the townspeople quickly subscribed the 785 guineas required. The golden statue of 'King Billy', situated prominently in Market Place, was unveiled with great ceremony on 'Town Taking Day' in 1734. Although the Town Taking Day holiday is now defunct, the statue installed to celebrate Hull's roles in these political upheavals remains in situ.

David Neave and Susan Neave

Sources: A. Browning, *Thomas Osborne, Earl of Danby* (Glasgow, 1951), vol. 1, pp. 409–10; T. Gent, *History of Kingston-upon-Hull* (York, 1735), pp. 188–89; A. Howes and M. Foreman, *Town and Gun* (Hull, 1999), pp. 129–31; R. Barnard, 'The Old White Hart, Hull', *East Yorkshire Historian*, 6 (2005), pp. 69, 75–76.

The medieval town defences

For at least a century after its foundation by the monks of Meaux in the late twelfth century, the town of Hull was without any serious defences. It was bounded to the south and east by the rivers Humber and Hull, but was open to the surrounding countryside to the north and west. All this changed over the course of the fourteenth century. In 1321 King Edward II granted a licence to crenellate, and the first defensive circuit was probably started shortly after this and completed by about 1330.[9] Archaeological evidence suggests that the defences consisted of a wide ditch (of up to 12 metres in places) backed by an earthen bank topped by a timber palisade. It was known in the early fourteenth-century Chamberlain's Account Roll as the 'great fossatum'. Access to the town within was via four main gates: North Gate next to the River Hull, Beverley Gate at the north-west angle of the defences, Myton Gate just to the south and Hessle Gate on the River Humber. The gates were mostly constructed of timber with some brick and stone used, probably primarily in their foundations.[10]

The town walls themselves were not constructed until some time later in the fourteenth century, probably over a relatively extended period between the 1330s and around 1406. The first of the defences to be rebuilt in brick may have been that to the south of the town running along the River Humber, and was perhaps in part intended to provide flood protection against the sea. The defensive walls to the north and west of the town were built some time later in the century and the walls alone incorporated as many as 4.7 million bricks, most or all of them fired at the brickworks just outside the town.[11] The gates were most likely rebuilt in brick at the same time and up to 30 interval towers constructed along the walls. There were also postern (secondary) gates at various mid-points along the walls, some of which were periodically blocked up.[12] Beverley Gate was probably the most substantial of the gates and was of at least two stages and topped with a substantial spire.[13] It projected forward from the town walls and was approached via a drawbridge across the ditch.

The walls as they stood in the early sixteenth century are shown clearly on a plan in the British Library (Figure 3.3).[14] These were largely as constructed more than a century earlier, although further minor defensive works had been undertaken in the autumn of 1460, including the construction of earthworks outside the main gates and the addition of an iron chain across the mouth of the River Hull, intended to protect the ships in the haven and the otherwise

3.2 The mock Beverley Gate erected for the visit of the Prince of Wales (later George V) in 1903.
Harry Cartlidge © Maritime Museum: Hull Museums

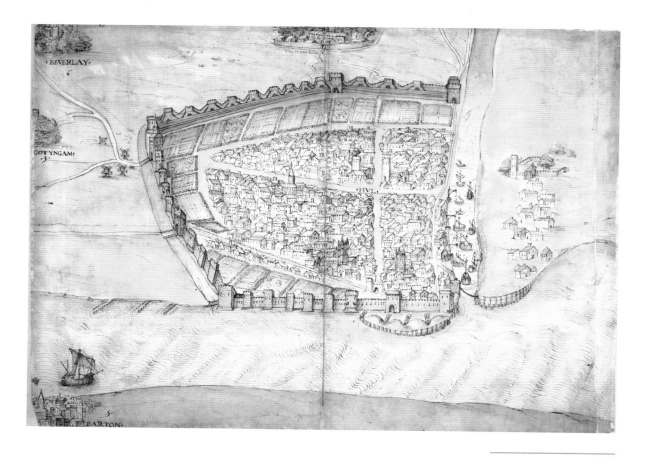

3.3 Plan of Hull *c.* 1537
(British Library, Cott Aug
I.i.83).
Briony McDonagh © British Library

unprotected staiths on the east bank of the river.[15] The early sixteenth-century plan
shows the tower on the west of the River Hull to which the chain was fastened, along
with the chain guarding the mouth of the Hull and a number of ships offloading
their cargo via cranes on the wharves. The defensive circuit of the walls, main gates,
postern gates and intervening towers are all shown, along with the bank on the
inside of the northern section of the walls, presumably the earlier bank on which
the mid-fourteenth-century brick wall was built. It also clearly depicts the fifth of the
town's main gates which was known as Humber Gate and let out on to the foreshore
where four cannons protected the southern wall of the town.

The plan is undated, but internal evidence suggests it was probably drawn in the
first few decades of the sixteenth century, most likely in the late 1530s. The towers
of both churches in the town are depicted on the plan and given that Holy Trinity's
tower was not finished until *c.* 1500 and that St Mary's was said to have collapsed
in 1541, the plan would seem to date to the first four decades of the century.[16] It
was probably drawn up in the aftermath of the Pilgrimage of Grace (on which more
below) and may have been the 'plat' or plan mentioned as being commissioned in
February 1537.[17] It gives us a good idea of what the town looked like at the time.
The two churches, two friaries and the Guildhall and prison are all visible, as is
the de la Pole manor house (later known as King's Manor). The centre of the town

was then densely built up along the two north–south axes of High Street and Low/ Marketgate as well as east–west along Whitefriargate and Myton Gate. The plan depicts extensive gardens and as-yet-undeveloped plots inside the town walls to the north, west and south-west of the town. At least some of this green space was probably artifice on the part of the mapmaker, perhaps intended to show off the town walls and inner bank unencumbered by housing. There were certainly extensive gardens in the north-west of the town associated with the de la Pole manor house, but the archaeological evidence suggests that the town was by then otherwise fairly closely settled (see Chapter 1). By contrast, there was very little settlement in the area outside the walls, with the exception of the former Carthusian friary known as the Charterhouse to the north and a scatter of buildings on the eastern bank of the Hull. Three windmills stood outside Beverley Gate along with the town gibbet, depicted in the plan in macabre fashion with three corpses adorning it. The causeway leading north from Beverley Gate towards Cottingham and Beverley is also visible as are the towns themselves, along with Barton-upon-Humber on the south bank of the estuary. So appeared the town on the eve of the Pilgrimage of Grace, the largest and most serious of all the sixteenth-century rebellions, in which the gentry and commons of Hull and the East Riding played an important part.

The Pilgrimage of Grace

The Pilgrimage started in Lincolnshire in early October 1536 and quickly spread into Yorkshire, eventually drawing in communities from across the north of England. Hull was one of several Yorkshire towns to play a key part in the rebellion and to witness the later wrath of King Henry VIII. The causes of the rebellion were various but included a complex constellation of religious, economic, social and political factors including unrest over Henry's decisions to break with Rome and dissolve the monasteries, as well as the northern gentry's discomfort with an increasingly centralised Tudor state administered from Westminster. Rumours that communion vessels and other goods were going to be seized from the parish churches were also important in galvanising support for the uprising in both Lincolnshire and East Yorkshire. We know a considerable amount about the events of the Pilgrimage of Grace thanks to the survival of a large body of letters written by Henry and his privy councillors, published as *The Letters and Papers of Henry VIII* more than a century ago. Additional information about both the causes and aftermath of the rebellion comes from the petitions written to the king by the pilgrim leaders at the height of the rebellion and from the trial papers preserved at the National Archives as KB8, a collection evocatively known as the *Baga de Secretis* (the Bag of Secrets).

The unrest had begun in the Lincolnshire town of Louth at the beginning of October 1536, but the first sign of trouble north of the Humber came a week later on Sunday 8 October.[18] That morning the common bell of Beverley was rung, a proclamation was read in the Market Place and the people of the town were told to assemble on the Westwood. News of the growing rebellion had reached the town over the previous couple of days, and the events at Beverley seem initially to have been a show of support for the Lincolnshire rebels. Little happened that night, but over the next few days men from Cottingham, Hessle and Holderness arrived in the town in response to the lighting of beacons on the Wolds and elsewhere. On Friday 13 October a large force mustered at Market Weighton where they were joined by men from Howdenshire and the Vale of York commanded by the lawyer Robert Aske, the so-called 'captain' of the commons. Many of the gentry had by then fled to the perceived safety of either Hull or various Yorkshire castles including Scarborough and Pontefract.

Aske quickly recognised the importance of securing major towns and split his force, with one part marching to York and the rest taking up strategic positions around Hull. Initial negotiations had already taken place between the Pilgrims – as the rebels now began to be known – and the mayor, aldermen and gentry of Hull, but the latter had refused to give up the town, with Sir John Constable of Burton Constable saying bluntly that he would rather die than live with the shame of joining the rebels. A five-day siege ensued in which the rebels from Holderness, Beverley, Cottingham and 'Hullshire' – that is, the villages lying in a rough triangle between Willerby, Hessle and North Ferriby – took up positions around the town. No serious violence occurred and the defences were not really tested, though the men of the Beverley Water Towns (Thearne, Woodmansey, Weel and Tickton) threatened to set fire to the ships sheltering in the River Hull, a threat which no doubt much concerned the merchant community in Hull. The arrival of further rebel troops seems to have swayed the aldermen and gentry, who on 19 October agreed to yield on the condition that no unwilling man be sworn to the rebels' cause. The rebel army – in reality, a fairly rag-tag bunch of farmers, labourers and craftsmen led by minor gentlemen – entered the town the next morning, claiming it for Aske and the Pilgrims.

Having secured Hull for the rebels, two local lords – Sir John Constable and Sir Christopher Hilliard – were put in charge of the town while much of the Pilgrim army moved on to a muster at Hunsley Beacon and from there on to the siege of Pontefract Castle. Pontefract fell to the rebels a day later and it was there that many of the Yorkshire gentry sheltering in the castle were eventually drawn into leading the rebellion. Among their number was Sir Robert Constable, lord of Flamborough and Holme-on-Spalding-Moor, the head of an important East Yorkshire family (but unrelated to Sir John Constable). Sir Robert Constable had by then been active in East Riding affairs for more than thirty years, serving as a Justice of the Peace and as a member of the Council of the North as well as holding the stewardships of various royal and ecclesiastical manors, though he had more recently also become embroiled in a series of court cases which had done little to put him in the good books of the king. Having been persuaded – or forced – to join the rebel cause, Constable quickly became a key figure in the Pilgrimage.[19] He was one of the four men representing the rebels at negotiations with the king's representatives at Doncaster in late October – where a temporary truce was agreed between the parties and a list of the Pilgrims' grievances sent to the king – and was later installed as 'ruler' of Hull.

November was an uneasy month in Hull and much of the north of England, with the Pilgrims and their leaders awaiting the king's response to their demands. Tensions were further heightened when Constable refused to hand over to the king rebels from Lincolnshire who were being held in gaol in Hull. He and the other Pilgrim leaders also worried that the king would use the forces stationed on the south bank of the Humber (at Grimsby, Barton-upon-Humber and elsewhere) to invade the East Riding via Hull.[20] Reports that reached the king suggested that Constable was garrisoning the town against him – he almost certainly was – and preparing to bring ordnance and powder into Hull on ships from Flanders.[21] He also requisitioned ships and duties on behalf of the rebels, though the townsfolk later claimed that this had happened against their will. Constable certainly spoke passionately in favour of an aggressive militarisation of the north during discussions among the rebels at York in late November, but the general feeling among the gentry was to move for an end to the conflict.

A peace was eventually agreed in early December, with the king promising a future parliament in the north to discuss the Pilgrims' complaints and issuing pardons to all involved. In return, the rebel army disbanded and returned home. The Pilgrimage was thus brought to a peaceful and (as yet) relatively bloodless conclusion. Henry, however, had already made up his mind to punish Constable for his role in the rebellion. To the minds of the king and his chief councillors, Constable, Aske and Lord Darcy (the man who had yielded Pontefract Castle to the rebels) were 'the three most arrant traitors' involved in the rebellion, men whose continued presence in the north was worse than 'hemlock … in a good salad'.[22] Exactly why Constable and the other gentry were drawn into leading the rebellion is unclear, though their adherence to the old Catholic religion and their distaste for the political changes of the 1530s no doubt played a major part in their decision making. Yet whatever

3.4 Watton Priory. The oriel window of the room where Hallam and Bigod planned the second rebellion is on the right.
Briony McDonagh

his personal and political allegiances, Constable certainly did his best to calm local nerves as a second rebellion threatened to break out in the East Riding early in 1537.

This second rebellion was precipitated in part by a conviction among the local population that the king was intending to garrison Hull and Scarborough as part of his move to subdue the countryside, as well as by a general feeling that the king had gone back on his promises to the Pilgrims.[23] Rumours that the Duke of Norfolk was advancing north with a force of 20,000 men did little to help matters.[24] On Plough Monday (8 January 1537), a yeoman farmer called John Hallam started to plot a second uprising, discussing his plans with his neighbours in Watton church 16 miles north of Hull and later over dinner at Watton Priory, a house of Gilbertine canons (Figure 3.4). Here he talked with Sir Francis Bigod, lord of Settrington in the northern Wolds and the second key figure in the renewed rebellion.

Their plan as it solidified over the next few days was to seize Hull and Scarborough for the rebels and hold them against the king. Hallam was to capture Hull and Bigod Scarborough, each with only a small company of men. Both attempts utterly and completely failed. On Tuesday 16 January, Hallam and around 20 men entered Hull, probably through Beverley Gate. His plan was to proclaim for the rebels in the Market Place and have his men take the town, but many of those who promised to come failed to materialise and Hallam quickly realised that he was vastly outnumbered. As it turned out, the town authorities had also been warned of the danger by Hallam's advance party when they reached Hull that morning. Finding the townspeople unsupportive, Hallam rode out of the town just as the gates were being shut against the rebels. Rather strangely, he almost immediately turned back to the now-closed Beverley Gate and demanded it be opened, presumably in an attempt to rescue the men he commanded. The two aldermen at the gate quickly identified Hallam, one of them crying 'thou art the false traitor that I look for' as he grabbed the bridle of Hallam's horse.[25] A swordfight ensued and Hallam was captured only after his horse stumbled into the Busdike, the main watercourse bringing fresh water into the town from springs in Willerby (from close to the site where the recently restored Springhead pumping station stands today).[26]

Hallam's accomplices in the town were rounded up, tried rapidly and condemned by a special commission of local gentlemen including Sir John Constable and Sir Christopher Hilliard. Hallam and two of his men were executed a fortnight later, almost certainly hanged at the scaffold outside Beverley Gate close to the site of his capture.[27] It is probably their three corpses that we see swinging from the gallows in the early sixteenth-century town plan. This was swift and decisive justice by the gentry at Hull, keen as they were to prove their loyalty to the king after their earlier decision to yield the town to the Pilgrim army. The two aldermen who had captured Hallam – men by the names of Knolles and Elland – were knighted later in the year, and this despite the fact they were the very men who had yielded the town to the rebels in autumn 1536. Thus the civic authorities at Hull and the town's wider population effectively came through the most serious of the Tudor rebellions relatively unscathed.

The same could not be said for the captains of the autumn uprising. The renewed unrest in January 1537 was exactly what Henry VIII needed to pursue the leaders of the first rebellion. Constable, Aske and Darcy were all summoned to London in the spring but, recognising the danger, they procrastinated as long as they could before journeying south. They were tried in May and found guilty of treason after the pardon, in reality a trumped-up charge based on fabricated evidence that they had supported Bigod and Hallam's second rebellion, when in fact both Constable and Aske had done their best to keep the populace calm in the heady days of January. Both were eventually sent north for execution, Aske to York and Constable to Hull, where he was hanged in chains from Beverley Gate in early July 1537. After the execution, the Duke of Norfolk reported that 'His bones will hang there this hundred year'. His putrefying corpse was apparently still on display in 1541 when Henry visited the town, a grisly reminder to townspeople and visitors alike of the fate of traitors.[28]

Beverley Gate thus functioned both as a place of rebellion and as the site at which the town authorities redeemed themselves by capturing Hallam. It was also one of the key sites from which kingly justice and authority was projected out on to what was – in Henry VIII's view at least – a troublesome and unruly region. The second rebellion ended with the execution of Hallam and his men at the gallows outside the gate, and the whole sorry affair of the Pilgrimage was brought to a close in July with the execution of Constable (at Beverley Gate) and Aske (at Clifford's Tower in York). Henry very deliberately sent them north to be executed in the towns that they had controlled during the rebellion and both mounted the scaffold on market days so as to ensure the most public of executions in front of the largest possible audience. In doing so, Henry hoped to flush out any further rebels and thus 'knit up this tragedy': in other words, to end the spectre of popular disorder in the northern counties once and for all.[29]

The sixteenth- and seventeenth-century fortifications

In the wake of the Pilgrimage of Grace, Henry VIII rapidly ordered improvements to Hull's fortifications. In this the king was no doubt motivated by a determination to ensure that the town would not so easily fall to a hostile force in any future rebellion. He was perhaps shocked at how quickly the besieged town had yielded to the Pilgrim army in the autumn of 1536: the siege lasted only five days and there had been no real assault of the defences, yet the town authorities had quickly opened the gates. The corporation later claimed that they had resisted the rebels 'until the poor people of the town, being much more numerous than the rest of the inhabitants, daily cried out that their wives and children would perish for lack of victuals' and that they 'were credibly informed also that the rebels intended to have fired the town'.[30] Yet if these sounded like slightly lame excuses to Henry, he apparently accepted them, and the civic authorities' actions during the second rebellion eventually earned the town a letter of thanks from the king followed by two royal visits.

Works to improve the town's defences were mentioned as early as December 1536 in the days immediately after the royal pardon was issued, and again in the New Year when local concern that by further garrisoning the town the king would be better able to subdue the surrounding countryside was apparently a contributing factor in Bigod and Hallam's second rebellion.[31] Reference was made to the commissioning of a new 'plat' or plan of the town in February 1537 and Henry twice visited the town in 1541 to inspect the defences and order additional works.[32] These included improvements to the walls and gates enclosing the town as well as the construction of new defences on the east bank of the Hull. Thus a new bulwark was constructed outside the Humber Gate, the tower on the east bank of the Hull (on to which one end of the chain fastened) was enlarged, the North and Beverley gates strengthened and extended, the town ditch scoured and the earthern ramparts improved. Repairs to the sluice gates on the rivers were also undertaken. These could be opened if the town came under attack and the land outside the walls flooded as an additional defence. On the east bank of the River Hull at Drypool three new blockhouses were constructed connected together by a long curtain wall. The central blockhouse was known as Hull Castle, though it was never really any more than a gun platform, as were the blockhouses to the north and south. The bridge over the Hull connecting the new Drypool defences with the west bank close to North Gate was built at the same time. The new fortifications cost a staggering £23,000 – equivalent today to not far off £12 million – but they substantially improved the town's defences, as did the

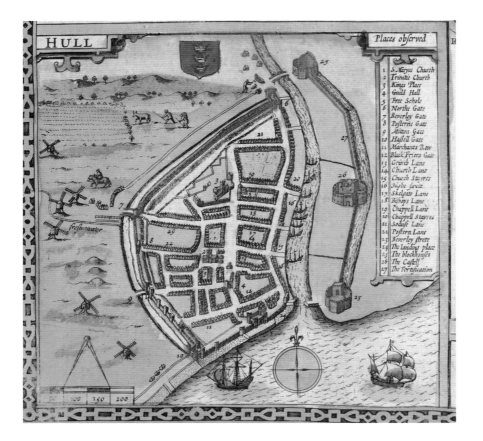

3.5 An insert from a seventeenth-century map taken from John Speed's atlas *Theatrum Imperii Magnae Britanniae* (*The Theatre of the Empire of Great Britain*), showing Hull and its environs. The inclusion of the insert is a marker of the important place that Hull occupied in the context of the larger Yorkshire region.
© The British Library Board.
Theatrum Imperii Magnae Britanniae, London: I. Sudbury et G. Humble, 1616

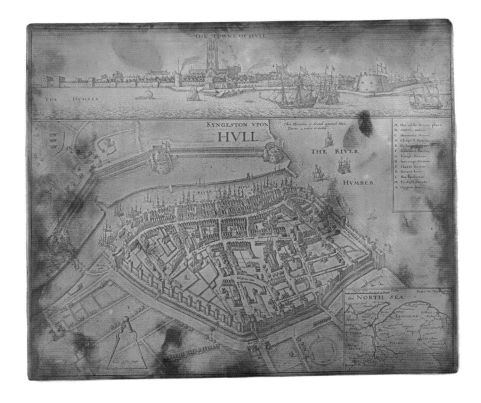

3.6 The original brass produced by Wenceslaus Hollar for his Hull map.
© British Library

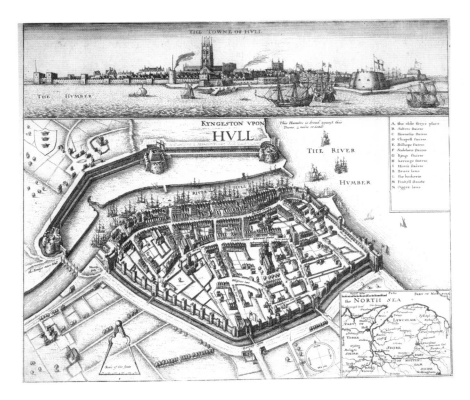

3.7 Hollar's map of Hull
c. 1640.
Courtesy of University of Toronto Wenceslaus Hollar Digital Collection

construction of a gun battery downstream at Paull. This lay six miles to the east of the town and from here enemy ships in the Humber could be attacked long before they came close enough to fire on Hull.

Further repairs to the walls were undertaken in the last quarter of the sixteenth century – in part a response to fears about the Spanish Armada – followed in the late 1620s and 1630s by another phase of defensive works. A new fort known as the South Battery was built in 1627 at the southern extreme of the town and the gap between North Gate and the River Hull finally stopped up with a wall. The latter is clearly visible in Figure 3.5 and appears to have consisted of a brick wall backed by an earthern bank but no palisade or parapet. In 1638 the town ditch was scoured once again, new drawbridges were erected before the three main gates and six new cannons (lent to the town by King Charles I) were installed.[33] In 1639 and 1640 an outer ditch and bank were thrown up around the north and west sides of the walls and gun batteries built in front of the main gates.

Thus by the time Wenceslaus Hollar's map was engraved, both the fortifications and the town looked rather different than they had a century earlier (Figures 3.6, 3.7). Hollar apparently surveyed his map some time in 1639 or 1640, just before work started on the new ditch and gun batteries (shown in Figure 3.8), but his plan shows some of the other new defensive works including the extended Beverley and North gates and the new drawbridges. The castle and the blockhouses commissioned by Henry VIII are also clearly visible on the Drypool bank of the Hull, as is the bridge over the river. The town itself had also expanded to some degree in the century since *c.* 1537: there were now fewer gardens and vacant plots within the walls, although both the northern section and the area around the Ropery (inside the wall along the Humber) remained less closely developed than other parts of the town. The former de la Pole manor house was by now used to store the royal magazine, a convenient halfway point between London and Scotland where Charles I was engaged in the so-called Bishops' Wars.[33] The additional defensive works at Hull of 1639–40 were almost certainly ordered in response to the large amount of arms then stored in the town, rather than as a reaction to the worsening relations between Charles I and Parliament in the late 1630s which eventually led to the Civil War. Yet the town authorities and Parliament were soon grateful for the improved defensive capability of the town. The king, by contrast, must almost certainly have rued his decision to authorise the new works.

The Civil War

The English Civil War as it erupted in the summer of 1642 had multiple long-term political, religious and constitutional causes. These are variously explained by modern historians, but were clearly exacerbated by Charles I's determination to push through various religious and fiscal reforms during his eleven years of personal rule (that is, during the period he reigned without Parliament between 1629 and 1640) and by the wars with Scotland in 1639 and 1640 and Ireland in 1641. Charles recalled

3.8 1668 map of Hull attributed to Joseph Osborne and showing the new ditch and gun batteries completed *c.* 1640. Reproduced from Thomas Sheppard, 'An unpublished manuscript map of the River Hull, dated 1668', *The Antiquary*, 38 (1880), p. 150.

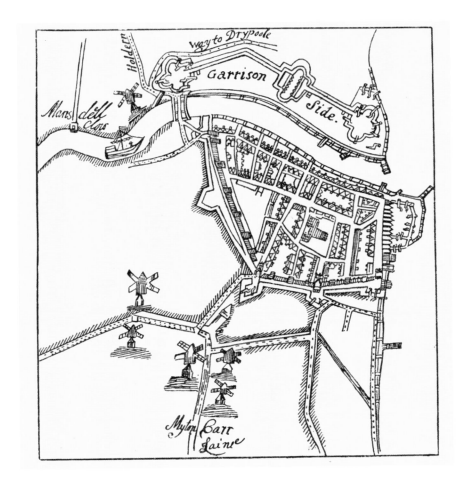

Parliament in autumn 1640 – the so-called Long Parliament which sat until 1660 – but relations between the king and Parliament continued to deteriorate, and by January 1642 the situation had reached breaking point. Early in the month, Charles attempted to arrest five MPs who were critical of him and his policies, but failed. Realising that his authority had been compromised and that his personal safety was in jeopardy, he left London, heading first for Hampton Court then onwards to York.[35]

War was not yet inevitable but both sides immediately recognised the importance of securing the large arsenal at Hull that had been amassed during the war with Scotland. With Portsmouth and London, Hull was one of the three largest arsenals of the pre-war period. As a defensible east coast port with good access to London and the Continent, it was also a town of strategic military importance to both king and Parliament. This ultimately led to the stand-off at Beverley Gate that is so integral to popular historical imaginations within the modern city and is hailed by many local historians as the first major action of the English Civil War.[36]

After Charles left the capital, both he and Parliament quickly appointed a governor to rule Hull – the Earl of Newcastle for the king and Sir John Hotham for

Parliament – and ordered them to seize the town. The mayor and aldermen of Hull initially resisted both parties, in part because they were reluctant to bear the costs of supporting a garrison (something they continued to complain of later in the spring of 1642), but also because they claimed that appointment to the governorship was theirs by ancient right.[37] When Hotham's son arrived outside the town with 300–400 trained militiamen on 18 January, the mayor shut the gates and refused to admit him and his soldiers, telling him – according to a later historian of the town – 'to remove further off or to expect to be treated like an enemy'.[38] Yet the town yielded a few days later, probably in response to Parliament's personal threats against the mayor and aldermen, and the young John Hotham then held the town until his father's arrival in mid-March.[39]

Sir John Hotham had been governor of Hull from 1628 until 1639, when he was apparently removed from the post after a disagreement with the king (Figure 3.9). Hotham later opposed ship money and presented his region's grievances to the Crown, including complaints about the costs of billeting royal troops sent by Charles to Scotland. His previous disagreements with the king may help to explain why he accepted Parliament's appointment of him as governor in opposition to the king's wishes. That he had previously been governor may also help to explain why the town finally yielded to his authority, despite the fact that many of the townspeople were said

3.9 Sir John Hotham by an unknown artist.

to support the king. When Sir John Hotham arrived there in March he reported that as many as five-sevenths of the townspeople were loyal to the king, though this may have been something of an exaggeration intended to underline his own authority and powers of persuasion. Importantly, Parliament's commission included the specific order that Hotham was not to surrender the town or its armoury without the authority of both Houses of Parliament.[40]

On Friday 22 April, the Duke of York (later James II), with about 50 followers, arrived at Hull to inspect the town and its defences. They entered unannounced, but once recognised were received and entertained by the mayor. Hotham was immediately suspicious but was assured that the duke and his party intended to stay only one night. Early the next morning news arrived that the king intended to dine in the town. He was said to have already set out from York with 200–300 attendants and perhaps another 400 men following him at a distance, which compared to 927 foot soldiers in the town under Hotham's command plus

the townspeople whose allegiance was unclear.[41] Whichever way he looked at it, this put Hotham in an impossibly difficult position: either he turned the monarch away at the gates or he let in the king and his followers and thus went against his orders not to admit a large force or deliver the town or magazine 'without the King's Authority, signified unto him by the Lords and Commons House in Parliament'.[42] Having discussed the matter with the aldermen and local MP Peregrine Pelham, Hotham resolved that he had no choice but to refuse the king entry. He sent a messenger to intercept the king – by now only three miles away – but Charles continued in his path towards Hull.

Told that Charles was by now approaching the town, Hotham ordered the new bridge at Beverley Gate to be drawn up and the gates shut. The mayor and townspeople were instructed to return to their homes – as Reckitt notes, this is evidence of Hotham's uncertainty about exactly where popular sympathies in the town lay – and the Duke of York and his party were confined to Trinity House where they were served with an impressive banquet but refused permission to go down to the gate. The king arrived mid-morning and Hotham appeared on the walls next to Beverley Gate. No doubt much affronted to find the gates shut against him, Charles demanded entrance (Figure 3.10). Hotham steadfastly refused, pledging his personal loyalty to the king but insisting that his orders from Parliament meant that he could not admit the king and his followers. All talk of compromise failed and at 4 p.m. the king gave Hotham one hour to reconsider his position and retired to tea in a house outside the walls. An hour later Charles returned to the gates only to be again refused entry, at which point he angrily declared Hotham and all who obeyed him traitors to the Crown, then begrudgingly returned to Beverley.[43]

In refusing the king entry, Hotham had denied him access to Hull's substantial arsenal. Barbara English has made the point that the events at Hull were only one of a number of triggers in the months leading up to the official declaration of war, though it is clear that had Charles managed to command the arsenal at Hull, hostilities would probably have been brought to a much more rapid resolution. Instead, Hotham and Parliament maintained control of the port and magazine at Hull, both crucial factors in Parliament's eventual victory.[44] Charles too recognised this. As the probable author of *Eikon Basilike*, he later reflected that

> my repulse at Hull seemed at first view an act of so rude disloyalty, that my greatest enemies had scarce confidence enough to abet or own it: It was the first overt essay to be made ... This was but the hand of that cloud, which was soon after to overspread the whole Kingdom, and cast all into disorder and darkness.[45]

With the king back in York, Hotham set about further garrisoning the town. He was sent money and ordnance by Parliament and himself sent arms to parliamentary troops in the West Riding of Yorkshire commanded by Lord Fairfax. By early July 1642 there were 1,300 soldiers in the town, and by the end of the month more than 2,200.[46] Much of the magazine, however, was removed to London by ship between May and September 1642, leaving only a relatively small arsenal at Hull to be used as necessary in the defence of the town. In early July, Charles attempted to take Hull by force. The windmills outside Beverley Gate were set alight by the king's soldiers, presumably with the intention of starving Hull into submission, though it seems to have had the opposite effect of rallying support for Hotham and the parliamentary cause among the townspeople.[47] Royalist forts were set up at Hessle and Paull in an attempt to control the River Humber, but supplies continued to reach Hull by sea. Hotham oversaw repairs and improvements to the town's defences, cannons were mounted on the walls, batteries constructed before three of the gates and two of the more minor gates earthed up.[48] On the night of 6 July, the banks of the rivers Hull and Humber were broken, so that the low-lying land outside the town walls was flooded and all landward access to the town was cut off. A couple of minor skirmishes followed – one in Anlaby where the royalist forces were caught off guard in the night and much of their magazine destroyed – and the siege was given up later in the month. The Civil War proper had not yet started – Charles did not raise the royal standard at Nottingham until 22 August that year – but this failed action must certainly have underlined to the king the difficulty of effectively laying siege to a port-town like Hull, not least because access by water left Parliament able to easily provision and reinforce the garrison.

The next year was a relatively quiet one in Hull, though nationally the campaign of 1643 was a successful one for the king, with large swathes of territory in the south-west, the Midlands and Lincolnshire seized for the Crown. By autumn 1643 Hull was a parliamentary outpost in an otherwise royalist north of England, hence its strategic importance to both sides. Sir John Hotham, however, was by now starting to regret his earlier enthusiasm for the parliamentary cause. He was strongly opposed to Puritanism and increasingly anxious about the course of the Civil War, particularly about the threat to the established social order posed by mob rule. As he noted in a letter to the Earl of Newcastle in January 1643 (with whom he was negotiating about defecting to the royalists), 'the necessitous people of the whole kingdom, will presently rise in mighty number and whosoever they pretend for at first, within a while they will set up for themselves, to the utter ruin of all the nobility and gentry of the kingdom'.[49] He was also increasingly paranoid about attempts on his own life, all of which led him to rethink his allegiance to Parliament. His change of sympathies did not go unnoticed by parliamentary leaders, and at the end of June 1643 both father and son were arrested on suspicion that they were planning to yield the town to the royalists. Both were imprisoned in the Tower of London for treason and eventually executed in January 1645. Several of Hotham's officers were also arrested in the wake of his capture, and such were local suspicions that the garrison was temporarily staffed by townspeople in place of soldiers.[50]

Lord Fairfax assumed command in Hull soon after the arrest of the Hothams and the town authorities quickly petitioned Parliament for more arms and additional ships to protect the Humber and counter royalist plans to build new fortifications from which to attack the town.[51] This was prescient given the second siege of Hull, which unfolded in the autumn of 1643. Royalist troops commanded by the Earl of Newcastle sacked Beverley in late August, then marched onwards to Hull, bringing with them the famous guns known as *Gog* and *Magog*. The royalist bombardment of the town began on 2 September, but was largely ineffective: red-hot cannon balls were fired 'fast and frequently into the town' from siege forts along the causeway to Beverley, though a contemporary source suggests that few townspeople were killed as a result.[52] On 14 September the parliamentary warships *Lion* and *Employment* arrived in the Humber, from where they were able to resupply the town with men, arms and provisions from Lincolnshire and beyond. On the same day, Fairfax ordered that the sluices be broken, once again flooding the surrounding land just as had been done a year earlier. Several minor actions took place over the ensuing three weeks, but when the royalist army tried to storm the town on 9 October, they captured but could not hold the town's outlying defences. Two days later, the parliamentary forces counter-attacked, pushing back the royalist troops and capturing their gun emplacements. The earl admitted defeat and the siege was lifted on 12 October, a date marked by a public holiday in Hull until the restoration of Charles II in 1660.

On the same day the royalists were also defeated at Winceby in Lincolnshire, thus ending their advance on London and effectively checking the royalist gains of 1643. For historian Peter Gaunt, the abortive siege at Hull was a 'grave mistake ... wasting time and dividing resources which should have been focused on the royalist push to London'.[53] Thus the Earl of Newcastle's failure to capture Hull was an important event in the turning of the tide in Parliament's favour, ultimately leading to the capture of York in July 1644 and the decisive victory at Marston Moor which brought much of the north under the control of Parliament. Further successes across royalist territory over 1644 and 1645 led to the eventual surrender of the king at Newark in May 1646. At the same time, although the failed siege of autumn 1643 was the last military action Hull saw – a full two-and-a-half years before the end of the Civil War – the town continued to be an important garrison for parliamentary forces throughout the remainder of the conflict. As the only northern town never to fall to the king and an important east coast port, Hull was strategically and symbolically important to Parliament. Thus while the town saw relatively little in the way of major action – compared, for example, to other Yorkshire towns such as Leeds or Wakefield – and survived without ever being sacked and pillaged unlike Beverley, it was nevertheless a place of considerable importance in the wider geographies and histories of the English Civil War. In other words, its importance went well beyond the events at the gates in April 1642, however iconic that episode has since become within historical imaginations in the city and beyond.

By the Tide of Humber: Andrew Marvell

Andrew Marvell was born on 31 March 1621 at Winestead-in-Holderness, 14 miles south-east of Hull. Three years later, his family moved to Hull when his father was appointed master of Hull Charterhouse, an almshouse for the poor just north of Hull's town walls. Marvell attended Hull Grammar School between 1629 and 1633, leaving for Trinity College, Cambridge, in December 1633 and travelling in mainland Europe throughout the Civil War years in the 1640s. Marvell's Yorkshire connections later led him to Nun Appleton, near York, where in 1650–52 he worked as tutor to the daughter of Thomas, Lord Fairfax, the former general of the New Model Army. He also tutored William Dutton, ward of Oliver Cromwell, and worked as a civil servant in Cromwell's protectoral government, assisting the poet John Milton in his work as Latin Secretary. In 1659 Marvell was elected a Member of Parliament for Hull, a post he held until his sudden death in August 1678 of a fever he had contracted on a visit to Hull 'about the Towns affaires'.

The town's influence on Marvell's poetry and prose can be perceived through three key landmarks from his boyhood life in Hull – the Charterhouse, Grammar School and Holy Trinity church. These centres of instruction, charity and faith had served generations before Marvell and were pivotal to the people of Hull during the seventeenth century, as were their counterparts to the people of many towns and cities in medieval and early modern England. By weaving memories of these landmarks into his literature, Marvell was not only breathing creative power into the Hull he knew; he was also linking Hull to the rest of the country and the formative communities that had helped to cultivate his belief in corporate citizenship – a form of citizenship that thrived in Marvell because of his profound sense of place and attachment to Hull.[1]

The Marvells lived at the Charterhouse from 1624 until the Revd Marvell's tragic death by drowning in the River Humber in January 1641. Subsequently, the Charterhouse was all but destroyed during the First English Civil War in 1643. However, in Marvell's poem *Upon Appleton House, to my Lord Fairfax* (c. 1651), a work largely in praise of country life, the Charterhouse – and its destruction, and place in the political machinations of the time – leaves a deep impression on the poet.

Upon Appleton House also reflects Marvell's fears of another royalist siege of Hull. John Shawe, the new master of the Charterhouse in the early 1650s, had celebrated Hull as a 'Virgin Town' for its victory over the royalists in 1643.[2] But in August 1651 Hull faced a new threat from Scotland's newly crowned king, Charles II, whose invasion of England had sparked fears of a royalist uprising around the city. England's Commonwealth government wrote to Fairfax at Nun Appleton on 12 August 1651, calling upon him to defend Hull, 'of which you are now governor'.[3]

Fairfax's role as Hull's new governor is marked in the poem by his appearance as 'governor' of Nun Appleton's fortress-like garden, a garden that also stands in *Upon Appleton House* as a symbol of Fairfax's virtuous soul.[4] Marvell contrasts Fairfax's virtues with the 'virgin buildings' of Nun Appleton nunnery: its ruin a century earlier is attributed in the poem to rumours of sexual scandals among its not-so-virginal nuns (l. 86). The poem asks Fairfax to learn a lesson from Nun Appleton's nuns. It calls on him to use moral virtues as well as military prowess to defend God's 'Virgin Town' in August 1651, just as Fairfax's father had when he was governor of Hull during the 1643 siege.

When Marvell's father was appointed master of the Charterhouse, he also

Portrait of Andrew Marvell by Vincent
Galloway (1894–1977)
Guildhall, Hull: Hull Museums

became a lecturer at Hull's Holy Trinity church, which at the time was officially
'a chapel of ease' attached to the much smaller mother church at nearby Hessle.
The post of lecturer was established to allow for regular sermons to be preached
at Hull when the vicar – in Marvell's father's day, Richard Perrot – was in Hessle.

A number of Marvell's father's sermons survive in manuscript; ten appear in
his own hand in the unique sermon book preserved at the Hull History Centre.[5]
This sermon book also contains a reading list and a section headed 'Thinges
to be Considered about [the] Hospitall called Gods-House', in which Marvell
Senior proposes building a 'competent library' above the 'Common hall' at Hull
Charterhouse. Marvell's father pledged his own books to this library, which he
wanted to make accessible to all: 'It will be some honour to the towne, that
men may say they have a good library', he writes. 'I know no publike place
north-ward, of which it can be so spoken.'[6]

Several of Marvell's poems contain suggestive echoes of images from
sermons collected in his father's sermon book, prompting questions about the
whereabouts of this manuscript after 1641. The sermon book builds an image
of Marvell's father as a tolerant and open-minded churchman.[7] Alongside the

sermons, it contains a medieval life of Christ, notes on Hull puritans, and even a banned heretical text, the Racovian Catechism. Marvell's later writings in defence of religious freedoms may well have been shaped by his early exposure to his father's eclectic religious tastes.

The Old Grammar School that Marvell attended still stands today on South Church Side. Marvell's memories of the Grammar School are recorded in two prose works from the early 1670s. They defend freedom of worship for Protestants outside the Church of England, in the process attacking two Anglican churchmen – Samuel Parker and Francis Turner – who had argued against such freedoms in print. Marvell's schooldays in Hull also leave their mark on his later poetry. Among the poems he wrote at Nun Appleton in the early 1650s are two 'to his Worthy Friend Doctor Witty'. Witty was born and educated in Beverley, near Hull, and after attending Cambridge University was appointed usher at Hull Grammar School in 1634. He left the school in 1642 to pursue a medical career, moving to York in 1651. Marvell's poems to Witty were printed in *Popular Errours. Or the Errours of the People in Physick* (1651), which contains a preface that Witty signs 'From my house at Hull, Decemb. 2, 1650'.[8]

Marvell's poetry has not always been as well received as it is today. Few poems were published in his lifetime, and before the twentieth century he was better known as a political controversialist and as the author of several prose pamphlets attacking establishment figures in Church and state in the 1670s. So incendiary were Marvell's later prose writings that in February 1678 the press censor, Sir Roger L'Estrange, offered a reward of £50 for information leading to the discovery of the author or printer of Marvell's anonymously published *An Account of the Growth of Popery and Arbitrary Government* (1677). L'Estrange's agents were hot on Marvell's heels at the time of his death in August 1678.

Marvell's childhood and civic activism was deeply embedded in Hull. He benefited from a very good education in Hull and Cambridge and through his exposure to tolerant ideals, such as those hinted at in his father's sermons, he sought to engender the same in others, using the skills that came most naturally to him, his skills with language and words. Hull, its community edifices, its landscape and its estuarial river had a profound impact on Marvell's life and that of his family; it left a deep imprint on his creative imagination, which he made artful use of in his poetry and prose political writings.

Stewart Mottram

Notes

1   See Phil Withington, 'Andrew Marvell's Citizenship', in Derek Hirst and Steven N. Zwicker (eds), *The Cambridge Companion to Andrew Marvell* (Cambridge and New York, 2011), pp. 102–21 (p. 112).

2   John Shawe, *Britannia rediviva* (London, 1649), p. 9.

3   Council of State to Thomas, Lord Fairfax, 12 August 1651, in Mary Anne Everett Green (ed.), *Calendar of State Papers, Domestic Series, 1649–1660*, 13 vols (London, 1875–86), III (1877), pp. 323–24 (p. 324).

4   Andrew Marvell, 'Upon Appleton House, To my Lord Fairfax', in *The Poems of Andrew Marvell*, ed. Nigel Smith (London, rev. edn, 2007), pp. 210–41, l. 297.

5   Hull History Centre, DIAM/1 (*c.* 1624–1640).

6   Hull History Centre, C DIAM/1.

7   Nigel Smith, *Andrew Marvell: The Chameleon* (New Haven, CT, 2010), pp. 20–25.

8   Marvell, *The Poems of Andrew Marvell*, p. 178.

With the exception of the excavated remains of Beverley Gate, little is now visible of the walls and gates that once protected the medieval and early modern town. The former fortifications were all demolished between 1776 and the 1820s, knocked down and filled in as the town eventually expanded out beyond them (Figure 3.11). Yet the course of the walls is preserved in the modern street plan and occasional street names – North Walls, for example. This is perhaps clearest in relation to the layout of the town docks and the modern Queen's Gardens (formerly, Queen's Dock), which follow the line of the earlier fortifications (on the docks, see Chapter 5). Archaeological investigations also suggest that the bottom few courses of the town walls survive in places, though this material is mostly buried below modern urban and industrial development.[54]

Yet for all that they are now lost to view, the walls, gates and other fortifications loom large in the history of the city. In mapping out the walls and gates of the early modern town, I have focused here on the two major episodes in which the defensive capability of the fortifications came into play: first when the town fell to the rebel Pilgrim army in 1536, and secondly when the town three times held firm against the king and his forces in 1642 and 1643. In doing so, I have sought to gently

3.11 Beverley Gate before it was taken down in 1776, by Benjamin Gale.
© Gott Collection

reassess the idea of Hull as a rebellious city, arguing that in both 1536–37 and 1642, opinion in the town was actually more divided and political allegiances much more complicated than is sometimes acknowledged. In both cases, armed forces critical of the king were initially resisted by the town authorities, who kept them outside the walls for some days before eventually admitting them, though on both occasions without any serious assault on the defences having taken place. Moreover, on neither occasion was public feeling in the town decisively in favour of the rebels: in 1536 the townspeople clearly wished to avoid taking the Pilgrims' oath, and in 1642, Hotham thought that as many of five-sevenths of the population supported the king. Having admitted the rebels, the town authorities and population were quickly drawn into rebellion, overseeing the garrisoning of the town and repairs to the fortifications under the command of Constable and Hotham, respectively. Neither man met with a happy end – Constable hanged from Beverley Gate, Hotham executed in London – but the town authorities actually survived both incidents relatively unscathed, a sign perhaps that Hull was not perceived as quite as much of a rebel town as later narratives have claimed.

At the same time, in telling these stories, I have also reflected on some of the ways in which historical events come to be bound into twenty-first-century identities. As others have noted, such identity-making is often articulated in relation to specific heritage sites. Constructed in the fourteenth century, elaborated and rebuilt several times in the fifteenth, sixteenth and seventeenth centuries, demolished in 1766, buried though not forgotten, excavated in the 1980s, and 'saved' by the public in 2016, Beverley Gate has become an important focus for the making of local identities in twenty-first-century Hull. Whatever the truth of the town's early modern rebelliousness, the *idea* of 'Rebellious Hull' continues to have a powerful afterlife both within the city and outside it. As a result, Beverley Gate remains a key site at which 'Hullness' is produced, reproduced and articulated for wider consumption, a place at which the town's early modern history can be retold and reimagined not only in the City of Culture year, but also across the decades and centuries beyond.

Notes

1   Paul Heaton, 'Hull is no King's Town', *The Guardian*, 20 March 2011.

2   'This City Belongs to Everyone', a Nova Studios film made in Hull for Hull City Council, 2013.

3   Yorkshire Post and Leeds Intelligencer, 15 October 1901, http://www.britishnewspaperarchive.co.uk/viewer/bl/0000687/19011015/094/0005; Yorkshire Post and Leeds Intelligencer, 28 April 1903, http://www.britishnewspaperarchive.co.uk/viewer/bl/0000687/19030428/100/0006; Leeds Mercury, 29 April 1903, http://www.britishnewspaperarchive.co.uk/viewer/bl/0000747/19030429/076/0004; Hull Daily Mail, 15 October 1937, http://www.britishnewspaperarchive.co.uk/viewer/bl/0000324/19371015/052/0008.

4   See, for example, Nuala Johnson, 'Cast in Stone: Monuments, Geography, and Nationalism', *Environment and Planning D: Society and Space*, 13.1 (1995), pp. 51–65; James Duncan, 'Elite Landscapes as Cultural (Re) productions: The Case of Shaughnessy Heights', in K. Anderson and F. Gale (eds), *Inventing Places: Studies in Cultural Geography* (Melbourne, 1992), pp. 53–70.

5   See, for example, Facebook groups under the names *Action for Hull* and *Stop Hull's Beverley Gate Being Filled In By Hull City Council*, and media appearances by campaigners Mike Covell and Mike Parkinson on ITV News (14 September 2015, http://www.itv.com/news/calendar/update/2015-09-14/hundreds-sign-petition-to-keep-beverley-gate/, and 17 September 2015, http://www.itv.com/news/calendar/update/2015-09-17/hull-councillors-refuse-to-rule-out-filling-beverley-gate/).

6   Elizabeth Mackley, 'Hull's Historic Beverley Gate Protected by "Scheduled Monument" Status', *Hull Daily Mail*, 21 January 2016.

7   Online contributions drawn from the comments section of the *Hull Daily Mail* website between 30 November and 1 December 2015. Quoted contributions by *qualitychap*, *Hull47* and *Unoimmrrite*.

8   Hull City Council Planning Committee Update Sheet, 2 March 2016, https://cmis.hullcc.gov.uk/CMIS/Document.ashx?czJKcaeAi5tUFL1DTL2UE4zNRBcoShgo=jXwEzXTshEF9zL50tWdgeGDFEaNWE93mNl9LrXl3ETWX9nmLt6PqXA%3d%3d&rUzwRPf%2bZ3zd4E7Ikn8Lyw%3d%3d=pwRE6AGJFLDNlh225F5QMaQWCtPHwdhUfCZ%2fLUQzgA2uL5jNRG4jdQ%3d%3d&mCTIbCubSFfXsDGW9IXnlg%3d%3d=hFflUdN3100%3d3d&kCx1AnS9%2fpWZQ40DXFvdEw%3d%3d=hFflUdN3100%3d3d&uJovDxwdjMPoYv%2bAJvYtyA%3d%3d=ctNJFf55vVA%3d&FgPllEJYlotS%2bYGoBi5olA%3d%3d=NHdURQburHA%3d3d&d9Qjj0ag1Pd993jsyOJqFvmyB7X0CSQK=ctNJFf55vVA%3d&WGewmoAfeNR9xqBux0r1Q8Za60lavYmz=ctNJFf55vVA%3d&WGewmoAfeNQ16B2MHuCpMRKZMwaG1PaO=ctNJFf55vVA%3d

9   *Calendar of Patent Rolls Preserved in the Public Records Office, Edward III, Vol. IV, 1321–1324* (London, 1904), p. 7.

10 On the town defences, see David Evans, 'The Fortifications of Hull between 1300 and 1700', in M. Gläser (ed.), *Lübecker Kolloquium zur Stadtarchäologie im Hanseraum VII: die Befestigungen* (Lübeck, 2010), pp. 47–70.

11 K. J. Allison (ed.), *A History of the County of York East Riding: Volume 1, the City of Kingston upon Hull* (London, 1969), pp. 412–13 [hereafter *VCH*]; Evans, 'Fortifications'.

12 *VCH*, p. 413; W. Foot Walker, *The Walls and Gates of Hull* (Hull, 1981).

13 The gate had been rebuilt and the spire had been replaced with a tower by the time John Speed and later Wenceslaus Hollar drew their maps of the town in 1611 and *c.* 1640, respectively. The tower had in turn been taken down in 1735 (Evans, 'Fortifications').

14 British Library, Cott.Aug.I.i.83.

15 Evans, 'Fortifications'.

16 *VCH*, pp. 291, 296–97; List of Buildings of Special Architectural and Historic Interest.

17 *Letters and Papers of Henry VIII* [hereafter *LP*], XII.i, no. 338. Available online at http://www.british-history.ac.uk/search/series/letters-papers-hen8').

18 The following paragraphs draw on the *Letters and Papers of Henry VIII*. Readers interested in an overview of the Pilgrimage should see Madeleine Hope Dodds and Ruth Dodds, *The Pilgrimage of Grace 1536–1537 and the Exeter Conspiracy 1538* (Cambridge, 1915), and Richard Hoyle, *The Pilgrimage of Grace and the Politics of the 1530s* (Oxford, 2001).

19 For more on Constable and his role in the Pilgrimage, see B. McDonagh, 'Fragments from a Medieval Archive: The Life and Treacherous Death of Sir Robert Constable', *Journal of Historical Geography*, 42 (2013), pp. 50–61.

20 *LP* XI, no. 1046 and 1086; Dodds and Dodds, *Pilgrimage*, I, pp. 283–85; Hoyle, *Pilgrimage*, p. 307.

21 *LP* XI, no. 998.

22 *LP* XI (note 27), no. 1120 and no. 1138; *LP* XI.i (note 27), no. 698. Hemlock was a deadly poison.

23 *LP* XII i, no. 201 (i), 81, 64; cited in Hoyle, *Pilgrimage*, p. 373.

24 *LP* XII i, no. 369; cited in Hoyle, *Pilgrimage*, p. 377.

25 *LP* XII i, no. 141.

26 Dodds and Dodds, *Pilgrimage*, II, p. 65. This suggests it was Beverley Gate at which Hallam was captured.

27 Dodds and Dodds, *Pilgrimage*, II, p. 82; *LP* XII i, no. 338. Bigod – who had fared no better at Scarborough – was eventually captured in Cumberland in March and executed in London at Tyburn. The rest of the East Yorkshire rebels were imprisoned to await the arrival of the Duke of Norfolk.

28 *LP* XII ii, no. 229; XVI, no. 1232 and appendix no. 6. Henry's subsequent orders about improving the fortifications of the town referred to the gate 'where Constable hangeth'.

29 *State Papers: Henry VIII* (London, 1831), Vol. I, 555. This section of Henry's letter does not appear in the edited copy published in *LP* XII.ii (note 27), no. 77.

30 *LP* XI, no. 1285.

31 *LP* XI, no. 1224; *LP* XII, no. 67.

32 *LP* XII, no. 338; *LP* XVI, no. 1232.

33 *VCH*, p. 414; Evans, 'Fortifications'.

34 Basil Reckitt, *Charles the First and Hull 1639–1645* (London, 1952), p. 7.

35 For a useful overview of the English Civil War and its causes, see Peter Gaunt, *The English Civil Wars 1642–1651* (Oxford, 2003), pp. 13–23.

36 Barbara English also makes this point in her article, 'Sir John Hotham and the English Civil War', *Archives*, 20.88 (1992), pp. 217–24.

37 I. E. Ryder, 'The Seizure of Hull and its Magazine January 1642', *Yorkshire Archaeological Journal*, 61 (1989), pp. 139–48 (p. 141).

38 A. De La Pryme, *A History of Kingston upon Hull* (Hull, 1986), II, p. 72.

39 Ryder, 'The Seizure of Hull', p. 145.

40 On Hotham, see English, 'Sir John Hotham', pp. 218–20. Further useful primary source material appears in the Hotham family papers at Hull History Centre.

41 Andrew Hopper, *The Papers of the Hothams, Governors of Hull during the Civil War* (Cambridge, 2011), Appendix II, p. 238.

42 *Commons Journal*, 12 January 1641/42, p. 372; cited in English, 'Sir John Hotham', p. 219, note 9.

43 These two paragraphs are based on Reckitt, *Charles I and Hull*, pp. 26–34.

44 English, 'Sir John Hotham', pp. 217–18.

45 *Eikon Basilike, Or, The King's Book*, ed. Edward Almack (London: A. Moring, Limited, At the De la More Press, 1904), http://anglicanhistory.org/charles/eikon (accessed 29 November 2016).

46 Hopper, *Papers of the Hothams*, pp. 249 and 253.

47 Reckitt, *Charles I and Hull*, p. 55.

48 Reckitt, *Charles I and Hull*, p. 57.

49 BL Add. MS 32096, fo. 248; cited in English, 'Sir John Hotham', p. 141.

50 Andrew Hopper, '"Fitted for Desperation": Honour and Treachery in Parliament's Yorkshire Command, 1642–1643', *History*, 86.282 (2001), pp. 138–54 (p. 147).

51 Reckitt, *Charles I and Hull*, p. 91.

52 Reckitt, *Charles I and Hull*, p. 95 cites the contemporary pamphlet *Hull's Pillar of Providence* as a source.

53 Gaunt, *English Civil Wars*, p. 40.

54 Evans, 'Fortifications'.

CHAPTER FOUR

The Merchants' Golden Age, 1650–1775

DAVID and SUSAN NEAVE

The century and a quarter between the end of the Civil Wars and the building of Hull's first dock was a golden age for Hull's merchants. They broke free from the domination of York, and the passing of the Navigation Acts allowed them to exploit the lucrative trade of the Baltic at the expense of the once-mighty Dutch. The goods they imported included the vital raw materials that fuelled the industrial revolution taking place in the port's extensive hinterland, now reached more easily by a network of improving navigable rivers and canals, which in turn allowed the ready export of manufactured goods, coastwise and abroad. The prosperity of the port at this time and the wealth of the merchants have left their mark on the landscape of Hull, not least in the fortunate survival of a handful of merchants' houses along the High Street in the Old Town, particularly Wilberforce House and Maister House, which provide the backdrop to this chapter.

'A fine town, with a great many good buildings'

On 23 August 1701 William Byrd from Virginia, in the company of Sir John Percival, arrived at Hull on a tour of England, having crossed the Humber 'in little more than an hour by the favour of a good wind … it blew fresh, and was rough-water, but for all that we could not be sick, tho we thought of all the nasty images in the world to provoke us to it'. Recovered from the hazards of the crossing, Byrd, like other visitors at the time, was full of praise for this 'fine town, with a great many good buildings, and inliven'd by a very good trade'.[1]

Until the last quarter of the eighteenth century, travellers approaching Hull by boat or by land would see a town that in many ways looked more Dutch than English, still confined by its medieval brick walls and surrounded by water.[2] To the north and west, as well as the walls and water-filled ditch or moat, there were the earthworks of the outer defences, with five projecting bastions, constructed during the Civil Wars, beyond which was the Bush Dyke. As Celia Fiennes found in 1697, having journeyed by horse along the causeway from Beverley, to enter the town one had to cross two drawbridges and pass through two gates.[3] The defences were often reported as neglected and in decay, and during the panic caused by the Jacobite rebellions of 1715 and 1745 emergency repairs had to be carried out. On the second occasion, 3,000 people, paid workers and volunteers, the latter distinguished by cockades in their hats, were summoned each morning by the beat of a drum to restore the ramparts and deepen the moat.[4]

A comparison between Hollar's bird's-eye view of around 1640 (Figure 3.7) and a plan of 1772 (Figure 4.2) shows that despite the population having risen from around 6,000 to about 14,000 over that period, there had been only limited development outside the walls. Most of this took the form of warehouses and industrial buildings north along the River Hull,

4.1 The Master's House, Charterhouse, Hull from the west. The master's house, with almshouse adjoining, was built in 1649–50 to replace buildings demolished at the beginning of the Civil War. The shaped gable and pantile roof reflect the port's trading links with Holland. David and Susan Neave

and housing and commercial premises to the west and north-west at the beginning of the turnpike roads that were established in the mid-1740s leading to Anlaby and Beverley. The greatest change was on the east side of the River Hull where the Citadel, a great triangular fort covering some 30 acres, was built between 1681 and 1690. Incorporating the Tudor castle and south blockhouse, it had substantial clay ramparts and brick gateways, with projecting bastions at each corner. The whole was surrounded by water, with a broad moat, known as the New Cut, to the east, west and north and the Humber estuary to the south (Figure 4.2).

One of the few medieval buildings outside the walls, the almshouse known as Charterhouse Hospital, which had been demolished in 1643 to prevent it being taken by the royalists, had been rebuilt, in three stages, on its old site north of the town. The rebuilding had begun in 1649–50, suggesting that there was a swift revival in prosperity and confidence in the port. Elsewhere in the town, houses were built or rebuilt from the early 1650s; all were of brick and most likely roofed with pantiles imported from Holland, as was the master's house at the Charterhouse, the shaped gable of which gave it a distinct Dutch appearance (Figure 4.1). As well as the houses, described by Sir John Percival in 1701 as being 'large, new fashioned and very neat', civic and other public buildings were rebuilt or 'improved' in the late seventeenth century.[5] The merchants' meeting place or exchange, with custom house above, on the High Street was 'beautified' in 1673, as was the Guildhall, at the southern end of the Market Place, in 1681. The following year the market cross, 'a mean building disgustful to the Corporation', was replaced by a handsome cupola and octagonal lantern on a base of open arches (Figure 4.4).[6] Merchants endowed new almshouses, and in 1698 the corporation built a large Charity Hall to accommodate the poor. The tower of St Mary's church, demolished in the early sixteenth century, was rebuilt in brick in 1697 and, as befits a town where 'sectarys' were 'very numerous', the Presbyterians built a new chapel in Bowlalley Lane in 1692, and the Independents one in Dagger Lane in 1698.[7]

The 'well ordered' streets of Hull, 'well paved' with cobbles from the Holderness coast, were admired as much as the new buildings, but by the 1720s the town had become 'extra-ordinary populous, even to an inconvenience, having really no room to extend itself by buildings'.[8] The western half of the town, which had been much more open a century earlier, was filled with close-built streets and yards by the mid-eighteenth century, and the extensive lands of the demolished Manor House,

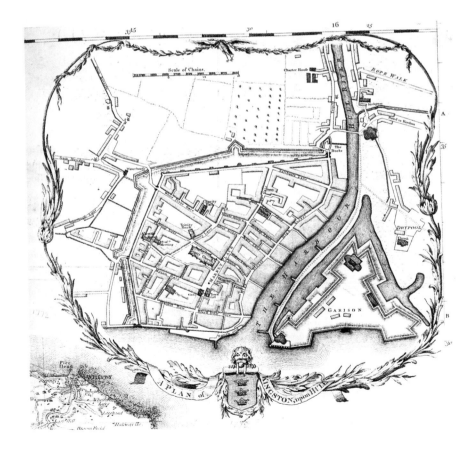

4.2 Thomas Jefferys' plan of Hull, 1772. By this date there had been some development to the north along both sides of the River Hull, and to the west on the main roads leading from the town. The great triangular Citadel is the most prominent new feature to appear in the landscape since the mid-seventeenth century.
David and Susan Neave

4.3 The Citadel and South Blockhouse from Samuel Buck's panorama of Hull, 1745. A flag is flying on the blockhouse and the Old Harbour, along the River Hull, is shown packed tight with ships.
David and Susan Neave

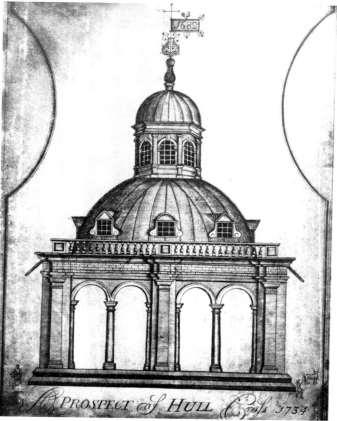

A PROSPECT of HULL Cross 1734

4.4 Market Cross, Market Place, Hull, engraving by J. Hilbert, 1734. Erected in 1682, the cross was demolished in 1761.
Wilberforce House, Hull Museums

4.5 Prince Street, looking east towards Holy Trinity church. The street was laid out in the early 1770s.
Visit Hull and East Yorkshire

to the west of Lowgate, and those of the former Carmelite friary, to the south of Whitefriargate, now belonging to Trinity House, were built upon. Throughout the town large houses, such as the 'great messuage' built by alderman Thomas Raikes on the south side of Posterngate *c.* 1660, had been subdivided into tenements and their yards filled with mean terraced cottages.[9]

From the mid-eighteenth century the corporation began a series of improvements, tackling first the Market Place, where more space was needed. It was overflowing with stalls 'with an infinite plenty of all sorts of provision', and packed with cattle, sheep and other livestock, and a 'vast concourse of people' who gathered from Holderness, north Lincolnshire and the villages west of Hull on market days.[10] The erection of the gilded statue of King William III there in 1734 had added to the congestion. In 1761 the market cross was demolished; so too were the market hall and tenements at the east end of Holy Trinity church, to be replaced by a butchers' shambles, and in 1768 the 'mountebank' stage, a venue for strolling players and other performers, was removed.[11]

Attention then turned to the west end of Holy Trinity church where the ancient Priest Row was demolished and a new street, King Street, was laid out 'commodious for carriages, passengers, travellers and the inhabitants' in 1771. Only the west side of the street remains with its archway leading to the delightful curving Prince Street (Figure 4.5). Both streets were the work of the architect Joseph Page who was to design the grand court room and council chamber of the nearby Trinity House in 1773. The associated almshouses, grouped around a courtyard with a handsome pedimented façade to the street, had been rebuilt in the 1750s (Figure 4.13).

If the town was overcrowded, then so too was the River Hull, in this case with shipping. Here the answer was a new dock, the building of which from 1774 necessitated the demolition of the northern stretch of the medieval walls, allowing the town to expand at last.

A place of great trade[12]

the commodious situation of this town, hath made it a place very well inhabited, and much resorted unto by merchants, being furnished with shipping and all sorts of commodities in great plenty, which they have from foreign parts, as well as from other parts of this kingdom, being inferior to none in England, except London and Bristol.

Richard Blome, 1673[13]

After the difficulties of the Civil Wars, when Hull's economy was severely hit, the trade of the port revived surprisingly quickly. Moreover, the overseas trade entered a period of vigorous growth, which owed much to the Navigation Acts of 1651 and 1660. The latter Act made it illegal to import into England most Norwegian and Baltic goods from anywhere other than their place of origin, and required that they must be carried in ships belonging to England, Norway or the Baltic countries. This excluded the use of Dutch ships and put an end to Amsterdam's role as the port through which much of Hull's Baltic trade had been channelled. Hull merchants were then able to take advantage of their long connection with the Baltic and Scandinavia area to establish direct trade links there. The numbers of foreign ships entering Hull decreased sharply, most being Norwegian vessels carrying timber, while an increasing number of English ships, chiefly from Hull, brought iron, pitch and tar directly from Sweden, and flax, hemp, linen, timber and iron from the Baltic ports.

After 1660 imports into Hull from Holland were largely confined to manufactured goods from the Low Countries and its German hinterland. It was said in 1668 that 'Hull ships seldom bring anything from Holland but pantiles, iron pots, frying pans and such things of small value'.[14] In contrast, exports to Holland increased in importance at this time because Amsterdam was the chief market for the products of the rapidly expanding Yorkshire woollen and worsted industry, which were shipped through Hull. By 1700 Hull was handling a tenth of England's total exports of cloth.[15] Holland was also the main overseas market for lead, mined in Derbyshire then carried by packhorse to Bawtry in south Yorkshire, where it was loaded on boats for transhipment from Hull.

Throughout the first half of the eighteenth century, Holland, and to a much lesser extent Hamburg, remained the main overseas destinations for exports from Hull, particularly manufactured goods, but the source of imports of raw materials, the demand for which was rapidly increasing, moved eastwards in the Baltic. From Russia came iron and unsawn timber and from Königsberg (Kaliningrad), then in Prussia, linen yarn and linseed, the latter supplying Hull's developing oilseed-crushing industry. The increasing demand for oil also encouraged the revival of whaling. Hull merchants had been actively engaged in the whaling trade in the 1650s, and as late as 1674 a 'Greenland house' for the processing of whales had been built on the River Hull above North Bridge. However, the English whale fishery soon collapsed and although Hull ships were sent out again to the Arctic in the mid-1750s, it was not until a decade later that the whaling trade, so important to the port in the early nineteenth century, was securely established.

Although trade with foreign ports was of great importance to Hull's economy, coastal and inland trade played an even greater role in the eighteenth century. Goods were sent by sea from London and other ports along the east coast to Hull for

4.6 Plan of Hull from Thomas Gent, *Annales Regioduni Hullini: or The History of the Royal and Beautiful Town of Kingston-upon-Hull*, 1735. The map is orientated with north to the left. The building shown at the top left is the eight-storey sugar refining house built in 1731.
David and Susan Neave

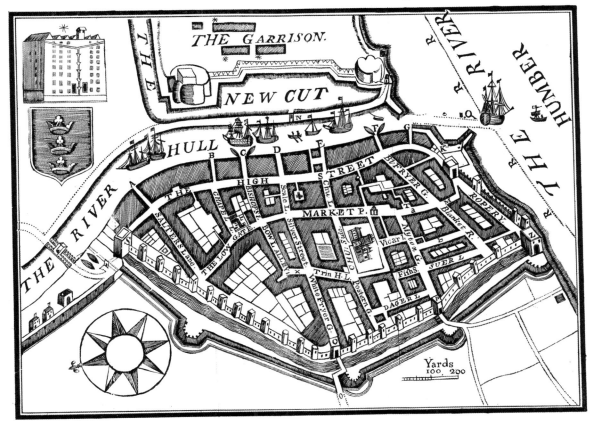

A PLAN OF KINGSTON - upon - HULL.

transhipment to a large part of central England. Mid-century, the tonnage of imports coastwise from British ports was much the same as that of foreign imports, while coastwise exports were double the amount going to foreign ports. From London came luxuries and other goods from the Mediterranean, the Americas, India and the Far East; from Newcastle and the north-east came coal, glass and salt; and from East Anglia, wool, corn and fish. Lead was an important export coastwise, along with iron goods, cloth and particularly foodstuffs, chiefly corn, butter and cheese and, by the 1770s, potatoes. The great range of imported goods meant that anything that was required throughout a large area of Yorkshire and the Midlands could be obtained through the port directly from abroad, or indirectly through London. Such richness in supplies encouraged the development of processing industries in Hull, including sugar refining, and the expansion of the port's role as the leading wholesale supplier and marketing town for east Yorkshire and north Lincolnshire (Figure 4.6).

The improvement of access to its hinterland was essential to the expansion of Hull's trade in the eighteenth century. It began in the early years of the century with the development of the Aire and Calder Navigation, reaching Wakefield and Leeds, and the improvement of the River Don beyond Doncaster and the Trent as far as Burton, and was followed from the 1750s with three decades of canal building. By the late 1770s direct water communication was possible with all the industrial areas of Yorkshire and the Midlands, including Sheffield and the potteries district of Staffordshire, the source of the exports and market for the imports that enabled the trade of Hull, like that of Liverpool, to grow faster than at other British ports during the century.[16]

Just before the outbreak of the Civil Wars it had been claimed of Hull, with some exaggeration, that all the merchants who traded through the port lived in York or Leeds. York merchants did indeed dominate the trade of Hull from the late Middle Ages, but this dominance, based chiefly on the export of York-produced cloth, was rapidly curtailed in the late seventeenth century as the West Riding became the centre of Yorkshire textile production. Hull merchants or their agents could deal directly with the West Riding textile producers as they did with the owners of the Peak District lead mines, without the involvement of their York rivals. By the early eighteenth century Hull had achieved complete independence from York, and this led to a rapid growth in the trade and wealth of its merchants.

But who were the merchants who benefited by the great expansion of trade? Port books show that 116 merchants exported through Hull in 1702, but many of these made only one or two shipments. Only 22 made ten or more shipments; the greatest number were made by William Crowle (85), John Thornton (80), Philip Wilkinson (68) and Daniel Hoare (48). The leading merchant families importing goods at this time were the Maisters, Sykes, Moulds, Somerscales and Broadleys. By 1751 almost two-thirds of the imports of iron through Hull – the most lucrative trade in the town – were handled by just two firms, those of Thomas Mould and Richard and Joseph Sykes. Mould was succeeded by his nephews Joseph and William Williamson, and by the 1780s their firm was the most important in eighteenth-century Hull.[17]

To maintain their leading position Hull merchants needed to secure markets

4.7 Francis Cotes, *Arthur Maister*, c. 1764–66. Maister, who spent many years in St Petersburg as an agent for the family firm in Hull, is shown as a Russian merchant with a fur-lined scarlet cloak. Fisher Museum of Art, University of South California

for the cloth, lead, ironmongery and the other goods being produced in increasing quantities by the industries of the port's hinterland, and locate new sources of raw materials for these expanding industries. To do so, they increasingly relied on their personal representatives resident in the Baltic ports. Many sons of Hull merchants found themselves working abroad for a few years as a factor or agent for the family firm; younger sons and other relatives might settle there permanently. Thus, there was a Maister – from the best-documented of Hull's Georgian merchant families – in one or other of the Baltic ports for almost 150 years. As early as 1636 William Maister was at Helsingore; the Henry Maister who was at Danzig twenty years later was probably his son; and the Henry Maister who settled at Gothenburg in 1699 was his grandson. Gothenburg on the west coast of Sweden was the main focus for British factors trading with the Baltic in the early eighteenth century, and for thirty years Henry Maister was the most important English merchant there.[18] Henry's nephew, William Maister, was based in Stockholm by the late 1720s and, save for some time in St Petersburg, spent most of his life there until his death in 1776. The potential of the newly founded St Petersburg as a trading base had been explored in 1727 by Thomas Grundy, a Hull merchant who was to go into partnership with Henry Maister at Gothenburg. Another William Maister (1731–58), second son of Henry, who built Maister House on the High Street in Hull, joined the firm Shairp and Swallow in St Petersburg in 1753, but sadly shot himself five years later, 'fearing that he had bought financial ruin to the firm'. He was succeeded there by his brother Arthur, who remained a partner in the firm until 1772 (Figure 4.7).[19] Among others from Hull who settled in St Petersburg at this time were John and George Cayley, sons of Cornelius Cayley, Recorder of Hull. John Cayley (1730–95) became British Consul in St Petersburg and his family remained there for nearly a century.

Holland, where members of Hull merchant families had been resident from the early seventeenth century, was not entirely abandoned in favour of the Baltic. The Pease family in particular maintained their long-established links. Theirs was a special case, for around 1663 Robert Pease (1643–1720), a young Hull merchant, had emigrated to Holland, apparently for religious reasons. He married Esther, daughter of George Clifford, the founder of an Anglo-Dutch merchant house which developed into one of the foremost banking houses in eighteenth-century Amsterdam. Robert Pease set up his own merchant house there, and in 1708 he sent his third son, Joseph Pease (1688–1778), back to Hull to establish a subsidiary to the main Amsterdam

firm (Figure 4.8). Pease received financial backing from his Clifford cousins and invested in shipping, banking, whaling and the development of oilseed crushing, the last with expertise, and initially seed, from Holland. Joseph Pease, who became a leading figure in Hull's merchant community, placed his son, sons-in-law and grandson, at various times, as his representatives in Amsterdam and Rotterdam, encouraging them to learn Dutch, which he continued to use when corresponding with his Clifford relatives in Holland.[20]

Merchant families

Anyone wanting an introduction to the influential merchant families of Hull in the century after the Civil Wars can do no better than to walk around the fine medieval churches of Holy Trinity and St Mary, reading the inscriptions on the elegant wall tablets or the many black marble grave slabs on which the merchants displayed their real or assumed coats of arms (Figure 4.9). At Holy Trinity, for example, there is a whole series of monuments to members of the Maister family. The earliest to Henry Maister, who died in 1699, states that he was 'twice mayor of this town and deputy governor to the Hamburg and Eastland Companies', while that to his son William

Maister, who died in 1716, records that he 'served his country and this corporation in seven successive Parliaments with a disinterested fidelity' (Figure 4.10). Through their wealth and close family ties, the merchants dominated and controlled the trade and social and political life of the town during this period. Between them, they provided most of the aldermen on the corporation and, for much of the time, at least one of the two Members of Parliament.

Some of the merchant families had been established in Hull from the sixteenth or early seventeenth centuries, including the Maisters, Fields, Moulds, Crowles, Wilkinsons and Blaydes, but others were newcomers, mostly from Hull's trading hinterland.[21] The Sykes family, for example, came in stages from Leeds and Knottingley (West Riding of Yorkshire), the latter then a thriving port on the River Aire. The first of the family to settle permanently was Samuel Sykes, son of the Leeds merchant William Sykes, who was apprenticed to Daniel Hoare of Hull (see below) in 1679. A few years later, Samuel's cousin Richard Sykes (1678–1726), son of Daniel Sykes of Knottingley, came to Hull as apprentice to the merchant George Crowle. In 1704 he married Mary, the daughter of Mark Kirkby, another wealthy Hull merchant. Their son Richard Sykes succeeded to the country estate that his mother's brother had built up, centred on Sledmere on the Yorkshire Wolds, and by the late nineteenth century the Sykes of Sledmere were the East Riding's greatest landowners.

Also from near the River Aire came John Thornton (1664–1731), the founder of what was probably the most prestigious merchant house to emerge from Hull at this time. He came from Birkin, near Knottingley, where his father was rector. Thornton was apprenticed in 1680 to John Field (d. 1689), merchant, alderman and mayor of Hull, and in 1686 he married his master's daughter, Jane. By 1701 the Thorntons were living in the fine house on the High Street known today as Wilberforce House. Their children included Robert (1692–1748) and Godfrey Thornton (1701–51), who ran the London branch of the business, trading chiefly with Russia, and William Thornton (1705–82) who remained a merchant in Hull, and who with his brothers and others established a sugar refinery there in 1732. In 1711 their sister Sarah (1690–1777) married William Wilberforce (1690–1774), the son of a Beverley mercer, who had been apprenticed to John Thornton in 1706. They were the grandparents of William Wilberforce the emancipator.[22]

4.9 Floor slab to Alderman William Ramsden, died 1680, in Holy Trinity church. Ramsden, Deputy of the Merchant Adventurers, was an MP for Hull, and twice mayor.
David and Susan Neave

Hull's trading links with Derbyshire may have brought Daniel Hoare (d. 1689) to the port, since he had connections there. The son of a Puritan brewer and alderman of Gloucester, he had gone to America around 1640 with his widowed mother and other siblings, settling at Braintree, Massachusetts. Daniel and his brother Leonard, later president of Harvard College, had returned to England by the early 1650s (the latter only temporarily) and Daniel settled in Hull from where he was exporting lead and cloth by 1658. Mayor in 1674 and 1688, Hoare was dismissed as an alderman in 1680 for his nonconformity. His son Daniel (d. 1722), who took over the business in 1687, shared the family home at No. 35 High Street. He too became an alderman and one of the port's leading merchants, but in 1712, 'greatly embarrassed by his circumstances', he sought permission to resign from the bench. The request was granted and, somewhat surprisingly, the corporation gave him the money to pay off his creditors. The elder Hoare took on at least seven apprentices, chiefly from areas with which he traded including Gainsborough, King's Lynn, Derby and Leeds.[23]

A number of the merchants had their origins across the Humber in north Lincolnshire, some the younger sons of gentry families including Erasmus Darwin and William Skinner (see below). Darwin (1659–1736), whose brother was the direct ancestor of the scientist Charles Darwin, came from Cleatham, a hamlet in the parish of Manton, five miles south-west of Brigg. Mayor of Hull in 1707 and 1720, Darwin had married Elizabeth, daughter of former mayor Robert Mason and sister of Hugh Mason, controller of customs for the port. Her great-nephew, the poet William Mason, was born at Hull in 1724.[24]

From the rural East Riding came William St Quintin (c. 1662–1723) who as a young merchant was taking on apprentices at Hull by 1688. A member of one of East Yorkshire's oldest landed families, he was the grandson of Sir Henry St Quintin of Harpham, Bt. (c. 1605–95), whom he succeeded as 3rd baronet in November 1695. Less than a month earlier St Quintin had been elected as one of the MPs for Hull. He served as mayor of Hull in 1700 and then again in 1715 when he was also Lord of the Treasury, a senior government position that he held from 1714 to 1717. The London lifestyle of Sir William St Quintin, who acquired a number of other lucrative government posts and built himself a grand country house at Scampston near Malton, was very different from that of the more provincial Hull merchant in the mid-to-late seventeenth century.[25]

A snapshot of the standard of living and lifestyle enjoyed by the merchant families can be gleaned from their wills and inventories. The will of Hugh Lister,

4.10 Monument to William Maister, merchant, and his wife Lucy, by Robert Hartshorne of London, 1717, in Holy Trinity church. Maister was MP for Hull.
David and Susan Neave

4.11 Silver tankard by Thomas Mangie, 1677. It has the monogram of Alderman Anthony Lambert, grocer, who was mayor of Hull in 1667 and 1682.
Guildhall, Hull: Hull Museums

the builder of Wilberforce House (on which see below), a wealthy merchant who died in 1666, is not untypical. He left to his 'dear and loving' wife Jane 'the gray mair she usually rides upon, as also the largest of the silver cups with cover, and one of the largest silver plates, and the silver cann which my father gave us att our marriage and six silver spoones we use daily', his watch and the 'bracelett rings and other jewells which I formerly gave unto her'. As long as she remained a widow, Jane could live in the house and have 'the use of the garden and stable on the backside', and the brewing vessels, pictures, hangings and curtains. His three sons and two daughters were each to receive silver and jewellery, including a silver gilt cup with a cover 'nut fashion' (probably fashioned out of a coconut shell), a toasting fork tipped with silver, twelve Apostle spoons, a French silver porringer, a silver sugar box, some broad flat wine bowls and two diamond rings. His daughter, Elizabeth, was also to have his 'harpsicalls', presumably a harpsichord, a musical instrument similar to the pair of virginals that the merchant John Field had at his death in 1689.[26] Field, like Lister, had a substantial amount of silver plate, some of it presumably made by local goldsmiths such as the Mangies of Church Lane, whose successful business no doubt depended on plenty of custom from the merchant community (Figure 4.11).[27]

The merchants are likely to have had furniture and other goods from Holland in their homes; houses in the High Street certainly had Delft tiles in their fireplaces and Dutch landscape paintings in their overmantels. Other pictures may have been imported from Holland or painted by Dutch artists visiting Hull, and included portraits of the merchants themselves. The delightful portrait of *c.* 1665 of George and Eleanor Crowle and their six children depicts them in similar clothes to those of Dutch merchant families of the time (Figure 4.12). Unfortunately the painting is not of a quality to have been painted by the great Dutch master Rembrandt, who Vertue, writing in the early eighteenth century, noted had 'liv'd at Hull in Yorkshire about sixteen or eighteen months, where he painted several gentlemen and seafaring men's pictures'. Rembrandt could certainly have been in Hull from November 1661 to July 1662, escaping creditors, for he is not recorded elsewhere at that time.[28] In the opening decades of the eighteenth century it is possible that Hull merchants were among those painted by the French artist James Parmentier (1658–1730), who lived in Yorkshire for twenty years from 1700. Part of his time was spent in Hull, where his commissions included an altarpiece for Holy Trinity church depicting the Last Supper, which survives in a truncated form.

By the mid-eighteenth century the status of the wealthier Hull merchant families was very different from that of a century earlier. Many were now accepted as members of county society, and their social life and leisure pursuits reflected this. The journal of the young merchant Robert Broadley for 1768–73 is much concerned with his leisure activities, which included hunting and racing, attending assemblies, concerts and plays at Hull, Beverley and York, and visiting Scarborough and the grander country houses. He was a great reader and with his close friends and fellow merchants Arthur Maister, Joseph Williamson, Benjamin Blaydes and Abel Smith played cards and gambled on anything. They were members of the Hull town hunt, with kennels just outside the town walls in Carr Lane.[29]

Hull was then a vibrant cultural centre drawing in the gentry, professionals and leading farming families from Holderness. As William Wilberforce noted:

It was then as gay a place as could be found out of London. The theatre, balls, great suppers, and card parties, were the delight of the principal families in the town. The usual dinner hour was two o'clock, and at six they met at sumptuous suppers … As grandson to one of the principal inhabitants, I was everywhere invited and caressed: my voice and love of music made me still more acceptable.[30]

The first known theatre, mentioned in 1743, was off Lowgate, and in 1768 Tate Wilkinson, the manager of the York circuit, built a 'well-contrived and handsome' theatre in Finkle Street. It became the Theatre Royal the following year on receiving a royal patent. The season ran from October to January when the merchant families were back from their summer excursions and the mariners back from the sea.[31] In 1733 it was reported that there was 'a polite assembly' once a week, then held in the upper room of the grammar school, but in 1752 a purpose-built assembly rooms was opened in Dagger Lane.[32]

Both parish churches had small libraries with some works other than theology and the classics, but a wider choice would have been available from the circulating library established by 1740, and the Subscription Library founded in 1775. There

4.12 Portrait of George and Eleanor Crowle and family, c. 1665. Alderman George Crowle (1631–82), merchant, was the builder of Crowle House, 41 High Street.
Hands on History Museum: Hull Museums

were booksellers and printers, one of the latter founding the town's first newspaper, the *Hull Courant*, by 1746. Many sons of merchants, professionals and tradesmen, most notably William Wilberforce and the poet and landscape gardener William Mason, were educated at the grammar school which had a succession of able masters including John Clarke (1720–32), a noted educationalist, and Joseph Milner (1767–97), ecclesiastical historian.[33]

William Wilberforce

William Wilberforce was born in what is now known as Wilberforce House on High Street in 1759. In the eighteenth century, the High Street was the city's economic core: its fine houses were the headquarters of many powerful merchant families whose commercial endeavours enhanced their wealth and the influence they were able to exert on the wider world. The fortunes of the Wilberforce family were closely linked to Hull's prosperity and they often worked in partnership with other leading High Street merchant families. The firm of Wilberforce and Smith did exceptionally well, and young William Wilberforce was able to use the company's wealth to pursue wider political and philanthropic interests and ideals. He was educated at Hull Grammar and Pocklington schools before entering St John's College, Cambridge, where he made many influential friendships, not least with William Pitt the Younger, a future prime minister.

Wilberforce entered Parliament as MP for Hull shortly after his twenty-first birthday in September 1780. In the late 1780s, with the encouragement of Pitt, he embraced the campaign for the abolition of the slave trade. Wilberforce worked with the newly formed Committee for the Abolition of the Slave Trade, becoming the recognised leader of the parliamentary abolition campaign. Though troubled by bouts of ill health, he proved a passionate and unrelenting advocate of abolition.

Wilberforce was not the first Hull MP to speak out in Parliament against the slave trade. David Hartley started that struggle in 1766 and the emancipation of slaves became a popular and heartfelt cause in Hull. Many townsfolk were inspired by Hartley's example, with some, such as the Cookman and Thompson families, making their respective marks in abolition movements and allied controversies on both sides of the Atlantic.

Wilberforce emerged as the leading voice in the campaign. Encouraged by the ailing John Wesley (a founder of the Methodist Church), Wilberforce moved his first abolition bill in 1791. This was defeated by 163 votes to 88, but his initiative sustained the abolitionist campaign, both inside and outside Parliament. Wilberforce also began working closely with key allies to form the Sierra Leone Company. Despite numerous parliamentary setbacks, Wilberforce and fellow campaigners finally secured the passage of the Slave Trade Act in 1807, which abolished the trade in slaves in the British Empire. Afterwards he worked tirelessly for the complete abolition of slavery until ill health forced his retirement from Parliament in 1825. His inspirational role helped ensure the durability of the campaign, which gained such moral and political strength that the Slavery Abolition Act was passed in 1833.

Wilberforce died just three days after hearing that its passage into law was assured. He was buried near his friend Pitt in Westminster Abbey, and in the following year the townsfolk of Hull raised the Wilberforce monument in his memory. Then, as now, the monument is a highly prominent landmark in the centre of the city.

William Wilberforce had a truly global impact. He inspired his contemporaries, and has continued to inspire campaigners against the evils of slavery to this day. Wilberforce House on Hull's High Street is now a museum of the slave trade and its abolition, while the University of Hull's Wilberforce Institute for the Study of Slavery and Emancipation (WISE), housed next door, is a world-leading centre for research into slavery and human rights in the past and the present.

Robb Robinson

William Wilberforce, 1794
Wilberforce House Museum:
Hull Museums

Mansions of merchant princes

Few, if any, of the merchants of Hull in the century or more after the Civil Wars achieved the great wealth of those of Bristol and Liverpool, who grew shamefully rich on the profits of the Atlantic trade. Nevertheless, many were able to build grand town houses, a handful of which survive along the High Street in the Old Town. As Sheahan wrote in the mid-nineteenth century: 'The advantages of situation that this street offered both for residence and business, induced the merchant princes and other principal inhabitants of the town to fix there abode there.'[34] Four houses in particular are discussed here.

In 1650 the narrow curving street was still dominated by medieval two- and three-storey timber-framed houses, those on the east side the most prized because they backed on to the private staiths or wharves on the River Hull where the merchants landed their goods straight into their yards and warehouses. The relationship of the merchant's house to the river can best be experienced today by a visit to Wilberforce House. Here you enter by a passageway that leads through the house to a rear yard, beyond which is a garden once filled with warehouses, and at the end you see the staith or wharf and the river, known at this point as the Old Harbour, although no longer crammed with shipping.

Wilberforce House was built around 1660 and demonstrates how quickly prosperity and confidence had returned to the Hull merchant community after the Civil Wars (Figures 4.14, 4.15). It was built for Hugh Lister, the fourth son of Sir John Lister, the wealthy merchant who had entertained King Charles I at his house elsewhere in High Street in September 1640 when the king came to inspect the town's defences (see Chapter 3). In his will, made later that year, Sir John directed that Hugh 'should live two years beyond sea vizt. one year in Holland and one year in France to learn his languages and book-keeping there, and that afterward when he is fit for it, he should live and continue in Hull and follow the course and trade of a merchant'.[35] It is not known whether Hugh Lister did as directed, but he would have had trading links with

4.14 Wilberforce House, High Street. Built *c.* 1660, this was the birthplace of William Wilberforce in 1759.
David and Susan Neave

Holland, and with its classical references and use of stone details and decoration in the brickwork the façade of Wilberforce House exhibits the strong influence of the Netherlands.[36] The house was almost certainly designed and built by William Catlyn (1628–1709), a Hull bricklayer, who must have been responsible for the other buildings in this distinctive style in Hull, the East Riding and north Lincolnshire. Catlyn clearly had skills as an architect and owned a 'book of architecture of ancient Rome' which he bequeathed to the library of Holy Trinity church.[37]

After Hugh Lister's death in 1666 his widow, Jane, continued to live in the house, which is recorded as having twelve hearths in 1673, and later became, for a time, the official residence of the governor or lieutenant governor of the garrison. As such it was occupied by Thomas Hickman, Earl of Plymouth, governor 1682–87, and Lionel Copley, lieutenant governor 1681–90 and then governor of Maryland. It was then leased in turn by the merchants William Mould and John Thornton, the latter purchasing the house in 1709. It was his son Godfrey Thornton who sold the property in 1732 to his brother-in-law William Wilberforce, the grandfather of William Wilberforce the emancipator, who was born there in 1759.[38]

The architectural style of Wilberforce House is known as 'artisan mannerist', referring to the unsophisticated use of classical detail by a bricklayer, stonecarver, woodworker or other craftsman. The most distinctive aspect of the building is the three-storey projecting entrance porch with its elaborate indented Corinthian pilasters decorated with rectangular and diamond stone 'jewells'. This feature is echoed in the façade of Crowle House, which is reached along a passage entered through a gate to the right of No. 41 High Street. Undoubtedly by the same architect, this house was built in 1664 for Alderman George Crowle and his wife Eleanor; the date and their initials are shown on decorative plaques on either side of the entrance bay.[39] Crowle founded an almshouse in 1668 which was also built in an artisan mannerist style; it stood in Sewer Lane and contained the poignant portrait of the merchant and his family referred to earlier (Figure 4.12).

4.15 Chimneypiece in the banqueting room, Wilberforce House, High Street. In the centre are the arms of Hugh Lister, who built the house 'new from the ground'.
Wilberforce House Museum: Hull Museums

4.16 Olde White Harte Inn, situated in a narrow passage off Silver Street. The upper part retains its artisan-mannerist detailing of *c.* 1660. It was the residence of the deputy governor and the place where the plot was made to overthrow the governor in November 1688.
David and Susan Neave

The Olde White Harte Inn, off Silver Street, is also in the same style and of a similar date (Figure 4.16). Originally a house, it was built for Alderman William Foxley, a wealthy grocer and 'good and kind friend' of Hugh Lister, who made him one of the supervisors of his will and an adviser to his widow. Altered externally in the 1880s, the inn has many original internal features including a substantial staircase and an elaborate chimneypiece on the first floor.[40] It was being used as the residence of the lieutenant governor Lionel Copley when it was the scene of the plot to overthrow the Catholic governor in 1688.

A fourth artisan-mannerist house, later known as Etherington House, was built on the east side of High Street by Foxley's son-in-law, William Skinner (1626–80), alderman and merchant, in 1672.[41] Skinner, mayor of Hull in 1664, was well connected. He was the grandson of Sir Vincent Skinner of Thornton College, Lincolnshire, and his mother, Bridget, was the daughter of Sir Edward Coke, Lord Chief Justice, and a patron of the poet Andrew Marvell. Skinner's sister was drowned crossing the Humber along with Marvell's father in 1641 and his brother, Cyriac Skinner, was a close friend of John Milton. William Skinner (d. 1724), who succeeded his father as a merchant in Hull, lacked his family's literary interests, for he gave a collection of Marvell's letters to his 'pastry-maid, to put under pie-bottoms'![42]

A detailed picture of the layout and contents of a large seventeenth-century merchant's house is provided by the probate inventory of Alderman William Dobson, a wealthy merchant who died in 1666. His house stood on the east side of High Street, to the south of Bishop Lane Staith; behind was a garth, or yard, then the garden and finally the staith or wharf, where Dobson had a 'study' with a chamber above. Storage was provided by a 'grayne house', a wine cellar and a 'presse seller' with a great cloth press, suggesting that Dobson traded in cloth, corn and probably wine. The arrangement of the rooms in the house is not clear, but on the ground floor there were great and little parlours, a counting house where business was conducted, a kitchen, a gallery and a 'great' back kitchen. Above there were six chambers, including great and little, and accommodation for maids and menservants. The parlours were sitting rooms, well provided with chairs, and the chambers were bedrooms. The great chamber also had plenty of chairs, suggesting that it was used for more than sleeping.[43]

Dobson's garden was seemingly a pleasure garden, since it had an arbour and beyond a 'grass plot' with five pairs of bowls and a jack. There was also a 'garden house' that contained two tables and frames, a pair of tables, one chair and four high chairs of Russian leather, a form, twelve little pictures, a 'hanging glass case', a copper warming pan, two garden knives, a pair of garden shears and 'some other odd implements'. Such garden houses were a common feature in Hull at this time, with twelve recorded in the hearth tax assessment of 1673, of which five had two hearths, suggesting substantial buildings. Eight of the garden houses were listed separately from the householder's main property and were seemingly in detached gardens, a feature of close-built towns such as Hull where many large houses had little or no open space adjacent to them.

In the summer months the wealthier families would set out to spend leisure time in their gardens on the edge of the town where the garden house provided a place to cook, eat and shelter. Alderman Francis Dewick, whose house was on the east side of High Street, had a garden and garden house on the south side of Jesus Gate (Robinson Row) in 1652.[44] In the later seventeenth century some of the land of the Manor House off Lowgate was divided into gardens. Robert Scott leased a garden and

4.17 Blaydes House, 6 High Street. Largely rebuilt around 1750 for Benjamin Blaydes, merchant and shipbuilder. The small window of the look-out can be seen between the chimneystacks. David and Susan Neave

garden house there in 1683 and Christopher Bayles, merchant, who lived on the east side of High Street, had a garden and garden house in 'the manner' in 1718. The gardens were often referred to in deeds as 'garden rooms', suggesting that they were walled. In 1711, for example, reference was made to 'a garden or garden room with a little garden house thereon built and all the brick walls … wherewith the same are inclosed' on the east side of High Street.[45]

As the merchants became wealthier their houses along High Street became grander and more fashionable. One of the most impressive would have been Nos. 42–43 High Street, built soon after 1727 by Richard Sykes (d. 1761), who was to inherit the Sledmere estate. The house, destroyed by fire in 1827, was set a little way back behind railings, with marble steps up to the front door, and across the road a coach house and stables.[46] Further south on the east side of High Street stood No. 66, built by Thomas Broadley, merchant, about 1740 and considered the 'best built' in the street in the mid-nineteenth century, by which time it had become a grocery warehouse but still retained 'the black and white marble pavement in the hall, the noble staircase, oak panelled rooms' and rich plasterwork. A staircase led up to the top of the house where there was a turret built on the roof, with views all round 'enabling the inmates to enjoy the surrounding scenery and imbibe the refreshing air' and the merchants to observe the shipping entering and leaving the port.[47] Many other houses along High Street were said to have had similar lookouts, and a more modest version survives at Blaydes House, No. 6, at the north end of the street. Here a secondary staircase leads up to a small window located between the chimneystacks with a view south (Figure 4.17).

Blaydes House, with its elegant five-bay façade and handsome Doric porch of around 1750, appears to incorporate part of an earlier building. A house on this site was acquired by Benjamin Blaydes (d. 1720), shipbuilder, in the 1690s, and it was evidently his son, Benjamin Blaydes (1709–71), merchant, who rebuilt it. The ornate plasterwork of the ceiling to the grand staircase, with its handsome Venetian window looking towards the River Hull, contains the monogram BB. The rooms on the ground floor were probably reserved mainly for business, with the panelled room to the south of the marble-floored entrance hall the merchant's office and study, while that to the north of the staircase, with a side entrance nearby, may have been occupied by the chief clerk. Upstairs were the family rooms, the grandest of which, with its fine chimneypiece, plaster cornice and superb carved doorcase, dado moulding, skirting and window architraves, would have been the drawing room.

The architect for the rebuilding of Blaydes House was probably Joseph Page of Hull, known to be responsible for the splendid plasterwork and possibly the design of Maister House, No. 160 High Street (National Trust). This was built for Henry Maister (1699–1744) to replace the house that was destroyed by a fire in April 1743 that killed his wife, young son and two maidservants. Maister sought advice on the rebuilding from Lord Burlington, the great patron of the arts, skilled amateur architect and promoter of the Palladian style. The connection was probably through Maister's fellow Hull merchant and MP, George Crowle, the younger, a regular guest when Lord Burlington was at his estate at Londesborough near Market Weighton. The spectacular staircase at Maister House, such a surprise after the plainness of the house's exterior, can be attributed to the influence of Burlington and perhaps that of William Kent. The broad stone staircase with an elaborate wrought-iron balustrade by the celebrated Derby ironsmith, Robert Bakewell, rises round three sides of the stairwell, the walls of which are decorated with stucco panels, brackets for busts, festoons of shells and swags of drapery. From the first-floor landing a separate staircase goes up to a gallery which has an ornate coved ceiling with octagonal opening to a glazed roof lantern (Figure 4.18).[48]

This lavish interior may have been the reason why other merchants improved or built their houses with the unnecessarily grand staircases that are a feature along the High Street. The most lavish were at No. 51 High Street (demolished), part of the mid-eighteenth-century additions to the earlier house for Henry Etherington. One staircase had a baroque plaster ceiling and elaborately decorated balusters while the other, more sophisticated, was set in an apse with a large Ionic Venetian window and topped by a shallow dome.[49] Around 1760 Robert Wilberforce, not to be outdone, added a fine staircase at Wilberforce House, with a rich Rococo plaster ceiling and an impressive Venetian window, which probably never had much of a view. The same can be said of the similar but less ornate matching staircases in the Georgian houses adjoining Wilberforce House (Figure 4.19). This pair of houses with their unusual double doorcase were built by James Hamilton, a tar merchant and whaling promoter, in 1759. Until the Second World War these Georgian merchant houses were the last of a run that stretched north along the east side of High Street as far as Alfred Gelder Street. The last but one, No. 18 High Street, the home of Robert Nettleton and his wife Lydia (niece of Andrew Marvell) in the late seventeenth century, was bought by the Anglo-Dutch merchant Joseph Pease in 1731.[50] Soon afterwards he rebuilt the house, and here in 1754 established Hull's first bank. The entrance to the bank is now marked by a dummy doorcase in the rebuilt wall of the former house, but behind, fronting the River Hull, are two four-storey warehouses built for Pease in 1745 and 1760 (Figure 4.8).

4.18 Maister House, 160 High Street. The grand staircase of 1744 with elegant balustrade by Robert Bakewell, and statue of Ceres by Henry Cheere.
Historic England

The layout and furnishings of a typical Georgian merchant's house can be recreated from the letters of Nathaniel Maister (1703–72) and a detailed inventory of his home. Maister, who ran the family business following the death of his brother Henry in 1744, initially lived in No. 160 High Street (Maister House), the building of which he had overseen, but in 1761 he bought another house, No. 154, a little further south on the same side of the street. His 'new habitation' comprised counting house and kitchen on the ground floor, the drawing room, middle dining room and fore dining room on the first floor, and four bedrooms on the second floor called the front chamber, middle chamber with closet, and the white and green rooms. At the top of the house were the garrets, one for maidservants, another for menservants and a third called the meal garret. The walls of the drawing room were covered in yellow paper, the two armchairs and nine single chairs were upholstered in yellow and the curtains were of yellow silk damask. On the floor there was a Wilton carpet, between the windows mirrors in carved gilt frames, and over the chimneypiece a landscape painting. The counting house contained a writing desk, two Windsor chairs and a walnut bookcase with glass doors that held the ledger books. Nathaniel had a library of around 150 books, including sets of plays with titles such as *The Provoked Husband*, *She Would if She Could* and *Sir Fopling Flutter*, the works of Racine, Molière and Rabelais in French and, reflecting his interest in science, *Baker on the Microscope*.[51]

Like many Hull merchants, Nathaniel Maister also had a country house, where he could go to escape from the increasing noise and smells of High Street. This was at Winestead in Holderness to the east of Hull, but most of the merchants had their rural retreat in one of the villages to the west. North Ferriby was a particularly favoured location. Here in the early to mid-eighteenth century could be found houses owned by John Field, William Wilberforce, Thomas Broadley and Henry Etherington, who each had their town house and business premises in High Street in Hull. In the country they took on the lifestyle of the landed gentleman. When Broadley bought what became Ferriby Hall in the 1720s, he consulted the celebrated landscape gardener Stephen Switzer about a design for the modest grounds of his

4.19 Georgian houses, 22–23 High Street. Built for James Hamilton, tar merchant, about 1759.
David and Susan Neave

'hunting seat', and a few years later Henry Etherington (d. 1760) commissioned a portrait of himself on horseback and in hunting gear.[52] Some merchant families, such as the Sykes, moved permanently to the country, in their case to Sledmere and West Ella, and their town house became just a business premises.

The abandonment of High Street by the merchant families that had gathered pace from the mid-eighteenth century entered its final phase after the opening of the first dock in 1778, when there was no longer any advantage in living close to the private staiths, and land was released for the building of grand terraced houses and villas outside the Old Town. Then, in the words of a mid-nineteenth-century commentator, the 'elegant houses' of the High Street were 'metamorphosed into tenements and merchants' counting houses'.[53] The golden age of the merchant was coming to an end, to be replaced by that of the shipowner and industrialist in the nineteenth century.

The *Bounty*

The shipbuilding firm owned by the Blaydes family built the *Bethia* in their North End Yard on the River Hull, close to their base at Blaydes House, High Street (now Hull University's Maritime Historical Studies Centre). The *Bethia* was an 85-foot-long, three-masted wooden sailing vessel deployed in carrying cargoes around the North Sea. In 1787 she was purchased by the Admiralty for £1,950, fitted out for a voyage to the South Seas and renamed *Bounty*. The expedition was intended to collect breadfruit from Tahiti and transport them to the West Indies, to be planted and grown as food for plantation slaves in another corner of the British Empire.

Bounty was smaller than either *Endeavour* or *Resolution*, which had been commanded by Captain James Cook on earlier South Seas voyages. *Bethia* had been worked by 15 men in her role as a merchant vessel. But after being modified at Deptford Royal Dockyard, His Majesty's Armed Vessel *Bounty* sailed from Spithead for the Pacific on 23 December 1787, under the command of Lieutenant William Bligh, with a 46-strong crew in cramped and overcrowded conditions.

The story that unfolded is now the stuff of maritime legend. After a ten-month voyage in atrocious conditions, featuring an aborted attempt to round Cape Horn, the exhausted ship's company dropped anchor off Tahiti in late October 1788. They spent the following five months collecting breadfruit in what seemed like a tropical paradise – a complete contrast to the hardships of the voyage. Strong relationships were forged between the seafarers and the Tahitians, and many crew members were reluctant to leave when their overcrowded ship, now stacked with breadfruit, sailed in early April 1789.

This scale model of HMAV *Bounty* was constructed from original plans by David Easterbrook, who donated it to the Maritime Historical Studies Centre (MHSC), University of Hull. The model is photographed here on the first-floor landing of Blaydes House, now home of the MHSC, but originally the dwelling and business premises of the Blaydes family, builders of the *Bethia*, the merchant ship purchased and converted into the *Bounty* by the Admiralty in 1787.

© Rebecca Hiscott

Once back on board tensions intensified. Three-and-a-half weeks after setting out on the return voyage, Acting Lieutenant Fletcher Christian and some armed companions seized HMAV *Bounty* and forced Bligh, and 18 of those who remained loyal to him, into the ship's launch (a large rowing boat). They then threw the breadfruit overboard and returned to Tahiti. Later, Christian and nine of the mutineers, together with 18 Tahitians, including 11 women, sailed southwards, finally settling on the remote Pitcairn Island where they ransacked and burned the *Bounty*. Meanwhile, against all the odds, Bligh pulled off an amazing feat of seamanship by covering over 3,500 nautical miles in 47 days in the oar-powered launch to reach the Dutch settlement at Timor. Another naval expedition was sent to capture the mutineers who had remained on Tahiti, ten of whom were court-martialled, with three being executed for piracy and mutiny. However, the whereabouts of Christian and those who had sailed south remained a mystery for many years. In the event, all bar one of them suffered violent deaths, but their descendants still live on Pitcairn Island.

Bligh led another expedition to Tahiti and successfully transported breadfruit to the West Indies. Later he carried out important hydrographical work, which included charting the shifting channels and sandbanks of the Humber estuary. Little remains of the *Bounty* today, but more than 240 years after *Bethia* was first launched into the River Hull the story still attracts considerable global attention, not least because the reasons why the mutiny took place have been disputed by contemporaries, historians, authors and film-makers ever since the fateful events of 28 April 1789.

Robb Robinson

1   Mark Wenger (ed.), *The English Travels of Sir John Percival and William Byrd II* (Columbia, MO, 1989), p. 185.

2   David Neave, *The Dutch Connection: The Anglo-Dutch Heritage of Hull and Humberside* (Hull, 1988).

3   Donald Woodward (ed.), *Descriptions of East Yorkshire: Leland to Defoe* (East Yorkshire Local History Society, 1985), p. 49.

4   Audrey Howes and Martin Foreman, *Town and Gun: The 17th-century Defences of Hull* (Hull, 1999), p. 151.

5   Wenger, *English Travels*, p. 102.

6   George Hadley, *New and Complete History of Kingston upon Hull* (Hull, 1788), p. 247.

7   Wenger, *English Travels*, p. 102.

8   Woodward (ed.), *Descriptions*, pp. 28, 56; Jan Crowther (ed.), *Descriptions of East Yorkshire: De la Pryme to Head* (East Yorkshire Local History Society, 1992), p. 14.

9   East Riding Archives and Local Studies [hereafter ERALS], Deeds Registry A 610/867.

10 Woodward (ed.), *Descriptions*, p. 56; Crowther (ed), *Descriptions*, p. 14.

11 Kenneth A. MacMahon, 'The Street in Eighteenth Century Kingston upon Hull', *Transactions of the Georgian Society for East Yorkshire*, 5 (1961), pp. 43–66.

12 This section is largely based on Ralph Davis, *The Trade and Shipping of Hull 1500-1700* (East Yorkshire Local History Society, 1964), and Gordon Jackson, *Hull in the Eighteenth Century* (London, 1972).

13 Woodward (ed.), *Descriptions*, p. 28.

14 Davis, *Trade and Shipping*, p. 27.

15 Davis, *Trade and Shipping*, p. 27.

16 Gordon Jackson, *The Trade and Shipping of Eighteenth-Century Hull* (East Yorkshire Local History Society, 1975), p. 14.

17 Jackson, *Hull in the Eighteenth Century*, pp. 96–97.

18 M. Edward Ingram, *The Maisters of Kingston upon Hull 1560–1840* (Reighton, 1983), p. 9; John R. Ashton, 'Henry Maister of Gothenburg: His Life and Times', *Yorkshire Archaeological Journal*, 70 (1998), pp. 93–99.

19 Anthony Cross, *By the Banks of the Neva: Chapters from the Lives and Careers of the British in 18th-century Russia* (Cambridge, 1997), p. 62.

20 Neave, *Dutch Connection*, pp. 6–7.

21 Jackson, *Hull in the Eighteenth Century*, p. 97.

22 Hull History Centre [hereafter HHC], C BRG/6/410, C BRG/6/1238; Lambeth Archives, IV/104/2/1.

23 Henry S. Nourse, *The Hoar Family in America and its English Ancestry* (Boston, 1899), pp. 12–17, 25–26; Frederick Brookes (ed.), *The First Order Book of the Hull Trinity House 1632–1665*, Yorkshire Archaeological Society Record Series, 105 (Leeds, 1942), pp. 133–34; Keith Allison (ed.), *A History of the County of York East Riding: Volume 1, the City of Kingston upon Hull* (London: Victoria County History, 1969) [hereafter *VCH*], pp. 119, 183, 194; ERALS, DDX 508/43; HHC, C BRG/6/33-4, 42-3, 84, 354-5.

24 Thomas Noble (ed.), *History, Gazetteer and Directory of the County of Derby* (Derby, 1829), pp. 154–55.

25 HHC, C BRG/6/812; Eveline Cruickshanks and Ivar McGrath, 'William St Quintin (c.1662–1723)', http://www.historyofparliamentonline.org/volume/1690-1715/member/st-quintin-william-1662-1723 (accessed 28 February 2016).

26 HHC, C DMX/328; Borthwick Institute for Archives [hereafter BIA], York Wills, Holderness, Jan. 1690.

27 Ann Bennett, 'The Mangies of Hull', *Yorkshire Archaeological Journal*, 57 (1985), pp. 149–63; Ann Bennett, 'The Goldsmiths of Church Lane, Hull: 1527–1784', *Yorkshire Archaeological Journal*, 60 (1988), pp. 113–25.

28 Christopher Wright, *From Medieval to Regency: Old Masters in the Collection of the Ferens Art Gallery* (Hull, 2002), pp. 16–17.

29 HHC, U DP/146; Jackson, *Hull in the Eighteenth Century*, pp. 265–66; Iris Middleton, 'An Investigation into Early English Fox Hunting with an Account of Hunting with Hounds in the East Riding of Yorkshire 1700–1850', unpublished MPhil thesis, University of Hull, 1995, pp. 79, 142.

30 Robert Wilberforce and Samuel Wilberforce, *Life of William Wilberforce*, 5 vols (London, 1838), I, p. 8.

31 *VCH*, p. 418; Crowther (ed.), *Descriptions*, p. 22.

32 Crowther (ed.), *Descriptions*, p. 14; Jackson, *Hull in the Eighteenth Century*, p. 268.

33 R. S. Tompson, 'Clarke, John (bap. 1687, d. 1734)', *Oxford Dictionary of National Biography* (Oxford, 2004), http://www.oxforddnb.com/view/article/5509 (accessed 5 March 2016); D. B. Hindmarsh, 'Milner, Joseph (1745–1797)', *Oxford Dictionary of National Biography* (Oxford, 2004), http://www.oxforddnb.com/view/article/18792 (accessed 5 March 2016).

34 James Sheahan, *History and Description of the Town and Port of Kingston upon Hull* (London, 1864), p. 301.

35 BIA, York Wills, Holderness, Feb. 1640–41.

36 Hugh Lister helpfully records in his will, made in 1664, that he built 'the house wherein I now live in Kingston upon Hull ... new from the ground'. HHC, C DMX/328.

37 David Neave, 'Artisan Mannerism in North Lincolnshire and East Yorkshire: The Work of William Catlyn (1628–1709) of Hull', in C. Sturman (ed.), *Lincolnshire People and Places* (Lincoln, 1996), pp. 18–25.

38 David Neave and Susan Neave, 'Wilberforce House, 25 High Street, Hull', unpublished report for Hull City Council, 2004.

39 David Neave and Susan Neave, *The Building of a Port City* (Hull, 2012), p. 15.

40 Robert Barnard, 'The Old White Hart, Hull', *East Yorkshire Historian*, 6 (2005), pp. 65–77.

41 Robert Barnard, *High Street Properties*, CD (Hull, 2003); Thomas Tindall Wildridge, *Old and New Hull* (Hull, 1889), pp. 12–26, pl. 69; Rupert Alexander Alec-Smith, 'Two Houses of the Etherington Family', *Transactions of the Georgian Society for East Yorkshire*, 2.2 (1948), pp. 34–38. Etherington House, 51 High Street, was demolished after being damaged in the Second World War.

42 Cedric Brown, 'Milton, the Attentive Mr Skinner, and the Acts and Discourses of Friendship', in Edward Jones (ed.), *A Concise Companion to the Study of Manuscripts, Printed Books, and the Production of Early Modern Texts* (Chichester, 2015), pp. 106–28; *Letters of eminent men addressed to Ralph Thoresby* (London, 1832), II, p. 103.

43 ERALS, DDHI/58/5/14. The house stood on the site of Pacific Exchange. There is a fine monument to William Dobson, with portrait bust, in St Mary's church, Lowgate.

44 David Neave, Susan Neave, Catherine Ferguson and Elizabeth Parkinson (eds), *Yorkshire East Riding Hearth Tax 1672–3* (London, 2015), pp. 94–96; HHC, C M.583; ERALS, DDCC/53/2.

45 HHC, C D.944 (f); ERALS, DDSA/399; Deeds Registry, A 638/91.

46 Sheahan, *History*, pp. 313–15.

47 Sheahan, *History*, pp. 318–19; John Symons, *High Street, Hull* (Hull, 1862), pp. 168–70. Fireplaces and other fittings were taken from the house in the 1880s and incorporated into Brantinghamthorpe Hall: Alec-Smith, 'Two Houses', pp. 34–38.

48 Rupert Alexander Alec-Smith, *Maister House* (National Trust, n.d.); David and Susan Neave, *Hull*, Pevsner Architectural Guides (New Haven, CT, and London, 2010), p. 90.

49 Alec-Smith, 'Two Houses', pp. 34–38; I. Hall and E. A. Hall, *Georgian Hull* (York, 1979), pp. 32, 39, 41.

50 Barnard, *High Street Properties*.

51 Ingram, *The Maisters*, pp. 48–50.

52 HHC, C DFB/1/54-55, C DFB/2/5; Wright, *From Medieval to Regency*, p. 18.

53 Sheahan, *History*, p. 301.

he Humber F.F. & Co.

CHAPTER FIVE

Dock Development, 1778–1914

MARTIN WILCOX

Nothing has more contributed to the extension of commerce in Hull than the docks.

White's Directory of Hull, 1882

Hull owes its existence to water transport. Located at the mouth of the River Hull, where the deep-water channel of the Humber sweeps along its north bank, it is a natural transhipment point, and although the town (as it is properly called until 1897, when Hull gained its city status) did become an industrial centre during the nineteenth century, it was always first and foremost a port. Between 1778 and 1914 its scale and operations were revolutionised. At the beginning of the period it was simply a river port, exploiting the natural harbour of the River Hull, but thereafter the port was transformed, and with it the town. The growth of trade and the industries it fostered drove Hull's economic development, and with it the expansion of its population and thus its urban sprawl. Meanwhile, the location of the various docks shaped the centre of the town, led its expansion east and west along the Humber and north along the Hull, and determined the location of its key industries. Through their influence the medieval town became a modern city.

Causes and influences

The development of Hull was driven fundamentally by the same factors as at other major ports: the industrialisation of the British economy, the growth of seaborne trade and with it the emergence of new commodities and trade routes, and developments in shipping.[1] Yet every port is distinctive, and Hull's evolution was shaped its geography, by its pre-existing trade links both at home and overseas, and by the priorities and needs of its political and commercial communities (Figure 5.1).

All ports depend on their hinterland, from where goods for export are sourced and in which imported goods are sold. From medieval times, Hull had reaped the benefits of being linked to inland Yorkshire and the Midlands via the Humber and its tributaries, such as the River Ouse, which was navigable as far as York and therefore saw much of the city's wool exports routed through Hull. During the eighteenth century major rivers were improved and linked to one another via the growing canal network, connecting ports more closely with the industrial areas of Britain.[2] Improvements to the Trent and Don linked Hull to Nottingham and Birmingham, while the Aire and Calder Navigation improved links with west Yorkshire. Later phases of canal-building, especially the Grand Trunk and Leeds and Liverpool canals, added further linkages.[3] All of this placed Hull in prime position to benefit from the rapid expansion of an array of industries across the north and Midlands. Hull also had a thriving coastal trade, mainly with London and other east coast ports, whence Hull imported goods from parts of the world with which its own ships did not trade and exported the foodstuffs and raw materials of Yorkshire and the Midlands.[4] The inland waterways continued to transport large quantities of goods into and out of Hull into the twentieth century, but by then the hinterland had been widened greatly by the railways.[5] An abortive scheme for a Hull–Leeds line was proposed as early as 1825, and although the railway did not actually reach Hull until 1840 it did exert an influence, as riverboats from Hull connected with it at Selby. When the railway arrived, it shared traffic in bulky goods with waterways and coastal shipping, but it also allowed rapid transport of passengers and lighter cargoes, and perishable goods such as fresh fish.[6] Later, the railways played a vital role in fostering the coal trade.

The 'transport revolution' fed into wider industrialisation which saw Britain evolve from the agrarian society of the early eighteenth century to the urban, industrial one

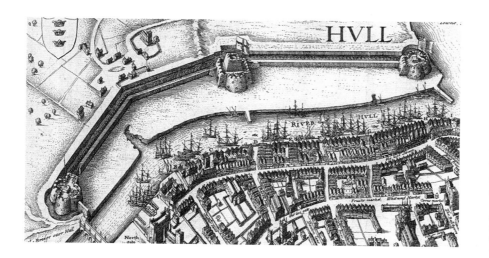

5.1 Detail from Wenceslaus Hollar's plan of Hull, clearly illustrating how, before the docks developed, the trade of the port was done along the river. This image dates from *c.* 1640: by the 1770s the river had become seriously congested.
Courtesy of University of Toronto Wenceslaus Hollar Digital Collection

of the nineteenth. Many key industrial areas lay within Hull's hinterland, and it was their early development that caused trade through the port to grow quickly from the mid-eighteenth century.[7] Then, as now, the principal business of Hull was trade with northern Europe, especially Scandinavia, Russia and the Baltic. Fundamentally, raw materials came in through the port and finished goods were shipped out (Figure 5.2). The principal imports were of iron ore, wood and raw materials for the textile industry. Iron ore came mainly from mines in Sweden. Imports rose from around 6,000 tons (6,100 tonnes) per annum in the late 1760s to 8,000 tons (8,100 tonnes) at the turn of the nineteenth century, and then accelerated in line with industrialisation: imports through Hull stood at 39,000 tons (39,600 tonnes) in 1857, and more than doubled to 113,000 tons (115,000 tonnes) by 1900.[8] Wood came mainly from Russia and the Baltic, and at times also from Canada. Imports here also boomed: 120,000 loads of deals were imported in 1857, and 613,000 by the turn of the twentieth century. Raw textile imports grew more slowly, but even here, for instance, raw wool imports doubled from 15,000 lb (6,800 kg) to 32,500 lb (14,700 kg) during the second half of the nineteenth century.[9] Linseed and similar products were imported on a large scale, as at times in the later eighteenth century was wheat from Russia, Poland and Prussia, and sundry other consumables such as fruit, wine and tobacco.[10]

The most important export in the late eighteenth century was the old staple: textiles. Shipments increased quickly as the west Yorkshire and Lancashire mills expanded, and continued to grow through the nineteenth century. Although exports of cotton yarn shrank, this was offset by an increase in manufactured cotton goods, which went up from 79.4 million yards (72.6 million metres) to 123.8 million yards (113.2 million metres) between 1850 and 1914. The late eighteenth century saw a boom in exports of earthenwares, heavy and fragile goods which came to Hull as the canals linked the potteries of Staffordshire to the port. Finally, iron and steel goods from the furnaces and forges of Sheffield and the Midlands saw a fivefold increase in the last decades of the eighteenth century. Hull is often thought of as a port based mainly on imports, but in fact exports were of greater value, although lesser weight.[11]

Most trades of the eighteenth century remained important throughout the nineteenth, but some previously small ones assumed large proportions. Among them were wheat imports, which grew from 242 quarters in 1840 to 4,300 in 1910; livestock and foodstuffs such as butter, pork and beef became major imports for the first time.[12] Some completely new trades appeared too, among them petroleum and coal. Hull was insignificant as a coal port before the 1870s, but the development of the south Yorkshire coalfield, with excellent rail links to Hull, saw the town become the third biggest exporter of British coal by the outbreak of war in 1914.[13] Finally, the railway and the steamship made people a lot more mobile during the nineteenth century, and led to a boom in the numbers travelling by sea. Hull was at the forefront of this, with the first river steamers entering service just after the end of the Napoleonic Wars and a large number of coastal and short-sea services being established in the following decade,[14] until by 1914 a network of steamship services connected Hull with ports around the UK and all over Europe, while the port's largest shipping firm, the Wilson Line, was running regular services to the United States, Australasia, India and North Africa.[15] Table 5.1 illustrates something of the scale of the port's growth.

Table 5.1: Average annual tonnage of vessels on which dock dues were paid, 1810–1900 (000 tons)

1810–19	337
1820–29	351
1830–39	460
1840–49	725
1850–59	942
1860–69	1,233
1870–79	2,032
1880–89	2,568
1890–99	3,422

Source: Hull History Centre, C DPD 12/1/23, Notebook of W. H. Huffam.

Hull was one of the few major ports to combine seaborne trade with harvesting the sea's living resources. The ancient business of whaling was revived in the 1770s and grew to a peak in 1818, when 63 ships were sent out. Decline then set in due to heavy losses of ships, overfishing, and the substitution of coal for whale oil in gas production.[16] Some, too, felt that the money invested in it could be better used. John Greenwood claimed in 1835 that it was 'greatly overdone and injurious to the general trade of the port', and blamed whaling for Hull's lack of trade to the Mediterranean. There was a short-lived revival in the 1840s, but by 1869 there was just one whaler left, the *Diana*, and with her grounding on the Lincolnshire coast, whaling from Hull ended.[17] By then, however, fishing was growing rapidly. Trawlers from south-west England had been working seasonally in the North Sea since the 1820s, but began to settle permanently at Hull from around 1840, as the railways allowed fresh fish to reach the working classes of Yorkshire and the Midlands in good condition and at a price they could afford.[18] Despite competition from Grimsby, the fishing industry grew strongly between the 1840s and 1880s. There were just 21 trawlers in Hull in 1845, but 535 by 1881, employing more than 2,500 men. From 1883 steam trawlers began to replace sailing vessels and the number of boats fell to 377 in 1901, but catching power and the numbers employed continued to grow.[19]

All of this created demand for dock space, and throughout the period Hull, like all major ports, struggled to provide adequate facilities and reduce congestion. The crowded state of the River Hull provided part of the rationale for building the first dock, but within just fifteen years another was needed.[20] By the 1840s the river was again so crowded that it could reportedly take a ship as long to cover the mile from the dock entrance to the Humber as to sail to St Petersburg. Within the docks, too, there were problems. Stored bundles of timber created obstructions and hazards to shipping, while in its early years the fishing industry had space enough in Humber Dock for just five trawlers to land, and many had to discharge their catches into boats in the Humber.[21] Developments in ships themselves also posed problems. The entrance to Humber Dock was built to accept a 50-gun warship, but was too narrow for many paddle steamers to pass through, while by the 1850s the Town Docks were too shallow for the newest and largest steamships. Later, the building of the large docks to the east was driven by the need to accommodate the 10,000-ton ships then coming into use.[22] Ships also became more specialised and required facilities tailored to their needs. The Alexandra Dock was built for the coal trade and featured the latest in conveyor belts and cranes to handle it, while the Riverside Quay was built

5.3 The Riverside Quay, opened in 1907 to provide quick turnaround times for ships carrying passengers and perishable cargo.
Contemporary postcard

to provide quick turnaround times for passenger ships and those carrying perishable cargoes (Figure 5.3).[23]

Another spur was competition with other ports, and the persistent fear that Hull was losing out. Early in the nineteenth century contemporaries fretted about Hull's ability to compete effectively with Liverpool, although such concerns ignored the fact that Liverpool was orientated towards the Atlantic trade whereas Hull faced Europe.[24] More realistic were complaints that high dock charges were losing the port business, especially in the face of growing competition from other east coast ports. Goole, established by the Aire and Calder Navigation company in 1826, made inroads in Hull's coastal trade, as did Grimsby in both commodity trade and fishing once the railways reached it and gave it the hinterland that it had previously lacked.[25] From 1912 Immingham represented another local competitor. Further north, Hartlepool was alleged to be creaming off trade that rightfully belonged to Hull.[26] Real or imagined, the threat from other ports was regularly invoked in campaigns for new and expanded port facilities, or used to justify investment.

The course of development was also influenced by often fractious relationships between different interest groups within the town, each seeking to protect its own position and impose its own view of what would be best for the port. The Dock Company, which had a monopoly on dock provision until the 1880s, took a conservative approach to providing facilities and was frequently accused of neglecting the port and allowing it to lose ground to competitors (Figure 5.4).[27] Some of its shares were owned by Hull Corporation, which could put pressure on the company to improve its facilities and oppose plans it thought ill-advised, but was itself sometimes blamed for not working in the interests of the port.[28] Various private interest groups naturally sought to advance their own aims. On several occasions, such as in the later 1830s and 1850s, consortia of local interests were formed to promote rival dock schemes and break the Dock Company's monopoly.[29]

5.4 Monument Bridge, *c.* 1910, with the Hull Dock Company offices in the foreground. The Dock Company offices, which opened in 1870, demonstrated the wealth and influence of the company. Since 1974 the building has housed Hull Maritime Museum. Contemporary postcard

None succeeded until the 1880s, when the Hull, Barnsley & West Riding Junction Railway and Dock Company created not just the largest dock in the port, but an entirely new railway line. Part of the impetus for the venture came from opposition to another powerful interest, the North Eastern Railway, which monopolised rail services to Hull from the early 1870s. The interplay between these forces, and less prominent ones such as Trinity House, was central to how the port developed and why its facilities expanded where and when they did.

Whaling

Stimulated by a government bounty designed to encourage whaling ventures, Hull whaling ships sailed north to Arctic waters from the 1750s onwards. The business grew rapidly, and by 1822, at the peak of the British whaling industry, Hull stood alone as the country's most successful whaling port in a lucrative global business. Over 60 whalers sailed from the town, and a substantial whale-processing industry developed on the banks of the River Hull.

The whalers hunted the Greenland Black or Bowhead whale, commonly called the 'right whale' because they were slow, passive and profitable, and hence the 'right' species to catch. Whale products were increasingly vital to the emerging consumer capitalism of industrialising Britain. Blubber oil was used for lighting and cooking, for processing leather and fabrics, as soap, as an industrial lubricant and for many other commercial applications. It was highly valuable. 'Whalebone' (baleen – the membranes in the whale's mouth that strain food from seawater) was used to make brushes, nets, upholstery and corsets; it sometimes realised ten times the profit of blubber oil. Other whale products provided base materials for medicines and perfumes and were still more prized.

Whales therefore yielded a host of commodities, the trade in which enriched Hull. This business further fuelled the local economy by stimulating shipowning and seafaring, rewarding the initiative of merchant families and companies, and boosting the city's industrial sector. Less salubrious aspects of the trade included the blubber yards that developed along the River Hull to the north of the Old Town. Whale carcasses were processed initially aboard returning ships, the procedure being concluded in port where the blubber was boiled in the yards until it reduced into oil. In Hull, as elsewhere, these were called 'Greenland yards' after the Greenland Black whales and the 'Greenlanders' (whalers) who hunted them. Ancillary and connected industries, such as paint manufacturing, also began to cluster around these noxious yards. Given its importance, the industry was supported by government subsidies and tariffs on imported whale products. The government 'bounty' was also payable to whaling ships that met certain criteria (including having medical cover on board). This bounty helped

PLATE XVII.

DANGERS OF THE WHALE FISHERY.

An early representation of a whale boat being upended by the prey, which would become a common theme in nineteenth-century marine art. From W. Scoresby, *An account of the Arctic regions with a history and description of the northern whale-fishery* (1820), vol. II, p. 588.

to ensure whale oil supplies for the British market, it guaranteed against fluctuations in catches and it sustained a ready pool of hardy, experienced sailors for naval service in wartime.

The whaling industry declined in the mid-nineteenth century, however. The emergence of gas lighting (in preference to smokier oil lamps) and alternatives to blubber oil and baleen began to undermine the market for whale products in the 1830s. Government bounties had ceased in 1820 and whale populations were diminished by the frenzied hunting of previous years. As a result, whaling became a more marginal business, and although Hull held on as the last major British whaling port, the final whalers sailed in the late 1860s.

Whaling bequeathed significant legacies for the town. The Greenland yards evolved alternative functions including oilseed crushing and oil processing. Other traces of this former world-leading industry are found in Hull Maritime Museum, which hosts a whaling gallery and a world-class collection of scrimshaw – the decorative carving of whale tusks and bones that seafarers produced in their spare time. Few would support commercial whaling today, but for eighteenth-century Hull, it brought wealth, employment and prestige.

David Atkinson

The course of development

The River Hull provided adequate space for trade and whaling from Hull for more than five centuries, but as a meeting organised by leading merchants put it as early as 1756: 'By the Increase of Trade the Present Harbour for Ships at this Port is become not large enough for the shipping and the want of sufficient room there in is found to be very detrimental and hazardous.'[30] The Seven Years War, which broke out that year, depressed trade and relieved the pressure, but the return of peace in 1763 saw the situation worsen again. Not only was this damaging to trade, but in the absence of a legal quay the Commissioners of Customs became concerned about the amount of smuggling being conducted in Hull. Leading merchants, operating from houses on the river, naturally rejected this, while the corporation procrastinated, before beginning to consider proposals to build a dock in 1772. It was the Customs which brought matters to a head by threatening to establish a port at Gainsborough and 'do such other things in the neighbourhood of Hull as for the trade of the country it appeared to them they ought to do'.[31] Faced with this threat, but also the offer of financial assistance and a grant of land on which to construct a dock, the corporation gave in. Rather than constructing the dock under its own auspices, as Liverpool had done, it was turned over to a private company, a decision whose consequences would be felt for more than a century. Hull Corporation and Trinity House held ten of its 120 shares each, with the remainder distributed among merchants and other interests, mainly in Hull and London. In 1774 an Act of Parliament authorised the building of the first dock, which duly opened four years later (Figure 5.5). It was an immediate success: 88,000 tons of shipping used it in 1780 alone.[32] Yet within a decade of its opening it was inadequate.

By 1786 there was a consensus that 'from the great increase of trade at this place, an extension of the Dock, or a new Dock, is become absolutely necessary'.[33] There was no consensus, however, over what should be built or who should pay for it. In the ensuing pamphlet war, the Dock Company was attacked for making large profits while having

5.5 Shipping in the River Hull, by the entrance to the first dock, 1829. Note the ship being built just beyond the dock entrance, and the windmill in the background. The remains of the dock entrance can be seen on Dock Office Row behind Hull College, whose main buildings cover the eastern end of the filled-in dock.

'impeded the improvement of the trade … diminished the conveniences of the port, and … prevented the useful, as well as ornamental extension of the town'. For such 'high crimes and misdemeanours' some went so far as to try to 'annihilate' it via a Parliamentary Bill that would force it to sell off land, restrain its profits and dividend payments, fix its rates and provide for its transfer to public ownership.[34] This was never likely to succeed, and nor were the first proposals for an alternative company, which had no support from the corporation.[35] It was true that the Dock Company had done little to plan for future growth, but the 1774 Act had made no provision for doing so and debate raged over whether the company had been granted the dues from the first dock as reward for its enterprise in building it or whether it was obliged to make further provision for the good of the town.[36] This question was unresolved when the French Revolutionary War broke out in 1793, as was the question of where a second dock should be sited, with some proposals favouring the west side of town and others, including the Dock Company itself, a site to the east of the Citadel.[37] The questions of where docks should be built, who should pay for them, and what the Dock Company should and should not do would flare up repeatedly during the nineteenth century. For now, though, they were resolved by the decision to build Humber Dock, authorised by Act of Parliament in 1802. Half of the cost was borne by the corporation, while the company was allowed to increase its shares from 120 to 180.[38] Construction began in 1807, with the famed civil engineer John Rennie in charge, and it opened in 1809. The spoil was used to build up the foreshore on the south side of town, upon which Wellington Street and Nelson Street were laid out, and later a small dock and then a pier for the Humber ferries were added.[39]

The 1802 Act included provision for a third dock, once trade in the first two rose above a certain level. Although the end of the Napoleonic Wars in 1815 saw a national economic depression, the tonnage of shipping entering Hull from overseas increased by 80 per cent between 1815 and 1818, sufficient to activate the clause allowing a third dock. A committee of shipowners and merchants was formed to press the Dock Company and the corporation to put it into effect.[40] The company's reluctance and a subsequent depression in trade postponed the issue, but when prosperity returned a new committee was formed, and in 1824 it persuaded the Dock Company to go ahead, this time financing the project entirely out of its own resources. The foundation stone was laid in 1826, and Junction Dock opened with great ceremony on 1 June 1829.[41] These three docks, collectively known as the Town Docks (Figure 5.6), circuited the Old Town, following the lines of and obliterating the remaining medieval fortifications. Thus, as James Sheahan wrote, 'have these formidable military walls and ditches … given way to industrious establishments of commercial appliances'. They were augmented in 1846 by Railway Dock, a westward arm of Humber Dock connected directly to the railway. Less than a hectare in area, some ridiculed it as a 'fish pond'.[42] Nevertheless, it represented a useful increase in space, and an invaluable inland link via the adjacent railway terminal.[43] Junction Dock and what was by then known as the 'Old Dock' were renamed Prince's Dock and Queen's Dock, respectively, in honour of Queen Victoria's visit to the town in 1854 (Figures 5.7, 5.8).

5.6 The tug *Edith* tows Humber keels out of the Town Docks, *c.* 1900. Despite the railways, riverboats continued to play an important role in transporting goods to and from Hull well into the twentieth century.
© Maritime Historical Studies Centre

Well before the foundation stone of Railway Dock had been laid it was clear that something separate and much larger than the Town Docks would soon be needed, and better facilities for steamships.[44] This sparked further debate over what should be done and by whom. The Dock Company initially denied the need for more space, and then in 1836 offered to sell the docks to the town, effectively washing its hands of the problem. This was rejected by ratepayers unwilling to shoulder the costs. Two years later a rival company was formed to promote a dock east of the Citadel. This failed for lack of support, but did provoke the Dock Company into developing a similar scheme, which it presented to Parliament in 1840.[45] Here it met the opposition of a group of influential merchants with property on the River Hull, who in 1836 had formed a committee to advance plans to enclose the river and turn it into a dock, something which the company's chairman, Joseph Robinson Pease, argued would 'involve the company in ruin'. The committee succeeded in getting amendments made to the Bill, prompting the company to withdraw it. The company later considered suing a prominent member of the committee for the costs it had incurred.[46] Nor were these the only plans, for others still were advanced for a 'railway dock' to the south-west, sharing its basin with Humber Dock. These had no real financial support, however, and once the merchants' committee's opposition had been quieted the Dock Company returned to Parliament and in 1844 finally succeeded in obtaining an Act of Parliament which authorised both Railway Dock and its venture east of the river.[47] The foundation stone of what became Victoria Dock was laid in 1846, and it opened in 1850.

Pease, who by then had stood down from the chairmanship of the Dock Company and whose opinion was perhaps coloured by a desire to protect the value

49824. Hull: Princes Dock. PP & Co.

of his High Street property (the same motive that had animated the committee whose schemes he had opposed), felt that building docks east of the River Hull was 'a sad mistake'. In truth it was an essential addition, increasing the docks' area by nearly 50 per cent, and more when it was extended in 1863 and additional timber ponds added.[48] These also helped to alleviate the 'nuisance' of timber being stored in floating bundles in the other docks and on the river, which everyone had admitted was a problem. More importantly still, it provided facilities for the larger ships then coming into use.[49]

Victoria Dock quieted calls for additional accommodation, and for a few years in the mid-1850s the business of the port was also disrupted by the Crimean War. When normal conditions resumed, however, the port again came under pressure and old disputes flared up once more. In the 1840s the Dock Company had explored the possibility of purchasing the Citadel site, despite Pease's feeling it was 'all nonsense' and that the government would never sell. When in 1858 it was put up for sale the company moved to buy it, but on this occasion was opposed by the corporation, which wanted to redevelop the site as a public park for the crowded town.[50] Neither scheme came to pass. The Dock Company had never been very popular, and at a 'numerous and highly influential' meeting convened by the corporation, one shipowner spoke for many when he lamented:

the absence of any forecast for providing for the wants of their customers, and seeking only to realise large benefits for the monopolisers; it was in consequence of the delay on the part of the Hull Dock Company in providing the requirements of the trade of this port that Goole, Grimsby, and Hartlepool had arisen.[51]

The company had never been closely connected to the town's commercial community, and it became more remote as the merchant dynasties of the eighteenth century – some of whom had invested and been involved in it – were supplanted by more specialist traders and shipowners. All too often it aggressively promoted its interests even when these were seemingly incompatible with those of the business community. The Bill it placed before Parliament for a dock on the Citadel site also included provision for extending its monopoly, due to end in 1865, for a further 21 years, a proposition decried by the *Hull Packet* as 'monstrous'.[52]

The alternative for some, once again, was the establishment of a rival, and during 1859 proposals circulated for a West Dock Company which would revive, in modified form, the plan for a south-western dock. This attracted promises of support from both Hull Corporation and the North Eastern Railway. The Dock Company countered with its own plan for the same site, and succeeded in obtaining the Hull Dock Act of 1861. This authorised the 'west dock' and extended the company's monopoly, but did acknowledge the opposition to it via the inclusion of clauses restricting its dividend payments (often attacked as excessive) and even making provision for the docks to be transferred to a public trust. Two unsuccessful attempts were made to do just that in 1865 and 1866, but foundered on the opposition of the North Eastern Railway, the parsimonious ratepayers, and of course the company itself.[53] By then construction of the dock was well under way, and it opened in 1869. Albert Dock, as it was named, began the port's sprawl to the west, but was far from an unqualified success (Figure 5.9). It was long and narrow, and its entrance too shallow for large ships to enter at most states of the tide. In that sense it was grist to the mill of those who argued that the Dock Company was building its facilities 'upon the same plan and in the same position as would have been provided fifty years ago, for the lumbering old ships which used to carry on the traffic of that day'.[54] On the other hand, it answered the fishing industry's demands for more space, especially after its westward extension, the William Wright Dock, opened in 1880, and for the first fifteen years of its existence it served well as the base for Hull's trawler fleet.[55]

Until the 1860s the town's business and shipowning interests had tended to treat the railway companies as allies against the Dock Company, but as the North Eastern Railway's influence grew, attitudes hardened. In 1865 it attempted unsuccessfully to buy out the docks, which is why it then found itself opposing the counter-proposal to transfer them to a public trust. Thereafter it began to work more closely

5.8 Queen's Dock, seen from Lowgate in the early twentieth century.
© Maritime Historical Studies Centre

with the Dock Company, placing them on the same side in forthcoming struggles over future provision. Its acquisition of the remaining independent railway line into Hull in 1872 gave it a monopoly on railway services. This did not work in the port's favour, given that the railway's heartlands were to the north while Hull mainly shipped goods to and from the south and west. At a time of rising inter-port competition, it fuelled allegations that Hull was losing out, especially to Hartlepool. 'You only have to unfurl a flag with "Hartlepool" on it,' noted one local dignitary, 'and Hull takes fire immediately.'[56] Nor was the North Eastern's reputation enhanced locally when its overstretched services 'completely broke down' in 1872, creating 'a state of block and confusion … seldom, if ever, witnessed in the history of a major trading port'.[57]

The idea of building a new railway to serve Hull had been floated periodically since the 'railway mania' of the 1840s in a variety of more or less realistic schemes. During the 1870s these crystallised into a plan for a railway to connect Hull to the developing south Yorkshire coalfield, to provide an alternative route to the Midlands, and to break the monopolies of both Dock Company and North Eastern Railway. Combined with this was a deep-water dock to accommodate the coal trade and other large ships. The venture had financial support from prominent shipowners, bankers and businessmen, as well as the corporation and Trinity House.[58] The Hull, Barnsley & West Riding Junction Railway and Dock Company, as it had become, got the necessary Bill through Parliament in 1880, and its Alexandra Dock opened in 1885 (Figure 5.10). It was the largest and most modern in Hull, and at 46 acres (18.6 hectares) four times the size of the Dock Company's latest venture, St Andrew's Dock, opened in 1883. This had initially been intended for the coal trade, but by 1882 the decision had been made to turn it over instead to fishing, answering renewed demands from what was by then a large and influential interest for better facilities. This did not pass without some resistance, both from those reluctant to uproot their

5.9 Victoria Pier, around the turn of the twentieth century. In the background a steamship prepares to enter Albert Dock. The pier in this picture was replaced with a smaller and simpler structure during the twentieth century, and lost its function as terminus for the Humber ferries with the opening of the Humber Bridge in 1981.
© Maritime Historical Studies Centre

5.10 Alexandra Dock, opened by the Hull, Barnsley & West Riding Junction Railway and Dock Company in 1885 to break the monopoly of the Hull Dock Company and provide facilities for the larger ships then coming into service, although here most of the users are sailing ships. Contemporary postcard

businesses around Albert Dock, and others who attempted to promote a controversial and ultimately unrealistic venture for a new facility at Saltend.[59]

Despite the complex manoeuvring and often unedifying conflict, Hull had done well in the preceding twenty years. The tonnage of shipping using the port rose by 130 per cent between 1862 and 1882, much faster than at either Liverpool (97 per cent) or London (83 per cent), and the value of its trade had increased. During this period, too, Hull's steamship services to Europe and beyond had flourished, and a series of new trades developed, especially in foodstuffs and petroleum. This expansion, periodic depressions excepted, continued until the First World War.[60] But although the local economy was doing well, the future for both dock companies was not so bright. Hull Dock Company had often struggled to raise capital, and now its income had been cut by the need to reduce dock dues in the face of competition from the Hull & Barnsley. As the need for another large dock became more pressing, the company's inability to finance it became increasingly obvious. The North Eastern Railway, too, had reacted to competition by slashing charges, triggering a rate war which the Hull & Barnsley did not have the financial resources to win. Within a decade of opening, Alexandra Dock was handling half as much traffic as the other docks in Hull combined, but both dock companies were showing signs of financial strain and began to look for allies, triggering off another round of manoeuvring between interest groups. The Hull & Barnsley's negotiations with first the Midland and then the North Eastern Railways came to nothing as the corporation fought to maintain its independence, and nor did a subsequent attempt by the corporation to create a public trust to take over both companies and pay off the Hull & Barnsley's debts. The corporation was fighting old battles, and the shipowning interest was tired of being caught in the crossfire. Led by Charles Wilson, shipowners supported a renewed attempt by the North Eastern to take over the Dock Company. After two years of negotiation this was finally agreed in 1893.[61]

The Act of Parliament that authorised this ended the rate war by forbidding the North Eastern from reducing dues below those of the Hull & Barnsley, and opened the way for the firms to cooperate in future on a new eastern dock.[62] Neither the corporation nor many in the town's business community were happy with the deal, and their continuing suspicion of the North Eastern saw them veto its plans to improve the Town and Victoria Docks, although they did allow it to extend St Andrew's. Such attitudes even surfaced when it produced a collaborative scheme with the Hull & Barnsley for an eastern dock, the need for which was increasingly urgent as ships grew larger and rising timber imports and coal exports put pressure on Victoria and Alexandra Docks. A corporation representative insisted before the Parliamentary Committee that the 'freedom' given to the town by the Hull & Barnsley had allowed Hull to 'advance by leaps and bounds'.[63] 'Freedom' did not provide the capital to build docks on the scale that were now needed, however, and both shipowners and the North Eastern ridiculed the corporation's parochial attitude. The Bill passed, and the dock was duly built, although it was delayed by difficulties in construction and the concerns of the Humber Conservancy Commission about its effect on the deep-water channel in the Humber. Nevertheless, King George Dock finally opened in June 1914 (Figure 5.11). It was the largest dock in north-eastern England, and the first with machinery powered wholly by electricity. In its original form it was 53 acres (21.5 hectares) in area, with the potential for further expansion with arms to the south-west and south-east.[64] Alongside its protracted construction went less spectacular developments. Cargo-handling facilities were steadily updated across the port. The Riverside Quay was built along the southern wall of Albert Dock, to allow North Sea passenger and cargo steamers to make quick turnarounds and to berth at any state of the tide.[65] Finally, petroleum had been imported in bulk since the early 1890s via a depot at the eastern end of St Andrew's Dock, which was augmented in 1914 by a large storage facility and jetties at Saltend.[66]

5.11 Ships loading coal in King George Dock. The coal trade was negligible before the 1870s, but by 1914 Hull was the third largest coal-exporting port in Britain.
Port of Hull Annual, 1911

5.12 The River Hull, *c.* 1910. During the nineteenth century the river came to form one of the main industrial axes of Hull, with factories and warehouses lining both banks. Some of the warehouses survive as residential and commercial developments.
Port of Hull Annual, 1911

Hull in the 1770s had conducted most of its business along a one-mile stretch of a narrow river. By 1914 the port stretched for 7 miles (11 kilometres) along the Humber. Its 11 docks covered 247 acres (100 hectares), with a total quay length of around 14 miles (22.5 kilometres). The port's steamship fleets traded all around Europe and further afield, while the size of its first-class trawler fleet made it the second fishing port in the country. Only London and Liverpool handled more cargo than Hull, which thus ranked as 'the world's gateway to the manufacturing centres of England', and Britain's third port (Figure 5.12).[67]

Hull's Bridges

Bridges have played a vital role in Hull's historical and geographical development since the sixteenth century, when the defence of the prospering and strategically important port required the construction of the first bridge across the River Hull. Erected in 1541 on the orders of Henry VIII, the crossing provided better access to the newly built fortifications on the east bank of the river. The original bridge was replaced by a firmer structure, known as North Bridge, which was developed further over the next 200 years as the town increased in population, importance and as a hub of commercial maritime activity.

From the 1850s, planners faced the challenge of providing access to Hull's expanding dock system and rapidly growing industries to the east of the River Hull. In 1865 the South Bridge, or 'ha'penny' bridge, was built across the river from Humber Street to Garrison Side, thereby improving access to Victoria Dock and its timber industries. Links between east and west improved further between 1875 and 1905 with the construction of bridges at Sculcoates, Drypool and Scott Street. In 1885 the Hull & Barnsley Railway Company built a high-level rail line as part of a direct connection between the south Yorkshire coalfields and the newly opened Alexandra Dock. Railway bridges were erected over several of the city's major roads, while Hull Bridge extended over the River Hull in an infrastructural development that is still used by rail freight today.

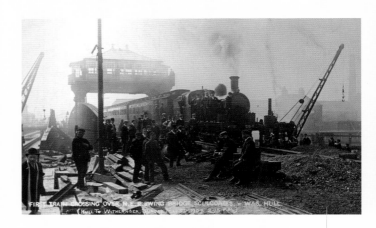

First train crossing over the North Eastern Railway's swing bridge, Sculcoates, Hull, 1907
Courtesy of the Maritime Historical Studies Centre

Road rather than rail links to the eastern docks dominated planning after 1945. The huge growth of motor transport, particularly during the 1950s, prompted the reconstruction of Drypool Bridge between 1958 and 1961. This soon proved inadequate, however, as the rapidly expanding volume of traffic precipitated bridge construction on an unprecedented scale in and around the city. A major road traffic route across the River Hull to the new container and roll-on/roll-off terminals in the eastern docks entailed the construction of Myton Bridge in 1981. A year later, following a century of campaigning, the Humber Bridge opened to provide the first direct road link between Hull and the south bank of the Humber. It was the longest suspension bridge in the world, an iconic structure that came to symbolise the city and region. By this time, suburban expansion to the north and east of the city had created a need for improved east–west connections upstream from the historic bridges. Accordingly, to complement Sutton Bridge, which had been completed in 1939, the Stoneferry and Ennerdale Link bridges were opened in 1991 and 1997 respectively.

In the twenty-first century, bridge building in Hull has entered a new and very different era with the construction of quirky and iconic footbridges, which contrast with the utilitarian and functional designs of earlier steel constructions. The Millennium Bridge was opened in 2001 to offer pedestrian access to The Deep, while 2013 witnessed the unveiling of Scale Lane Bridge, which links the Old Town to the east bank.

This array of bridges testifies to the ability of Hull's inhabitants to respond effectively to their ever-changing transport needs, as well as their ingenuity in overcoming obstacles such as the rivers Hull and Humber, and the roads that hindered railway operators in their efforts to reach the eastern docks from the west and the north.

Alex Ombler

The effects of dock development

The port was, and remains, Hull's *raison d'être*, and its transformation inevitably shaped the town. First, and most visibly, it did so in geographical terms. Hull in the early eighteenth century had been an 'exceeding close built' place confined within its defensive walls.[68] Some limited development had taken place beyond them by the 1770s, but it was the docks that released the town from its medieval confines. On land to the north of the first dock the Dock Company laid out a series of streets known as the New Town, which started the process of urban expansion to the north.[69] Along the river, the whaling yards and some shipyards had long been sited to the north of the town walls on the west bank of the river, but the late eighteenth century saw ribbon development intensify on both banks, in the form of ship- and boatyards, timber storage, roperies and similar industrial developments. The docks also provided the early stimulus to development to westward, once the walls on that side of town had been demolished to make way for Humber Dock. By 1817 the Beast Market, which had lain just outside the walls to the north-west, was surrounded by buildings. A decade later the market area was cleared for Junction Dock.[70] Subsequently the docks supported and sometimes led expansion east and westwards along the Humber. To the west of Humber Dock there was little in 1817 beyond garden plots and small potteries, and, some distance away, the fashionable residential suburb around St Mark's Square. Urban development had extended this far by the 1850s, and speeded up further with the opening of Albert Dock. Fifteen years later St Andrew's Dock was added to the west. The need to house the thousands of dockworkers, seamen, fishermen and others led to intensive residential development all along the Hessle Road, and further north towards Anlaby Road (Figure 5.13).[71]

Before 1800 Hull had been confined to the west side of the River Hull, and on the east side there was little apart from the Citadel and the small village of Drypool.

5.13 Hessle Road, seen here c. 1900, developed from the 1870s and was known for its population of fishermen and dockworkers.
Contemporary postcard

5.14 Hedon Road between the wars. Despite the tram and the roadside shops, Hedon Road was and remains more an industrial than a residential area.
Contemporary postcard

The development of the docks from 1850 seems to have had relatively little effect on residential development, for Drypool and Witham, just to the north, had grown into residential suburbs by the 1840s, and for the rest of the century most housing was built further to the north around the Holderness Road.[72] South-eastern Hull developed instead as a mainly industrial area (Figure 5.14). During the 1870s some of the vacant land was used for the sort of municipal establishments that the corporation preferred to keep out of town, such as a new cemetery, the sanatorium and the new prison. By 1914 these were surrounded by industrial and some residential development as the town expanded west towards the new King George Dock.[73] 'Nothing,' noted a directory in 1882, 'has more contributed to the extension of commerce in Hull than the docks.' Their influence was felt throughout the local economy. Hull in the eighteenth century was a commercial centre and it remained so, but during the nineteenth century it also grew into a sprawling industrial city, an outlier of the West Riding industrial conurbation. The port shaped its economic geography, determining the location of many of the industries that grew up around it.[74]

There had always been some industrial activity in and around the town, most notably shipbuilding. Hull was the third largest shipbuilding centre in the country in the eighteenth century, and in 1820 produced 6.1 per cent of total shipbuilding output. By 1913 this had slipped to 2.1 per cent, but Hull retained one of the few large steamship-building firms outside the giant clusters that had developed on the Clyde and Tyne.[75] Earle's Shipbuilding and Engineering Company, originally C&W Earle, was founded in 1853 and gained a reputation for turning out fine steamships. In peak years it was one of Hull's largest employers, but it later ran into financial difficulties and in 1901 was purchased by the Wilson Line, which needed to maintain facilities for servicing large steamships, although it continued to build for other owners. As with Hull's smaller shipbuilders, Earle's main customers were local shipping firms, but it also built for owners elsewhere in Britain and overseas, and continued the tradition of building warships for the Royal Navy.[76]

Much of the rest of Hull's industrial sector processed the goods brought into the docks.[77] Whaling had long supported processing industries that died out with the catching sector, but the growth of fishing provided raw material for a whole new cluster of smokehouses, filleters and fishmeal plants, mainly concentrated around

Hessle Road. There were 55 curing firms alone in 1897. Every man employed on the trawlers supported several more jobs ashore, and by 1915 it was estimated that one-sixth of the city's population depended directly or indirectly on fishing for their livelihoods.[78] More important still were the manufacturing industries whose raw materials came in through the docks. Timber went through a network of timber yards and sawmills and a thriving furniture-making industry, seeds supported a cluster of oil-extraction businesses and paint manufacturers, while some of the imported wheat was milled into flour by several local firms, most prominently Joseph Rank & Company (Figure 5.15).[79]

The port also supported many of the town's service industries, most prominent among which was shipping. Hull was the fourth largest shipowning centre in Britain in 1790, with just under 55,000 tons registered.[80] Its relative position declined during the nineteenth century, and by 1913 it was the eighth largest, albeit with a registered fleet of over 283,000 tons. Of this, just under 238,000 tons consisted of steamships operated by 19 firms, down from 72 in 1878, and the majority of the largest and most modern ships were owned by just one firm, the Wilson Line. Wilson's dominated the port, operating almost all of the long-distance liner services from the port as well as numerous European routes, and it also had interests in fishing and, after 1901, shipbuilding.[81] Wilson's and other large steamship operators were complemented by a plethora of companies operating river and coastal services, and the ubiquitous keels which carried goods around the east coast and down the inland waterways as far as Sheffield and even Nottingham.[82] All of these supported a dense network of shipbrokers, freight forwarders, agents and dealers in the commodities arriving in the port (Figure 5.16).

5.15 Clarence flour mill, *c*. 1900. Flour milling was one of the major industries supported by the port during the nineteenth century, and was directly dependent on river transport. The mill was partly rebuilt between the wars, closed in 2005 and demolished in 2016 to make way for a hotel.
Reproduced by kind permission of Houlton & Co.

Economic and industrial growth fostered rapid population growth. Hull had just 19,500 inhabitants in 1780, but 95,000 in 1851 and 297,000 by 1911. During the 1860s and 1870s booming manufacturing industries and fishing drew in migrants, and Hull grew twice as fast as Liverpool, Leeds and Manchester.[83] Where these people lived – Hull's social geography – was shaped partly by the docks. This began right at the start of the period, when the Dock Company's land north of the dock was developed into a fashionable residential suburb. This triggered the decline of the High Street as a residential area, as many of the merchant dynasties moved their town residences to the New Town, leaving the High Street to assume a mainly commercial function.[84] Some of the town's later middle-class suburbs were also linked directly to the port, such as the large houses along the Boulevard that housed trawler owners and successful skippers. At the other end of the social scale, the docks, mainly built on the edge of town or on land reclaimed from the Humber, did not entail the clearance of swathes of working-class housing in the way the railways often did. Rather, they tended to call for its construction, especially in the developing suburbs of south-west Hull, whose close-packed terraces housed thousands of fishermen and seamen, and many who worked in related industries.[85]

Many of the older working-class suburbs in southern Hull also had a strongly maritime character, none more so than the crowded courts of the Old Town, inhabited in large measure by sailors, dockers and their families, and the area just to the west of Humber Dock around Waterhouse Lane.[86] These maritime suburbs were poor areas, often with a reputation for squalor and vice. Hull did not possess the classic 'sailortown' areas, into which young men came ashore from long-distance sailing ships with several months' pay in their pockets and where crimps, lodging-house keepers, pubs and brothels sought to relieve them of it.[87] Most of Hull's seafarers worked in European shipping and the fishing industry, and came home regularly. Nevertheless, its maritime suburbs offered some of the same attractions, and many of the pubs, music halls and brothels of southern Hull catered at least in part to the seafaring population, as did many of the town's churches (Figure 5.17).[88] At the other end of the social scale, figures from the maritime industries featured prominently among Hull's elites, and served as councillors, aldermen, mayors and, in the case of Charles Wilson, its most prominent MP.

5.16 The Fruit Market, 1913. The docks supported the work of dozens of agents, freight forwarders and commodity dealers, such as the fruit and vegetable merchants around Humber Street who distributed the produce landed at the Town Docks.
Port of Hull Annual, 1914

5.17 The Mariners' church on Prince's Dock Side, built in 1828, as sketched by Thomas Tindall Wildridge in 1884. It was one of many churches which ministered to the town's seafaring population. No trace of this building remains. From T. T. Wildride, *Old and New Hull: A Series of Drawings, with Descriptive and Historical Notes* (Hull, 1884).

Maritime trade and its related industries had always dominated the economy, society and politics of Hull. In this sense the period between the opening of the first dock and the outbreak of war in 1914 was no different. Yet this period did see unprecedented changes in the scale of Hull's trade and shipping, and with it qualitative change in the town's economy. This was led and shaped by the port, which between 1778 and 1914 played the most important part in creating the modern city of Hull.

Zachariah Pearson

There have been few more controversial or enigmatic figures in Hull's long and varied history than Zachariah Pearson. On the one hand, he was a self-made man, a sea captain, shipowner and then a civic leader and philanthropist with an apparently well-developed social conscience who tried to improve the quality of life of his fellow townsfolk. On the other hand, he was a reckless gambler who tried and failed to run the Union blockade of the slave-owning Confederate South in the American Civil War – with all this implied about supporting slavery. In so doing, Zachariah Pearson also sowed the seeds of his financial downfall.

Pearson was born on High Street in 1821, and was raised by his uncle after his mother died when he was only four years old. Educated at Hull Grammar School, he was apparently drawn to the sea from an early age, unsuccessfully stowing away on a vessel at the age of 12. He went to sea legally at 16, becoming a captain five years later in 1842. By the time he acquired his first ship in 1847 he was a seasoned and experienced seafarer.

During the 1850s Pearson expanded his maritime interests in partnership with James Coleman. Their firm, Messrs Pearson, Coleman and Company, traded into the Baltic as far as St Petersburg and ran a mail packet service in the Antipodes. Already a man of substance in business circles, Pearson became a town councillor in 1856 and his energy and wealth brought another rapid rise – this time up the civic ladder. He became an alderman in 1857, Town Sheriff the following year, then Lord Mayor in 1859.

Pearson was committed to improving Hull, promoting initiatives such as the building of the new town hall and a water works. He was popular because of his philanthropic endeavours, the most notable of which was the donation of land for the creation of the town's first public park, now known as Pearson Park, though he retained, and probably profited from, the development land around the edge of this new green space. In 1862 he was made Lord Mayor again.

In 1860 he parted company with partner James Coleman and, once he was on his own, all restraint seems to have fallen off his business ambition. He borrowed heavily to expand his fleet, being persuaded by the Overend and Gurney banking house to acquire six steamers from a Greek shipowner. In 1861 the American Civil War broke out and Pearson was lured by the chance of making huge profits by running the blockade imposed by the Union on the Confederate South. While some blockade runners did make big profits, Pearson's endeavours met with ill luck of every kind. Seven of his ships were seized or lost running the blockade, with cargoes evidently including munitions, but his misfortunes went further. On just one day in June 1862 it was reported that he received news of one ship wrecked, another accidentally burnt and a further vessel captured. These losses alone were said to have cost him £85,000.

Within months he was bankrupt with huge debts of over £600,000. He resigned as Lord Mayor, retired from public life, and lived with his wife in a small house by the park he had created. He died in 1891 and his memory faded from local consciousness – although Pearson Park has endured and remains a popular, green oasis in a busy part of Hull.

Robb Robinson

In 1860 Zachariah Pearson purchased 37 acres of land to the west of Beverley Road for £7,400, and donated 27 acres to the town for the establishment of the first public park in Hull. Initially dubbed the 'People's Park', the deeds to the land were presented at a public ceremony on 27 August 1860. Over the next two years, the park was laid out and equipped with a substantial ceremonial gateway made by Young and Wood of Hull. The iron gates fitted to the gateway – which were removed for war purposes in 1940 – bore the Pearson motto: *Providentia fido* (I trust in Providence).

Notes

1. G. Jackson, *The History and Archaeology of Ports* (Tadworth, 1983), p. 31.

2. W. R. Childs, *The Trade and Shipping of Hull 1300–1500* (Beverley, 1990), pp. 5–7; P. S. Bagwell, *The Transport Revolution from 1770* (London, 1974), pp. 14–17.

3. G. Jackson, *Hull in the Eighteenth Century: A Study in Economic and Social History* (Oxford, 1972), p. 51; H. Calvert, *A History of Hull* (London and Chichester, 1978), p. 315.

4. K. J. Allison, 'Hull, 1700–1835', in K. J. Allison (ed.), *A History of the County of York East Riding: Volume 1, the City of Kingston upon Hull* (London, 1969) [hereafter *VCH*], pp. 174–214, http://www.british-history.ac.uk/vch/yorks/east/vol1/pp174-214 (accessed 30 May 2016).

5. *Port of Hull Annual* 1911, p. 33.

6. E. Gillett and K. A. MacMahon, *A History of Hull* (Hull and Oxford, 1980), p. 271; G. Head, *A Home Tour through the Manufacturing Districts of England in the Summer of 1835* (London, 1836), pp. 211–13; J. Simmons, *The Victorian Railway* (London, 1991), pp. 351–55.

7. G. Jackson, *The Trade and Shipping of Eighteenth-Century Hull* (Beverley, 1975), pp. 19–20.

8. Jackson, *Trade and Shipping of Eighteenth-Century Hull*, Appendix 2; Annual Statement of Trade and Navigation of the United Kingdom, 1857; Annual Statement of Trade of the United Kingdom, 1900.

9. J. M. Bellamy, 'Some Aspects of the Economy of Hull in the Nineteenth Century with Special Reference to Business History', unpublished PhD thesis, University of Hull, 1965, Appendix B.

10. Jackson, *Trade and Shipping of Eighteenth-Century Hull*, pp. 23–24.

11. Bellamy, 'Some Aspects of the Economy of Hull', Appendix B; Jackson, *Hull in the Eighteenth Century*, Appendix 9; Jackson, *Trade and Shipping of Eighteenth-Century Hull*, p. 20; Allison, 'Hull, 1700–1835'.

12. Bellamy, 'Some Aspects of the Economy of Hull', Appendix B.

13. T. Sheppard, *City & County of Kingston upon Hull: The Third Port of the United Kingdom* (Hull, 1925), p. 12; Bellamy, 'Some Aspects of the Economy of Hull', p. 89.

14. F. H. Pearson, *The Early History of Hull Steam Shipping* (Hull, 1894), pp. 2–5.

15. *Kelly's Directory of the North and East Ridings of Yorkshire*, 1913.

16. W. Gawtress, *A report of the inquiry into the existing state of the corporation of Hull* (Hull, 1834), p. 382; A. G. Credland, *The Hull Whaling Trade: An Arctic Enterprise* (Beverley, 1995), pp. 38–47.

17. J. Greenwood, *Picture of Hull* (Hull, 1835), pp. 41–42; Credland, *Hull Whaling Trade*, pp. 81–84.

18. R. N. Robinson, *Trawling: The Rise and Fall of the British Trawl Fishery* (Exeter, 1996), pp. 23–33.

19. E. J. March, *Sailing Trawlers: The Story of Deep-Sea Fishing with Long-Line and Trawl* (Newton Abbot, 1970), p. 177; British Parliamentary Papers (BPP) 1882 XVII, Report of Committee of Board of Trade relative to Sea Fishery Trade, and Relations between Masters and Crews of Fishing Vessels, Appendix 29; Annual Report of the Inspector of Sea Fisheries, 1901.

20. T. Wood, *Tidal Harbours Commission: The Humber, its roads, shoals, and capabilities. Importance and improvement of the Port of Hull. A report of the proceedings at the Town Hall, Hull, on the 23d. day of October, 1845* (Hull, 1845), p. 45.

21. Wood, *Tidal Harbours Commission*, p. 59; BPP 1841 IX, Committee on Kingston-upon-Hull Docks Bill: Minutes of Evidence, q.266; *Hull Packet and East Riding Times*, 20 December 1867; Robinson, *Trawling*, p. 44.

22. Wood, *Tidal Harbours Commission*, p. 47; K. J. Allison, 'Modern Hull', *VCH*, pp. 215–86, http://www.british-history.ac.uk/vch/yorks/east/vol1/pp215-286 (accessed 18 May 2016).

23. *Port of Hull Annual* 1911, p. 51; A. G. Credland, 'The Dock System of Hull: Eighteenth to Twentieth Centuries', in D. Neave and S. Ellis (eds), *An Historical Atlas of East Yorkshire* (Hull, 1996), p. 90.

24. J. M. Bellamy, *The Trade and Shipping of Nineteenth-Century Hull* (Beverley, 1971), p. 28.

25. J. D. Porteous, 'The Company Town of Goole: An Essay in Urban Genesis', *University of Hull Occasional Papers in Geography*, 12 (1969); G. Jackson, 'Port Competition on the Humber: Docks, Railways and Steamships in the Nineteenth Century', in E. M. Sigsworth (ed.), *Ports and Resorts in the Regions: Papers Submitted to the Conference of Regional History Tutors Held at Hull College of Higher Education in July 1980* (Hull, 1980), pp. 45–58.

26. *Hull Packet and East Riding Times*, 18 May 1855, 5 November 1858; *Port of Hull Annual* 1911, p. 4.

27. See, for example, Hull History Centre, C DPD/1/29, Second Report of the Committee Appointed to Obtain Additional Dock Room at the Port of Hull, 24 February 1820; Report of the Proceedings of the Committee of Owners of Property on Both Banks of the River Hull, 1836.

28. BPP 1841 IX, Committee on Kingston-upon-Hull Docks Bill: Minutes of Evidence, q.1,590; Wood, *Tidal Harbours Commission*, p. 18.

29. HHC, C DPD/1/29, Fourth Report of the Proceedings of the Committee of Owners of Property on Both Banks of the River Hull, 1841; *Hull Packet and East Riding Times*, 4 May 1860.

30. Quoted in Jackson, *Hull in the Eighteenth Century*, p. 238.

31. HHC, C DPD/1/30, 'Free Thoughts on the present proposed Plan for Erecting a Quay at the Port of Kingston-upon-Hull, in a Letter offered to the consideration of Inhabitants, by a Well-wisher to the Prosperity of the said Town', c. 1773; C DPD/1/29, 'Remarks on a Publication Intitled the Case of the Merchants &c of the Town of Kingston-upon-Hull', 1787; Jackson, *Trade and Shipping of Eighteenth-Century Hull*, p. 52.

32. Jackson, *Hull in the Eighteenth Century*, p. 243; HHC, C DPD/1/29, 'Dock Company at Kingston-upon-Hull, 1789', list of shareholders; Jackson, *Trade and Shipping of Eighteenth-Century Hull*, p. 53.

33 HHC, C DPD/1/29, 'Mercator', 'To the Merchants, Ship-owners and Others of the town of Kingston upon Hull', 9 March 1786.

34 HHC, C DPD/1/29, 'Charges intended to be Exhibited in Parliament against the Dock-Company at Kingston-upon-Hull', 5 January 1787; 'A Defence of the Rights of the Dock Company at Kingston-upon-Hull', 1787.

35 HHC, C DPD/1/29, Public Notice by Hull Dock Company, 26 October 1787.

36 See, for example, HHC, C DPD/1/29, 'Publicola', 'To the Right Worshipful the Mayor of Kingston-upon-Hull', 15 September 1787.

37 HHC, C DPD/1/29, Letter from the Principal Merchants at Hull to the Collector and Comptroller of His Majesty's Customs at Kingston upon Hull, 15 February 1793; Memorial Presented by the Dock Company at Kingston upon Hull to the Lords Commissioners of H.M. Treasury, 30 January 1793.

38 42 Geo. III, cap.xci; *Hull Packet and Humber Mercury*, 2 June 1829.

39 J. J. Sheahan, *History of the Town and Port of Kingston-upon-Hull* (Beverley, 2nd edn, 1866), p. 381; M. T. Wild, 'The Geographical Shaping of Hull', in S. Ellis and D. R. Crowther (eds), *Humber Perspectives: A Region Through the Ages* (Hull, 1990), p. 254.

40 HHC, C DPD/1/29, Letter to Thomas Thompson Esq. MP, Chairman of the Dock Company at Kingston-upon-Hull, on the subject of making a Junction-Dock at that Port, by John Wray Esq., 1814; First and Second Reports of the Committee Appointed to Obtain Additional Dock Room at the Port of Hull, 22 February 1819, 24 February 1820.

41 HHC, C DPD/1/29, Report of the Committee for Obtaining Additional Dock Room, 30 March 1825; *Hull Packet and Humber Mercury*, 2 June 1829.

42 Sheahan, *History*, p. 373; *Hull Packet and East Riding Times*, 5 February 1847.

43 G. Jackson, 'Shipowners and Private Dock Companies: The Case of Hull, 1770–1970', in L. M. Akveld and J. R. Bruijn (eds), *Shipping Companies and Authorities in the 19th and 20th Centuries: Their Common Interest in the Development of Port Facilities* (Amsterdam, 1986), p. 50.

44 HHC, C DPD/1/29, Report of the Proceedings of the Committee of Owners of Property on Both Sides of the River Hull, 1836.

45 Sheahan, *History*, p. 376; *The Civil Engineer and Architect's Journal*, II (1839), p. 16.

46 HHC, C DPD/1/29, Fourth Report of the Proceedings of the Committee of Owners of Property on Both Banks of the River Hull, 1841; J. D. Hicks (ed.), *The Journal of Joseph Robinson Pease 1822–1865* (Beverley, 2000), p. 110.

47 HHC, C DPD/1/29, An Examination of the Report of the Proceedings of the Committee of Owners of Property on Both Sides of the River Hull, by 'Agathon', 1836; *Hull Packet*, 23 December 1842; W. Wright, 'The Hull Docks', *Proceedings of the Institution of Civil Engineers*, XLI (1875), p. 87.

48 Hicks (ed.), *Journal of Joseph Robinson Pease*, pp. 180 and 190; after Sheahan, *History*, p. 377; E. Wrigglesworth, *Brown's Illustrated Guide to Hull* (1891, repr. Goole, 1992),

p. 209. Victoria Dock in its original form covered 12 acres: the combined area of the other enclosed docks was 25.75 acres.

49 *Hull Packet and East Riding Times*, 5 July 1850.

50 Hicks (ed.), *Journal of Joseph Robinson Pease*, p. 123; BPP 1859 XXV, Correspondence between Corporation of Kingston-upon-Hull, Treasury, Hull Dock Company, War Dept., and Office of Woods and Forests on Sale of Citadel Site, Hull.

51 *Hull Packet and East Riding Times*, 5 November 1858.

52 Bellamy, 'Aspects of the Economy of Hull', pp. 151–52; *Hull Packet and East Riding Times*, 24 September 1858.

53 24 & 25 Vict., cap.lxxxix; Bellamy, 'Aspects of the Economy of Hull', p. 152; Sheahan, *History*, p. 767.

54 *Hull Packet and East Riding Times*, 4 May 1860; G. Jackson, 'The Ports', in M. J. Freeman and D. H. Aldcroft (eds), *Transport in Victorian Britain* (Manchester, 1988), pp. 228–29.

55 C. Hellyer, 'The Fishing Trade from its Commencement at the Port of Hull', in J. Franks (ed.), *Hull as a Fishing Port* (Hull, 1915), pp. 49–53.

56 Jackson, 'Shipowners and Private Dock Companies', p. 54; *Hull Packet and East Riding Times*, 26 May 1865; W. W. Tomlinson, *The North Eastern Railway: Its Rise and Development* (Newcastle and London, 1915), p. 705.

57 G. G. MacTurk, rev. K. Hoole, *A History of the Hull Railways* (Hull, 1880; repr. Knaresborough, 1970), p. 151.

58 Bellamy, 'Aspects of the Economy of Hull', pp. 153–54; J. Simmons, *The Railway in Town and Country 1830–1914* (Newton Abbot, 1986), pp. 204–07.

59 *Hull Packet and East Riding Times*, 22 February 1878, 1 March 1878.

60 'The Humber', in E. Rowland Jones (ed.), *Industrial Rivers of the United Kingdom* (London, 1891), p. 198; Bellamy, 'Aspects of the Economy of Hull', Appendix B.

61 Jackson, 'Shipowners and Private Dock Companies', p. 55; Bellamy, 'Aspects of the Economy of Hull', p. 165.

62 Tomlinson, *North Eastern Railway*, pp. 712–16.

63 Quoted in Jackson, 'Shipowners and Private Dock Companies', p. 56.

64 *The Engineer*, 19 June 1914, 26 June 1914; M. Thompson, *Hull Docklands: An Illustrated History of the Port of Hull* (Beverley, 1990), p. 62.

65 *Port of Hull Annual* 1911, pp. 17–29; *The Engineer*, 1 July 1910; Thompson, *Hull Docklands*, p. 58.

66 HHC, C DPD/12/1/4, Hull Dock Company: Extracts of Minutes of the Board and Committees, 1888–93, undated entry c. July 1889; *The Engineer*, 26 June 1914.

67 Sheppard, *City and County of Kingston upon Hull*, p. 21; *Annual Report on Sea Fisheries*, 1914; *Port of Hull Annual* 1911, p. 11.

68 Daniel Defoe, *A Tour Through the Whole Island of Great Britain* (London, 4th edn, 1748), p. 198.

69 I. Hall and E. Hall, *A New Picture of Georgian Hull* (Hull, 1978), p. 19; J. Markham, *The Book of Hull: Evolution of a Great Northern City* (Hull, 1989), p. 19.

70 J. Craggs, *Craggs's Guide to Hull: a Description, Historical and Topographical, of the Town, County, and Vicinity of*

the Town of Kingston-Upon-Hull (London and York, 1817), pp. 38–39.

71   *White's General Directory and Topography of Kingston upon Hull and the City of York*, 1851; A. Gill, *Village Within a City: The Hessle Road Fishing Community of Hull* (Hull, 1986), pp. 5–6; J. Watts, *Hessle Road: A History* (Hull, 1984).

72   Wild, 'Geographical Shaping of Hull', p. 259.

73   *Port of Hull Annual* 1914, p. 55; Markham, *Book of Hull*, p. 95.

74   *White's General and Commercial Directory of Hull*, 1882; G. De Boer, 'The Evolution of Kingston upon Hull', *Geography*, 31 (1946), pp. 145–46; W. G. East, 'The Port of Kingston-upon-Hull during the Industrial Revolution', *Economica*, 32 (1931), p. 191.

75   A. Slaven, *British Shipbuilding 1500–2010* (Lancaster, 2013), pp. 19–20, 51; Allison, 'Hull, 1700–1835'.

76   J. M. Bellamy, 'A Hull Shipbuilding Firm', *Business History*, 6 (1963), pp. 27–47; A. G. Credland, *The Gibsons: A Shipbuilding Family of the 18th and 19th Centuries* (Beverley, 2006), pp. 9–10.

77   S. R. Palmer, 'The Ports', in M. Daunton (ed.), *The Cambridge Urban History of Britain Volume 3: 1840–1950* (Cambridge, 2001), p. 144.

78   J. H. Hargreaves, 'Introduction', in Franks (ed.), *Hull as a Fishing Port*, p. 9.

79   A. G. Credland, *Artists and Crasftsmen of Hull and East Yorkshire* (Hull, 2000), pp. 82–128; Bellamy, 'Aspects of the Economy of Hull', pp. 244–45, 317–20, 323–25.

80   Jackson, *Hull in the Eighteenth Century*, p. 136.

81   D. J. Starkey, 'Ownership Structures in the British Shipping Industry: The Case of Hull, 1820–1916', *International Journal of Maritime History*, VII (1996), p. 73; M. G. Barnard and D. J. Starkey, 'Private Companies, Culture and Place in the Development of Hull's Maritime Business Sector, *c.*1860–1914', in G. Harlaftis, S. Tenold and J. M. Valdalaiso (eds), *The World's Key Industry: History and Economics of International Shipping* (Basingstoke, 2012), p. 205.

82   See F. Schofield, *Humber Keels and Keelmen* (Lavenham, 1988).

83   Allison, 'Modern Hull'; Bellamy, 'Aspects of the Economy of Hull', pp. 49–52.

84   Markham, *Book of Hull*, pp. 61–62.

85   S. Capes, 'The Contribution Made by Devonian and Kentish Migrants to the Fishing Industry and Community of Hull during the Late Nineteenth Century', *Maritime South West*, 18 (2005), pp. 33–60.

86   BPP 1882 XVII, Sea Fishing Trade Committee, Minutes of Evidence, q.26 & 248; R. Gurnham, *The Story of Hull* (Stroud, 2011), p. 99.

87   See S. Hugill, *Sailortown* (London and New York, 1967).

88   J. Tickell, *History of the Town and County of Kingston upon Hull to the present Time* (Hull, 1798), p. 737.

Neil Hadlock's sculpture depicts a family from Northern Europe having left ship before continuing to Paragon Station then on by train to Liverpool then by ship to America

Over 2,200,000 people passed through Hull and other Humber Ports to America between 1836 and 1914

CHAPTER SIX

The Making of a Mosaic:
Migration and the Port-city of Kingston upon Hull[1]

NICHOLAS J. EVANS

When the results of the 2011 UK Census were made public in 2013, the BBC's *Six O'Clock News* ran a live television broadcast from Hull to herald a remarkable transformation – the city was now home to a migrant population of 12,000 European migrants, 5 per cent of the total.[2] Despite being one of the UK's largest passenger ports and home to a university recruiting large numbers of overseas students, that Hull had been settled by European workers seemed to be a cause for national concern. Although the workers filled employment shortages in low-paid sectors and bolstered under-populated areas along the Beverley Road district to the north of the city centre, the media portrayed the city as being deluged by a sizeable number of immigrants for the first time in its history. Numerous maritime metaphors were used to explain to 'alarmed' audiences what was happening. Although the city had proudly branded itself as a Gateway to Europe for the previous two decades, and urban planners had sought to persuade Europeans arriving and embarking through the North Sea ferry terminal to 'stop off' in Hull, the 200 per cent increase in the number of EU workers choosing to work in the city was deemed newsworthy locally and nationally. A handful of outsiders or 'aliens' had been associated with Hull since the foundation of the medieval port in the thirteenth century, but 'difference' was always seen as transitory and not part of the place's DNA.[3]

In fact, however, the cultural, religious and linguistic influences of foreign merchants, artists and refugees have given the area its outsider character and unique linguistic identity for over a millennium. Danish-speaking Vikings, who landed in the ninth century, are recalled in place names of villages surrounding

Hull such as Anlaby, Kirk Ella, Willerby, Ferriby and Skidby. French-speaking merchants, such as the de la Poles, helped shape the early commerce of the port during the fourteenth century.[4] Flemish cloth merchants expanded trade during the fifteenth century. The Elizabethan Aliens Rolls record the town's first black migrant to have been the servant of Bartholomew Burnett in 1599 (Figure 6.1).[5] Peter Scheemakers, a Dutch sculptor, created the much-loved statue of King William III (King Billy) that has dominated the Market Place since the mid-eighteenth century. The creative talents of Giuseppe Cortese, an Italian stucco artist, embellished the architecture of Wilberforce House.[6] 'Hullness' has been shaped by the continual influence of outsiders throughout the port's long history, and it can be argued that the continual presence of new aliens has been an enduring feature of Hull's maritime identity, a symbol of its entrepreneurial vigour. The ebb and flow of every high tide brought people with new skills who have enriched the expanding conurbation. This chapter seeks to explore this forgotten aspect of the making of the city – Hull's acceptance and absorption of outsiders throughout its past. From the Revolutionary and Napoleonic

6.1 This portrait photograph was taken at the studios of Sunley and Toogood at 10 Caroline Place around 1880, and highlights the small, often forgotten black population who had resided in Hull since the Tudor era. The clothing suggests that this was a poorer resident, but it is interesting that he was photographed so far from the dock area, where so many black seafarers lived while ashore. At sea, most of Hull's early black population worked as seafarers rated as cooks or donkeymen (stokers).
Collection of Nicholas J. Evans

Wars that convulsed Europe during the 1790s and 1800s to the War on Terror at the end of the twentieth century, various river-, sea- and ocean-going vessels brought multitudes of migrants of various identities, nationalities, ethnicities and cultures. Following the opening of the first dock (later Queen's Dock) in 1778, Hull's importance as a commercial centre was underpinned by outsiders. In turn, the success of maritime trade drew traders and potential settlers from further afield. From the Corporation Pier to Hull Fair, from Market Place to the affluent suburbs, men, women and children from outside of the city have collectively made a mosaic that has enhanced Hull's commercial prowess, cemented its cultural diversity and bolstered the physical expansion of the urban landscape beyond the confines of the fortified medieval town. Hull would arguably be nothing without the continental migrants who expanded its commercial and cultural horizons, the transmigrants who for decades made Hull one of the most important transport hubs in the world, and latterly the economic migrants, refugees and university students who have made Hull a truly global city.

Sensationalising Hull: Mary Elizabeth Braddon's Theatrical and Literary Connections[1]

Best-selling and prolific Victorian sensation fiction author Mary Elizabeth Braddon was born in London in 1835 to a Cornish father and an Irish Protestant mother. However, the heart, soul and certainly the creative spirit of this writer were most at home in Yorkshire. Braddon became (in)famous for novels depicting female bigamists, attempted murder, arson and bribery – anything and everything that shocked Victorian sensibilities. Her career as a writer spanned from the outbreak of the American Civil War to the start of the First World War, encompassed a broad range of literary genres and won her international fame with *Lady Audley's Secret* (1862) and *Aurora Floyd* (1863).

Life circumstances and the very real threat of poverty compelled Braddon to take on acting work as a means of providing for her single mother early in her life. Her father left the family when she was four and her siblings' lives took them abroad. Nevertheless, as an actress during the 1850s Braddon's work

William Powell Frith, *A Private View at the Royal Academy* (1881). Mary Elizabeth Braddon stands with her back to the viewer on the left side of the picture in a brown or deep red dress. She appears to be talking to the musician, Sir Julius Benedict. Braddon and Benedict stand to the left of a tall figure with a full-white beard, top hat and notebook– this is Anthony Trollope (d. 1882). The subject of the picture is the contrast between lasting historical achievement and ephemeral trends, such as the aestheticism embodied in the figure and set-up of Oscar Wilde in the image (right, framed by female figures in fine dress). The portrait of Benjamin Disraeli hanging at the back of the room (to the right of the doorway) is suggestive of lasting historical legacy and achievement. The ephemeral is reiterated in the colourful outfits worn largely by the women in the picture. It is interesting to note that Braddon appears as a subtle figure in contrast to the other women.
https://upload.wikimedia.org/wikipedia/commons/7/7f/Frith_A_Private_View.jpg

carried her far and wide and enabled her to achieve independence, while still taking on a great deal of responsibility. She toured the country, performing in theatres at Hull, Beverley and Brighton, and her mobility certainly enriched her knowledge of people and places, giving her insight into the tastes and interests of the people who would later form her substantial readership.

In 1856–57 Braddon joined the theatrical company of Messrs Wolfendon and Melbourne, the owners of Hull's Queen's Theatre on Paragon Street, reputed to be the largest theatre outside London. Braddon's acting ability earned her parts in comedies, tragedies, Shakespearean plays and a pantomime – literary and dramatic exposure that she would later draw on in her own writing career for stage and popular fiction. Wolfendon and Melbourne's company also played Beverley's Assembly Rooms and it was while she was in Beverley that Braddon befriended the actor, Wybert Rousby, who, almost twenty years later, starred in the leading role of one of her own plays, *Griselda* (1873).

There was a period of transition in Braddon's life at the end of the 1850s when she was still acting to earn a living while simultaneously pursuing a writing career and taking on other work suitable for a single, literate and practical woman in order to make ends meet. It was while she was living in Black House Farm, Beverley Parks, for six months as a governess that John Gilby, a Yorkshire squire, helped Braddon to publish her first collection of poems, *Garibaldi and Other Poems* (1861), after reading her first forays into publishing in *The Beverley Recorder and General Advertiser*. During this time she also published her first novel, *Three Times Dead* (1860), with the printer Charles Empson of Toll-Gavel.

Braddon returned to Hull after moving to work in Brighton for a time, and on her return she played an active and vocal role in the town's community enterprises, including the endeavour to raise funds for the People's Park – renamed Pearson Park after Hull's mayor. For a special benefit night on 25 June 1860, Braddon performed in a comedy, as well as writing a poetic address. In her speech she couched Pearson's offering of the park in language that evokes both the shipowner and Hull's maritime interests, and, in the process, conflates the identities of the self-made man and his home town. Pearson had 'never launched a better, braver barque/ Than when he charted this the People's Park', Braddon declared – a masterful example of her skill as a rhetorician and her shrewd ability to manipulate language. The event raised £70 which went to fund the entrance gates, lake and bandstand.

Braddon moved to London in 1860 and in 1861 moved in with John Maxwell, her long-term lover. But she never forgot her time in Hull and the East Riding, which featured as a

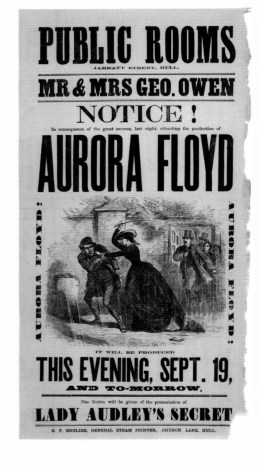

backdrop to her fiction over the next fifty years. Braddon's fiction depicts the county's rough beauty, the people, their habits, hobbies and food, illustrating the long-lasting impression the area made on her imagination and creative output. Indeed, the county of Yorkshire becomes a character in its own right in Braddon's work, changing over time. After the phenomenal success of her 1860s sensation fiction, Braddon continued to publish two novels per year, flooding the London literary market. To widen her readership and appeal, from the 1870s Braddon began syndicating her novels to newspapers in the major industrial cities of the north through William Tillotson of Bolton.[2] This led to her publishing her 'new and powerful' novel *Phantom Fortune* in the *Hull Packet and East Riding Times* from 9 March to 26 October 1883.[3] This was over twenty years after she had left the city, again demonstrating how Hull stayed with her, and how she stayed loyal to Hull.

It is worth noting that this successful, well-travelled, worldly woman looked back to her short time living in Beverley and described it as the 'happiest half-year of my life'. The same warm, friendly, welcoming and homely atmosphere shines through in her literary depictions of Hull and the East Riding, for Hull, like Beverley and Yorkshire in general, had welcomed and sheltered Braddon and given her opportunities to carve out a diverse and successful career in literature and the performing arts. Furthermore, in providing Braddon with materials and subject matter to engage her readers, the county, its towns and its people had helped her to secure international fame and recognition.

Janine Hatter

Notes

1 This article is based on Janine Hatter, 'Closing the Curtain: M. E. Braddon's Last Performance as Mary Seyton', *Notes & Queries*, 62 (2015), pp. 426–29.

2 Jennifer Carnell and Graham Law, '"Our Author": Braddon in the Provincial Weeklies', in Marlene Tromp, Pamela Gilbert and Aeron Haynie (eds), *Beyond Sensation: Mary Elizabeth Braddon in Context* (New York, 1999), pp. 127–63.

3 'New Story of the Highest Rank and Excellence', *Hull Packet and East Riding Times*, 9 February 1883, p. 1.

Foreign immigration and the emergence of an ethnic mosaic

Where once Hull had a 'uniquely Dutch feel', by the outbreak of the Napoleonic Wars it was becoming a major European gateway.[7] Traders, mariners and migrants from a number of different European nations settled in Hull from the 1790s onwards. They were not the only ethnic minorities who visited the town. The black abolitionist Olaudah Equiano is said to have visited John Sykes – Hull's mayor and Wilberforce's cousin – in late 1792, and he would have encountered people of all colours, creeds, ethnicities and nationalities, visiting or living and working in the port-town (Figure 6.2).[8] Although racial diversity was less advanced than in the larger ports of London, Liverpool, Bristol and Glasgow, some paintings now held in the Ferens Art Gallery and

Wilberforce House Museum capture the growing diversity of the maritime community.[9] The size of any 'alien' group never exceeded the hundreds before the 1850s, and the thousands before the 1880s, yet the alternative name of Dagger Lane, Ten Faiths Lane, suggests that a range of foreign faiths worshipped there. It was certainly the home of Hull's first synagogue, which opened in 1766; subsequently, ecclesiastical buildings for German and Scandinavian migrants were opened in Osborne Street in 1848 and 1871. A constantly changing European mosaic settled around the edges of the historic town, increasingly surrounded on all sides by maritime activity. As gravestones across the surrounding region indicate, people came from as far away as India, Jakarta, Russia, Latin America, Africa and, of course, Europe.[10] Aliens Lists and passport controls introduced to protect the harbour during the conflict with France further reveal the arrival of migrant men, women and children between 1793 and 1828. Included in the records were 'Italian pedlars', 'negroes' and Polish, Danish, German and Russian 'Jews' and 'Jewesses',[11] who all landed at the western confluence of the rivers Hull and Humber. While many, like the Cohen sisters, were in transit for Sheffield, others remained for the duration of the war, reporting to the Custom House situated in the former Neptune Hotel on Whitefriargate.

While the maritime workforce was inherently diverse, the people who permanently settled were, until at least the mid-Victorian period, drawn from the merchant or artisan classes. Usually possessing both capital and social networks established through seaborne trade with Hull, they were part of dynasties handling port commerce between Hull and the North Sea ports of Amsterdam, Gothenburg, Oslo, Rotterdam, Hamburg and the Baltic ports of Riga, Åbo (now Türkü) and Hangö (Hanko). Men such as John Cankrien from Rotterdam and Frederick Helmsing from Riga augmented the already strong commercial links between ports from rival imperial powers. Except during wartime, papers proving identity were not an

6.2 Ticket for the opening of St Charles Borromeo church, 1829. When it opened on 29 July 1829, St Charles Borromeo was one of the first purpose-built Catholic churches to open in Hull since the Reformation. It marked an important moment in the emancipation of Catholics in Britain. The price of the ticket was probably an attempt to recoup the costs of the elaborate Italian baroque building. Opening just three months after the Roman Catholic Relief Act, the building played an important role in distributing aid to people fleeing the Irish potato famine in the 1840s.
Collection of Nicholas J. Evans

impediment to movement.[12] Identities were often deliberately changed so that traders appeared, to all intents and purposes, British. Yet full citizenship – including the ability to own freehold property and vote in parliamentary elections – was both rare and expensive. Obtaining citizenship required an immigrant to secure an individual Act of Parliament at that time. Only a handful of merchants achieved what the grave of John Cankrien, the former Dutch Consul, memorialised: 'Naturalised by Act of Parliament'.[13] The wealth of these merchants enabled them to integrate into local society, and following the expectations of the time for people 'of means' they often had fine residences erected in the rural suburbs surrounding the town.[14]

Rather than retarding settlement, the Napoleonic Wars served to expand Hull's largest alien group, the Jewish community. Although the largely foreign-born community was formally established in 1766, it was the establishment of Hull as a naval prize court during the Napoleonic Wars that persuaded Jews resident in southern ports, and Hampshire in particular, to migrate north, as gravestones in the Jewish cemetery on Hessle Road attest. Money was to be made in the buying and selling of these naval prizes, and for the Georgian Jewish community it made Hull an attractive place to live and work.[15] As research by David Lewis has revealed, throughout the early Victorian era Hull's isolated Ashkenazi Jewish community buried Jews from as far away as Kings Lynn to the south, Sheffield and Leeds to the west, and Scarborough to the north.[16] These early Jewish residents were joined by a smaller number of Mediterranean Jews wearing the exotic clothing of the Levant, who worked as pedlars hawking their wares in the surrounding villages. Thus we find reference to Philip Solomon of Selby appearing in court records at Beverley in 1796; Joseph Jelson, a Sephardic Jew from Gibraltar, was charged at the Beverley Assizes in 1839 for criminal activity; and the Baghdadi Jew Reuben Sassoon witnessed the infamous Baccarat Scandal at Tranby Croft in 1890. Yet despite such 'exotic' Jews occasionally visiting the town, most of Hull's Jewish community was made up of Ashkenazi Jews from central and eastern Europe.[17]

With the peace of 1815, Hull's foreign-born migrant community expanded further as technological innovation reduced journey times and increased the reliability of North Sea travel. The General Steam Navigation Company, Gee and Company, Bailey & Leetham, and the Wilson Line all plied the North Sea routes from the 1820s onwards. Running scheduled services, the frequency and regularity of movement enabled people and goods to traverse the North Sea with an ease unimaginable during the age of sail. Journey times were reduced on an almost yearly basis as local shipbuilders such as Pearsons and then Earles, coupled with the local engineering company Amos & Smith, improved the design and reliability of steamship services. Like the infrastructure that enabled Hull to expand, the supply routes – on land and along waterways – in central and eastern Europe meant that from the 1840s onwards traders, craftsmen and immigrants from as far away as Scandinavia, Russia, Finland and Italy were arriving through Hull's expanding dock estate. From the late 1820s, the new harbour and steam packet wharf near the entrance to Humber Dock improved landing facilities for passengers and circumvented the need to navigate the crowded River Hull completely. Immigrants settled

close to where they landed on reclaimed land near the edge of the former walled town. Those settling came predominantly from or via Hamburg and were aided by John Hurst, the former captain of the early steamship SS *Lion*, who operated an emigrant, passenger and victualling business from the Minerva public house from 1854 (Figure 6.3).[18] The triangular-shaped premises, erected in 1829, were perfectly situated between the Humber Dock basin and what later became the Corporation Pier.[19] The latter had regular Humber ferry passenger services to nearby Grimsby and thus the area became the central point of arrival for most early Victorian migrants.

Given the regular sailings of steamers to and from both Hamburg and later Bremen, a growing number of highly skilled artisans began to settle during the 1840s. Hairdressers, sugar bakers and butchers all served the expanding Hull population.[20] Although their arrival coincided with the opening of the Hull to Selby railway line in 1840, there is little evidence to suggest that the railway was used by any of the early immigrants. Yet what had been a steadily paced rate of immigration changed dramatically in 1848 with the failure of harvests and revolutions across central Europe. While the Irish potato famine was a central factor in Britain and Ireland, agrarian failure in the late 1840s, coupled with failed political revolutions in Europe, also precipitated large-scale German emigration.[21] Most Germans were bound for the industrial centres of Leeds, Bradford and Manchester, but a growing number established themselves and their families in Hull. By 1851 Germans formed the largest foreign-born population in Hull. They established their own church services from 1844, with donations from the Royal House of Prussia.[22] The population was affluent, and from 1848 it sustained both a permanent German Lutheran Church on Nile Street and a charity for distressed foreign migrants.[23] Being wealthy and highly cultured, they expanded the cultural aspirations of the town and facilitated the visits of talented, classically trained musicians. Although removed from their native homeland, most retained a strong command of the German language. Professional tradesmen also visited trade fairs in Germany, where they won awards for their crafts – all of which were proudly displayed to their non-German clientele in Hull shops.

Many female immigrants, and a significant number of immigrant children, entered the service of local gentry and aristocratic families as German culture became *de rigueur* for aspiring Victorians. The Barnards of Cave Castle in the west Hull village of South Cave typified this trend by employing German-born governesses to educate their children at home before the First World War. Meanwhile male migrants and their children, such as the Hohenreins, entered the East Yorkshire Militia and became members of the Humber Masonic Lodge – Hull's oldest – situated off Dagger Lane. Other successful German-born merchants entered the Hull and Humber Chamber of Commerce as part of their commercial assimilation into the business elite of the town. Until the First World War hampered German settlement, Hull retained one of the country's largest German communities after London, Manchester, Dundee and Bradford. The census reveals that in 1891 at least 906 Germans, or 33 per cent of the foreign-born population, lived in the town; this declined to 576 (18 per cent) by 1901, before growing again to 738 (20 per cent) by 1911.[24] Unlike the case of the early generation of immigrants, naturalisation had become easier and more affordable, and so around 10 per cent of the Germans arriving sought British citizenship.[25] They gave generously to local good causes and, like the early migrants, moved to some of the elite residential districts of the city, including Coltman and Linnaeus Streets, the Avenues and Beverley Road. Very much an upwardly mobile population, they made an important cultural imprint in terms of music, food, drink and language.[26] They cemented important commercial ties between the Humber and the global trading centre of Hamburg. It is thus of no great surprise that the future shipping magnate John Reeves Ellerman, described by William Rubinstein as the richest man in England when he died in 1933, was born to German immigrant parents on Hull's Anlaby Road in 1862.[27]

By far the largest and most influential migrant group in terms of Hull's development as a city were the Jews from eastern and central Europe, who reached the town between 1848 and 1914 (Figure 6.4). They changed both the religious and the economic landscape of Hull, and although most studies of British Jewish history, and indeed the Jewish diaspora, begin their coverage with the outbreak of the Tsarist persecutions, or pogroms, in 1881, Hull's Ashkenazi population mushroomed following the expansion of the German railway network during the 1840s. The opening of a direct rail route between Berlin and Hamburg in 1846 enabled Jews to reach North Sea ports within hours. Most of those bound for Britain originated in the area of eastern Poland or western Russia known at the time as the Pale of Settlement. The Jews of Russia had faced mobility and occupational restrictions since at least the 1790s. Despite the repression and hardship facing all who lived under the brutality of imperial Russian rule, the community grew during the mid-to-late nineteenth century. The Jews who came into Britain between the 1880s and 1914 entered mainly via Hull and Grimsby and were mostly transients, crossing the country on their way to the United States and Canada. The majority came on a through-ticket that included the cost of travel from continental Europe, a train journey across Britain, and then the steamer across the Atlantic. Yet in addition to those bound for further afield, Jews wishing to settle permanently in Britain landed at either Hull (from Bremen, Libau and Hamburg) or Grimsby (from Hamburg, Antwerp or Rotterdam). Although later descendants often believed they had been tricked into stopping off in Hull, from 1851 onwards their tickets clearly stated the ultimate destination to which they were bound.[28]

Despite its role as a major immigrant and transmigrant terminus for Jewish migrants during the period of mass migration in the mid-to-late Victorian period, Hull did not develop a Jewish migrant ghetto. Unlike the Red Bank area of Manchester, Leylands in Leeds, or the East End of London, the port-city never had a migrant ghetto and, according to analysis of the 1861 and 1891 censuses by Michael Smale, no street had more than 22 per cent of its population born elsewhere.[29] Even Osborne Street, recalled by third- and fourth-generation Jewish immigrants as the centre of Jewish Hull, was a cosmopolitan space within which foreign migrants of many religions and nationalities settled and worshipped. At its height the Jewish immigrant generation was supported by kosher bakeries, butchers, delicatessens, fish shops, six synagogues and numerous Jewish charities. Yet, as with the children of immigrants elsewhere, those born in Hull rapidly began to enter the professions and eventually dominated the legal profession in Hull.[30] The Jewish community made a vital contribution to civic life as councillors, mayors, lord mayors, sheriffs and aldermen (Figure 6.5).[31] As with affluent German immigrants, over the next 150 years Hull's Jewish population suburbanised. Ultimately, some would argue, the success of these immigrants lay in their ability to assimilate and integrate, in

6.4 The Hull Western Synagogue was built and formally consecrated in 1903. Officially opened by O. E. D'Avigdor Goldsmid, a plaque to mark the occasion can be seen in the bottom right of the photograph. The building was designed by B. S. Jacobs, the son of the president of the synagogue, Bethel Jacobs. Jacobs's buildings often used a combination of brick colours, with examples including what is now Cafe Nero in Queen Victoria Square and Pacific Court in High Street. As the Jewish community grew, so did the number of synagogues needed for the religious community, to a total of six during the interwar period. This synagogue remained in active use until 1994 and was frequented by assimilated members of the 'established' community. Above the entrance are displayed the ten commandments in Hebrew. The synagogue combined with the Old Hebrew Congregation in Osborne Street in 1994, and relocated to a new building in Anlaby to be nearer to the homes of congregants.
© Nicholas J. Evans

part because of the piecemeal and gradual nature of their settlement. This largely explains why Jews who lived in the town escaped the type of persecution directed towards ethnic minorities living elsewhere. They added, moreover, to the fluidity and vitality of Hull as a great port-city. After the Alien Immigration Act in 1905 attempted to curtail European immigration to Britain, each vessel arriving in the Humber was visited by an immigration officer. At Hull in the early twentieth century, the officer concerned was Paul Julius Drasdo. An immigrant from Berlin in 1880, Drasdo married the daughter of one of Hull's emigration agents, and by the time the Aliens Act was passed he had become Hull's leading emigration agent.[32] He was then appointed Hull's official immigration officer. In this role he met (for a fee) every vessel bringing aliens to Hull, and arranged transport for those who had not already paid for onward rail travel. Drasdo spoke several languages, including German, Yiddish and Russian, and could help the immigrants during their medical inspections and on disembarkation.

Immigrants from most European countries found a home in Hull during the long nineteenth century. Swedes, Norwegians, Danes and Finns rubbed shoulders with Russians, Poles, Austro-Hungarians, Italians, Greeks, Romanians, Germans, Dutch, Belgian, French, Spanish and Portuguese settlers. The cultural sophistication of those inhabiting the port-town also developed as every high tide brought new cultures, foods and styles. While fish, bread and potatoes remained the staple diet for most, exotic spices from Asia, rice from slave plantations in the Americas, bananas and pineapples from the Caribbean, and oranges and lemons from the Mediterranean all changed the culinary palate of Hull's growing urban population.[33] As mariners and merchants settled, they were joined by other migrants from most European countries. However, although 612 Belgians found temporary refuge in Hull during the First World War, the era of mass immigration came to an abrupt end.[34] Only those transiting the port *en route* to foreign countries would be welcomed in the decades that followed. As Hull developed a truly ethnic mosaic during the nineteenth century, the port remained a very European space, with few settlers from the British Empire or other places further afield. Hull, unlike most British ports, remained an overtly white city – something that remained unchanged for most of the twentieth century.

6.5 Merchant tailor, councillor and later alderman, Solomon Cohen was a leading member of Hull's Jewish community. The length of his civic service earned him the title 'Father of the Corporation'. As well as being a town (later city) councillor for thirty-seven years, he was an active Freemason, a member of the Hull Board of Guardians, and a merchant operating on King Edward Street. Hull has one of the oldest Jewish communities in Britain, and some of the earliest elected Jewish politicians.
Collection of Nicholas J. Evans

Alderman S. COHEN,
Born April 27th, 1827,   *Died March 20th, 1907.*

Madame Clapham

Madame Clapham, née Emily McVitie, was born in Cheltenham in 1857. She moved north to live in Scarborough at a young age and trained as a dressmaking apprentice at the Marshall and Snelgrove department store. It was here, in 1886, that she married Haigh Clapham, a clerk from Wakefield. They moved to Hull just one year later and set up a dressmaking salon at 1 Kingston Square, a well-to-do area and the location of Hull's Assembly Rooms where fashionable dances took place. Within a few years they had established a remarkably successful business, enabling them to acquire 2 and 3 Kingston Square.

Ambitious and determined, Madame Clapham was the public face of the business and soon nurtured a strong customer base in Hull and the East Riding as well as establishing a national and international reputation. Her list of high-society clients lengthened considerably to include Muriel Wilson, the renowned Edwardian beauty and daughter of the shipping magnate Arthur Wilson (co-owner of the Wilson Line), and Queen Maud of Norway, daughter of King Edward VII and by far her most famous customer.

Madame Clapham knew intuitively which style, colour and fit would suit a client. She had an eye for detail and the business acumen to match. She regularly visited Paris and London to find inspiration for her bespoke designs. Her team of dedicated dressmakers would then turn her designs into dresses of exquisite quality. She was a perfectionist and a hard disciplinarian who expected absolute loyalty from her workforce, but she was also known for genuine displays of kindness, especially to family and friends. Working for her was deemed prestigious, and her employees were proud to be 'Clapham girls'.

Madame Clapham's business was at its height from 1890 until the outbreak of the First World War. Thereafter, social codes changed and fashions became less elaborate. Simpler, ready-to-wear

Made of bottle green velvet and ivory silk brocade, this Clapham creation was worn by Caroline Jameson at the wedding of her son, Frank Wordsworth Jameson, to Ethel Maude Marion Ayre, at All Saints church in Hessle in 1891. Caroline was the wife of Robert Jameson, thrice mayor of Hull in 1870–73, after whom Jameson Street in Hull city centre was named. The Jameson family lived at East Ella Hall on the corner of Anlaby Road and Calvert Lane, a property that was later home to the White City skating rink on the eve of the Second World War.
© Hands on History Museum: Hull Museums

Emily Clapham, *c.* 1910. Madame Clapham had blue eyes and a rosy complexion. She dressed typically in black or navy with her blonde hair arranged elaborately on top of her head. Her commanding presence in the dressmaking salon was noted by all who worked for her.
Courtesy of Hull Museums

styles became the norm and were much easier to mass-produce and retail in Hull's emerging department stores. Despite the arrival of strong competition Madame Clapham's business remained largely stable, but change was inevitable and she increasingly struggled to attract the patronage of younger generations. The 'make-do-and-mend' ethos of the Second World War further diminished demand for extravagant fashion, and as Madame Clapham aged the business continued to contract. Following her death in 1952, Emily Wall, Madame Clapham's niece, maintained the business until its closure in 1967.

Emily Clapham is still widely revered in Hull and beyond by aficionados of *haute couture*. She dedicated her life to her business, employing and training hundreds of local women and girls in the skills that underpinned their craft. Her creative flair, tenacity and sheer determination helped to make Hull a leading fashion centre. Madame Clapham's significant legacy lies in the stunning dresses that are held in Hull Museums' collections (see www.hullcc.gov.uk/museumcollections), while the name 'Clapham' is prominently displayed in the ironwork above the entrance to her former salon at 1 Kingston Square.[1]

Susan Capes

Notes

1   This article draws upon previous published work by Ann Crowther, *Madame Clapham: The Celebrated Dressmaker* (1976); Jayne Tyler and Clare Parsons, *Madame Clapham: Hull's Celebrated Dressmaker* (1999); unpublished notes by Lydia Saul, former Assistant Keeper of Social History at Hull Museums; and an entry on Madame Clapham by Susan Capes in the 2016 edition of the *Oxford Dictionary of National Biography*.

The staging post to America: transmigration through Hull

Because of its location on the shortest rail route across Britain, Hull developed in the mid-nineteenth century as a major gateway for transmigrants. Those arriving were not destined to settle in Hull, nor to live in Leeds, Manchester or Liverpool. Instead, they already possessed a ticket to a final destination further afield. The combined influence of geography, transport infrastructure and foreign merchants able to assist every boatload of migrants arriving at the port ensured that for nearly a century Hull was one of the world's largest migrant handling ports. Like New York, Boston, Philadelphia, Liverpool, Hamburg, Bremen, Rotterdam and Le Havre, Hull facilitated millions of European migrants bound for the United States, Canada, Latin America and southern Africa. All were hoping to better their economic, political or religious well-being by migrating to the other side of the world, and Hull developed into a secure staging post along this aspirational route – a stepping stone to far larger cities. So central was the traffic to the prosperity of the city that when a statue to Queen Victoria was unveiled in 1903, the profile of a Wilson Line vessel carrying transmigrants was chosen to symbolise, on its pedestal, one of the means through which Hull had emerged as Britain's third port during Victoria's long reign. Although a significant and constant feature in the port's traffic from the 1840s to the First World War, transmigration was a largely forgotten story until the late 1990s, when attempts were made by Hull City Council to rebrand the city as a both a gateway to Europe and a fount of freedom.[35]

During the period between 1851 and 1914, Hull played a pivotal role in the movement of transmigrants via the UK,[36] with over 2.2 million European migrants passing through *en route* to a new life in the USA, Canada, Latin America, South Africa and, to a lesser extent, Australasia.[37] Originating predominantly from

TYPES OF GERMAN EMIGRANTS

6.6 'Types of German Emigrants' originally appeared in the *Daily Graphic*, 26 November 1881.
Collection of Nicholas J. Evans

Denmark, Finland, Norway, Russia, Sweden and Germany (Figure 6.6), the transmigrants disembarked in Hull, and then proceeded by train to Glasgow, Liverpool, London or Southampton. The latter cities were the real destination, for they were the departure points for steamship services to the New World. Before 1848, the traffic was small and insignificant, with less than a thousand European migrants arriving annually. Whether the European emigrants came from the Baltic, Germany or Scandinavia, the experience of the voyage from mainland Europe to the UK was the same – an ordeal. The journey varied in length according to the weather and the vessel, but it generally took between three and five days. Yet economic and political crises in Europe in 1848, together with the introduction of improved transport facilities, stimulated and facilitated the growth of emigrant passenger services via the UK.

Although the trade was cyclical, and emigration to America collapsed during the American Civil War (1861–65), once peace was restored America again became the distant magnet for the transmigrants on the steamers that arrived every Sunday and Wednesday evening. The Hull-based Wilson Line dominated the Scandinavian business, but it faced constant competition from German, Dutch and Danish transatlantic steamship companies, which all sought to transport migrants directly from the European continent to the USA. Wilson's dominance was not accompanied by improvements in the quality and standard of the service provided for transmigrants, with Hull Board of Health communicating frequently with the company between 1864 and 1884 about the poor and unacceptable standards of accommodation it offered to its transmigrant customers. In the case of SS *Argo*, the board claimed that the migrants, who were supposed to be third-class passengers, were treated more like cattle than humans. In another instance, the board reported that human excrement was running down the sides of ships in which 200 migrants were to be housed for four days until their train for Liverpool was ready. Something had to be done, and ultimately action was taken by Hull's sanitary authority.

Because of the perceived risks to the town's health from the large numbers of European migrants passing through the port, the North Eastern Railway Company built a waiting room near Paragon Railway Station in 1871. This waiting room had facilities for the transmigrants to meet the ticket agents and take shelter from the weather. At no time throughout the age of mass migration did the authorities in Hull provide purpose-built emigrant lodging houses for the migrants. Although twenty emigrant lodging houses were given licences to accommodate or feed transmigrants by the town council in 1877, these differed from common lodging houses only in their description and size – the emigrant lodging houses licensed after 1877 were much larger and able to accommodate between 20 and 80 people at a time (Figure 6.7). Most only stayed in these lodging houses when necessary and most departed from Hull within 24 hours of their arrival. Although the majority of migrants were only in Hull for a short period, the emigrant waiting room at Paragon Railway Station was doubled in size in 1882 due to the numbers of transmigrants passing through the town (Figure 6.8). The extension provided a separate waiting room, and discrete toilet and washing facilities, for women and children. A second emigrant railway platform was constructed in 1885 by the Hull & Barnsley Railway Company as part of its new facilities at Alexandra Dock, with deeper docks to cater for larger steamships. This was the first purpose-built dockside railway platform for emigrants, long enough to enable large numbers of people to board the specialist 'emigrant trains' that conveyed them to Liverpool.

Most transmigrants travelled from Paragon Railway Station to Liverpool via Leeds, Huddersfield and Stalybridge, near Manchester. Sometimes so many migrants arrived at one time that there would

6.7 Harry Lazarus Hotel, Posterngate. Lazarus originally settled in London during the early 1860s. A former tailor, he relocated to Hull in 1864 where he opened a lodging house for immigrants and transmigrants arriving in the port. The premises served two distinct functions. Transmigrants were fed on the first floor in batches of 80 at a time, while immigrants were housed overnight on the top floor. Around 1887 Lazarus relocated to nearby Nile Street when the Scandinavian transmigrant trade was restricted to the Albert Dock area.
© Nicholas J. Evans

6.8 Originally designed and constructed by Norbert Prossor for the North Eastern Railway Company in 1871, the six-windowed emigrant waiting room was extended to its left-hand side in 1882 to accommodate a surge in migration from Eastern Europe, and to compete with facilities being erected on the Hull & Barnsley Railway's Alexandra Dock. The facility ensured a physical divide between immigrants using the main Paragon Station and transmigrants bound for Liverpool, Glasgow, Southampton and London.
© Nicholas J. Evans

be up to 17 carriages being pulled by one steam engine. All the baggage was stored in the rear four carriages, with the passengers filling the carriages towards the front of the train. These trains, which usually left Hull on a Monday morning around 11.00 and arrived in Liverpool three or four hours later, took precedence over all other rail services because of their length. In 1904 the number of transmigrants travelling through the UK via Hull was so great that the Wilson Line leased a separate landing station called Island Wharf (Figure 6.9). This was located just outside Humber Dock and was one of four separate landing stations used to disembark passengers. Although the Allan, Cunard, Dominion and White Star Lines sold tickets throughout rural and urban Scandinavia to would-be migrants travelling to America, it was Wilson ships that brought almost all of these migrants to the UK, thereby generating profits for the family members who owned what was dubbed at the time the 'largest privately owned shipping line in the world'. The scale of this firm, and the agencies it had established across northern Europe, explained the dominant role it played in the migration of thousands of Scandinavian emigrants between 1843 and 1914.

After 1905 the numbers of immigrants travelling via the UK was severely restricted by the Alien Immigration Act. Although this legislation did not initially inhibit the scale of transmigration, by 1914 the level of migration via Hull had declined (Figure 6.10). With the outbreak of the First World War and then the passing of immigration acts in South Africa and America, the era of mass transmigration via the UK, and from Europe in general, ended. Although transmigration on a smaller scale did resume after 1918, it never approached the volume witnessed in the seventy or so years preceding the First World War. During that time, transmigration generated business and income in Hull. It stimulated demand for the building, victualling, coaling and servicing of steamers; it increased dock dues, berthing fees and agency commissions; it created employment for seafarers and stevedores, both British and foreign; and it contributed to the extraordinary hold that Thomas Wilson Sons & Co. was able to exert over Hull's maritime interests, a role that permeated the city through the investments, philanthropy and civic service of the Wilson family members. Transmigration also temporarily expanded the population of the port area of the city by up to 50 per cent in waves that strained

6.9 The adjacent entrances to two of the city's most important docks – Humber Dock (on the right) and Albert Dock (towards the rear of the image) – provided constant interest for visitors and residents alike. In the foreground is Island Wharf, often used to disembark transmigrants by the North Eastern Railway during the Edwardian period. It explains the presence of the Wilson Line passenger vessel in the foreground. The photograph dates from around 1910.
Collection of Nicholas J. Evans

6.10 Although most immigrants and transmigrants landed at docks situated west of the River Hull, from the 1890s a growing number of vessels arriving from the Baltic ports of Hango, Abo, Riga and Libau discharged their passengers at Victoria Dock to the east of the river. The vessels of the Finnish National Steamship Company were distinctive because of their white hulls. The *Arcturus* (shown here *c*. 1905) carried tens of thousands of Finns to Hull between 1892 and 1914. Upon arrival they were assisted by John Good and Sons, who also served as Honorary Finnish consuls.
Collection of Nicholas J. Evans

the city's provision. In response, foreign-based charities, including those funded by the German, Danish and Jewish communities, assisted those staying temporarily in Hull, whether as passengers or crew. Indeed, reports published between 1897 and 1899 show that the Hull Hebrew Board of Guardians paid more than any trans-Pennine Jewish community to keep the migrants moving – either back to Europe or onwards to America. Together, these transients and support agencies collectively expanded the racial and cultural diversity of the city. By 1924, when transmigration came to an end with the closure of US borders to immigrants under the Quota Acts, Hull had become a major player in the flow of people, cultures and money along the commercial highways and seaways that connected the Old World with the new lands of opportunity across the oceans (Figure 6.11).

6.11 Hull was one of a handful of ports to take part in the sesquicentennial anniversary of the gathering of Latter-Day Saints or Mormon converts to Utah between 1851 and 1894. Most of these ports had historic ties to Mormon emigration, and so were given a statue marking this connection when eight tall ships recreated the emigrant journey in 2001. The majority of European converts to the Mormon Church emigrated through Hull or Grimsby and bolstered the fortunes of local shipping companies. From 1868, the Wilson Line dominated the business. The Sea Trek statue was sculpted by Mark DeGraffenried of Utah and based on his ancestors who had emigrated to the US state 150 years earlier. It looks west to Liverpool and Utah, the latter being the spiritual centre of Mormons around the world.
© Nicholas J. Evans

Charles Henry Wilson, 1st Baron Nunburnholme

'My family has created a business unique in the world's history' was how Charles Henry Wilson described the shipping firm of Thomas Wilson Sons & Co. (TWSC), which he and his younger brother, Arthur, managed from 1869 to 1907. While perhaps somewhat exaggerated, Charles's assertion is nevertheless correct in its implication that this was no ordinary business. TWSC truly was a large-scale enterprise. With a fleet of over 100 steamships operating over 25 lines to North America, the Far East, the Mediterranean, north-west Europe and Scandinavia, TWSC competed and negotiated with Norddeutscher Lloyd, DFDS, Cunard and other significant players in the global shipping industry of the early twentieth century. Yet TWSC remained a quintessentially family firm in an age when mergers, takeovers and amalgamations characterised big shipping business; indeed, TWSC was the 'largest privately-owned shipping firm in the world' according to *The Times* in 1912. The company, moreover, was securely anchored in Hull, where it dominated shipping, shipbuilding, engineering and port activity to such an extent that the adage 'Hull is Wilsons, Wilsons are Hull' reflected a monopolistic reality that was not apparent in any other major European port.

TWSC had its origins in a partnership formed by Charles's father, Thomas Wilson, in the 1820s with the object of importing Swedish iron. By the early 1840s Thomas controlled the enterprise, which he ran in collaboration with David Wilson, his eldest son. Charles, who had been born in 1833 and educated at Kingston College, Hull, joined the family business in the mid-1850s, together with Arthur, the youngest of the 16 Wilson children. In 1861 Charles and Arthur formally entered into a partnership with their father, who

Edward Hughes, *Charles Henry Wilson, 1st Baron Nunburnholme* (c. 1880)

henceforth played a 'sleeping' role, as did David Wilson. In these mid-century years, iron-hulled, steam-powered vessels were increasingly deployed by British shipowners, especially in ports like Hull, which had major interests in the short-sea and coastal trades. The Wilson family firm was one of the organisations that invested early and substantially in steamers, thereby expanding its interests in the north European and Scandinavian trades.

When Thomas died in 1869, the Wilson Line, with Charles and Arthur now fully at the helm, rapidly expanded the scale and scope of its activities, with new lines established with the Black Sea, Adriatic, India and New York. The Wilson Line played a prominent role in the movement of European people to North America, cornering and growing the transmigrant trade, which saw more than 2 million people cross the North Sea from eastern Baltic ports such as Libau and Riga to Hull between the 1840s and 1914. Alighting at Hull, the migrants travelled by train to Liverpool, where they boarded transatlantic liners bound for New York.

The phenomenal rise of their company brought great wealth, influence and honours to Charles and his family. He married Florence Jane Helen Wellesley, acquired a large country estate at Warter Priory, near Pocklington, and properties in Grosvenor Square (London), Nice and Scotland. Charles was Liberal MP for Hull from 1874 to 1906, when he was created Baron Nunburnholme. He died in the following year, and when Arthur died in 1909, their dependants and descendants continued to own the company, with Oswald Sanderson serving as managing director from 1906. In 1916 the Wilsons sold their family firm for £4.3 million to the Hull-born tycoon, Sir John Reeves Ellerman, who called his new acquisition, Ellerman's Wilson Line, a name that remained prominent in British shipping until the 1970s.

Robb Robinson

While both the city and the port of Hull grew steadily during the long nineteenth century, the outbreak of the First World War stalled its commercial and urban expansion. Although the war provided an important economic stimulus and full employment for men and, increasingly, women, the end of mass migration had begun. The Aliens Act of 1905 was augmented by wartime restrictions on aliens under the Defence of the Realm Act of 1914. When the war ended in 1918, two new measures – the 1919 Aliens Restriction (Amendment) Act and the 1920 Aliens Order – further limited immigration.[38] From then on the scale and character of migration – whether by immigrants, transmigrants, sojourners or increasingly refugees – was conditioned by legislation. Hull became an increasingly inward-looking and isolated space and outsiders already resident in the town assimilated and integrated into the host society. Supported by so-called 'paper walls' (legislation prohibiting aliens from living or working in the UK after 1919), the city's alien population stabilised and at times decreased. Although many visitors continued to use the port, they transited without engaging with the city at all. There was now a discernible disconnect between the port and the city – whether real or imagined. Those who did come – black seafarers, refugees from Nazism, displaced persons from the Second World War, the Hong Kong Chinese, and Kurdish asylum seekers resettled during the Gulf War – were all seen as outsiders. Although these arrivals were notionally welcomed by the city and its communities, the earlier waves of internal migrants from Scotland, Wales and Ireland, as well as European immigrants and transmigrants, were all forgotten, and amnesia quickly set in about the central role that migration had played in the city's life. Hull remained, to all intents and purposes, a monocultural city.

With the outbreak of the First World War, Hull's position as one of the world's great migrant entrepôts came to an abrupt end. The infrastructure, both in the UK and on the European continent, that had previously aided transcontinental migration was quickly commandeered to support the military effort. British crews of migrant vessels intent on sailing to Hull, with both transmigrants and immigrants aboard, were interned following the declaration of war. They were then imprisoned for the duration of the conflict at Ruhleben in Germany, a transit point through which many European emigrants bound for Hull had once passed.[39] Closer to home, the crews of foreign vessels berthed in Hull's docks were also interned, the majority on the Isle of Wight. Meanwhile, the British-registered SS *Borodino*, belonging to the Wilson Line, was used as a makeshift internment camp for adult male Germans between the ages of 17 and 42.[40] Even those who had been resident in Hull for many years now found themselves rounded up, ostracised and unable to financially support their wives and children. The maltreatment of aliens intensified as the war progressed, as the Defence of the Realm Act impeded migration, while Hull was identified as a possible landing place for the anticipated German invasion of Britain. Anti-German prejudice surfaced on a number of occasions and was targeted at people who had served the city economically and philanthropically for several generations. Blatant and more subtle prejudice compelled Germans not only to naturalise, but also assimilate their personal and commercial identities. The German Church on Nile Street was quickly closed for the duration of the war and all things German were cleared from public view. Wartime propaganda denigrated 'the Hun', and thus everything German was susceptible to attack – especially men of military age.

After an outburst of anti-German activity on the day war was declared, things in Hull appeared peaceful. Even the bombardment of Scarborough, West Hartlepool and Whitby in December 1914 failed to generate any response from the population of Hull. Yet in spring 1915, after first trawlers were torpedoed and then the *Lusitania* was sunk, small-scale attacks – window smashing, verbal assaults and boycotting – on German-owned businesses were seen as a form of revenge. Order was quickly restored, but in June 1915 the destructive bombardment of numerous parts of the city by Zeppelins prompted one of the largest acts of anti-German agitation in British history. Crowds and individuals targeted not only foreign-born enemy aliens but also innocents mistaken for foreigners, including Hannah Feldman, the Liverpool-born former Lady Mayoress of Hull.[41] The attacks were not just reprisals for the civilian air attacks, but attempts to loot food and valuables from businesses in the city centre, Princes Avenue, Hessle Road and Holderness Road. The Hohenrein family (Figure 6.12), who owned four properties and had shown unstinting loyalty to Hull for over sixty years, were compelled to close their business after a series of violent and very personal attacks. Sympathy for the family was expressed by the constabulary and former employees, yet anti-immigrant sentiment had manifested itself as never before in Hull. The city lost the German cultural influences that had prevailed in city centre and suburban landscapes for some time. Even patriotic families, such as Max Schultz's, who had seen their patriarchs interned in pre-war Germany as punishment for allegedly spying for the British, found that they had to assimilate and use the name of the British branch of their family – Hilton – even after the war.

6.12 Charles Henry Hohenrein, a successful British-born pork butcher, photographed here with his family *c.* 1910, suffered extensively from prejudice during the First World War. Although he offered his business vehicles for the war effort, changed his name to 'Ross' on the first anniversary of the war, and joined the East Yorkshire Militia, he was still the victim of at least three anti-German attacks in the city during the conflict.
Collection of Nicholas J. Evans

6.13 A black sailor observing the damage inflicted upon Hull trawlers during the so-called North Sea incident of 1904. On the night of 21 October 1904, the Russian Baltic fleet mistook a trawling fleet from Hull for the Imperial Japanese Navy and fired on them. Three British trawlermen died and a number of seamen were injured.
Courtesy of Hull History Centre

By the end of the war, the German community had been reduced to one-quarter of its pre-war size, just 254.

During the First World War, merchant shipping operations continued on a reduced scale, and the complement of seafarers who had not been called up into the Royal Naval Reserve was supplemented by non-white seamen, known as lascars. Deployed especially on long-haul routes to Asia and Africa, lascars valiantly staffed vulnerable steamers ploughing through bomb-ridden waterways for lower rates of pay than their white counterparts. At the end of the conflict, most were dismissed when white seafarers returned from military service. For the non-white seafarers based in Hull, further misery was to follow, as waves of xenophobia swept through the city between 1919 and 1921. Despite being British subjects, in Hull, as in Liverpool, Glasgow and other port-cities, blatant prejudice was directed towards the non-white seafarers. As Jacqueline Jenkinson has observed, this was not just related to the war, for there was 'evidence of a persistent anti-Black sentiment in British society which, at times, in specific circumstances, spilled over into violence'.[42] In Hull during mid-June 1920, Osborne Street, Pease Street and Lower Union Street all became areas where violence towards black seafarers occurred. Although Hull had tried forcibly to repatriate mariners to Africa or the Caribbean where the authorities felt they belonged, a colour bar on vessels bound for those destinations meant that these seafarers could not work their passages home. In one instance, over 200 people were seen attacking a 'negro child', while pubs banned non-whites, and the wives and children of interracial unions were harrassed. In total, accounts indicate that Hull's non-white population was between 60 and 100 at this time (Figure 6.13).

During the interwar era Hull became more intolerant of ethnic and religious minorities. Despite its long, proud record of accepting waves of migrants and refugees, the economic challenges of the interwar period made life for ethnic minorities challenging. That racism emerged as the economic well-being of the port-city diminished suggests that there was much concern within the community about the precarious future of the 'Third Port of England'. In response, with the election of Hitler to power in March 1933, protests against prejudice were held across the city. Yet such liberal sentiment did not prevent the surge of intolerance that broke out in the mid-1930s. One of the largest crowds in British history gathered in 1936 at the city's Corporation Field to hear Sir Oswald Mosley, head of the British Union of Fascists, deliver a racist speech just a stone's throw from one of Hull's Jewish synagogues in Park Street. The assembled thousands included fascists and anti-fascists. After shots were fired at Mosley he was forced to flee, yet he returned in the following year to speak again. Hull was now divided between those who sympathised with Hitler and those fighting prejudice in all its forms. Despite the pockets of intolerance, the city once more became a refuge for people escaping religious and political persecution in Europe. Children fleeing Nazism, or some of the 10,000 Kindertransports arriving via Harwich, settled in the city, alongside leading academics who came on work visas as refugees. Some 63 children found safety and toleration in Hull after their flight from Nazism in 1939.[43] By then, support for fascism had all but ended as the Second World War brought carnage to the city.

The end of the war witnessed the arrival of so-called 'displaced persons' from Latvia, Lithuania, Poland, Estonia and Ukraine. While the fabled arrival of migrant workers from the Caribbean on the MV *Empire Windrush* changed the demographic profile of Britain from 1948, for Hull and northern England it was the landing of the SS *Empire Halberd* on 23 April 1947 that paved the way for the entry of hundreds of thousands of migrants from Eastern Europe.[44] Helping to stem labour shortages, they came under the 'Westward Ho' scheme, which was designed to help rebuild

6.14 One of many temporary camps used to house people left homeless as a result of bombing during the Second World War, Priory Road Camp was also used to accommodate eastern and central Europeans arriving in Hull from 1947. Many of these 'displaced persons' stayed in Hull for a short time before settling in the west Yorkshire mill towns of Huddersfield, Bradford and Dewsbury, with those who remained reinforcing the Polish community that had established itself in Hull from the 1830s. This bus sign from an East Riding Motor Services vehicle was complemented by multilingual bus signs for the routes connecting the city centre and the docks.
© Nicholas J. Evans

war-torn towns and cities, as well as supply workers to contribute to the revitalisation of agricultural production.[45] Hull once more provided a temporary residence for many of these people. A temporary National Hostel Corporation Camp, located on Priory Road, served as a transit camp for the National Assistance Board, which then dispersed refugees to hostels across Britain (Figure 6.14). Most had been forced labourers in Russian 'gulags', but had been freed when Russia changed sides to support the British–US coalition in 1941. During the war, most of these former prisoners ended up in East African countries under British rule. After hostilities ceased, they returned to Europe via Hull, where they received a friendly welcome. Many of the 1,018 Polish refugees who disembarked at King George Dock from the SS *Dundalk Bay* on 2 September 1950 had come from Mombasa in Kenya. The Priory Road camp, like others situated in Hessle and Anlaby in the rural belt surrounding Hull, housed the refugees for a night or two, before they were moved to other camps, after which many settled in Huddersfield, Dewsbury and Bradford. Large numbers of transients were handled; for example, the camp on Wymersley Road housed over 16,000 'displaced persons' between April and August 1947 alone.[46] Some married into local families and were absorbed into Hull's population, but in general these were 'forgotten migrants', despite many retaining their Eastern European surnames.

Although the short-term impact of the 'displaced persons' was considerable, for over five decades the largest ethnic community in Hull was the Chinese, particularly those from Hong Kong. Although many British towns and cities were demographically altered by post-1945 decolonisation, Hull remained a city that the so-called 'Windrush generation' largely missed, as only a few non-white settlers arrived. A sizeable Chinese community did emerge, however. It was concentrated in the north-west of the city, near the university, and along the Hessle and Holderness roads, where Chinese laundries were rapidly eclipsed by Chinese food takeaways and restaurants. The signage of these places was multilingual, with food being offered in a form familiar to local tastes. Like the Hong Kong diaspora in general, the community grew slowly. All were members of the British Commonwealth, and therefore UK passport holders, until changes in sovereignty occurred in 1989.

The arrival of the Hong Kong Chinese was nothing new. Aside from seafarers noted in the censuses of 1881, 1891, 1901 and 1911 as being born in China, the earliest resident Chinese population dated from 1910. As a journalist for the *Hull Daily Mail* observed:

> When in Leeds recently I noticed a Chinese laundry, and said to myself that it would not be long before there was one in Hull. Now the expected had come to pass, and a yellow man started a business recently in one of the best parts of the city. Thus do we get discovered?[47]

A few months later, the newspaper reported a 'Chinese invasion' of the city, portraying the community in a negative way, in keeping with prejudices towards the Chinese across the UK at that time (Figure 6.15). The earliest Chinese laundry opened on Hessle Road in 1910, shortly followed by Gong Wing Sing's Chinese laundry, based on Spring Bank.[48] Though Sing married an English woman, he was later prosecuted for failing to comply with the 1914 Aliens Restriction Act in that neither he nor his five Chinese workers could speak a word of English.[49]

The older Chinese settlers did not linguistically assimilate because their children, born in the UK, assimilated for them. Their bilingual family life served as a bridge between home and Hull.[50] When the population did mature enough to need specialist care charities, the Hong Lok Senior Association catered for the needs of the elderly. Just a stone's throw from the first Chinese laundry of ninety years earlier, the purpose-built community hall prominently displayed Chinese culture in the form of a three-masted Chinese junk standing four metres high (Figure 6.16). It also proclaimed, in Mandarin, 'Hung Lok Happy Association', on what remained one of Hull's busiest thoroughfares. Alongside the communal space, a further nine single-storey homes for the elderly, and ten double-storey family properties, were built, each with a 'good luck' symbol above every window. Between 1911 and 2011, the decennial census recorded the increasing size of the Chinese population in Hull. And yet its statistical significance was neither seen as overwhelming nor threatening. The lack of prejudice towards the Chinese community was perhaps explained by the spatial dispersal of the 'outsiders' across the city. The sobriety of the community – who only took Monday or Tuesday evenings off work – meant that they were never accused of being an economic burden. Instead, the city embraced once more the cultural contributions made by migrants.

Whether selling English or Chinese food, Chinese takeaways and restaurants became hugely popular – especially for new residents to the city, such as Philip Larkin, who liked to dine at Hull's first Chinese restaurant, the Hoi Sun, which opened in 1959 on Jameson Street, and was owned by the Yun family (Figure 6.17).[51] Fellow diners included Larkin's partner, Jean, who later recalled that the 'regular haunt … used to have lanterns in the window and lots of Chinoiserie'.[52] It was not only the educated elite who dined there, for it offered working-class couples a rare chance to eat out in the post-war city.[53]

For most of the twentieth and early twenty-first centuries, Hull's growing diversity was never statistically significant and this set the city aside from most other cities of a similar size. In the decades following the Second World War, the size of Hull's Chinese population caught up with those of other leading maritime centres such as Liverpool, Cardiff and London. However, there was no real expansion in other ethnic groups, despite the growing number of foreign medical professionals who moved to Hull to work in the National Health Service, and the increase in the population of international staff and students at the city's universities. Although

ILLUSTRATED HULL.

(BY ONE OF OUR SPECIAL ARTISTS.)

CHINESE INVASION OF HULL.

Two or three Chinese Laundries have recently been opened in Hull, and are getting custom.

6.15 'The Chinese Invasion of Hull', *Hull Times*, 2 August 1910.
Courtesy of Hull History Centre

6.16 The Hung Lok Cultural Association Building, Beverley Road. Erected in 2001, this building was the brainchild of Luana Smith, who received on MBE for her work with the Chinese community in Hull. As well as the impressive four-metre high Chinese junk, the Cantonese on the side of the building, 隶樂苑, translates as the Hung Lok Happy Association.
© Nicholas J. Evans

decolonisation and globalisation left no major visible imprint on the city's ethnic make-up, the Iraq War in the 1990s, and the enlargement of the European Union in 2004, both had a strong bearing on the composition of Hull's population.

The Iraqi conflict and subsequently the War on Terror led to an increase in migration. In the 1980s the beginning of a permanent Muslim community was evident in the city. Although Hull's first mosque had opened in 1945, it closed with the decline in the number of Yemeni seafarers visiting the port after the Second World War (Figure 6.18). In the mid-1980s a group of Muslims formed the Hull Mosque and Islamic Centre, which opened on Berkeley Street in 1984, while a second, largely Bangladeshi community formed the Jame Masjid and Madrasah Darul Marif Al Islamia at Pearson Park in 1987.[54] While the former sought to provide a gathering place for Muslim worship, the latter, comprising just a small number of families, sought to provide spiritual education for the children of Bangladeshi migrants in their mother tongue. Both situated their operations in close proximity to the growing number of international shops and curry houses along Princes Avenue and Spring Bank where many community members worked. In the aftermath of the Second Gulf War, and in particular the War on Terror, they were joined by over 1,000 young, unmarried Iraqi Kurdish males who were seeking asylum in the UK.[55] Unlike earlier refugee flows which had been directed by transport links, the government directed this refugee flow from Kent, where the Kurds had originally been sent upon claiming asylum, to northern cities. In Hull, they settled in private housing in the greater Pearson Park area and their concentrated settlement, in areas ill equipped for so many refugees, fuelled community tensions and was labelled a 'disaster' by scholar Gary Craig.[56] Spring Bank (or 'Spring Bankistan', as it was known locally) quickly became a multicultural corridor connecting the city centre and the university, as Hull finally became home to a sizeable and permanent multi-ethnic population; but this was not without negativity, as riots between rival groups of refugees in 2001 and accusations of institutional racism in the police increased socio-political tensions in the city.

The multiculturalism visible along Spring Bank, Princes Avenue and Newland Avenue is recent testimony to Hull's transformation into a global city. This has intensified since 2004, as changes to regulations within the European Union have enabled workers to move freely across borders and work in other member states. With countries such as Latvia, Lithuania and Poland joining the EU, Hull is one of many UK towns and cities that have become home to Eastern European workers and their families, so much so that between 2001 and 2011 the census recorded a 200 per cent rise in the number of so-called 'Accession 8' migrants. The 'ethnic' corridors along some of the city's main arterial routes – Beverley Road, Hessle Road and Anlaby Road – reflect this significant change in the composition and socio-cultural configuration of the city. The new arrivals quickly opened their own shops, restaurants and community organisations, yet did not need to establish their own religious infrastructure, as many simply bolstered the congregations of local Catholic churches, which had once catered for the spiritual needs of Irish famine workers. Once more, negativity has surrounded the newly arrived, most obviously in the campaign and result of the EU membership referendum of 23 June 2016. This is partly because of the additional pressures migrants have placed on social, educational and health services and partly a result of the competition they have introduced into local labour markets. But negativity has also arisen because Hull seemingly had no tradition of migration from Eastern Europe. Yet in fact, Poles, Lithuanians and Latvians had occupied different parts of Hull over the previous two centuries, if not longer. What such negative episodes in the changing ethnic make-up of the city reveal is that the period from 1918 to the early twenty-first century created a chasm in which linguistic skills, communal and philanthropic institutions, and cultural bodies able to adapt and care for outsiders had all disappeared. Hull's remoteness made it a city that neither Windrush nor multiculturalism, at least on the face of it, had reached.

MOHAMMEDANS IN HULL are seen at yesterday's festivities, their equivalent of our Christmas Day. This "Mail" photograph taken at the Hull Mosque of the Islamia Allaouia Religious Society, shows the priest-in-charge, Abdul Hassen, reading the scriptures to others of his faith.

Mary Charlotte Murdoch

Dr Mary Murdoch, Hull's first female GP, lived at 102 Beverley Road, Hull. She was internationally known as a specialist in children's health and an activist for women's rights. Born in 1864, Murdoch studied medicine at London School of Medicine for Women. After working at Tottenham Fever Hospital, she moved to Hull as senior physician at Victoria Hospital for Children, Park Street. She had a private practice, with consultations extending to Grimsby. In Hull, she founded a school for mothers, a crèche, the Girls' Patriotic Club and a lodging house for women in Lister Street. She was involved in public education as well as the formal training of others, notably one of the most famous British female doctors, Dr Louisa Martindale, who worked in Murdoch's Hull practice until 1906.

Murdoch was innovative in her understanding of the connections between health and environment, and was an advocate of improvements in housing as well as childcare. The significant and long-lasting contributions she made to Hull concerned not only the health and welfare of its citizens, but also their education and civil rights. In her public speaking and campaigning, she looked beyond her immediate duties as a doctor and considered the social circumstances of her patients. She raised awareness about the significance of hygiene and good practices in childcare for the improvement of the health and well-being of the community as a whole. This laudable educational strategy was combined with Murdoch's fearless commitment to political and philanthropic organisations to ensure that these ideas were implemented.

1911 Census schedule for the household of Mary Charlotte Murdoch, 'Physician & Surgeon', 102 Beverley Road, Hull

Murdoch's understanding of the role of women in working-class households was greatly enriched by her experiences in Hull. She encouraged men to become more aware of the needs of their children and promoted men's direct involvement in childcare. According to Louisa Martindale, Murdoch would stand on an upturned box in order to speak to crowds at Hull docks, exhorting the men to 'hold their babies for two hours every Sunday, saying it was as good for the babies. Perhaps, too, she was thinking of obtaining a little relief for the tired mothers.' Murdoch's public discussions of poor housing conditions in Hull were controversial. She provoked a 'storm of abuse' in 1911 by outlining the need for housing reform supported by quotations from a Fabian Society pamphlet on 'How the People of Hull are Housed'. After scandalous denials by the local press, the corporation and landlords, the statistical evidence and Murdoch's persuasive arguments won.

The connectedness of these issues was of great concern to Murdoch and she was highly motivated to bring about wider social change. She was founder and president of the first Hull branch of the National Union of Women's Suffrage Societies and founded the local branch of the National Union of Women Workers. Her influence extended to lobbying in national political campaigns. She was invited to speak at the International Suffrage Alliance (London) and was an elected delegate to the International Council of Women (Toronto, The Hague and Rome).

Driving was a great passion for Murdoch, but rarely a relaxing experience for her passengers. She was apparently the first woman in Hull to own a car and she drove it at speed. The car appeared at a suitably slow pace at her funeral at All Saint's church in 1916, witnessed by thousands of people who lined the streets. As Dr Martindale recalled, 'She had won the heart of an entire city.'

Katharine Cockin

Cockin, Katharine, 'Mary Murdoch', *Oxford Dictionary of National Biography* (2004)
Malleson, Hope, *A Woman Doctor: Mary Murdoch of Hull* (London: Sidgwick & Jackson, 1919)
Martindale, Louisa, *A Woman Surgeon* (1951)

A city of diversity

Cultural absorption has been one of the defining characteristics of Hull since its genesis. Indeed, it is impossible to differentiate between Hull and the constantly changing mosaic that makes up its population. Although the once sizeable Welsh, Scottish, Irish, Italian, Jewish, German and Scandinavian communities are now dwindling, other newer migrant communities have replaced them (Figure 6.19). Hull's largest ethnic population is once more Polish – as it had been in the early, mid and late Victorian eras, and again in the immediate aftermath of the Second World War.[57] In turn, the 'outsiders' have helped maintain some of Hull's vernacular architecture because they have enhanced congregations in the city's many religious buildings. In this sense, it might be argued that the modern migrant brings something alien to the city – that is, religious belief – in an era of secularisation. Their settlement near the city centre, which has largely been vacated by long-established residents now intent on living in the suburbs or beyond, has also helped ensure that the Spring Bank and Beverley Road areas retain some economic vibrancy as enterprising migrants open new commercial outlets. Although some local people have undoubtedly resented Hull's emergence as a global city, the ebb and flow of communities, transients and travellers has sustained Hull's population and prevented further post-war economic deprivation. As members of the community often tell outsiders: 'it's never dull in Hull!'

6.19 Paid for by the Mahatma Gandhi Memorial Committee, this bust was unveiled by the film producer David Puttnam in 2004. It is a reminder of the size and growing affluence of the Hindu community in Hull. Its location reinforces how Gandhi started campaigning for human rights in British South Africa before returning to his native India. The work was sculpted by Jaiprakash Shirgaoankar, who is based in Mumbai.
© Nicholas J. Evans

Notes

1 Some of the research for this essay was funded through the EU's Comenius Regio Programme, 2009–11 and a Research Councils of the UK Fellowship held by the author between 2008 and 2011. I would like to thank Professor David Starkey, Susan Capes and Samuel North for advice on earlier drafts of this essay. Numerous members of Hull's communities have inspired or assisted with this research. In particular I would like to thank David Lewis and Helen Good for permission to use information from their researches here. Linda Lai and her family have also been very generous in sharing information about the Hong Kong community.

2 According to the 2011 UK Census the population of Kingston upon Hull had grown to 256,406. The non-UK born population represented 8.9 per cent of the population in 2011 – with non-EU migrants representing 4 per cent of the population. Office of National Statistics report, 2011, in *The Guardian*, http://www.theguardian.com/news/datablog/2011/may/26/foreign-born-uk-population#data (accessed 1 April 2016).

3 The medieval genesis of immigration to the town can now be easily explored online thanks to the University of York's 'England's Immigrants 1330–1550', www.englandsimmigrants.com (accessed 1 June 2016).

4 Jenny Kermode, *Medieval Merchants: York, Beverley and Hull in the Later Medieval Ages* (Cambridge: Cambridge University Press, 1999) provides a detailed exploration of the foreign merchants operating in the region.

5 Research by Helen Good found that he was described as 'his neager an aliant by the pole' in the Aliens Lists held at the National Archives in London (TNA, E 179/204/349).

6 David Neave and Susan Neave, *Hull: City Guide, The Buildings of England*, Pevsner Architectural Guides (New Haven, CT: Yale University Press, 2010).

7 David Neave, *The Dutch Connection: The Anglo-Dutch Heritage of Hull and Humberside* (Hull: Humberside Leisure Services, 1988).

8 Olaudah Equiano, *The Interesting Narrative of the Life of Olaudah Equiano* (London: Stationer's Hall, 7th edn, 1793), p. xiv.

9 See, for example, Bernard Hailstone, *Signing On in a Hull Merchant Marine Office c.1939–1945* and John Ward (style of), *Shipping Hull Garrison*, in Hazel Buchan-Cameron (ed.), *Oil Paintings in Public Ownership in East Riding of Yorkshire* (London: The Public Catalogue Foundation, 2010), pp. 108, 290.

10 The East Yorkshire Family History Society's series of monumental inscriptions has been an invaluable source of information. I am grateful to my former history students at the University of Hull for helping me find foreign-born memorials within the transcriptions produced by the society that are housed in the University of Hull Brynmor Jones Library.

11 Hull History Centre, BRE/7/1, 'Arrival Certificates and Declarations'.

12 The exception being Russian ports that required identity papers for those arriving or leaving every port in the realm.

13 The grave of John Crankien remains at the rear of the Kirk Ella churchyard.

14 K. J. Allison, *Hull Gent seeks country residence, 1750–1850* (Beverley: East Yorkshire Local History Society, 1981). Crankien's home, now called Wolfreton House, is still visible on the Beverley Road linking Anlaby and Willerby.

15 Hull Jewish Community, *250 Years of Jewish Life in Hull: 1766–2016* (Hull: Hull Jewish Community, 2016), p. 3.

16 Walking tour of Hull's Jewish cemeteries as part of the European Days of Jewish Culture, 2008. Lewis's transcriptions were published in East Yorkshire Family History Society, *Ella Street & Hessle Road Jewish Cemeteries, Hull: Monumental Inscriptions* (Beverley: East Yorkshire Family History Society, 2010).

17 Israel Finestein, 'The Jews in Hull, Between 1766 and 1880', *Jewish Historical Studies*, 35 (1996), pp. 33–91.

18 Robert Barnard, *The Minerva Hotel* (Hull: Local History Unit, 1999), p. 7.

19 Barnard, *The Minerva Hotel*, p. 2.

20 Michael Adrian Smale, 'Patterns and Processes of Migration to the Port of Hull in the Second Half of the Nineteenth Century: An Examination of the Movement and Settlement of Migrants from the Rural Hinterland and Continental Europe', unpublished PhD dissertation, University of Hull, 2006.

21 Russia's occupation of Poland had caused the arrival of a smaller number of Poles during the early 1830s. See Alan Deighton, *"A Shocking Case of Starvation in Hull" – A Short Memoir of the Life of "Count" Adolph de Werdinsky* (Beverley: Highgate Publications, 2014).

22 D. G. Woodhouse, *Anti-German Sentiment in Kingston upon Hull: The German Community and the First World War* (Hull: Kingston upon Hull Record Office, 1990), p. 15.

23 Barbara Robinson, *The Hull German Lutheran Church, 1848–1998* (Beverley: Highgate Press, 2000).

24 Robinson, *The Hull German Lutheran Church*, p. 87.

25 Robinson, *The Hull German Lutheran Church*, p. 87.

26 See in particular Norman Staveley, *Two Centuries of Music in Hull* (Cherry Burton: Hutton Press, 1999).

27 William Rubinstein, *Men of Property: The Very Wealthy in Britain since the Industrial Revolution* (London: Social Affairs Unit, 2nd edn, 2006), p. 61.

28 For examples of the myths surrounding Jewish immigration, see Elliott Oppel, *The History of Hull's Orthodox Synagogues: And the People Connected with Them* (Beverley: Highgate Publications, 2000); Michael E. Ulyatt, *Be Still and Know Thyself More: The Flight of Eastern European Jews to Hull and Beyond* (Hull: Michael Ulyatt Enterprises, 2012); and David Goodman, *Aspects of Hull: Discovering Local History* (Barnsley: Wharncliffe Books, 1999).

29 Research by Michael Smale presented to the Hull College 'Know Your Place' module field trip around migrant Hull, 2002.

30 Legal businesses with Jewish origins included Graham and Rosen, Max Gold, Gosschalks and Myer Wolff.

31 This was reiterated at events marking the 250th anniversary of the Hull Jewish Community at the Hull History Centre and the Hull Hebrew Congregation.

32 For further information on the role of foreign agents in the transmigration business, see Nicholas J. Evans, 'The Role of Foreign-born Agents in the Development of Mass Migrant Travel through Britain, 1851–1924', in Torsten Feys, Lewis R. Fischer, Stephone Host and Stephan Vanfraechem (eds), *The Impact of the Maritime and Migration Networks on Transatlantic Labour Migration during the 18th-20th Centuries* (St John's, Newfoundland: International Maritime Economic History Association, 2007), pp. 49–61.

33 Ann Bennett, *Shops, Shambles and the Street Market: Retailing in Georgian Hull, 1770 to 1810* (Wetherby: Oblong, 2005)

34 Oliver Baxter, 'Reception, Experiences and Departures of Belgian Refugees on the Yorkshire Coast, 1914–1918', *East Yorkshire Historian*, XVI (2015), pp. 61–88.

35 The exception were brief references in the works by local historians Edward Gillet and Kenneth MacMahon, *A History of Hull* (Hull: Hull University Press, 2nd edn, 1989), pp. 340, 375; John Markham, *The Book of Hull: The Evolution of a Great Northern City* (Buckingham: Barracuda, 1989), p. 100; and George Patrick, A *Plaque on You Sir* (Hull: George Patrick, 1981), pp. 71, 81–82, 95.

36 This topic has been discussed extensively in Nicholas J. Evans, 'Aliens en Route: European Transmigration through Britain, 1836–1914', unpublished PhD thesis, University of Hull, 2006.

37 For a breakdown of the statistics, see Nicholas J. Evans, 'Indirect Passage from Europe', *Journal for Maritime Research*, 3.1 (2001), pp. 75–84.

38 For the history of immigration restrictions in modern Britain, see Tony Kushner and Katherine Knox, *Refugees in an Age of Genocide: Global, National and Local Perspectives during the Twentieth Century* (London: Frank Cass, 1999).

39 Tobias Brinkmann, 'Traveling with Ballin: The Impact of American Immigration Policies on Jewish Transmigration within Central Europe, 1880–1914', *International Review of Social History*, 53 (2008), pp. 459–84.

40 Arthur Credland, *The Hull Zeppelin Raids, 1915–1918* (Croydon: Fonthill Media, 2014), p. 43.

41 According to reports from the Hull Police Court retold in the *Hull Daily Mail*, it was believed the 'riot' outside Feldman's home arose from an incident on Holderness Road earlier that day when her sister-in-law had been attacked by rioters and needed to be escorted to Linnaeus Street by the army. *Hull Daily Mail*, 21 June 1915, p. 6.

42 Jacqueline Jenkinson, 'The Black Community of Salford and Hull, 1919–1921', *Immigrants and Minorities*, 7.2 (1988), p. 166.

43 Ian Vellins, 'Kindertransport Children. Memory, Narration, Celebration and Commemoration: Reconstructing the Past', unpublished MA dissertation, University of Leeds, 2014.

44 *Hull Daily Mail*, 23 April 1947, p. 1, 'Farmers, Engineers in Hull Arrivals'.

45 Emily Gilbert, *Changing Identities: Latvians, Lithuanians and Estonians in Great Britain* (CreateSpace Independent Publishing Platform, 2013), p. 168.

46 *Hull Daily Mail*, 5 August 1947, p. 1, 'Hull to Close Centre for Displaced Persons'.

47 *Hull Daily Mail*, 7 June 1910, p. 2.

48 *Hull Daily Mail*, 11 July 1910, p. 1.

49 *Hull Daily Mail*, 29 August 1914, p. 1, 'Failing to Register'.

50 I. S. Watt, D. Howel and L. Lo, 'The Health Care Experience and Health Behaviour of the Chinese: A Survey Based in Hull', *Journal of Public Health*, 15.2 (1993), pp. 129–36.

51 I'm grateful to Linda Lai and her father, C. H. Chan, for this information. Lai's maternal grandparents ran the business, which employed her father after he married the owner's daughter in Harrogate in 1943. Such mobility, and the change of the family business from a Chinese laundry in Harrogate to a Chinese restaurant in Hull, reveals a lot about the long-term nature of Hong Kong Chinese settlement in the region. This restaurant habit of Larkin was also recalled on the letters page of the *London Review of Books*, 15.10, 27 May 1993, letter from Neville Smith, London W14.

52 *The Yorkshire Post*, 18 November 2002, 'At Last, Poetic Justice for Hull'.

53 Hull History Centre, 'Oral History with Mrs Gloria Evans' (2014).

54 The websites of both mosques provide a brief summary of their heritage. See http://www.hulljamemasjid.org.uk/mosque/about/ and http://hullmosque.com/ (accessed 1 July 2016).

55 Hannah Lewis, Gary Craig, Sue Adamson and Mick Wilkinson, *Refugees, Asylum Seekers and Migrants in Yorkshire and Humber, 1999–2008: A Review of Literature for Yorkshire Futures* (Leeds: Yorkshire Futures, 2008), p. 17.

56 Gary Craig with Mick Wilkinson and Johar Ali, *At a Turning Point? The State of Race Relations in Kingston upon Hull* (Hull: Centre for Social Inclusion and Social Justice, 2005), p. B.

57 Anna Krausova and Carlos Vargas-Silva, *BRIEFING: Yorkshire and the Humber: Census Profile* (Oxford: The Migrant Observatory, 2013), p. 11.

HULL FOOTBALL CLUB
N·U·CUP WINNERS.
19 14

NED ROGERS

BERT GILBERT (Capt.)

BILLY BATTEN

ALF. FRANCIS

A. J. BOYNTON Esq.
(Chairman)

JACK HARR...

BILLY ANDERSON

JIMMY DEVEREUX

T. MILNER

N·U· CUP

GREG. RO...

DICK TAYLOR

W. HOLDER

ALF. GRICE

TOM HERRIDGE

STEVE DARM...

SID. MELVILLE
(Trainer)

MR. CHARLESWORTH
(Sec.)

CHAPTER SEVEN

The Sporting Life of the City

TONY COLLINS and VICTORIA DAWSON

Since the early nineteenth century, Hull has developed a deep, rich and in many ways unique sporting culture that not only consumed the leisure time of much of its population but also made an important contribution to the city's sense of self. Indeed, much of the cultural geography of the city, especially its east–west rivalry, is expressed in, and shaped by, the way that sport has developed across the city. This chapter explores how, for over 150 years, sport has been a key strand of the cultural fabric of Hull and a vital part of its unique identity.

The emergence of modern sport 1850–1900

Cricket was the one sport in Hull that straddled the pre-industrial sporting scene of the start of the nineteenth century and the emergence of the mass spectator entertainment industry of the late Victorian era. Although it held the social cachet of being the national sport, it attracted all classes of society, and in northern urban areas was closely associated with the working classes. It was openly commercial, despite its rigid adherence to classifying its players as gentlemen 'amateurs' and working-class 'professionals', and it had benefited tremendously from the communications and transport revolution that had transformed Victorian society.

As the nineteenth century passed the half-way mark, cricket represented both the past and the future of sport. And, as Hull itself began to industrialise and its urban population expanded rapidly, the nature of the city's sporting activity began to change and grow too. The 1860s and 1870s saw Hull participate fully in what Robert Malcolmson described as the 'reshaping of popular leisure'. From that point, sport in Britain, and subsequently in the rest of the world, began to enter a new era. Refashioned by the influence of muscular Christians and educationalists such as Thomas Arnold, the headmaster of Rugby school, sport became something more than mere entertainment; it was now a moral and educational force, thanks to the huge popularity of Thomas Hughes's 1857 bestseller *Tom Brown's Schooldays*, in which rugby and cricket were portrayed as essential to the character-building of young English gentlemen. Moreover, the expansion of the middle classes in the mid-nineteenth century led to a corresponding demand for recreational activities from those engaged in white-collar work. In this 'new leisure world', there was a growing interest in physical activity, especially from those educated at public schools upon whom the importance of healthy minds and healthy bodies had been impressed from an early age.

Rugby clubs – although for much of the century the word 'football' was used as a synonym for both rugby and soccer versions of the game – had begun to be formed by ex-public school boys in the north of England in the late 1850s and early 1860s. In 1865 a group of the scions of some of Hull's leading business families followed this trend to form Hull Football Club. W. H. H. Hutchinson, the heir to his family's shipbuilding business and the first player from Yorkshire to play for the England rugby union side, was educated at Rugby; the Harrison brothers, of whom Gilbert also would play for England, were educated at Cheltenham; and Charles Beevor Lambert was educated at St Peter's in York. The five sons of the vicar of St Mary's church in Lowgate made up a quarter of the side, rugby teams comprising twenty players per side until 1876.[1]

The club was initially precisely that – a private association of young men who gathered to play rugby, and occasionally soccer, together. Initially the club played at the Harrison family home in North Ferriby but, as similar clubs sprang up across Yorkshire, it moved to play its games at Selby to facilitate easier travel for opponents. However, the success of the team and the rising profile of rugby as a source of civic pride saw Hull FC move into the city in 1871 and establish a home ground at the Rifle Volunteer barracks on Londesborough Street, conveniently close to Paragon Station. By this time the club could lay claim to be the leading rugby club in the county, becoming the first to join the Rugby Football Union in 1872, a year after its foundation. In 1874 it was one of five clubs that set up what became the Yorkshire Rugby Union.[2]

The burgeoning interest in rugby meant that considerable crowds now gathered to watch matches, and in 1877, Hull and the other leading Yorkshire teams decided to launch a county-wide knock-out trophy, the Yorkshire Cup, to further popularise the sport. It was an instant success, attracting thousands of spectators. When Hull visited Heckmondwike in West Yorkshire for a cup-tie, the players were shocked by the crowd. 'There was so much excitement over the match among the local public that we really were fortunate in getting away from the ground without having to fight our way out … the spectators swarmed all about the field and there was a scene that up to that time we had not been accustomed to', recounted William Hutchinson.[3]

Writing in 1896, Talbot Baines, grandson of the Liberal founder of the *Leeds*

Mercury, commented on 'the existence in Northern parts to a degree elsewhere unknown, of the "element of local corporate unity" … its presence begets a public spirit fruitful in all manner of good civic deeds, a wholesome rivalry between communities and a healthy local pride'.[4] The success of the Yorkshire Cup cemented rugby as the industrial north's sporting vehicle for civic pride, part of a wider quest that was embodied in the erection of town halls, municipal buildings and public utilities. In Hull, Cuthbert Brodrick's Town Hall was opened in 1866, Pearson Park was opened in 1860 (followed by West and East Parks in 1885 and 1887), the first tramway opened in 1872 and the town itself was granted city status in 1897.

The upward spiral in rugby's fortunes in the city and across the north was facilitated by these works of the municipal age. The creation of public parks extended the scope for both playing and watching football, while the provision of transport, especially the railways and tramways, expanded dramatically during this period, increasing the ability of teams and spectators to travel between and within towns and so enhancing the nature of local rivalry. Contests between different districts of towns could now take place with ease.

Alongside this expansion of facilities and transport came rising standards of living for the industrial working classes. Factory reform in 1874 meant that a significant proportion of industrial workers now finished work at one o'clock on Saturdays, and the 'Saturday half-day holiday' increasingly became the norm during the economic boom of the early 1870s. This upturn in economic fortunes also saw working-class standards of living begin to rise, providing working-class people with not only leisure time but also the means to enjoy it, and effectively laying the basis for the growth of most modern forms of working-class leisure over the following years. Along with the music hall and seaside trips, football of both rugby and soccer varieties became a focus of interest for those with new time to spend. In Hull this was seen in the number of clubs that were formed from the late 1870s that shared neither the social status of Hull FC's rugby pioneers nor their belief in the public school principles that had underpinned the game up to that point.

The late 1870s and early 1880s saw rugby clubs springing up throughout the city. These were often supported by local employers, such as Hull Dock Company FC and Earle's Engineers, formed around 1880, or based at local pubs, such as Hull Marlborough on Lower Union Street. Typical of the new generation of clubs was Hull Southcoates, formed by a local shopkeeper, publican and Board School teacher, and based in the Courteney Street area of east Hull. These clubs survived for a decade competing against other local Hull sides, and were 'invariably composed of horny-handed sons of toil'. Looking back at their history, an old player proudly remarked that the club had fulfilled one useful function, 'and that was in training the manual labourer and in educating his mate to take an interest in the game'.[5] This was overly modest. Southcoates was so successful that it was able to persuade players from as far afield as Wakefield to come to Hull to work and play for club.[6]

In 1884 the *Hull Times* began sponsoring a knockout tournament for Hull's junior clubs, as those clubs below the elite level were known. By 1888 there were 34 teams in the first round of the Hull Times Cup including five from as far afield as

7.1 Hull Football Almanack for 1889 showing the leading rugby clubs in the city.
Courtesy of RFL Archives

Goole, Selby and York.[7] Supporters that year could also purchase the *Hull Football Almanack*, a guide to the local game that printed full-colour illustrations of the captains of the city's leading teams (Figure 7.1). The following year saw the start of publication of the *Hull and East Riding Athlete*, a weekly paper devoted to local sports that spent a considerable amount of space reporting on the city's most popular sport.

The immense popularity of rugby in the town was such that in 1887 the first-ever recorded women's rugby match took place at the East End club's ground opposite the Elephant and Castle, Holderness Road, on 8 April, Good Friday. Given the dominance of rugby in Hull's sporting landscape it is perhaps not surprising that the women of Hull wanted to participate. As one might imagine, in a town that had for so long been dominated by puritan morality, these remarkable, unknown women players who seemed to threaten the frontier of masculine sport received widespread condemnation from both the Hull and District Rugby Football Union and the local press.[8] 'Full Back' in the *Hull Daily Mail* vented his disgust. Sport on such a holy day was deemed distasteful enough, but this particular match went further in pushing the boundaries of Victorian decency and was considered 'a low and demoralizing affair'. The author urged the 'football-loving public of Hull to withhold their support for a match that will only tend to bring the noble game into disrepute'.[9] However, many spectators did attend, though when they poured on to the pitch the women's display was unceremoniously halted.[10]

Hull sides were enthusiastic participants in Yorkshire-wide competitions. In 1888 Hull Britannia brought the Yorkshire Church Temperance Challenge Shield back to Hull. The competition had begun the previous year to 'promote an interest in football among the younger churchmen of Yorkshire and, secondly, to keep them out of the public houses'. Clubs that had pubs as team headquarters were barred from competing, but this didn't stop Britannia from proudly displaying the trophy in its local pub.[11] This flouting of the spirit if not the precise rules of the temperance competition had a deeper significance than mere over-enthusiastic celebrations. The huge influx of working-class players and supporters into rugby since the late 1870s had caused a deep rift in the game. The newcomers paid little heed to the muscular Christian principles that underpinned the sport for the middle classes. Working-class spectators did not watch and applaud politely, but were full partic-ipants, shouting, jeering and booing in a partisan way that shocked rugby's rulers. But perhaps the most worrying aspect of rugby's growth for its leaders was the fact that working-class teams could now regularly defeat those who had learned the game with their Latin grammar at school. This seemed to many to be an inversion of the natural order. Within eighteen months of the Football Association's legalisation of professionalism in soccer in 1885, the Rugby Football Union decided to make its game strictly amateur in an attempt to stem the proletarian tide.

But this was too late for the founders of rugby in Hull. The fortunes of Hull FC had been in decline in the late 1870s and its morale had been badly shaken by heavy defeats at the hands of local rivals Hull White Star in 1879 and 1881 (Figure 7.2). White Star played in Sutton, and was the first significant club in east Hull, having been formed in the mid-1870s by cricketers looking for winter amusement. Unlike FC, White Star was a much more socially open and mixed club – its committee included a plumber, a commercial traveller, a clerk and two publicans – which had quickly come to dominate the rugby pitches of the town.[12] For the patrician FC, its humiliation at the hands of those it perceived to be its social inferiors was too much to bear, and in May 1881 its annual general meeting decided that 'this club cease to exist, subject to the white star club taking our name and admitting our members without ballot'.[13] The merged club played on Holderness Road on Hall's Field, a site now occupied by Mersey and Severn Streets.

The fact that Hull's premier sports club could now be based on Holderness Road was an indication of the way in which Hull itself had changed over the previous decades. In 1885 Alexandra Dock had opened as the docks began to expand eastwards and major employers such as Reckitt's and Needler's had established themselves east of the River Hull. Up to the 1860s the centre of sporting and recreational life had focused on the west of the town, but now the rapid growth of the east side had given rise to new communities and rivalries. Between 1871 and 1901, Hull's population ballooned from 136,358 to 255,552, and for a significant proportion of those new citizens rugby was a means of integration into their new host society. Hull installed new grandstands at its ground in 1882 and 1883 to cope with larger crowds and even considered buying the Botanical Gardens on Spring Bank in 1887 in order to meet the increasing spectator numbers.[14]

The growth of the club also demonstrated how far rugby had travelled in the late 1800s. Until this was banned by the Rugby Football Union's new amateur regulations in 1886, Hull regularly paid its players compensation for time taken off work to play rugby. 'Broken-time' payments, as they became known, would become the rallying cry for those clubs with predominantly working-class players and the very thing that would cause a great schism in rugby in 1895. Hull's 1883/84 report and accounts actually listed as expenditure £18 spent on 'players' loss of time, through accident and attendance at matches' and the committee minutes for that season, in which the club reached the Yorkshire Cup final, show that broken-time payments were paid on at least three occasions during the cup run, including for the final itself when the club asked all players not to work on the morning of the game.[15]

Perhaps the most prominent example of the way in which rugby in Hull (and across the north of England) had become dominated by working-class players could be seen in the rise of the club that would become Hull Kingston Rovers (Hull KR).

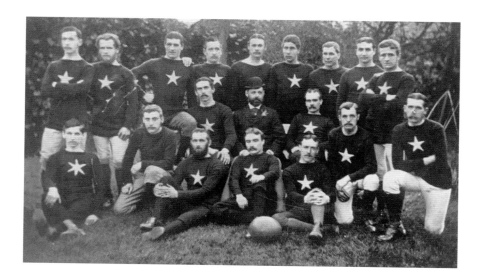

7.2 Hull White Star rugby club in 1879, shortly before the east Hull club merged with Hull FC.
Courtesy of RFL Archives

The club was formed as Kingston Amateurs in 1882 by apprentice boilermakers living on Hessle Road who worked for the ships' engineering companies C. D. Holmes and Amos and Smith, both based on Albert Dock. In 1885 the club changed its name to Kingston Rovers and in 1888 it won the Hull Times Cup, by which time its home ground was at the Hessle Road Locomotive cricket ground at Dairycoates. In February 1892 its status as Hull's second major rugby club was confirmed when it moved to the newly opened Hull Athletic Ground on the Boulevard, midway between Hessle Road and Anlaby Road. The Athletic Ground had been built by a consortium comprising local athletics and cycling clubs, led by Edward Robson, the Sheriff of Hull, to capitalise on the town's sporting boom, but despite the widespread appeal of these sports to participants, only rugby could provide sufficient spectators to finance the new stadium. And it would be the economics of commercial sport that would lead to the most remarkable change in Hull's sporting geography.[16]

When Kingston Rovers' three-year lease came up for renewal early in 1895, it found itself confronted by a rival offer that amounted to three times what the club could afford to pay. The counter-offer came from Hull FC, whose frustration at the limited crowds that its Holderness Road ground could accommodate led it to bid for the west Hull stadium. The Athletic Ground Company accepted the larger offer, forcing Rovers to look for a new home. The club found it in east Hull on the former ground of Hull Southcoates at Craven Street, just a few hundred yards from the vacated Hull FC ground, which had been sold for housing development (Figure 7.3). Although the switch from west to east caused some level of friction among the club's supporters, Rovers was able to integrate quickly into the east Hull rugby community, co-opting a number of former Hull Southcoates officials and supporters into the club.[17] Hull FC's mirror-image move also proved to be highly successful, with attendances in the first season at the new location increasing from 81,257 to 131,717. It eventually bought the ground from its ailing owners for £6,500 in 1899 and renamed it the Boulevard.[18]

But the move to west Hull was not the only reason for Hull FC's increased crowds. The civil war in rugby over the question of broken-time payments had come to a head in the summer of 1895. Hull was one of the founding members of the new Northern Rugby Football Union that was formed in August 1895 when the leading northern clubs resigned from the Rugby Football Union in protest at the governing body's refusal to allow broken-time payments to players. The new organisation not only brought more spectators to matches but also found deep support among Hull's sporting community. 'The clubs who have struck a blow for freedom are to be commended for throwing off the cloak of hypocrisy, conceit and subterfuge, and standing out for those essentially English characteristics – honesty and straight forwardness', said a correspondent to the *Hull Daily Mail* a few days after the split occurred. Two weeks later a special meeting of the Hull and District Rugby Union voted 33–24 to resign from the RFU in support of the Northern Union, the first of many local rugby bodies to do so.[19] When Hull KR joined in 1897, to all intents and purposes the old game of rugby union was dead in the region and the new Northern Union (which was renamed the Rugby Football League in 1922) reigned supreme.

Although not on the same scale, this sporting revolution had also affected cricket. Nationwide, this sport pioneered the modern sporting world of celebrity and international competition. Hull was not immune to its appeal. In 1875 W. G. Grace, arguably the most famous man in England at the time, appeared at the Argyle Street cricket ground when it was selected to host the North of England against the South of England match. Three years later 6,000 people crammed into the ground to see a Hull and District eleven unsuccessfully take on the might of the touring Australian team. In 1888 a grandstand was erected to accommodate the increasing number of people who wanted to watch the sport.

Demonstrating the extent to which sport had become a business, in 1896, after the North Eastern Railway Company, the owners of the original Argyle Street ground, asked the club to move, Hull Town cricket club formed a limited company in order to purchase a new ground adjacent to Anlaby Road and Walton Street. The last match at Argyle Street was played in September 1897 and the following season the club commenced playing at its new ground, known as the Circle, on Anlaby Road, after spending £6,000 on its purchase and development. In July 1899 the ground hosted the first of what would be 89 Yorkshire county matches when the county faced Somerset in front of 8,000 spectators. Five years later Yorkshire played the touring South Africans there and in 1909 an unusual joint Yorkshire & Lancashire side drew with Australia.[20]

The Circle was the second major sporting stadium to be built in west Hull during the 1890s, emphasising the extent to which the sporting and recreational heart of what was now a city lay in that area. This could also be seen in the development of athletics, for which Hull Athletic Club had been formed in 1879, holding its events at a ground on Coltman Street. Two years later it moved to a new ground at Spring

7.4 Cross-country runners awaiting the start of the Hull Harriers Monstre Meet at Stoneferry in 1913. The club had been formed in 1882 by a group of amateur athletes, the most prominent of whom were George Lidiard and Charles Campion Merrikin.
Courtesy of Robb Robinson

Lane, now the site of Hymers College, where it laid out a cinder running track. By 1888 the club was also benefiting from the sporting revolution that was taking place, as seen by the fact that its May meeting was watched by 14,000 spectators, who saw 265 athletes from as far afield as Nottingham, Leeds and Grimsby. The 1880s also saw a boom in cross-country running, with numerous 'Harriers' clubs being established, leading to the formation of the Hull and District Cross-Country Association in 1889. The fact that Hull Harriers had been formed in 1882 by two professional athletes, George Lidiard and Charles Merrikin, was one more example of the way in which sport was no longer the exclusive property of the muscular Christian gentleman amateur (Figures 7.4, 7.5).

7.5 Runners and officers of Hull Harriers at their clubhouse on the eve of the First World War.
Courtesy of Robb Robinson

Such a development was not to the liking of all sport aficionados. The Circle's magnificent pavilion and the high cost of membership set a social tone that differed markedly from the plebeian atmosphere that could be found a mile away across Anlaby Road at the Boulevard rugby league stadium. The fact that the Circle was also used for polo practice underlined the social gulf that separated the two stadia. Indeed, the development of the Circle was an example of the emergence of specifically middle-class sports and recreational spaces that began in the last decade of the nineteenth century. As John Lowerson has pointed out, the growth of golf and tennis clubs in particular were among the most visible examples of the development of discrete leisure spheres for the middle classes, and this was no less the case in Hull.[21]

The affluent belt surrounding the city saw golf clubs being formed as early as 1890 in Beverley, when the town club was formed, closely followed by Hornsea and Hessle, both formed in 1898. It was not until 1904 that the city acquired its own club, when the creation of Hull Golf Club was led by local solicitor Haggitt Colbeck, and its first course laid out on land at the corner of Boothferry Road and North Road, where Hull City's Boothferry Park ground would be opened in 1946. Tennis clubs, another great symbol of late Victorian middle-class sociability, also sprang up in the more affluent parts of the city. In 1901 rugby union was restarted in the city when the creation of the Hull and East Riding club was 'taken in hand by the sons of Hull and district's leading citizens' and made its home, appropriately enough, at the Circle.[22]

William Colbeck

People from Hull and the East Riding of Yorkshire played a significant role in the 'Heroic Age' of Antarctic exploration (1897–1922). Clements Markham, the president of the Royal Geographical Society, who envisaged and oversaw the British National Antarctic Expedition (1901–04), came from Stillingfleet, East Yorkshire. Much of the money required to fund the expedition was provided by Llewellyn Longstaff, owner of Hull's Blundell's Paints. And a key player in the celebrated Antarctic expeditions was Captain William Colbeck of Hull.

Colbeck was born in 1871 and educated at Hull Grammar School before signing as an apprentice, aged 16, on a sailing ship bound for India. As a talented mariner he rose through the ranks, and under the tutelage of Zebedee Scaping, headmaster of Hull Trinity House School, Colbeck gained his Master's Ticket in 1894. But his career shifted suddenly in 1898 when he was invited to serve as Magnetic Officer (taking scientific measurements) on the 'Southern Cross Expedition' led by the Norwegian explorer, Carsten Borchgrevink. Colbeck accepted the offer and became one of the pioneers of living and 'overwintering' on Antarctica. Colbeck and a Finnish colleague, Ole Larsen, set a new exploration record by travelling further south than anyone before them. He

William Colbeck in front of the magnetic observatory at Cape Adare during the Southern Cross Expedition, 1899
State Library of Tasmania

also mapped the Ross Ice Shelf and was convinced that he had found the best route to the South Pole. Roald Amundsen followed this route successfully in 1911 and subsequently sent Colbeck a letter of thanks.

Colbeck returned to Hull and took a command with the Wilson shipping line, but in 1902 he was commissioned by Markham to captain *Morning*, a steam yacht to be despatched south to relieve Captain Robert Falcon Scott's ice-bound *Discovery* expedition (1901–04). Many of Colbeck's crew were from Hull when *Morning* left London in July 1902 and steamed south via Lyttelton in New Zealand. On 6 December, they headed towards the Antarctic ice where, on Christmas Day 1902, Colbeck located the *Discovery* stranded in McMurdo Sound. She was locked solidly in the ice, so Colbeck's crew transferred provisions from *Morning*, working day and night to haul vital supplies across the five miles of ice that separated the two ships. After six weeks, *Morning* returned to Lyttelton, dodging out of the ice as conditions deteriorated.

Colbeck moored in New Zealand for the austral winter and then returned briefly to London to plan a second relief voyage. In 1903 *Morning* was joined by a second ship, *Terra Nova*, with Colbeck in overall command. The British Admiralty ordered that *Discovery* was to be abandoned if she could not be released. When *Morning* and *Terra Nova* got within twenty miles of Scott's ship on 5 January 1904, they used explosives to blast a path through the ice and, on 16 February, *Discovery* was finally freed.

After refitting in New Zealand, *Morning* returned to England. Thousands of people greeted Colbeck and the other Hull crew members when they arrived at Hull's Paragon Station in autumn 1904 after their two epic Antarctic voyages. Several Hull-based crew members, including Alfred Cheetham, returned south with later expeditions, but Colbeck went back to the Wilson Line. Cape Colbeck and Colbeck Bay in Antarctica are named after him and he was also awarded the Polar Medal, but he has been under-acknowledged in the literature about Antarctic exploration. This is gradually being redressed: in 2016 a plaque marking the achievements of Colbeck, Cheetham and the rest of the crew was unveiled in Hull's Paragon Station.

Robb Robinson

Although the late Victorian sporting revolution had transformed sport as it was played and watched in the city, Hull had not taken any part in its most distinctive feature. As in the rest of Yorkshire, with the exception of Sheffield, soccer, as the association code of football was known, was virtually unknown in nineteenth-century Hull. The town's only connection with the sport was the fact that Hull-born solicitor Ebenezer Cobb Morley had been the first secretary of the Football Association when it was founded in 1863 and had helped draw up its first set of rules, though by that time he was resident in the London suburb of Barnes.

Hull Town cricket club had formed a soccer section in 1879 but apart from a single match in the first round of the FA Cup in November 1883, the game failed to capture the imagination of the population and the section folded in 1887.[23] Part of the problem was that there was little top-class soccer played in the region – the closest sides that Hull Town played during the 1883–84 season were Grimsby and Scarborough. Whereas Hull's rugby sides had literally hundreds of potential opponents in Leeds and the other textile towns of west Yorkshire, the nearest city for high-calibre soccer opponents was Sheffield. The *Hull Packet* seemingly spoke for the vast majority of Hull's sporting public when it explained in 1883 that 'the "Rugby" is now generally preferred to the "Association" and the use of the hands in the former carries the monotony of the latter. The game of Rugby, under the revised rules, is made exciting from beginning to end, and as it is, is by far the best of all winter games.'[24]

However, by the turn of the century such a view seemed to be increasingly out of kilter with the rest of Britain. In 1901, 114,815 spectators packed into Crystal Palace

7.6 Hull City before their first ever match, a friendly against Notts County at the Boulevard
Courtesy of Victoria Dawson

to see Tottenham Hotspur draw 2–2 with Sheffield United in the FA Cup Final. The success of the FA Cup and the Football League in the 1890s had transformed soccer into the national winter sport, far outstripping the popularity of rugby, which was now split into two sports riven by class and geography. West and east Yorkshire were rugby anomalies in the face of a seemingly unstoppable tide of soccer. In 1903 Bradford City became the first Football League club in the rugby heartland and the dam had been breached. In 1905 Hull finally entered the world of top-flight professional soccer when Hull City were admitted to the second division of the Football League (Figure 7.6).

Soccer in Hull had slowly been growing in popularity since the 1890s. In 1894 a Hull and District Football Association had been formed and by 1901 it could boast 51 clubs, so by the time of Hull City's acceptance into the Football League in 1905 there was a ready-made audience for the new game. Even so, at the club's inaugural game the matchday programme and advertising posters featured a summary of the rules for those spectators more accustomed to rugby.[25] City's first matches before their first season in the Football League were played at the Boulevard, but the Northern Union's concern about encroachments into its traditional rugby heartlands led to it banning its clubs from allowing soccer sides to use their grounds. So when the Tigers, as they had been nicknamed by the *Hull Daily Mail*, kicked off their first season in the Second Division they played on the cricket pitch at the Circle.

In March 1906, as its first season was drawing to a close, the club moved to a rectangular pitch at the eastern side of the Circle. The Anlaby Road ground, as it became known, was the club's home for the next four decades. But the ground was never seen as a permanent base for the club and its officials spent considerable time searching for an alternative. In April 1914 the main stand was burned down and rumour had it that this was the work of the militant suffragettes. However, no immediate action to find a new ground was taken; the outbreak of the First World War meant that the club's search for a new home had to be suspended.

Women made one more significant appearance at the Anlaby Road ground, but this time for charitable causes, when Hull City Ladies took on the famous Dick Kerr's side in a game of association football on 5 May 1921. This was the only time the ground entertained women's soccer. The match came on the back of a successful game at the Boulevard two months earlier, when 16,230 saw Dick Kerr's beat Yorkshire 4–1. White City Pleasure Gardens also hosted Hull City Ladies on 14 May when they beat Huddersfield Atalanta by two goals to nil. Disaster nearly struck when Hull City Ladies travelled to Preston for a return match the following week, when a taxi carrying five of the women, including the captain, overturned just outside Ilkley, smashing the car to smithereens. Miraculously unscathed, the women managed to fulfil their fixture. The Boulevard was the brief home of women's soccer, thanks to rugby league ace Billy Batten. He coached a team from his home village of Kinsley, made up largely of young women and girls from the nearby pit villages, who dominated the game in the west Yorkshire area. The August bank holiday of 1921 saw his team unbeaten for their sixteenth consecutive game as they played Yorkshire in the high point of a grand sports meeting that included athletics and wrestling.

The Boulevard might have become a more permanent home for women's soccer had the Northern Union not agreed to uphold the FA's vote to ban women's soccer in December 1921, barring any women's team from playing on rugby league pitches.

In the early 1920s Hull City's directors considered moving to the White City Pleasure Gardens at the junction of Calvert Lane and Anlaby Road. This had been opened in 1920 as a multi-attraction leisure park boasting dance and concert halls, tennis courts, a roller-skating rink, athletics facilities and numerous bars. But despite the success of boxing and wrestling tournaments there, the Tigers' directors rejected the idea in favour of a purpose-built stadium (Figure 7.7). With hindsight (the fact that the White City complex was destroyed by fire in 1938), the club's decision in 1930 to buy a seven-acre site at the corner of Boothferry Road and North Road can be seen as wise.[26]

Boothferry Park, as the land became known, was just a short walk from the Pleasure Gardens. It had a sporting history going back to 1904, when the newly formed Hull Golf Club built a nine-hole course there, to be followed by the opening of tennis courts, which were home to the Imperial Tennis Club, and bowling greens. Hull Golf Club moved out to the western suburb of Kirk Ella in 1924 and the Tigers' acquisition of the former golf course – there is no evidence that they ever considered a move to the east of the city – underlined how Hull's sporting centre was moving further west beyond its traditional Anlaby Road core as new housing and industry pushed the boundaries of the city outwards. Indeed, North Road itself had only been opened in 1927 and the city's boundaries were formally extended beyond the traditional Calvert Lane/North Road border in 1929.

7.7 An early 1950s illustration of Hull City's state-of-the-art Boothferry Park.
Courtesy of National Football Museum

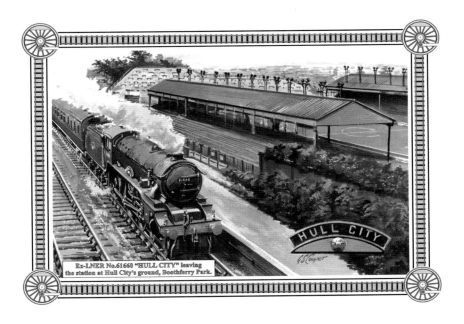

7.8 Train pulling into Boothferry Halt station. Illustration by G. S. Cooper, commissioned by Stuart Renshaw for a series of locomotive paintings featuring football clubs. Details at www.footballcover.co.uk

Ex-LNER No.61660 "HULL CITY" leaving the station at Hull City's ground, Boothferry Park.

7.9 Cover of Hull City vs. Southport match in 1950, featuring future Leeds United manager Don Revie
Courtesy of Tony Collins

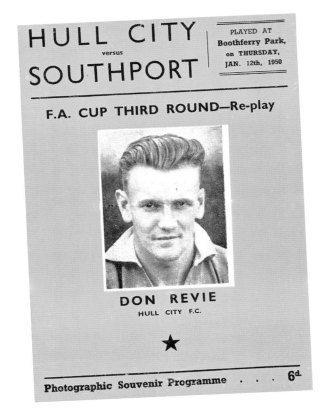

HULL CITY
versus
SOUTHPORT

PLAYED AT
Boothferry Park,
on THURSDAY,
JAN. 12th, 1950

F.A. CUP THIRD ROUND—Re-play

DON REVIE
HULL CITY F.C.

★

Photographic Souvenir Programme . . . 6ᵈ

Work on the new stadium began in 1932, but in the midst of the depression finance was difficult to obtain and work on the ground stalled. It would not be opened until 1946, which propitiously coincided with a huge post-Second World War boom in football attendances. For the time, it was a state-of-the-art stadium with a capacity said to be between 40,000 and 50,000 and, most revolutionary, its own railway station, Boothferry Halt, which was opened in 1951 (Figure 7.8). In 1949 a record attendance for any sporting event in the city was set when 55,019 crammed into the ground to see the Tigers – who would later be crowned Third Division North champions – lose 1–0 in the FA Cup quarter-final to the cupholders Manchester United. Managed by former England international midfielder Raich Carter, this would be seen as the club's golden age, rivalled only by the era of Terry Neill's management in the early 1970s, before the ascent to the Premier League in 2008 (Figure 7.9).

The rise of Hull City did little to dent the popularity of rugby league, and the city became one of the few to support three professional football or rugby sides playing at the top levels of their sports (Figure 7.10, 7.11). The early 1920s were a period of significant success for both rugby teams, with Hull being crowned champions in 1920 and 1921 and Rovers emulating this feat in 1923 and 1925. In 1921 Rovers moved from their Craven Street ground to take up residency in a new stadium in 1922, Craven Park, which is further east on Holderness Road (Figure 7.12). In 1936 Hull once again won the rugby league championship, but by this time rugby in east Hull had been badly hit by the depression and declining crowds saw Hull Kingston Rovers sell their stadium and rent it back from its new owners in 1938 (Figure 7.13).

The rugby ground was sold to a greyhound racing syndicate, underlining the popularity of the 'new' sports of the interwar years and a shift in sporting facilities in east Hull. Greyhound racing, which had been introduced to Britain in the mid-1920s, had started at Craven Park in 1928 largely as a new revenue stream for the rugby club, and soon attracted thousands of spectators. In the mid-1930s baseball was established during the summer months at Craven Park and it too proved to be successful, with Hull winning the national pennant in 1937 (Figure 7.14). This success, which was boosted by matches between American soldiers during the Second World War,

7.10 Poster celebrating Hull FC winning the Rugby League Challenge Cup for the first time.
Courtesy of RFL Archives

meant that by 1948 there were an estimated 80 sides in the city and Hull became one of the centres of baseball in Britain. One of the other 'new' sports of the interwar years, speedway, did not become established in Hull until the post-war years and it gravitated towards the east of the city.[27]

All of the sports that were established in Hull in the first half of the twentieth century were essentially commercial ventures. Sport had become big business and an important sector of the entertainment industry. But during the same period many industries in Hull had also made themselves part of the city's sports scene with the provision of extensive sporting facilities for their employees. The most famous of these was Reckitt and Sons Ltd, which opened its Garden Village in east Hull in 1908, providing not only high-quality housing but also extensive sports facilities for employees. As early as 1903, 38 local factory rugby league sides took part in the works competition organised by Hull KR that saw Earle's Shipyard defeat Reckitt's in the final.[28] After the First World War, many other companies embraced what became known as 'welfare capitalism' and opened sports and other recreational facilities for their employees. Many of these companies, such as Fenner's, Priestman's, Earle's

7.11 Cartoon commiserating with Hull City, Hull FC, Hull KR and rugby union side Hull and East Riding for all losing on the same day in 1924.
Courtesy of RFL Archives

7.12 Hull KR and Wakefield Trinity in 1922 before the inaugural match at Craven Park on Holderness Road.
Courtesy of RFL Archives

7.13 Hull FC's Boulevard ground after an attack by the Luftwaffe in 1941.
Courtesy of RFL Archives

Cement and British Oil and Cake Mills, were based in east Hull, reflecting the rapid industrial development and population growth that took place east of the River Hull from the late nineteenth century.

In 1930 ten of the local factory welfare organisations came together to form the Hull Works' Sports Association (HWSA), its founding president being George Earle of Earle's Cement. By 1938 it had 75 companies in membership and organised 15 different sports, including rugby league, cricket, hockey, netball, tennis and athletics.[29] The city became one of the leading centres for works' sport in Britain and in 1938 the HWSA was one of the founders of the National Council of Sport in Industry. In parallel to the extensive provision of sports facilities for employees, the city itself opened a municipal golf course in 1935 at Sutton Park with the intention of bringing the opportunity to play golf within the reach of working-class people. Reflecting the changing demographics of the city, it was not accidental that the course was in east Hull.

Another significant but smaller demographic change had been the growth of the city's Jewish population from the end of the nineteenth century. Anti-semitic pogroms in Tsarist Russia saw tens of thousands of fleeing Jews pass through the city on their way to America, but a considerable number made Hull their home, and sport proved to be no less important to the newcomers than it was for the native population. In 1919 Hull Judeans' cricket club was formed, but such was the enthusiasm that it soon became a multi-sports club, playing soccer, rugby league, table tennis, lawn tennis, hockey and swimming. The most prominent of the local Jewish athletes was Louis Harris, one of the cornerstones of Hull KR's championship-winning sides of the 1920s. Harris would later become one of the city's leading business and civic figures.

7.14 Hull take on Leeds at baseball in 1938.
Courtesy of *Hull Daily Mail*

7.15 Barbara Buttrick sparring in the early 1950s.
Courtesy of Victoria Dawson

Perhaps the heyday of Jewish sporting activity was the immediate post-war decades, when the Judean club acquired its own building and began a golf club. In 1958 the popular local doctor Lothar Seewald of Anlaby Park Road established Britain's first handball league in the city, which lasted four years, and organised the first-ever international match for the Great Britain handball team against Holland in 1959.[30] In the early 1960s Hull FC's star winger was Wilf Rosenberg, the South African son of a rabbi. Rosenberg wasn't the only indication of diversity in the city after the Second World War. In 1949 Roy Francis transferred to Hull FC to become the club's player-coach, in the process becoming the first black coach of any professional sports side in Britain. Under his leadership Hull were rugby league champions in 1956 and 1958. In 1961 Francis signed Clive Sullivan, who would emulate his coach's achievements in becoming the first black captain of a national sports team when he captained Great Britain to their Rugby League World Cup triumph in 1972. In 1974 Sullivan moved across the city to play for Hull KR and became an iconic figure for the entire city. He was memorialised when the Hessle to Hull section of the A63 was named Clive Sullivan Way.

The post-war years also saw the increasing involvement of women in the predominantly male kingdom of sport. Although middle-class women had been involved in local golf and tennis clubs from the 1890s – Beverley Golf Club staged its first Ladies' Tournament in 1897 and the Hornsea Club had formed a Ladies' Section in 1919 – it was not until the 1940s that women began to make a mark on sport in Hull (if we discount earlier controversies reported in the newspapers). The first, and to conventional opinion most shocking, was Barbara Buttrick (Figure 7.15). 'Girl boxers! Disgusting!' exclaimed an official of the British Boxing Board of Control (BBBC) in March 1949, when 18-year-old Buttrick caused a stir by being billed to spar with a man at an exhibition match at the Kilburn Empire theatre, London. In 1948 Buttrick had publicly called for other women boxers to take her on, but she only received three replies, and they were from women in Australia. Nevertheless, she was determined to become England's first professional woman boxer. The BBBC refused to consider granting her an exhibition licence, but Buttrick refused to give up on her dream: 'My plan is to make boxing my career, and I shall go on with it', she declared.[31]

In her teenage years, Buttrick began boxing by joining a gym and sparring with a friend at her Cottingham home. She moved to London to work as a shorthand typist and trained every day, but her much-publicised exhibition match was cancelled due to the overwhelmingly adverse press coverage. Instead 'Battling Barbara' had to give a demonstration of training techniques and shadow boxing. A tour of the provinces beckoned in May 1949, but Buttrick struggled to find opposition. Her first professional fight was fixed for 25 July 1950, against a German, Elsa Hoffman, who was living in Dewsbury. The Dewsbury mayor objected to the fight, but 500 spectators turned up, only to be disappointed when Hoffman didn't arrive. Fairground boxing wasn't enough for Buttrick and she was lured to the USA in 1952, where women's boxing was becoming popular, by the promise of a professional career. She never looked back, and in 1956 she beat Phyllis Kugler in the first official women's boxing world championship. She was only beaten once in her career, by Joan Hagan, who was 33 lb heavier. Buttrick retired in 1960 having fought 32 times and given over 1,000 exhibitions. She remained devoted to women's boxing, setting up the Women's International Boxing Federation and influencing the careers of generations of women boxers who followed in her footsteps.

In 1960, convinced of the social benefits of rugby league for young boys, East Hull's Kay Ibbetson not only set up a club, but coached them too, making her the first female rugby coach. The club was hugely successful and the *Hull and Yorkshire Times* lauded her as the 'belle of the egg-shaped ball'; journalist John Rodgers could not hide his admiration of Ibbetson's strength in adversity, and remarked that it was 'surprising not to find her as large and tough as a Sherman tank'. Her club faced many setbacks, but she said, 'Give me five years and I'll have a club house or my name's not Ibbetson!'[32] She had her club house in a mere ten months. The club spawned such great rugby players as Alan Burwell, John Moore, Trevor Carmichael and Roger Booth and won many trophies. In 1963 Ibbetson facilitated a five-day trip to France that saw East Hull become the first Yorkshire amateur club to play international rugby league, and she became the first woman on the Amateur Rugby League Council (Figure 7.16). Her example was followed in 1991 when Hull's Julia Lee became the first woman qualified to referee professional rugby matches in Britain and Australia.

Buttrick and Ibbetson were more successful than other women involved in Hull sport. A short-lived Hull Ladies' athletic club had been formed in the early 1950s but

EAST HULL RLFC FRANCE 1963

7.16 Kay Ibbetson and her East Hull amateur rugby league club on the way to a historic tour of France in 1963.
Courtesy of Victoria Dawson

7.17 Ken Wagstaff: Hull City cult hero of the 1960s and 1970s.
From *The Book of Football*

7.18 The day the city moved to Wembley: Hull KR vs. Hull FC Rugby League Challenge Cup Final programme 1980.
Courtesy of RFL Archives

this was essentially superseded by Hull Harriers' starting a women's section in 1956. Women were also prominent in the city's strong culture of competitive swimming, fostered by the corporation's provision of public baths. The first baths were opened at Stoneferry in 1845 but the late Victorian population boom led to new baths being built at Madeley Street (1885), Holderness Road (1898), Beverley Road (1905) and Albert Avenue (1908). As well as providing clean bathing facilities, the baths became centres for competitive swimming. The earliest beneficiary was Jack Hale, who swam for Britain at the 1948 London Olympics and won gold and bronze team medals at the 1950 British Empire Games, but the baths also provided many women with opportunities for sport. Jackie Brown represented Britain at both the 1968 and 1972 Olympics and the city produced many local and national champions. Hull women were also prominent in judo, with Sharon Rendle winning a bronze medal at the 1992 Olympics, as well as world championship golds in 1987 and 1989. Karen Briggs also competed at the Barcelona Olympics but failed to add to her four successive world championship medals and five European golds of the 1980s.

However, by the time that Briggs and Rendle were competing in Barcelona in 1992, the city's economic and sporting fortunes had changed dramatically. The 1970s witnessed the rapid erosion of Hull's industrial base, and with it the closing of many of the workplace recreational facilities that had provided the structures for recreational sport since the 1920s. Lack of investment, exacerbated not least by a lack of on-field success, led to major problems for the city's professional sports stadia. In 1974 Yorkshire played their last county cricket match at the Circle, and Hull City and Hull KR struggled financially to maintain the needs of the modern stadium. Even the rebirth of speedway in the city in 1971, when Hull Vikings made their debut at the Boulevard, was partly due to Hull FC seeking to support its ailing finances by promoting other sports.

Yet despite falling attendances, disappearing facilities and economic depression, the city's appetite for sport remained strong (Figure 7.17). By the end of the 1970s Hull and Hull KR were the two dominant sides in British rugby league, competing against each other in six cup finals between 1979 and 1984, including the memorable 1980 Challenge Cup Final in front of 95,000 people at Wembley (Figure 7.18). Indeed, it sometimes appeared that during the economic depredations of the 1970s and 1980s, sport was the only thing that kept the city's spirit of identity alive.

Clive Sullivan

Few individuals born outside Hull have captured the hearts of the city's people in the way that Clive Sullivan did. Sullivan was born in 1943 in Cardiff, and although he soon showed promise as a rugby player, he was beset throughout his early years by various physical problems and injuries. After one operation his family were told he might never walk properly again. Yet Sullivan overcame these difficulties and enlisted in the army, qualifying as a radio operator before becoming a paratrooper. He saw active service in Cyprus in 1964 and was afterwards attached to the United Nations peacekeeping force, earning a United Nations medal for his service. While stationed at Catterick in North Yorkshire,

Clive Sullivan in action for Hull FC. The first black player to captain a Great Britain international sporting team, Clive played with great distinction for Hull FC and Hull Kingston Rovers.

Sullivan started playing rugby union again, albeit with some initial reluctance because of his earlier injuries. But he quickly demonstrated his ability and attracted the attention of rugby league scouts.

Although a trial with Bradford Northern was unsuccessful, Sullivan made the most of a second trial with Hull FC. At that time any triallists turning out for rugby league matches were banned by the rugby union code, so Sullivan played in the match anonymously. His debut was a revelation: dubbed Mr X by the local newspaper, Sullivan scored three tries. He signed a professional contract the next day. Although military duties, injuries and a serious car crash restricted his rugby league outings, once Sullivan left the army in 1964 he became a key part of the Hull FC team.

Sullivan was noted for his phenomenal pace on the wing. Despite his spindly legs and misleadingly frail appearance, he had considerable upper body strength. He soon proved to be a very fine player and was selected for Great Britain in 1967, scoring a hat-trick against New Zealand in the World Cup during the following year. In 1972 he was appointed captain of the Great Britain World Cup side, becoming the first black captain of any major British sporting team. He proved an inspirational leader, leading his country to World Cup victory as well as scoring one of the best tries ever seen in the competition.

Sullivan was very much the heart and soul of the Hull FC side for a decade. He became player-coach during the 1974 season, but then shocked the local rugby world when he crossed the city to join Hull Kingston Rovers. He had success in east Hull too: he won a Championship medal with Rovers in 1979, and played in the legendary FC vs. Rovers Challenge Cup final at Wembley on 8 May 1980. Sullivan then returned to Hull FC in 1981 and was part of the team that won the Challenge Cup by beating Widnes in the replayed final in 1982.

During his long and illustrious career, Clive Sullivan scored 250 tries for Hull FC and 118 for Rovers. He died in 1985, aged only 42, but he is still held in great affection by both sides of Hull's deep rugby league divide. Although a rugby league superstar, his was an age before modern wages and sponsorship, and he worked during his sporting career on the shop floor of Hawker Siddeley Aviation in Brough. After his death, the main A63 road into the city was named Clive Sullivan Way and every year Hull FC and Hull KR play a pre-season derby match for the Clive Sullivan Memorial Trophy, a fitting reminder of a superb sportsman and a remarkable individual.

Robb Robinson

In hindsight, it is no surprise that the two Hull clubs' domination of rugby league came to an end in the mid-1980s or that Hull City stagnated throughout the 1980s. The Bradford City fire of May 1985 led to new safety and crowd controls being imposed on sports grounds and, already staggering under the weight of the cost of maintaining their dilapidated facilities, the city's leading clubs abandoned their historic stadiums one by one. The first was Hull KR, which moved to a new ground on the site of the former Shakespeare Hall High School in Greatfield in 1989. The financial impact of the move effectively throttled the club for almost two decades, during which it slipped into the lower divisions of the game and had to fight to resist suggestions that it should merge with Hull FC.

Indeed, when rugby league switched to a summer season in 1996, neither Hull side was in the rebranded first division, the Super League. That same year saw Hull City relegated to soccer's third division, where they would languish for the rest of the decade. For much of the 1990s, the city's only taste of sporting success came from its ice hockey side, Humberside Seahawks. In one sense the Seahawks were a throwback to the older traditions of municipal support for sport, having been established and partly financed by Humberside County Council in 1988, and based at the Hull Arena, itself one of the centrepieces of the city's regeneration of the Marina area. The side quickly became one of the leading clubs in Britain but the inevitable financial pressures of professional sport led to changes in ownership and fortune, with successive iterations being known as the Hawks, Thunder, Stingrays and Pirates.

That same lingering spirit of municipalism would also lead to the most significant development in the city's sporting history for over a century. In 1997 discussions began about a new stadium for the Tigers, whose Boothferry Park was increasingly expensive to maintain, and in 2001 the club once again went into receivership, posing the question of the stadium point blank. Hull FC also began to consider a move from the Boulevard due to the spiralling costs of the stadium. In a neat tying together of the historic threads of sport in west Hull, the city council decided to build a new stadium for the two clubs on the site of the Circle at the junction of Walton Street and Anlaby Road. Ironically, the continuation of the west Hull sporting tradition was facilitated by the dotcom bubble of the late 1990s, as much of the cost of the new stadium was met by the council's sale of part of its share of Kingston Communications. When it opened in 2002, the stadium was named after the company as the KC Stadium.

It was the signal for a sea-change in the fortunes of professional sport in the city. In 2005 Hull FC won the Rugby League Challenge Cup for the first time since 1982, and the following season reached the Super League Grand Final. That same year also saw Hull KR earn promotion to the Super League, returning to the sport's highest division having been absent since 1994. Perhaps even more remarkable was the rise of Hull City, which was in the fourth tier of English football when it moved into its new home. By 2008 they had fought their way up

7.19 Gipsyville's Dean Windass celebrates taking Hull City into the Premier League for the first time in 2008.
Courtesy of Victoria Dawson

the divisions to play in the Premier League, the first time that the club had ever played in the top division of English football. Their meteoric rise was sealed at the Championship play-off final at Wembley when promotion was won through a 1–0 victory over Bristol City. As if to emphasise the romance of the day, the winning goal was scored by Dean Windass, who was born and bred in Gipsyville and who had stood on the terraces of Boothferry Park to support City ever since he was a small boy (Figure 7.19).

In 2014 the Tigers played at Wembley in their very first FA Cup Final. For many supporters, it was a day that they thought they would never see. Previously thwarted by semi-final and quarter-final near-misses, this time the club stormed through the semi-final 5–3 against Sheffield United and finally took their place at soccer's showpiece occasion on 17 May 2014. Within ten minutes of the kick-off, goals from James Chester and Curtis Davies had put the Tigers 2–0 up against the favourites Arsenal. It was perhaps the most memorable ten minutes in the club's 110-year history, but they were eventually overtaken by their glamorous opponents and the FA Cup slipped from their grasp by three goals to two. City returned to the Premier League in 2016, confirming their status as a major English football side, but the year was also memorable for Hull FC breaking their hoodoo of never winning a cup final at Wembley when they defeated Warrington 12–10 in the Challenge Cup Final.

However, despite this unprecedented success at the professional level – in 2008, for the first time ever, all three of the city's professional sides played at their sport's elite level and by 2016 all had also won at Wembley – sport at Hull's grassroots withered. The loss of works-based sports grounds had a crippling effect on cricket in particular. Local summer evening leagues disappeared, and continuous cuts in local authority spending meant that public sporting facilities contracted. Endemic unemployment and low wage levels constricted the demand for sport. The numbers of local soccer and rugby clubs declined, and youth sport suffered from declining schools' interest and the atrophy and death of youth clubs.

The most notable loss was the closure of Hull Boys' Club in 2015. First opened in 1902 as a means of providing out-of-school recreation and training for working-class boys, the club specialised in rugby league and boxing, producing the 1957 Amateur Boxing Association lightweight champion Tommy Green and the 1966 Commonwealth Games light-heavyweight gold medallist and future professional Roger Tighe. Yet, in another paradox of the city's sporting culture, the profile of boxing in the city had never been higher, thanks to Luke Campbell's 2012 Olympics bantamweight gold medal and Tommy Coyle's 2013 International Boxing Federation lightweight title win. The consolidation of elite sport in the city was once again demonstrated in 2015 when Campbell defeated Coyle in a high-profile bout at Hull KR's stadium.

A unique city of sporting culture

The Campbell/Coyle fight was another demonstration of the importance that sport has to the city. In one of the most deprived areas in Britain thousands of people assembled to enjoy themselves and celebrate their collective identity as citizens of Hull. In that sense, little had changed since the Victorian era when thousands of people gathered together to watch and play sport for exactly those same reasons. The fact that the boxing match was held at Hull KR in the east of the city also served to emphasise the way in which sport had come to define the geographical division of the city; for those in the east, the fact that the fight was not at the KC Stadium in the west was a small victory in the ongoing rivalry. In an era where deindustrialisation and free-market economics had robbed much of Hull's population of their hopes for a better future, the success of the city's clubs and athletes had at least given them momentary cause for pride – demonstrating yet again that in the British sporting landscape, Hull's sporting culture was unique to the city and its people (Figure 7.20).

7.20 Sport – Hull's true religion?
Courtesy of RFL Archives

Notes

1   *Yorkshire Evening Post* (Leeds), 1 December 1900; Frank Marshall, *Football. The Rugby Union Game* (London, 1892), pp. 421–23.

2   *Athletic News*, 11 October 1876.

3   *Yorkshire Evening Post* (Leeds), 1 December 1900.

4   *The Times*, 30 October 1896.

5   Hull History Centre, W. Corlyon manuscript notebooks, C DBHM/11/9.

6   *Yorkshire Evening Post* (Leeds), 21 November 1903.

7   *York Herald*, 2 January 1888.

8   *Hull Daily Mail*, 6 April 1887 and 7 April 1887.

9   *Hull Daily Mail*, 6 April 1887.

10 *Hull Daily Mail*, 1 October 1908.

11 *Yorkshire Post* (Leeds), 18 July 1888.

12 Hull FC, *Annual Report and Statement of Accounts*, 1881–82, Hull History Centre, C DBHM/11/2.

13 *Yorkshire Evening Post* (Leeds), 1 December 2000 and 20 February 2004.

14 Hull FC, *Annual Report and Statement of Accounts*, 1882–83, 1883–84 and 1887–88, Hull History Centre, C DBHM/11/2.

15 Hull FC committee minutes, 10 March 1884, 17 March 1884 and 1 April 1884, Rugby Football League Archive, University of Huddersfield, RFL/CR/1/H3/1/1.

16 For details of the ground moves, see Trevor Delaney, *The Grounds of Rugby League* (Keighley, 1991), pp. 91–101.

17 *Hull Times*, 7 September 1895.

18 Hull FC, *Annual Report and Statement of Accounts*, 1894–95 and 1895–96, Hull History Centre, C DBHM/11/2.

19 *Hull Daily Mail*, 4 September 1895 and 20 September 1895.

20 Mike Ulyatt, *See You Down at the Circle* (Hull, 2004), pp. 8–9, 28.

21 John Lowerson, *Sport and the English Middle Classes* (Manchester, 1983), p. 140.

22 *Hull Daily Mail*, 15 January 1901.

23 David Goodman, *Hull City, A History* (Stroud, 2014), p.7.

24 *Hull Packet and East Riding Times*, 28 September 1883.

25 Goodman, *Hull City*, p. 11.

26 *Hull Daily Mail*, 10 August 1938.

27 Hull Angels began competing in Hedon, on the site of the old racecourse, for two-and-a-half seasons in 1947.

28 Hull KR, *Annual Report and Accounts*, 1904, Hull History Centre, C DBHM/11/1.

29 *Sport in Industry*, 1 (June 1938), pp. 22, 31.

30 *Hull Daily Mail*, 31 March 2003.

31 *Daily Mirror* (London), 30 October 2010.

32 *Hull and East Yorkshire Times*, 28 January 1961.

CHAPTER EIGHT

Distant-Water Trawlerman: William Oliver, 1884–1959

DAVID J. STARKEY

The last few hours of the 1930s were unremarkable in William Oliver's household. 'Wife and I,' ran his diary entry for 31 December 1939, 'sat by the fire waiting for the year to expire and at 12 o'clock wished each other luck for the coming year. Nobody came to let our New Year in, so I went outside and let it in myself.' Reflecting on the year just ending, he noted that there had been 'several removals and changes in our life', which he listed as follows:

> Removed to Ryehill bungalow from Pickering Road, September 6th
> Let our Pickering Road house, December 1st
> Lorrie [his son] took over White Swan Inn, January 25th
> War declared against Germany, September 3rd

In conflating global and personal events in this loose chronology, William Oliver might also have noted that on 3 August 1939 his career as a skipper in Hull's distant-water trawl fishery had come to an end when his vessel, the *Runswick Bay*, returned from Icelandic waters to land a catch of cod, haddock and flatfish at his home port. This was almost thirty-three years since he had had been awarded his skipper's certificate and taken command of the *Lord Salisbury*, a steam trawler that departed St Andrew's Dock bound for the fishing grounds off Iceland on 26 September 1906.[1] During that third of a century, Skipper Oliver commanded trawling voyages to fishing grounds in the North Sea, the White Sea (Murmansk coast), and off the coasts of Norway and west Scotland, as well as serving in the minesweeping branch of the Royal Naval Reserve, largely in Malta, for most of the First World War (Figure 8.1). By far the greatest part of his sea-going effort, however, was expended in removing cod, haddock, plaice and other species from the waters covering the continental shelves that lie to the south and west of Iceland.

In commanding these voyages, Skipper Oliver maintained a daily log of his vessel's course and bearings, descriptions of weather conditions, comments about catches and fishing grounds, and details of any extraordinary events. These personal logs appear to have been kept for two main reasons: first, they constituted a record that could be called upon to answer enquiries should the voyage prove to be unsuccessful or contentious; and, secondly, there was a business rationale, for the logs provided their author with a guide as to what had been caught in which location, and how much fish and money had been generated on each trip. Although no trace has been found of pre-1914 logs, eight volumes have survived to provide a virtually complete set of logs relating to the days he spent at sea from 8 October 1919 to 3 August 1939. Not content with compiling his logs, Oliver copied his shipboard record into diaries, augmenting his sea-going narrative with a daily account of his activities ashore between voyages. Twenty annual diaries contain entries for each day from 1 January 1920 to 31 December 1939, offering glimpses of the very full social, cultural and domestic life of a man who spent about 77 per cent of the period at sea, and had a spouse, Betsy Oliver, ten children and a home in Hull. Despite her significant role in his life – they were married for over fifty-five years – Betsy is scarcely identified by name in Oliver's personal record. Rather, apart from a single entry for 31 May 1921, in which he referred to her as 'the Missus', and two references to 'wife Betsy' in 1935, she is known as 'wife' throughout the logs and diaries.[2]

Skipper Oliver drew upon his own handwritten testimony to write an autobiographical account for publication as 'A Trawlerman's Reminiscences' in 11 monthly instalments in *World Fishing* during 1953 and 1954.[3] These printed recollections enhance the logs and diaries by taking their author's story back to his boyhood, and by providing detail that is lacking in his often stark and formulaic daily entries. Taken together, William Oliver's logs, diaries and 'Reminiscences' offer valuable personal insights into Hull's highly significant trawl fishery, how it changed during one practitioner's lifetime, and what it was like working aboard a trawler in distant waters, as well as living ashore with 'wife'.

8.1 William Oliver qualified to serve as skipper in the minesweeping branch of the Royal Naval Reserve on 11 July 1911. If enrolled, he would receive 9s per day plus 1s 8d messing allowance and a £10 per year retainer. In this photograph, he is wearing his RNR uniform and sporting a handsome moustache. Many reservist fishermen grew such moustaches when called up, for it served to distinguish them from naval seamen, who were only allowed to grow full beards or go clean shaven.
From William Oliver, 'A Trawlerman's Reminiscences (6)', *World Fishing*, 3 (1954), p. 112.

Hull, steam trawling and distant waters

A quest for food has largely motivated people to remove fish from marine habitats. This has given rise to subsistence fishing, with coastal dwellers hunting sea fish to meet their own nutritional needs since the earliest times. A commercial motive, however, has accounted for the bulk of the fish extracted from the seas over the long term. The food requirements of human societies have persuaded some people to make it their business to capture, transport and process sea fish, thereby transforming a natural living resource into a commodity that is sold to supply consumers from all ranks of society. Such transactions have generated personal income and profit for those engaged in catching, curing and marketing fish, an incentive that encouraged many thousands of Hull people, including William Oliver, to engage in commercial fishing activity during the nineteenth and twentieth centuries.

The extent to which Hull people engaged in fishing, and the form that this engagement took, was largely shaped by the interplay of environmental, economic and political factors.[4] In the late eighteenth century, stocks of cod, plaice, haddock, herring and other commercially viable species were abundant in the waters that surrounded the British Isles. Ashore, the size and distribution of Britain's population was undergoing significant change. With the absolute number of people rising rapidly, and a growing proportion dwelling in urban settings, fish suppliers, like other food merchants, faced generally buoyant demand conditions. But they were also faced with the difficulty of supplying the right product at an affordable price in areas where demand was high. In England, this essentially meant providing fresh white fish to low-income consumers congregated in towns and cities distant from the sea, a goal that was rendered largely unattainable by constraints in catching and transport technologies before the mid-nineteenth century.

Overcoming these obstacles entailed technological developments at sea, where the introduction and diffusion into the North Sea of trawl nets towed by relatively small wooden sailing vessels, known as smacks, enabled an increase in catches of white fish.[5] On land, delivering these catches in a fresh condition to urban working-class consumers was not economically feasible until the railways connected ports with inland cities during the 1840s and 1850s. At this point, Hull emerged as one of the foci in the dynamic expansion of the trawl fishery due principally to its proximity to key North Sea fishing grounds, especially the Dogger Bank, its port facilities and its rail links with Leeds, Manchester, Birmingham and other rapidly growing towns and cities. For the next thirty to forty years, Hull – like Grimsby, North Shields and Aberdeen – was home to a burgeoning trawl fishery undertaken by a fleet of over 420 sailing smacks that extracted substantial and growing quantities of cod, plaice, sole and other species of white fish from large areas of the North Sea.

A highly significant sea-change in the development of this industry occurred in the late 1880s and 1890s when the sail-driven, wooden-hulled smacks were swiftly supplanted by steam-powered, steel-hulled trawlers. This transition was driven by changes in the marine environment triggered by fishing activity and signalled by smackmen, whose reports of declining yields became louder and more convincing as the 1870s and 1880s progressed. While stock depletion was seemingly occurring in the North Sea, the growth in demand for fresh white fish continued apace in Britain and was now enhanced by the introduction of new retail outlets in the form of fried fish shops.[6] The rapid adoption of these modern vessels was facilitated by improvements in shipbuilding materials and marine engine construction, which allowed entrepreneurial smackmen and new investors to risk their capital in steel-hulled trawlers propelled by triple expansion marine engines – innovations that were also transforming the merchant shipping industry. Such economic and technological changes were encouraged, moreover, by a political situation in which Britain could exert diplomatic pressure and, if needed, naval force to ensure the rights of its citizens and vessels to extract fish from the inshore waters of Norway, Russia, Denmark and the Danish North Atlantic dominions. The net result of this process of investment, replacement and renewal – which was one of the most rapid and comprehensive transitions in British industrial history – was that British trawlers could now fish beyond the North Sea in the so-called 'distant waters' off the Faroes, Iceland, Norway and Russia (Figure 8.2). These waters remained the main fishing grounds for the trawling industry for the first three-quarters of the twentieth century, for it was not until 1976 that British trawlers were prohibited from fishing within the newly extended territorial waters of Iceland and other so-called 'coastal states'.[7]

Born in Hull on 1 June 1884, William Oliver witnessed at first hand the transition from wooden sailing smacks to steel steam trawlers. As a small boy he was an avid observer of the fishing smacks and early steam trawlers – some of which, like the one skippered by his father, were converted smacks – that entered and cleared St Andrew's Dock. Having completed a few voyages in his father's vessels during holidays from school, young Oliver determined to escape the tedium of his first paid employment, as a clerical worker in the North East Railway Fish Office, by enlisting as a cook aboard a fishing smack, the *Emperor*, in January 1898. Although he had claimed to be 16 when signing on, he was actually just 13½ years of age as the *Emperor* set forth on a fishing trip in the North Sea that was to last for over ten weeks. Oliver was retained for the *Emperor*'s next voyage, before transferring to another smack, the *Queensland*. By 1898, the *Emperor* and the *Queensland* were among the very few smacks still operating, both being deployed in one of Hull's two 'box fleets', so called because the catch was gutted, cleaned and packed in boxes for daily delivery in fast steam cutters to Billingsgate in London. This assignment did not last long, for Oliver's second trip on the *Emperor* changed course rather abruptly when the skipper was instructed after five weeks on the grounds with the

8.2 Hull trawlermen aboard an unknown ship in the interwar period.
Courtesy of the Maritime Historical Studies Centre (Robb Robinson)

8.3 Fish in 'kits' standing on the quayside, awaiting the early morning fish auction. Fish landed in Hull was invariably measured in kits. One kit is the equivalent of 140 lb (63.5 kg) of gutted fish.
Maritime Museum: Hull Museums

'Great Northern' boxing fleet that the smacks were to be replaced by steam trawlers. Although the *Emperor* sailed across the North Sea to join Hull's other boxing fleet, the 'Red Cross', off the Danish coast, the end was nigh for Hull's fishing smacks.[8]

In marked contrast, the port's complement of steam trawlers was increasing swiftly. Some of these vessels worked five-week stints in the box fleets according to the directions of an 'admiral', who decided where the fleet would fish and for how long. Many other steam trawlers worked as 'single boaters', their skippers deciding which grounds to fish, with the catch retained on board, where it was packed in ice in the fish hold for landing at market in Hull at the end of the voyage (Figure 8.3). Although the steam boxing fleets continued to fish the North Sea until 1936, the single boating mode of operation was largely deployed in more distant waters from the late 1890s. William Oliver swam with this tide. His trip as cook on the *Queensland* was his last box fleet venture, for he then enlisted as a deckhand ('decky') on the *Duke of Wellington* for a trip to Faroe that yielded a very good landing of plaice in November 1898. According to his published recollections, Oliver decided in 1899 'to concentrate on the Iceland trips, and at 15 years of age [I] was decky of the *Sylvia*, a fine type of vessel commanded by Tom Clarkson, one of the foremost skippers of the day'.[9]

Hindsight indicates that this was a wise decision. After less than two decades during which technical, managerial and operational changes had transformed the industry, British trawl fishing entered a longer phase in which the structure, *modus operandi* and working practices of the business altered little over nearly eighty years. Indeed, it was contended in the 1960s and 1970s that this was an 'antiquated industry' which had barely moved on since the climacteric of the 1890s and early twentieth century.[10] Oliver engaged in steam trawling for much of this period, his career progressing quickly from deckhand to mate to skipper, a status he held for over thirty-three years until he retired from the sea on the eve of the Second World War. His long engagement in distant-water steam trawling – which continued ashore from 1945 to 1954, when he served as secretary of the Hull Trawler Officers' Guild – as charted in his logs, diaries and 'Reminiscences', reveals how this business was conducted and how it shaped the lives of large numbers of Hull people.

William Papper

The murder of 14-year-old William Papper shocked the nation. Papper had been apprenticed to trawler owner and skipper Osmond Otto Brand in 1881. At first Brand treated him well, but shortly before they sailed in the *Rising Sun* in December, Papper apparently remarked that his sister was having an affair with Brand. That evening Brand beat Papper as they lay at anchor, and once at sea he subjected him to a fortnight of starvation and gross physical abuse, until he was so disfigured that Brand feared to take him back to Hull. Papper died in his berth and his body was thrown overboard on 1 January 1882. Brand threatened the rest of the crew into silence and reported on arrival in Hull that Papper had been knocked overboard by the foresail. There the matter rested until March, when two of the crew went to the police. The trial of Brand and third hand Frederick Rycroft attracted angry crowds and the attention of national newspapers. Rycroft was convicted of common assault and received three months' hard labour, while Brand was hanged for murder at Armley Gaol, Leeds, in May 1882.

The scandal exposed a side of the fishing industry that was little known. In Hull and Grimsby, trawler owners found it difficult to obtain sufficient labour and therefore recruited teenage boys from workhouses and reformatories, some of whom simply tramped to the ports and asked for work. Many were unruly, unhealthy and unsuitable, and many signed their apprenticeship indentures with no real idea of the commitment they were making. By the late 1870s, about 1,200 of the 2,300 fishermen in Hull were apprentices. Many owners were either unwilling or unable to accommodate them in their own homes, and instead paid them a small allowance and left them to fend for themselves.

The results were predictable. Ashore, apprentices tended to drift into the slums and resorted to heavy drinking, prostitution and brawling. At sea, training was minimal and accidents common: almost one in twenty Hull and Grimsby apprentices died at work in the 1870s. Moreover, crews were paid partly by share and therefore worked intensively in harsh and dangerous conditions. Some had little patience with frightened, clumsy and sometimes resentful apprentices.

A typical sailing trawler, or 'smack'. Built in 1867, and slightly larger than the vessel depicted here, the *Rising Sun* was one of over 1,000 smacks that worked from Hull and Grimsby by 1880. They usually carried crews of five, of whom two or three were teenage apprentices. Living conditions were cramped and the work was hard and dangerous. During the 1870s one in twenty Hull apprentices died in accidents at work.
Courtesy of the Maritime Historical Studies Centre, University of Hull

Bullying and petty intimidation were common, while serious violence and sexual assaults were not unknown. About a quarter of all apprentices absconded; many were caught, brought back and sent to prison for breaking their indentures. Some even preferred prison to the relentless labour of the Dogger Bank fishing grounds and the cramped cabin of a sailing trawler. Although many completed their apprenticeships and went on to become skippers themselves, an apprentice had a far greater chance of drowning than of owning his own boat.

The apprenticeship system had been in decline for some years when the murder of William Papper hit national headlines. In response, the government ordered an inquiry that informed legislation to bring fishing and its apprenticeship system under control. However, by then apprenticeship was in terminal decline and had all but disappeared from Hull by 1900, although at some other ports it survived into the 1930s.

The modern fishing industry was built on the often unwilling labour of thousands of teenage boys, without whom it could not have grown as quickly as it did. The murder of William Papper exposed the conditions they worked under, the risks they ran, and the appalling cruelty with which a few of them were treated. It also changed the industry forever.

Martin Wilcox

Skipper Oliver's sea time

Learning the ropes

Setting forth in 1899 to exploit new fishing grounds in a modern trawler commanded by a skipper with a reputation for landing large catches, William Oliver was presented with an exceptional opportunity to engage in a business that appeared to be on the brink of taking off. He succeeded in grasping this opportunity by enhancing his knowledge and understanding of the trawling business in three principal ways. First, he listened to, and heeded, the advice offered to him by experienced, effective skippers. Presumably he learned something from his father, who took him out on North Sea fishing voyages during school holidays. But William Oliver certainly gained much from the sage counsel of seasoned exponents of the craft of fishing, notably Tom Clarkson and John (Tommy) Gant, to whom he acknowledged an enormous debt for passing on hard-won information and insight regarding the fishing grounds, weather patterns, sea conditions and shiphandling techniques. Acquiring qualifications through training programmes was the second means through which Oliver sought to develop his expertise. Having accumulated the necessary four years' sea service, in 1904 he emerged from a week-long training course, delivered by a retired skipper and a Customs official, with a mate's certificate issued under the auspices of the Board of Trade. Two years later, in July 1906, he undertook more training and was rewarded with a skipper's certificate, after passing an examination that he completed just in time to embark as mate aboard the *Ocean Queen*, which was bound on an Iceland fishing trip. In 1911, while his trawler was undergoing its summer refit, Skipper Oliver became the first Hull seafarer to become a Royal Naval Reservist on completing a training course and examination administered by the Royal Navy.[11]

Such qualifications contributed to the attainment of the third element of Oliver's personal development plan, the assembly of a range of intangible assets that generally underpin progression in any career. In this respect, like masters of merchant vessels and captains of naval ships, trawling skippers required the trust, confidence and support of employers ashore and employees at sea. That William Oliver built up such reputational qualities is implied by his rapid rise from decky learner to skipper between 1899 and 1906. Such progression entailed promotion to mate in 1904, and then appointments successively as relief skipper, continuing skipper and leading skipper, a status he retained until the mid-1930s. Much of this was achieved over a period of twenty-four years in conjunction with Mr McCann, who managed both Pickering & Haldane Ltd and the Yorkshire Steam Fishing Company. Indeed, such was the strength of this working relationship, and such was the esteem in which Skipper Oliver was held by the trawler owners, that in 1926 he was invited to become a shareholder and co-owner of Yorkshire Steam Fishing, an invitation that he duly accepted. These shareholding and working ties were cut after a row in August 1933, which the skipper-shareholder later described as a 'demented' decision on his part.[12]

Skipper Oliver's reputation was an important professional attribute, especially in a relatively isolated, compact place like the Hessle Road fishing district of west Hull. Here, as in many business contexts, but especially in ports, reputations, interpersonal relations and social connections underpinned the networks that, in turn, were vital to the conduct of a comparatively high-risk business. Nevertheless, like his fellow skippers, Oliver's credibility in the highly competitive arena of the trawl fishery was largely based on his ability to manage a vessel and her crew, so that sufficient fish were caught and landed to generate earnings that exceeded the costs incurred in the catching operation – in other words, his ability to make a profit. That Oliver did so by engaging in 'Iceland fishing trips' over a prolonged period is evident in his logs and diaries.

The trawling routine

Skipper Oliver commanded 274 fishing voyages between 9 October 1919 and 3 August 1939, as Table 8.1 indicates. As a consequence, he was at sea for approximately 77 per cent of the 7,239 consecutive days covered by his logs and diaries during this period. This sea time comprised, as Table 8.2 shows, 1,445 'travel to work' days, 2,882 days spent fishing on the grounds, and 1,222 days steaming for home.

Table 8.1: William Oliver's voyages by fishing ground, 1919–39

Year	Trips	Iceland	White Sea	Norwegian coast	North Sea (herring)	West Scotland	'Broken' trips
1919	2	2	0	0	0	0	0
1920	14	14	0	0	0	0	0
1921	12	10	0	0	0	1	1
1922	13	13	0	0	0	0	0
1923	14	14	0	0	0	0	0
1924	15	14	1	0	0	0	0
1925	13	13	0	0	0	0	0
1926	14	14	0	0	0	0	0
1927	14	14	0	0	0	0	0
1928	12	12	0	0	0	0	0
1929	15	13	2	0	0	0	0
1930	23	11	1	0	11	0	0
1931	16	12	1	1	2	0	0
1932	15	15	0	0	0	0	0
1933	14	14	0	0	0	0	0
1934	14	12	2	0	0	0	0
1935	10	9	1	0	0	0	0
1936	15	14	1	0	0	0	0
1937	12	10	1	0	0	0	1
1938	11	10	1	0	0	0	0
1939	6	6	0	0	0	0	0
	274	246	11	1	13	1	2

Source: University of Hull, Blaydes House, William Oliver's logs, 1919–39

The objective of 246 of the 274 trips, 89.8 per cent of the total, was to catch fish off the southern and western coasts of Iceland. In charting the course of up to 15 Iceland voyages per year, the logs give an impression of routine and regularity – perhaps even a sense of the mundane – in their cursory daily reports of the progress of what were reckoned to be 2,074-mile round trips (see Figure 8.4). Leaving St Andrew's Dock at high tide, Oliver's vessel would proceed out of the Humber to test the compass and set the log at the Outer Bank buoy, and take bearings at Flamborough Head and Rattray Light, before steaming through Pentland Firth and across the North Atlantic to the Westman Isles, off the south-western coast of Iceland, where the fishing gear would be readied. According to the skipper's judgement of conditions, the trawl would be shot in the inner, middle or outer Westman grounds, or further to the north-west, which entailed steaming across Faxa and Brede bays to the western fjords that lie north of Stallberg Huk. Having taken between four and six days to reach the grounds, a further eight to twelve days were spent fishing, often for sustained periods at night – especially in the summer months when nights were light in northern waters – when the prey was deemed to be particularly amenable to capture.

Table 8.2: William Oliver's sea time, 1919–39

Year	Voyage out (days)	On fishing grounds (days)	Return voyage (days)	Total days at sea	% of year at sea
1919	21	37	13	71	–
1920	84	148	70	302	82.5
1921	79	161	53	293	80.3
1922	71	157	63	291	79.7
1923	85	157	68	310	84.9
1924	77	150	70	297	81.1
1925	77	144	60	281	77
1926	103	140	64	307	84.1
1927	65	124	71	260	71.2
1928	71	144	54	269	73.5
1929	74	157	70	301	82.5
1930	68	182	57	307	84.1
1931	79	166	60	305	83.6
1932	82	143	73	298	81.4
1933	69	156	59	284	77.8
1934	72	142	66	280	76.7
1935	51	112	45	208	57
1936	69	166	66	301	82.2
1937	67	120	55	242	66.3
1938	53	121	55	229	62.7
1939	28	55	30	113	–
	1,445	2,882	1,222	5,549	

Source: University of Hull, Blaydes House, William Oliver's logs, 1919–39

Equally, there were sustained periods when working on the grounds largely involved sheltering from the weather in Dyra Fjord or the main harbour of the Westman Isles, or resorting to such places to repair damaged trawl nets or, on a few logged occasions, to land a crew member for medical treatment (see Figure 8.5). Such eventualities meant, of course, that fish were not being caught and therefore money was not being made, sometimes causing Oliver's generally matter-of-fact tone to give way to frustrated exclamation: 'I am fed up', 'FED UP', 'Disgusted', 'worst trip I have

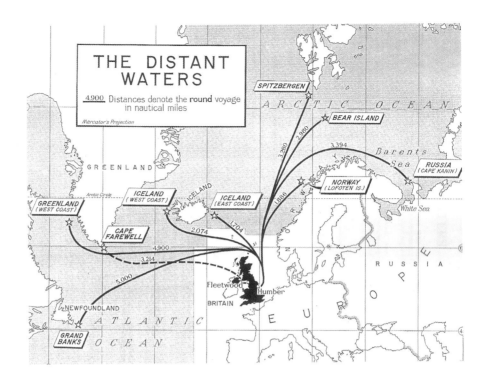

ever known'. Often such angst was followed by a decision to 'pack up and head for home'. Following a south-south-east course from the west or south coast of Iceland, a return voyage of four or five days' duration ensued, with bearings generally taken at Skule Skerries, Duncansby Head, Rattray Light and Flamborough Head, before Skipper Oliver steered his vessel into the Humber and alighted for home, leaving the mate to take the trawler into dock and supervise the landing of the catch, which usually took place at around 5 a.m., ahead of the morning auction.

The Iceland routine was interrupted by 28 voyages to other grounds during the interwar period. A single trip was undertaken to the fishing grounds off the west of Scotland in the midst of the 1921 coal strike, presumably because limited coal supplies restricted the *Lord Minto*'s operational range. Eleven voyages to the northern North Sea, where herring was the target species, took place during the summer of 1930, with two more 'herring voyages' completed in late July and early August 1931. These trips lasted from two to nine days and were executed in the *Waveflower*, a distant-water trawler equipped with specialist herring nets that Oliver and crew members had tested in a field near Hessle during the planning stage of these North Sea ventures (see Figure 8.6). There was a further single voyage in December 1931, when the *Waveflower* fished off the Norwegian coast in what might have been – like the herring voyages of the two previous summers, and the Bear Island voyage that departed on 16 December 1932 under the command of A. Smith while Oliver had a trip ashore – an exploratory attempt to diversify into different products, source areas and markets.

Another 11 of Oliver's fishing trips were conducted on what were termed the White Sea grounds, which were actually located off the Murmansk coast rather than in the White Sea itself. Such voyages were not favoured by Oliver, who concluded the log entry for one such trip – which yielded 870 kits worth £722 – by stating: 'So ends the White Sea trip. Never again if I can help it.' Such negativity was perhaps rooted in the memory of his mentor, Tommy Gant, enduring a difficult and unproductive trip to the Murmansk coast back in 1906. This was possibly because of the logistics of a White Sea voyage, which was some 1,200 miles longer than an Iceland trip,

and required a pilot to steer trawlers northwards 'through the fjords' from Londingen to Honningsvaag, pick up approximately 60 tons of ice at Tromso and then steam east around Finnmark and south into the Barents Sea (Figure 8.7). The most likely explanation, however, is that he had much less experience of White Sea voyages and therefore preferred to fish the Iceland grounds, where his accumulated expertise translated into a telling comparative advantage. Notwithstanding his reservations, Oliver steamed to Russian waters on ten further occasions between 1929 and 1938, with two such trips occurring in both 1929 and 1934.

It was not always plain sailing during these 274 voyages. After an Iceland trip in January 1928, chillingly logged as 'The Trip of Troubles', Oliver was obliged to attend a 'trial' in the Insurance Offices in Hull 'for being alongside and going ashore'. As a consequence, he 'got suspended for 2 months', though he did not appear to dwell on the verdict, for he 'was home at 1pm [and] in the afternoon went in company with Mr & Mrs Battersby for a motor run to Beverley'. 'The Trip of Storms' was perhaps more challenging for the skipper, who noted that gales, snowstorms and heavy seas led to a protracted 28-day Iceland trip, which had commenced on 14 December 1921 and ended on 10 January 1922. Two of the voyages enumerated in Table 8.1 were not completed. One was aborted due to the poor quality of the coal that was taken aboard the *Waveflower* at Hamburg in September 1926. With no coal available in Hull due

8.5 Oliver generally recorded his time at sea in terse diary entries outlining the weather, fish catches, navigational matters and incidental voyage details. Occasionally, he was more reflective; for instance, on Christmas Eve 1926, while on an Iceland fishing trip, he was 'thinking of home very much tonight' as his vessel 'remained at anchor until Christmas came in'.
University of Hull, Blaydes House, 'William Oliver's Diary, 1926', courtesy of the Maritime Historical Studies Centre

8.6 Having proceeded up the Humber in the early hours of the morning, on 29 July 1931 Oliver stayed on the dock to observe the landing of a catch of North Sea herrings, which eventually sold for £283. Perhaps this return, one of the lowest of his long career, put him in the rotten temper that resulted in him being 'very objectionable' that evening.
University of Hull, Blaydes House, 'William Oliver's Diary, 1931', courtesy of the Maritime Historical Studies Centre

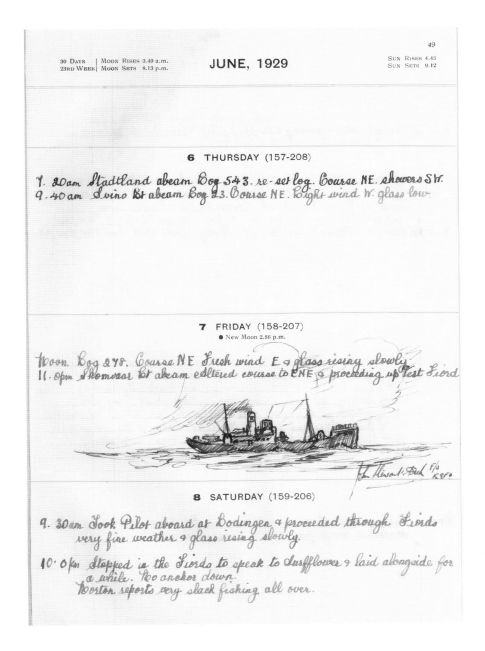

JUNE, 1929

6 THURSDAY (157-208)

7. 20am Stadtland abeam Log 543. re-set log. Course NE. showers SW.
9. 40 am Svino Lt abeam Log 23. Course NE. Light wind W. glass low.

7 FRIDAY (158-207)
● New Moon 2.56 p.m.

Noon. Log 278. Course NE Fresh wind E & glass rising slowly
11. 0pm Skomvaer Lt abeam altered course to ENE & proceeding up Vest Fiord

8 SATURDAY (159-206)

9. 30am Took Pilot aboard at Bodingen & proceeded through Fiords very fine weather & glass rising slowly.

10. 0pm Stopped in the Fiords to speak to Sunflower & laid alongside for a while. Too anchor down.
Boston reports very slack fishing all over.

to the miners' strike, Oliver had been obliged to cross the North Sea to seek fuel at the start of an Icelandic fishing voyage, a diversion he had had to make during the 1921 coal strike and more recently in the general strike of May 1926. However, whereas previous supplies of coal loaded at the 'near continent' ports of Schiedam, Ostend and Antwerp had been fit for purpose, the Hamburg consignment was poor in quality and therefore the *Waveflower* was unable to generate enough steam to make adequate headway or tow a trawl. She struggled to reach Scottish waters, where it was decided to terminate the voyage and return to Hull to land the fish – which fetched £9 8s – that had been taken during a trial tow. Ill health was responsible for the second 'broken' trip, as Oliver decided to turn back to Hull two days into an Iceland voyage on account of an outbreak of influenza that afflicted nearly all of the crew of the *Brimness*, including the skipper himself, who remained indoors for five days after he got home on 27 January 1937.

The intensity of particular phases of the work process is evident in the logs. At sea, Oliver sometimes felt it necessary to lay his vessel up to allow the crew to sleep, while he noted in one entry that he had not slept for 18 hours, and later reminisced that on difficult voyages he had not rested for up to 60 hours. But the rarity of references to excessively long working hours perhaps implies that such occurrences were either infrequent or part of a regime that was accepted and not worthy of comment. Ashore, Oliver's logs indicate that turnaround times in Hull were generally short, with trawlers frequently entering port during the evening or the early hours of the morning, landing their catch at dawn on the next morning and then being ready to depart on the morning after – a turnaround of less than 36 hours. Such swift arrivals and departures sometimes took place sequentially; for instance, in the five months (153 days) from 1 August to 31 December 1923, the *Lord Talbot* was only in port for ten days, while there was a similarly intensive sea-going phase during the equivalent five months of 1929, when only eleven days were spent in Hull landing fish taken in six Iceland trips.

Making a decent living

Although Skipper Oliver's personal logs and diaries do not include financial statements, profit and loss accounts or balance sheets, they provide a number of indicators relating to various aspects of his performance. For example, he won a number of awards during his career, which suggests that he was well regarded by his employers and his peers. In 1924, for instance, he received a £200 prize for achieving the second highest annual return in Hull, a reward he also earned in 1925, after which the port's trawler owners abandoned this particular incentive scheme. Ten years later, on 31 May 1935, he was one of three Hull skippers whose long service and outstanding performance were recognised in the presentation of a King's Silver Jubilee Medal at 'a very pleasant ceremony [at which] our wives were a great deal more excited than the men'. Unfortunately, just over a month later, the medal was stolen from the Olivers' car when they stopped for lunch at the Green Man Hotel in Edgware during a motoring holiday. This loss 'completely spoiled what was a splendid run and wife and I are very much upset about it'. In 1955 Oliver was further honoured by the award of an OBE for services to the fishing industry after retiring as secretary of the Hull Trawler Officers' Guild on health grounds. He received the award in person at Buckingham Palace, which prompted the *Yorkshire Post* to print a photograph of Skipper and Mrs Oliver under the heading: 'Northerners at the Palace'.[13]

Key to such accolades was Oliver's performance on the fishing grounds. Here, in contrast to the regularity of the sailing schedule, the catching effort was marked by the variability and uncertainty of the outcome of individual hauls (Figure 8.8), as the following sample entries from the logs suggest:

made a decent living last night …
shot off Dyra Fjord Bank and made a good living …
heaving in as many haddocks as we can take …
cod end split and lost a full bag of fish …
poor night's work …
steaming around looking for fish …

Luck, stamina and perseverance appear to have been as important as judgement in the operational sphere, while competition with other trawlers for sea space and catches was invariably a feature of the business. Although it is never overtly stated in the logs and diaries, there are signs that Oliver kept a watchful, and sometimes jealous, eye on his rivals, noting wistfully that the '*Woolborough* [is] going home

8.8 Oliver kept daily notes of the success or otherwise of each day's catching effort in a log book aboard ship. He then copied the entries into his annual diary. The four days on this particular diary page indicate that trawlermen might experience mixed fortunes in a short space of time on the fishing grounds; thus, after a split trawl and 'no fish', Skipper Oliver's men took 'as much as can have in for 2 hours', as well as 'decent bags cod with 1 & 2 plaice for two hours', before they 'had 2 hauls and got nothing'.
University of Hull, Blaydes House, 'William Oliver's Diary, 1933', courtesy of the Maritime Historical Studies Centre

with 900 kits & has only been out 11 days', 'the *Foamflower* is outfishing us', and, on anchoring at Dyra Fjord, that 'several trawlers are coming in. All seem to have been fishing much better than we have.'

The products of Oliver's labours are outlined in Table 8.3. A total of 232,158 kits of fish were taken during the 274 fishing trips he commanded during the 1919–39 period.[14] Cod constituted 75.7 per cent of the aggregate catch, with the remainder comprising plaice and flatfish, haddock and herring. On an annual basis, catches ranged from 8,940 kits taken in 1928 to a high point of 17,857 kits reached in 1930, when 5,518 kits of North Sea herring were landed as well as white fish from the distant grounds. The variability of returns was much pronounced at the voyage level, with a personal peak of 1,980 kits being landed by Oliver on 5 March 1936 contrasting with landings of 410 kits on 12 November 1923, and 412 kits on 2 November 1931, at the other end of the scale.

Table 8.3: Quantity and value of fish landed by William Oliver's trawlers, 1919–39

Year	Total	Cod	Plaice	Haddock	Herring	Value
	(kits)	(kits)	(kits)	(kits)	(kits)	(£)
1919	1,550	1,250	300	0	0	4,752
1920	12,645	10,111	2,534	0	0	21,435
1921	9,020	7,548	1,472	0	0	16,404
1922	10,785	8,369	2,416	0	0	16,079
1923	10,076	8,618	1,458	0	0	15,318
1924	11,312	9,579	1,733	0	0	15,842
1925	10,260	8,772	1,488	0	0	15,475
1926	10,826	9,546	1,280	0	0	14,048
1927	11,314	10,227	1,087	0	0	13,252
1928	8,940	7,946	994	0	0	11,531
1929	13,056	10,396	1,464	1,196	0	19,009
1930	17,857	4,410	6,532	1,397	5,518	16,378
1931	14,163	9,209	2,144	1,644	1,166	11,746
1932	13,217	10,012	1,240	1,965	0	12,809
1933	12,886	10,302	1,005	1,579	0	10,616
1934	13,691	10,849	967	1,875	0	13,483
1935	10,236	7,940	814	1,482	0	8,872
1936	14,517	11,683	1,002	1,832	0	13,364
1937	9,389	6,798	1,090	1,501	0	9,640
1938	10,480	7,756	797	1,927	0	10,815
1939	5,938	4,427	425	1,086	0	5,353
	232,158	175,748	32,242	17,484	6,684	276,221

Source: University of Hull, Blaydes House, William Oliver's logs, 1919–39

The amount of fish landed did not necessarily correlate with the value of the catch. For instance, as Table 8.3 shows, the 12,645 kits landed in 1920 fetched £21,435, whereas approximately 600 more kits were landed in 1932, but realised just £12,809 on the market. Presented in another way, the data indicate that the average value of landings ranged from just over £3 per kit in 1919 to 16 shillings per kit in 1933. Such single-year comparisons form part of a long-term pattern, for the annual price per kit comfortably exceeded £1 during the 1920s, while the equivalent figure dropped beneath £1 in 1930 when 17,857 kits generated a gross of £16,293, and it remained at that comparatively low level for much of the 1930s. Such divergence was even more pronounced at the voyage level; accordingly, at one extreme, the 801 kits landed on 3 January 1920 yielded £3,020, while at the other end of the spectrum, a mere £755 was generated by the 1,234 kits landed on 13 May 1930.

Various reasons for this price volatility can be discerned in the logs. There were short-term, local factors such as the market gluts precipitated by the arrival and landing of numerous trawlers on the same tide. On 29 August 1921, for instance, Oliver 'went down dock & saw Mr McCann. 9 Iceland ships landing & markets very bad. A lot of fish going to manure yard' (Figure 8.9). Conversely, if his vessel arrived and landed alone then an excellent return might result, as occurred on Maundy Thursday in 1913 when demand and prices increased dramatically ahead of Good Friday,[15] which was traditionally a fish-eating day for many English people. The poor quality of the product could also depress prices, as occurred on 22 May 1939 when a low return was blamed on the inadequate cleaning and gutting of the fish by crew members, who were summarily dismissed. Broader, less visible factors relating to the amount of fish available and the demand for fish in relation to other foodstuffs had a significant bearing on the income and profits of those engaged in the trawl fishery. This is apparent in Oliver's terse references to 'markets dropped 50%' in the log entries for 14 December 1928, 15 July 1932 and numerous other landing days.

Oliver was keenly interested in the catch and financial returns of his fishing trips because he had a significant stake in the gross worth of each voyage he commanded.

According to his own rough calculations, which he entered as handwritten notes in his personal logs, this stake amounted to 10 per cent of the net earnings of each voyage. Such performance-related payments were described as bonuses and were normally paid in the autumn. In October 1923, for instance, Oliver wrote in his log that he had received a bonus of £455 in respect of the 14 voyages he had completed in the *Lord Minto* during that year, while in 1924, his bonus amounted to £645. Although he is somewhat coy in the logs and diaries about how much he earned, there can be no doubt that Skipper Oliver's income was relatively high in the context of a port-city that was struggling to come to terms with a business environment that had altered significantly in the wake of the First World War. His earnings underpinned a lifestyle that hinted at relative affluence in the diary entries relating to the days he spent ashore during the 1920s and 1930s.

A City of Character: Winifred Holtby's Hull

Born in Rudston, East Yorkshire, on 23 June 1898, Winifred Holtby moved with her family to Cottingham in 1919. The city of Hull ('Kingsport') has a distinct and vibrant presence in her work – it informs the settings she creates, the characters we encounter in her writings and the issues her novels bring to life. Holtby registers the hardship and deprivation of a city severely hit by the depression of the 1930s, yet the pursuit of pleasure in the face of hardship and pain is at the heart of her understanding of a city insulated from the rest of the country, but with its face firmly set towards Europe and the wider world.

Shy and 'end-of the roadish', Hull nevertheless provides a vivid location for the dramatisation of one of Holtby's major themes – how art and the imagination enhance the quotidian realities of life and death. In her best-seller, *South Riding* (1936), for example, the schoolteacher Sarah Burton, newly arrived from London, takes a bus over North Bridge and catches sight of flashing water, masts and funnels, 'the blank cliffs of warehouses, stores and offices', tall cranes and walls 'powdered from the fine white dust of flour mills and cement works'. In the suburbs, east of the city, Sarah sees

> a street of little shops selling oilskins and dungarees and men's drill overalls, groceries piled with cheap tinned food, grim crumbling facades announcing *Beds for Men* on placards foul and forbidding as gallows signs. On left and right of the thoroughfare ran mean monotonous streets of two-storied houses, bay-windowed and unvarying – not slums, but dreary respectable horrors, seething with life which was neither dreary nor respectable. Fat women lugged babies smothered in woollies; toddlers still sucking dummies tottered on bowed legs along littered pavements. Pretty little painted sluts minced on high tilted heels off to the pictures or dogs or dirt track race-course.[1]

Holtby's Kingsport is a run-down port-city teeming with potential and with a lust for life.

Hull provided Holtby, and several of her characters, with pleasure in the form of its numerous theatres and cinemas such as the Grand Theatre and Opera House in George Street. Shortly after the end of the First World War, Holtby watched a film about T. E. Lawrence at the Hull Picture House with her friend Edith de Coundouroff, and in August 1925 she admired Charlie Chaplin in *The Gold Rush* in an unnamed cinema.[2] Holtby used her experience at the Palace of Varieties in March 1935 in *South Riding* to express her strong sense of the link between the ephemeral nature of life's pleasures and the reality of death. In the novel, Lily Sawden leaves the doctor's surgery in the fictional Willoughby Place, Kingsport, following confirmation that she is terminally ill with cancer, and is confronted by the 'bright gorgeousness' of the Kingsport Empire cinema. The sensuous opulence of the movie theatre draws her in and she buys 'a one and three-penny ticket' to watch a Mickey Mouse film, a slapstick comedy and Greta Garbo in *Mata Hari*. The transformative experience of the film lifts her out of the

Winifred Holtby's sketch map of South Riding illustrates the high degree of thought and planning that went into *South Riding*. Her detailed map also suggests that Holtby believed in the powerful influence of geography and place on character and in their potential to inform and guide narrative.
© Estate of Winifred Holtby, courtesy of Hull City Council, Hull History Centre

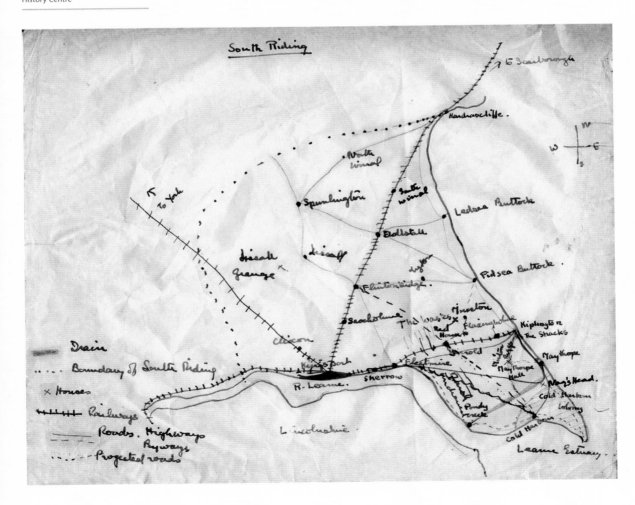

world of pain and illness into a mystical sense of her own imminent demise: 'where others guessed in panic, she knew, and knowing, feared no longer, and being redeemed from fear, she was invincible'.[3]

Holtby's third novel, *The Land of Green Ginger* (1927), features an actual street in Hull with a name so magical that she retained it as a symbol of the 'protest against the tangible world'.[4] In the story, eight-year-old Joanna accompanies her aunts up 'Friarsgate' (Whitefriargate) – 'a grey, narrow canyon between beetling cliffs … blank grey and angry brown' – and discovers a sign 'half hidden in the obscurity of the dirt and darkness':

'The Land of Green Ginger, dark, narrow, mysterious road to heaven, to Fairy Land, to anywhere.' Winifred Holtby, *The Land of Green Ginger: A Romance* (London, 1955 [1927]), p. 201.

> To be offered such gifts of fortune, to seek Commercial Lane and to find – the day before Christmas Eve and by lamplight too – The Land of Green Ginger, dark, narrow, mysterious road to heaven, to Fairy Land, to anywhere.[5]

At the novel's close, Joanna encounters the street again. Following her husband's funeral cortege through the narrow winding streets of the Old Town, where her carriage is momentarily delayed by a motor lorry, she glances through the window and sees the hearse 'flashing in sunlight, move round from Friarsgate and turn before her into the dark by-road called the Land of Green Ginger'. Denied the chance to explore the street as a child, she is carried into it as an adult fully experienced in the realities of love and hate, birth and death. 'The Land of Green Ginger' – as Hull's residents can testify – has its own prosaic reality, and yet in Holtby's novel it represents what her great friend Vera Brittain defined as 'the magic always lying just beyond the surface of life'.[6]

The River Humber ('Leame') is used by Holtby as a symbol of the expansive possibilities of life, and their extinction, in both *The Land of Green Ginger* and *South Riding*. In the former, it links Kingsport to Europe and the forests of Hungary. For Lydia Holly in *South Riding* it expresses the exhilaration of a future in the wider world; for Sarah Burton it spells the end of romance as the body of her would-be lover Robert Carne is discovered 'submerged in the mud, one arm floating limply along the water, its head mercifully buried in clay and weed'.[7] The river reminds the reader of the frailty and the preciousness of life, giving them something of the knowledge that all Hullensians learn to bear in mind.

Sadly, Winifred Holtby died prematurely in March 1935 from Bright's disease. However, the posthumous publication of *South Riding* in 1936 confirmed her as a Yorkshire novelist, specifically of the East and North Ridings, which she combines into a semi-fictional 'fourth' or 'South' Riding. For Holtby, Hull as a place, its geography and culture, enabled her to imaginatively explore universal experiences through the characters she created and narrated, and, indeed, to present the enriching possibilities of actively allowing place to direct the imagination.

Jane Thomas

Notes

1   Winifred Holtby, *South Riding, An English Landscape* (London, 1947 [1936]), pp. 64–65.
2   Holtby also mentions a lecture 'at Hull' on 2 August 1923. Winifred Holtby, *Letters to a Friend*, ed. Alice Holtby and Jean McWilliam (London, 1937), p. 205.
3   Holtby, *South Riding*, p. 225.
4   Winifred Holtby, *The Land of Green Ginger, A Romance* (London, 1955 [1927]), p. 250.
5   Holtby, *The Land of Green Ginger*, p. 201.
6   Holtby, *Letters to a Friend*, p. 222.
7   Holtby, *South Riding*, p. 485.

Skipper Oliver's trips ashore

Oliver's logs and diaries indicate that he was ashore on 1,690 days between 8 October 1919 and 3 August 1939, which amounted to roughly 23 per cent of that period (see Table 8.4). In 12 of these 21 years, he was ashore for fewer than one in five days, or less than 20 per cent of the year. He tended to spend more time home from the sea as the period progressed, with six of the nine years in which he was ashore for more than 20 per cent of the year falling after 1933; indeed, the leap year of 1936, during which Oliver spent only 65 days on land, stands out as the only year after 1931 in which he spent more than 300 days at sea.

The logic of distant-water trawling dictated that Oliver would spend a relatively small proportion of his time ashore. This was a business of margins. Fish consumers perceived fishing as an activity based on the remote margins of the English east coast and prosecuted in the cold, distant and alien margins of the North Atlantic. But to those directly engaged in the business, it was the financial margins that mattered most. As it was by no means guaranteed that a voyage would return a catch or a profit, investors of money and effort in distant-water trawling were obliged to work their resources intensively so that the rewards of good trips would provide a surplus to cover losses incurred in past or future voyages. Moreover, fishing in general, and trawling in particular, is invariably conducted on the environmental margins, for successful catching activity soon translates into overfishing and the depletion of formerly abundant fish stocks. Adding to these economic and environmental pressures, skippers faced competition from mates, relief officers and unemployed skippers eager to share in the profits of fishing trips. It was therefore in no one's interest for trawlers and trawlermen to be laid up in port for any longer than absolutely necessary – meaning that Skipper Oliver often spent less than 48 hours ashore between voyages.

Table 8.4: William Oliver's time at sea and ashore, 1919–39

	At sea (days)	% of year at sea	Ashore (days)	% of year ashore
1919	71	–	14	–
1920	302	82.5	64	17.5
1921	293	80.3	72	19.7
1922	291	79.7	74	20.3
1923	310	84.9	55	15.1
1924	297	81.1	69	18.9
1925	281	77	84	23
1926	307	84.1	58	15.9
1927	260	71.2	105	28.8
1928	269	73.5	97	26.5
1929	301	82.5	64	17.5
1930	307	84.1	58	15.9
1931	305	83.6	60	16.4
1932	298	81.4	68	18.6
1933	284	77.8	81	22.2
1934	280	76.7	85	23.3
1935	208	57	157	43
1936	301	82.2	65	17.8
1937	242	66.3	123	33.7
1938	229	62.7	136	37.3
1939	113	–	101	–
	5,549		1,690	

Source: University of Hull, Blaydes House, William Oliver's logs, 1919–39

Such shoreside interludes were generally very busy for Oliver, who had a large family, a keen interest in socialising and a range of leisure pursuits. His diaries describe days ashore full of seemingly frenetic activity – pitched in an unassuming, understated style – including family events, visits to the cinema, motor car rides to the coast, meals at Powolny's and other high-end restaurants and hotels, yarning in pubs, attendance at soccer and rugby league matches (Figure 8.10), and, invariably, a call at the dock to check the size and value of the catch. One eventful turnaround in November 1930 illustrates how 'brisk' these 'pit stops' could be:

5 November 1930:   anchored at midnight
6 November 1930, 1pm: Left Dock with wife in car and called at Dr
                                    Jackson's solicitors to make out a statement

	regarding disturbances by Norske Gunboat off Pes Fd last trip. Then to Rippons for bonded stores and called at Blue Bell until 3pm. Afterwards was very busy calling at various houses arranging for my daughter's (Elsie) wedding at 10.30am tomorrow
7 November 1930, 10.30am:	Attended my daughter's wedding at Hessle Parish Church. I would just as soon attend her funeral for all the happiness she will get out of it. I hope I am wrong but that is my opinion. Arranged a reception at Powolny's but Bride arrived alone the groom having gone home to his mother's to change. Everyone disgusted. Had a lie down in the afternoon and in the evening gave a dinner at Powolny's Restaurant with a dance afterwards. Some of the young people enjoyed themselves but I didn't. Glad when it was all over.
8 November 1930, 2am:	Arrived home after dance very tired
7.0am:	Ship left St Andrew's Dock and I joined her on the River at 10.30am.

Breaks between voyages were not always so disappointing. On 2 March 1922 Oliver returned from Iceland to discover that there had been an 'increase in family (son)', which persuaded him to spend a few extra weeks ashore, 'staying indoors' on most days, but going for the doctor on 17 March when 'wife suddenly taken very ill'. A further 'increase in family (girl)' – the Olivers' tenth child – greeted him when he docked in Hull on 23 October 1924, and again he stayed at home to assist his 'very ill' wife. Oliver was obliged to remain in Hull for various other reasons during the course of the interwar period. Labour shortages and disputes delayed sailing by a few days on a number of occasions, while the bureaucracy and fitting out entailed in transfers from one vessel to another generally took a week or so to complete. Ill health sometimes caused Oliver to remain ashore. In 1927, for example, he contracted bronchitis, and then pneumonia, which confined him to bed in a delirious state for much of January and February. Although this illness meant that he missed only two fishing trips, it left him with a permanent respiratory weakness that rendered him susceptible to bronchial coughs for the rest of his life, and caused him to be rejected when he volunteered for military service in 1940. Oliver missed a further voyage due to influenza in 1932, but there were times when he stoically went to sea despite suffering from gastritis, neuralgia, lumbago or, more often, a hangover. He also had extensive dental treatment, which he managed to incorporate into his working routine. In 1923, for instance, he dashed from ship to surgery to have four teeth extracted, while in 1938, having made a number of visits to the dentist in the interim, he reported to the surgery to have 'all my remaining teeth drawn', two days before he departed for Iceland.

JANUARY, 1935.

Saturday 12
(12-353)

Stayed indoors all forenoon and after dinner Frank and I went to see a football match Hull City versus Newcastle in Cup-tie. It was very cold but dry. A perfectly disgusting exhibition on the part of Hull City. The result was Newcastle 6 goals. Hull City 1 The first goal scored against Hull was by one of our own men who headed the ball into his own goal. After that Hull went all to pieces, & remained so until the rest of the game. Newcastle did just as they wanted Home at 5 pm to tea & stayed indoors all night.

8.10 Football's a funny old game! Eighty years on from the drubbing described in this diary entry, Hull enters its year as UK city of culture with its football team competing in the English Premier League, while Newcastle United play in what would have been the Second Division in Skipper Oliver's day.
University of Hull, Blaydes House, 'William Oliver's Diary, 1935', courtesy of the Maritime Historical Studies Centre

Longer breaks from work at sea – described as 'trips ashore' in the logs and diaries – were taken by skippers when their vessels were in dock for their annual refit during the summer. In Skipper Oliver's case, this generally occurred in July and was cast as a 're-fit and holiday' period in his log entry. He could also elect to take a trip or trips ashore, presumably with the agreement of the trawler owners and the assurance that he would resume his command after a relief skipper or mate had 'taken the ship out' during these sojourns. Oliver chose to remain ashore in 12 of the 21 years covered by the diaries and logs, with most of these leave periods embracing Christmas and New Year. Such trips ashore became more frequent during the late 1920s and through the 1930s, reflecting Oliver's seniority within the ranks of Hull skippers, and also his health problems and advancing years. In 1935, for instance, Oliver wrote that he 'didn't fancy' returning to sea and remained ashore for over three months. It is clear from his 'Reminiscences' that he had decided to retire from the sea at that point, as he was disappointed by a sustained fall in his earnings compared to those of other, younger skippers who were seemingly driving their vessels and their crews harder than he preferred to do. His diary entries reveal that during this prolonged stay ashore he held negotiations with Hull Brewery about taking up the tenancy of a country pub. He also implied that this prospect was proving troublesome at home, as he confided in his diary on 10 May 1935 that he 'cannot exactly understand wife lately. She seems as though she would like to have me at home but afraid to take the risk.' He was therefore a little disingenuous when he reminisced eighteen years later that in 1935 his wife had 'dropped a bombshell' by declaring at a meeting with Hull Brewery that she had no intention whatsoever of running a pub. As a consequence, Oliver returned to sea and in 1936 spent only 17.8 per cent of 366 days ashore.

Whatever the reasoning behind her decisive intervention in these pub tenancy discussions, there can be no doubt that Betsy Oliver contributed strongly to her husband's professional success by managing the domestic base and providing the majority of the childcare during his absences at work. This gendered division of labour is implicit in Oliver's logs and diaries, chiefly, and ironically, through his reticence on matters relating to their house and the ten children they reared. He was unequivocally the breadwinner, a role reflected in diary entries concerning the commodities he provided, and the events he funded, for his family. On 22 March 1929, for example, he 'inspected & tested a car & decided to purchase same. Wife & family very pleased. [At] 7.0pm Took a party to Powolny's & had a good dinner there & home 10.30pm', before leaving St Andrew's Dock for Iceland at 5.15 a.m. on the next day (Figure 8.11). There is a detached anonymity, moreover, in his descriptions of family events – 'took youngest two children to Hull Fair', 'went with wife & four children to see pantomime (painful)', 'took wife & some of the children for a motor drive' – although this altered as the children grew up, particularly when his sons followed in his wake and entered the trawling business. Oliver elaborated a little on Betsy's place in his world in his 'Reminiscences'. As well as taking a lead on life-changing decisions, she initiated house moves, sold cars, organised the children's schooling and, remarkably, travelled from Hull – where her house had suffered damage in a Zeppelin raid – across war-torn Europe with their eight children to join her husband in Malta. Perhaps even more remarkably, after spending two happy years in Floriana, just outside Valletta, in September 1918 she travelled with the children back to Hull, via Taranto, Rome, Paris, Le Havre and Southampton; as Oliver observed: 'Whatever war medals I afterwards received for my services were better earned by Mrs Oliver than I.'[16]

Respect bordering on affection is evident in log and diary entries that acknowledged on 28 January each year that it was 'Wife's birthday today' with

---

FEBRUARY 1 TUESDAY (32-333)
Partridge and Pheasant Shooting ends.

Stayed indoors all day. feeling rotten all over.

2 WEDNESDAY (33-332)
● New Moon 8.54 a.m.   Purification of B.V.M.   Candlemas.
Scottish Quarter Day.

Eldest daughter Emily 21 years old today. Am giving a birthday celebration at Dance-de-Luxe (Scala) tonight. At 3 pm completed arrangements for party & home at 4.30pm. Had an extremely jolly party about 100 guests turned up.

8.11 Having been unwell earlier in the week, Oliver organised a party to celebrate his eldest daughter Emily's birthday on Wednesday 2 February 1927, which proved to be 'extremely jolly' for the 100 guests who turned up.
University of Hull, Blaydes House, 'William Oliver's Diary, 1927', courtesy of the Maritime Historical Studies Centre

a note of her age, and references to wedding anniversaries such as that of 30 July 1935: 'My wedding day today 32 years. Sent wire home and also received one from home.' It would seem, moreover, that William and Betsy enjoyed each other's company, for they invariably spent most of his time ashore together. During the holidays and prolonged 'trips ashore', for example, Oliver and his wife took vacations in Ostend, London, Edinburgh, Blackpool, Brighton, Scarborough, Bridlington and Hornsea, generally staying in the more expensive hotels and dining in the more up-market restaurants and tea rooms in these places. Some of these were motoring holidays, with the Olivers touring south-west and south-east England during three weeks in the summer of 1931, which included a remarkable drive of 310 miles from Lowestoft to Blackpool in ten hours (Figure 8.12). When holidaying in London they generally took the train and stayed at the Regent Palace or Imperial hotels, with visits to Kew Gardens and Hampton Court interspersed with shopping in Oxford Street and meals in central London restaurants. Visiting West End theatres was a feature of these breaks in the capital, though not all of the shows appealed to Skipper Oliver, who felt obliged to leave the Prince of Wales Theatre in mild disgust on 5 July 1938 because he considered the 'Folies Bergere'

8.12 Having drawn £200 prize money for being the firm's second most successful skipper over the previous year, Oliver embarked on a week's holiday to Holland on 23 June 1926. He returned on 30 June, and set forth on the next day on a motor trip to the Highlands of Scotland with Mrs Oliver, Mr and Mrs Battersby, and Mr and Mrs Greaves. After driving an estimated 980 miles round Scotland, down to Blackpool and across the Pennines, the Olivers arrived home at 8.30 p.m. on 9 July, where they 'found children & everything else alright & ended up with what wife and myself agree was the best holiday we have ever had'.
University of Hull, Blaydes House, 'William Oliver's Diary, 1926', courtesy of the Maritime Historical Studies Centre

8.13 Skipper Oliver and 'wife' were regular patrons of Powlony's restaurant in King Edward Street during the late 1920s and 1930s. With its continental-style marble floors, mahogany doors and oak panelling, this became Hull's most exclusive restaurant – a veritable 'hit with the affluent Pearson Park and Avenues residents'. Opened in 1903, Powolny's was destroyed on 7 May 1941 during one of the worst air raids that Hull suffered in the Second World War, which left 203 people dead. Powolny's never reopened. https://fancythatofyorkshire.wordpress.com/2013/12/24/dinner-at-powolnys-from-the-book-spicy-green-ginger/ (accessed 5 November 2016)

review to be a 'leg show', in which 'the only attraction seemed to be the showing off of nearly naked women'.

Time ashore in Hull not only witnessed the couple socialising together, but also suggested that the Olivers were comparatively well-to-do. Powolny's in King Edward Street – Hull's high-class restaurant – was their eating house of choice (Figure 8.13), both between voyages and during longer breaks.[17] In a clear sign of affluence, they owned a car from 1920 onwards, even though Oliver was still being taught to drive by Lawrie, his second eldest son, in 1935 – implying that Betsy was at the wheel during their motoring holidays. Some socio-spatial progression can be discerned in their housing, as they moved from the Boulevard (on the fringes of the Hessle Road district) to 'Floriana' on Tranby Lane, Anlaby (one of Hull's 'much sought after' west villages), to the Sutton Park estate (in the new suburbs) and then on to Pickering Road (in west Hull). To Skipper Oliver, home was a place for dinners and bedtime, for entertaining friends in sometimes 'brisk' evenings, and more frequently for 'down time', denoted in his economical style by a simple statement: 'Stayed indoors all day'. There was probably more scope for such gentle recreation from September 1939, as he and his wife moved to a bungalow in Ryehill, a hamlet to the east of Hull. This downsizing was seemingly a rational response to children growing up and the significant reduction in earnings that came with retirement. William Oliver was now permanently home from the sea for the first time since he married Betsy Andrews on 30 July 1903, a 'change in our lives' that must have fundamentally altered the dynamics of the family at a time when total war had just commenced.

Lillian Bilocca

Lillian Bilocca (1929–88) was a seafarer's daughter who became a seafarer's wife and then a seafarer's mother. She had two children – Ernest in 1946, and Virginia in 1950 – with Carmelo 'Charlie' Bilocca (b. 1904), a Maltese sailor who later worked as a trawlerman. They lived in Coltman Street, Hull, and Lillian ended her days alone in a council flat after Charlie's death in 1981. Dubbed 'Big Lil' by the media, she became a household name when she and her 'headscarf protestors' highlighted the harsh conditions suffered by Hull's fishing community in the wake of the tragic events of the 'Dark Winter' of 1968. Their campaign led to changes in trawler safety that saved countless lives.

The 'headscarf protests' were precipitated by the loss of three Hull trawlers in atrocious weather in North Atlantic waters in the space of three weeks. Fifty-eight Hull trawlermen perished in the 'triple trawler tragedy' of 1968, the biggest peacetime fishing disaster of the twentieth century. The *St Romanus* sank with all hands on 11 January, and then on 26 January the *Kingston Peridot*

Lil Bilocca (1929–88)
Courtesy of *Hull Daily Mail*

met the same fate. On 4 February, only one man (the mate, Harry Eddom) survived the sinking of the *Ross Cleveland*, whose skipper sent a last desperate, poignant radio message: 'I am going over. We are laying over. Help us, Len, she's going. Give my love and the crew's love to the wives and families.' The message was heard by Skipper Len Whur of the *Kingston Andalusite*, who saw his friend's ship sink. Standing next to Whur in the wheelhouse was Lillian's son, Ernie, a 21-year-old deckhand. Incredibly, one of the three ships (the *St Romanus*) had no radio operator. There were no lifelines or adequate safety rails on the three trawlers and any protective clothing had to be bought by the men themselves. Remarkably, such limited safety provisions were within the law.

After the *Kingston Peridot* was declared lost, Lillian gathered thousands of signatures demanding better safety at sea, and she and her fellow 'fishwives' organised a meeting at the shack that was the Victoria Hall on Hessle Road. The women, with local union men, families and politicians, addressed an overflowing hall. The Hessle Road Women's Committee, comprising Lillian, Mary Denness, Yvonne Blenkinsop and Christine Smallbone (née Gay, sister of the *Ross Cleveland*'s skipper), was born. 'Big Lil' and her women's committee became household names as they travelled to Westminster to put their case for safety improvements to the government. Multiple changes were enacted in weeks. Their fame put the spotlight on an industry in which trawlermen died at sea at the rate of more than one a week, with over 6,000 lost since the late nineteenth century. Their successful struggle is remembered in a plaque on the site of the old Victoria Hall that reads: 'In recognition of the contributions to the fishing industry by the women of Hessle Road, led by Lillian Bilocca, who successfully campaigned for better safety measures following the loss of three Hull trawlers in 1968.' In 2015 four further plaques in honour of the women, two of whom are still alive, were unveiled in Hull's Maritime Museum.

Brian W. Lavery

An extraordinary typical career

When William Oliver died on 14 February 1959 the *Hull Daily Mail* commented that 'no British trawler skipper was better known or held in higher regard than Mr William Oliver … whose death this weekend leaves the fishing industry bereft of one of its most colourful characters'. A funeral service was held at Hull Fishermen's Bethel in the heart of the port's fishing community, with his widow – to whom he willed an estate worth £1,343 13s 11d[18] – ten children, five grandchildren and representatives of Hull trawling firms, trade unions and the Ministry of Transport among the mourners. This large gathering was addressed by Pastor T. Chappell, who remembered Skipper Oliver as a man who 'gave cheerfully, readily and quietly from his wonderful store of knowledge' in his work for the Hull Trawler Officers' Guild, and in the valuable services he rendered as a trustee of the Fishermen's Widows' and Orphans' Fund. The pastor also mentioned the presence at the funeral of trawler skippers from the deceased's generation: 'I believe he and they and their kind laid the foundations of the great industry we have in the port today.' In essence, while Skipper Oliver's career may have been extraordinary in terms of length, commitment, performance and service, it was typical of the contributions made by many of his contemporaries over the preceding six decades – a point that is confirmed in the striking similarity between the picture painted in this chapter and the portrait of the archetypal Hull skipper drawn by Jeremy Tunstall in 1962.[19]

The context in which 'he and they and their kind' operated was extraordinary in various respects. Although much of their working lives was spent in vessels steaming to and from, and fishing in, distant waters, these skippers were based in Hull, which was the only major commercial port in the United Kingdom that had a significant fishing industry in the twentieth century. In 1911, for instance, Hull was not only the third largest port in the British Empire in terms of traffic handled, but also the home of the Wilson Line, the world's largest privately owned shipping firm, and the place of registration of 411 steam-propelled first-class fishing vessels of 50 or more tons – amounting to 30,362 tons, 33.5 per cent of the total for England and Wales.[20] It was also remarkable that Hull's trawling interests continued to grow during the 1920s and 1930s in terms of fleet size, catches and market share. Alone in the nation's fishing industry in this respect, Hull's trawlers fed a buoyant market for cheap food in the midst of domestic depression, operating without the environmental pressures of stock depletion and largely unfettered by political constraints concerning access to the fishing grounds.[21] Given that these economic, environmental and political factors turned sharply against British distant-water trawling in the wake of the Second World War (giving Skipper Oliver 'more sleepless nights than he had ever had at sea'), it is extraordinary that it was not until 1976 that these distant waters were closed to trawlers from Hull and other UK ports. This durability was due in no small measure to the extraordinary efforts of trawler skippers, as typified by William Oliver, and illuminated by the 'wonderful store of knowledge' evident in his memorialisation of 7,390 days of his career in the diaries, logs and reminiscences that underpin this chapter.

Notes

1   William Oliver, 'A Trawlerman's Reminiscences', *World Fishing*, 3.1 (1954), pp. 20, 28.

2   Unless otherwise stated, the evidence used in this chapter has been drawn from two parallel and overlapping sources: William Oliver's logs, 1919–39 and William Oliver's diaries, 1920–39. Both sets of records are housed at the Maritime Historical Studies Centre, Blaydes House, University of Hull.

3   Oliver, 'A Trawlerman's Reminiscences', *World Fishing*, 2.10–12 (1953), pp. 401–03, 447–48, 473–75; *World Fishing*, 3.1–8 (1954), pp. 19–20, 28, 69, 78, 112–14, 139–40, 188–89, 229–30, 271–74, 303–05.

4   David J. Starkey, 'The North Atlantic Fisheries: Bearings, Currents and Grounds', and 'Fish: A Removable Feast', in David J. Starkey, Jón Thór and Ingo Heidbrink (eds), *A History of the North Atlantic Fisheries: Volume 2, From the 1850s to the Early Twenty-First Century* (Bremen: Hauschild, 2012), pp. 13–26, 327–35.

5   Margaret Gerrish, 'Following the Fish: Nineteenth-century Migration and the Diffusion of Trawling', in David J. Starkey, Chris Reid and Neil R. Ashcroft (eds), *England's Sea Fisheries: The Commercial Sea Fisheries of England and Wales since 1300* (London: Chatham, 2000).

6   John K. Walton, *Fish and Chips and the British Working Class, 1870–1940* (Leicester: Leicester University Press, 1992).

7   For a definitive study of trawling, see Robb Robinson, *Trawling: The Rise and Fall of the British Trawl Fishery* (Exeter: University of Exeter Press, 1996).

8   Oliver, 'Reminiscences', *World Fishing*, 2.10, pp. 401–03.

9   Oliver, 'Reminiscences', *World Fishing*, 2.11, p. 447.

10   Jeremy Tunstall, *Fish: An Antiquated Industry* (London: Fabian Tract 380, 1968).

11   The National Archives, Kew, London, BT 377/7, William Oliver, Royal Naval Reserve Service Record.

12   Oliver, 'Reminiscences', *World Fishing*, 3.7, p. 273.

13   *Yorkshire Post and Leeds Mercury*, 9 March 1955.

14   A kit is equivalent to 140 lb (62 kg) of gutted fish.

15   Oliver, 'Reminiscences', *World Fishing*, 3.3, p. 114.

16   Oliver, 'Reminiscences', *World Fishing*, 3.5, p. 189.

17   Robin Dermond Horspool, *The House of Powolny: Life and Death of a Hull Restaurant* (Beverley: Highgate, 2000).

18   National Probate Calendar, England and Wales, 'Index of Wills & Administrations', 1858–1956.

19   Jeremy Tunstall, *The Fishermen* (London: MacGibbon and Kee, 1962), pp. 176–224.

20   British Parliamentary Papers (cd. 6398, 1912), *Annual Statements of the Navigation and Shipping of the United Kingdom for 1911*, Table 14.

21   Robinson, *Trawling*, pp. 144–61.

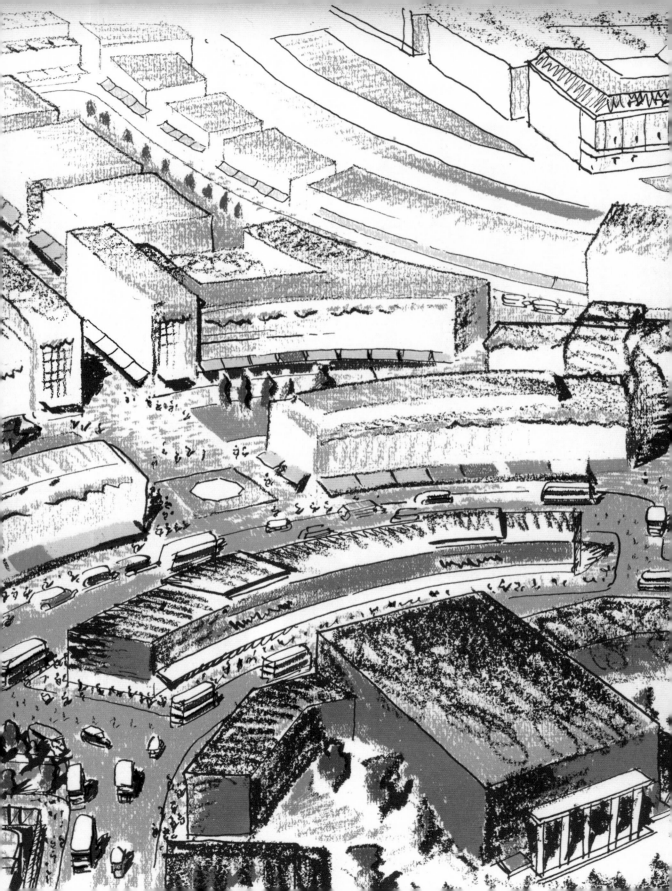

CHAPTER NINE

Trauma, Resilience and Utopianism in Second World War Hull

DAVID ATKINSON

When the fury of an enemy's assault was loosed upon our city and we saw our heritage shattered under the weight of air attack, the spirit of the people of Kingston upon Hull was unbroken … We resolved then that the only fitting tribute that could be paid to the devotion and courage of the brave people was to rebuild our city in a manner worthy of its citizens. Out of the ashes of the old would arise Phoenix-like a fairer and nobler city than we had ever known.[1]

The city of Hull suffered grievously in the Second World War. Its core maritime trades and routes were suspended, its trawling fleet was largely requisitioned or dock-bound and, as elsewhere around the UK, many citizens were enlisted, served and sometimes died in the various theatres of this global war. But Hull also suffered more direct and lasting trauma. By most estimates, Hull was the second most blitzed British city of the war and the casualties were considerable. The figures vary between different sources, but around 1,200 people were killed between 1940 and 1945, 20 per cent of whom were children, and 3,000 more people were injured.[2] In addition, many who escaped harm were still affected profoundly. Of Hull's 92,660 inhabitable houses in 1939, only 5,938 escaped damage, leaving 152,000 people (around half the population) homeless at some point during the war.[3] Three million square feet of industrial space was lost and, by extension, the associated employment and economic sectors disappeared too. In the spring and summer of 1941 Hull suffered enormous destruction from ferocious bombing. Although there were lulls in the blitz before and after this period, and no bombs fell in 1944, Hull also suffered aerial attacks into 1945. Hull lived with the threat and fear of bombing longer than other British cities. Virtually everyone would have been touched by the trauma and the devastation.

The theories of aerial warfare that developed in the interwar period argued that bombing cities would lead to the disintegration of civilian morale and the consequent defeat of enemy states. The sustained bombing and damage in Hull was so marked that it prompted government fears that this might be the first British city to experience 'civilian collapse'. When the phenomenon of trekking accelerated in the summer of 1941, whereby locals left the vulnerable city centre nightly for the relative safety of surrounding suburbs and countryside, this was seen as a sign of this imminent breakdown. In November 1941 Winston Churchill and the Royal Family visited Hull to boost the citizens' spirits. That same month, but in a more secretive move, the Ministry of Home Security also sent a team of psychologists northwards to assess morale and the likelihood of 'civilian collapse'. The London team evaluated over 700 people ranging from dockworkers to school children. They found evidence of clear trauma, but decided that collective psychological collapse remained unlikely. The findings of the Hull survey would have significant repercussions for later British bombing strategy, but meanwhile the population of Hull was deemed sufficiently resilient and the city was left to carry on beneath the bombs.

Hull's civic leaders responded to this traumatic episode in a more proactive and positive manner. In 1941 the city council commissioned Patrick Abercrombie and Edwin Lutyens, the leading planner and architect of the day, to draw up proposals to rebuild the city using modern, rational planning. The resultant *Plan for the City and County of Kingston-upon-Hull* (1945) envisaged a new, utopian city emerging from the fractured fabric of the earlier city.[4] This example of the best contemporary planning practice would, it was hoped, repair the trauma of the blitz and, in consequence, engineer a radical new urban structure to restore the city's pride, rebuild its communities, and generate better lives for post-war generations. Rather than planning for collapse and defeat, the city council, Abercrombie and Lutyens demonstrated sufficient optimism and fortitude to envision a bold, modern city that would forge a productive future from amid the bomb-sites and devastation. The political contingencies and economic budgets of post-war reconstruction meant that most aspects of the ambitious plan were never realised, but these proposals offered a confident, utopian response to the trauma of the war that reflected Hull's broader resilience to its wartime blitz.

The rise of aerial warfare

Hull was one of the earliest cities to experience the aerial bombing of civilians when it was subject to attacks by German Zeppelin airships in the First World War.[5] While we are now familiar with the idea and practice of aerial bombing, these attacks were entirely new and terrifying for early twentieth-century civilians. For generations, Britain had waged war overseas and military reports filtered home slowly. In 1915, however, the spaces of warfare constricted dramatically as enemy airships arrived overhead without warning to change the public's experience of warfare.

By dint of their geography, moreover, Hull and East Yorkshire became a focus for several aerial attacks because England's east coast was the safest and most accessible target for the Zeppelins. The first raid on Hull of 6 June 1915 left 25 dead and around 100 wounded, while further raids between March 1916 and March 1918 killed 51 more.[6] The city centre and the docks to the east of the River Hull suffered the worst destruction, and the damage was clearly visible. The new aerial threat brought the war to local doorsteps. Some people were traumatised and others began 'trekking' from the central districts each night to safer, rural spaces at the city's edge. By the Second World War therefore, Hull had recent experience of the new and unpredictable threat of aerial bombing.

Advances in technology shifted the scope and nature of aerial warfare further in the interwar years, and its military potential was debated extensively in political, military and public circles. In particular, the idea of winning wars by targeting and traumatising civilians was developed by theorists of air power.[7] These theories were tested to murderous effect during the later 1930s in the Spanish Civil War and the Sino-Japanese war. Despite the casualties, cataclysmic civilian defeat did not materialise, although evidence of the destruction circulated globally through newsreels and newspapers.[8] These accounts of this new form of warfare reinforced publics and politicians alike in the belief that cities and civilians were now inevitable targets for aerial bombing and that, because civilian morale would probably be fragile, at some stage cities would break.

Amy Johnson

Amy Johnson hailed from Hull, a port-city whose seafarers voyaged to every corner of the world. But Johnson blazed her own, very distinctive global trail through the skies. Crossing great continents and immensities of ocean, she was a key figure in the era of pioneering long-distance aviation between the two world wars.

Born in 1903, Johnson attended Boulevard Secondary School. She later graduated from Sheffield University in economics, although she also attended engineering lectures (despite hostility from the engineering professor) as her interest in aviation grew. After university, Johnson worked as a secretary in Hull's Old Town, but eventually moved to London to pursue her growing passion for flying. Although her first flying instructor said she would never make an aviator, Johnson persevered, and helped by comedian Will Hay, an experienced flyer, she obtained her pilot's licence after sixteen hours of flying. Johnson was unable to obtain work in what was a male-dominated profession. Frustrated, but undaunted, she became the first Englishwoman to gain an Air Ministry ground engineer's qualification. Johnson was determined to show that women were the equal of men in the air and decided to challenge the solo record for flying from England to Australia. Assisted by her father and Lord Wakefield (an oil magnate and philanthropist), she acquired a second-hand Gypsy Moth biplane, naming it *Jason* after her family firm's trade mark. On 5 May 1930 she was waved off from Croydon Airport by a handful of people – nobody knew who she was.

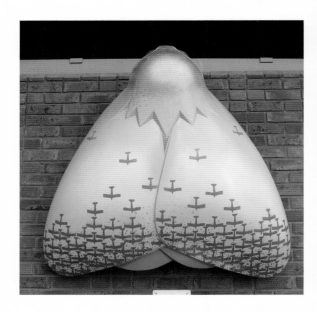

The dangerous flight headed south-eastwards in stages, by way of Vienna and Constantinople, then onwards through the Middle East to Karachi, Rangoon and Singapore. Repairs were needed *en route* after a couple of bad landings, while the engine required serious attention at Timor before the last 450-mile leg over shark-infested seas. Pilot and plane finally touched down on 24 May 1930 at Port Darwin, Australia, having covered 9,960 miles in 19½ days. Although the flight record was not broken, Johnson was the first woman to fly solo from Britain to Australia. Her feat made global headlines and brought her international celebrity and honours. After returning to England, she was met by huge crowds in Croydon. She later flew *Jason* up to Hull and was greeted by thousands of well-wishers and a civic reception.

Johnson subsequently reinforced her reputation for pioneering, long-distance flights. In 1931, for example, she set a record – with co-pilot Jack Humphreys – for the flight from England to Japan. In the following year, she set a solo flight record time on the England to Cape Town route. This record was later broken, but she recaptured it in 1936. She made other path-breaking flights with her husband, aviator Jim Mollison, most notably setting a record time for reaching India from Britain in 1934.

After the outbreak of war in 1939, Johnson delivered aircraft from factories to RAF airfields. In January 1941 she was lost when her aircraft went off course and crashed into the Thames estuary.

Johnson's determination and aeronautical success were an inspiration for many in the early days of aviation, particularly as she operated in male-dominated fields. A statue of Johnson stands in Prospect Street, Hull, and the Amy Johnson Cup for Courage is still awarded to local children who show exceptional bravery. In 2016 her home city hosted a festival to celebrate her life and achievements.

Robb Robinson

Amy Johnson's pioneering flight to Australia was undertaken in a De Havilland Gipsy Moth aeroplane. To commemorate this extraordinary feat, her home city commissioned a mass engagement public art project – 'A Moth for Amy' – that ran from 1 July 2016 until 31 March 2017. Created by Saffron Waghorn and 59 other artists, sculptures of moths, each designed to reflect the powerful inspiration of Amy Johnson and her amazing achievements, were exhibited on buildings across Hull. This moth, designed by local artist Dalo, was displayed on the exterior wall of the Streetlife Museum in Hull's Old Town.
© Nicholas J. Evans

Hull was bombed in the Second World war partly because of its strategic importance as a major port, transport hub and industrial centre, and partly due to accidents of geography. Alongside the emerging theories about destroying civilian bodies and spirits, interwar military strategy also argued that blitzing key industrial and transport infrastructure would cripple an enemy's war effort.[9] In this respect, Hull was a military target and it suffered accordingly. Hull's docks, railway junctions and yards, and other industrial districts were targeted by German aeroplanes, and the pattern of bomb damage across the city (Figure 9.1) shows some clustering around the docks and industrial districts alongside the River Hull. The German airmen knew where to locate these sites because they carried maps of their targets and guides that illustrated what they looked like from the air. The Luftwaffe bombing map of Hull (Figure 9.2) detailed 30 key targets: primary red targets (docks, railway junctions and barracks) and secondary purple targets (industrial sites, gasometers, wood yards, factories and mills). The pilots' guide included an image of the River Hull to help pilots find and identify their targets (Figure 9.3).

9.1 'Survey of bomb damage', from Lutyens and Abercrombie, *Plan for Hull*, Plate VII between pp. 16–17. The areas in black indicate bomb damage, grey areas are undamaged urban fabric.

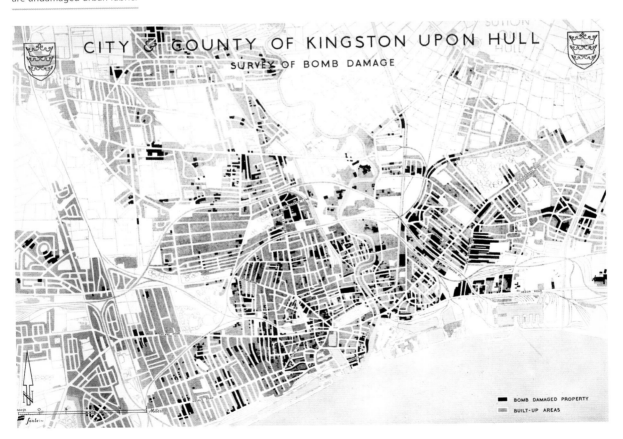

Bomb-aiming technology in the 1940s was imprecise and unreliable, however, and this, combined with wind, anti-aircraft fire and decoy systems on the ground, meant that bombs rarely hit their intended targets and often damaged adjacent areas.[10] The development of Hull's industrial districts and their surrounding working-class residential streets meant that housing was often hit by bombs aimed at industrial and transport sites. That said, several raids by isolated aircraft deliberately attacked civilian targets to fuel public terror. The mass bombing raids of spring and summer 1941 also hit residential districts, with the destruction of civilians and their morale as a key objective.

There were also geographical reasons for Hull's suffering. German aircraft flying across the North Sea towards northern and central England could navigate inland more easily once they identified the broad Humber estuary. Moreover, as the largest city on its banks and with the confluence of the River Hull and the extensive docks and railway yards reflecting any moonlight, Hull was often visible at night (despite 'blackout' and decoy measures to protect the city). In addition, when poor visibility, the weather or failed navigation prevented the completion of raids on Manchester, Liverpool, Leeds or Sheffield, surplus bombs were sometimes dropped on Hull as the Germans returned home.[11]

9.2 'Stadtplan von Kingston upon Hull mit Mil-Geo.- Eintragungen', 1942 [city map of Kingston upon Hull with military-geographical notifications, 1:10,000, 1942]. This map was recovered in Wuppertal, Germany, in 1945 by Fred Metcalf (British Army), and donated to the University of Hull in 1993. University of Hull Map Library UK(s) R29.

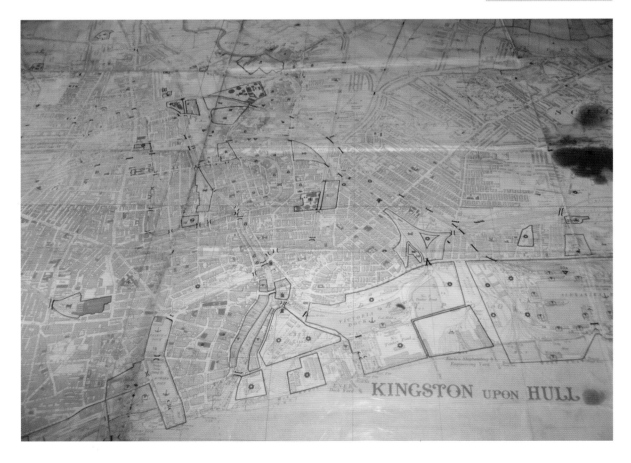

KINGSTON UPON HULL

9.3 'Mühlenwerk an der Mündung der Hull in Kingston upon Hull', in Generalstab des Heeres Abteilung für Kreigkarten und Vermessungswesen (IV. Mil.-Geo), *Militargeografische Angaben über England. Ostküste (Nördlicher Tiel vom Humber bis zum Firth of Tay)* (Berlin, 1941), p. 17 ['Mills at the mouth of the Hull in Kingston upon Hull', in General Staff of the Army Department for War Maps and Surveying (IV. Mil.-Geo), *Military-geographical Information about England. East Coast (The Northern Side of the Humber to the Firth of Tay)*]. This was recovered in Wuppertal, Germany, in 1945 by Fred Metcalf (British Army), and donated to the University of Hull in 1993. University of Hull Map Library UK(s) R29.

The bombing of Hull was sporadic, but stretched from 1940 to 1945. It was also shaped by the shifting rhythm and progress of the wider war. In 1940 German bombing prepared for potential invasion by attacking airfields and defences. After a seaborne invasion of Britain was abandoned in September 1940, the Luftwaffe switched to civilian and industrial targets to shatter fighting capacity and the population's resistance. Consequently, February to September 1941 saw the most lethal bombing of Hull. With the German invasion of the Soviet Union in June 1941, however, aircraft were increasingly diverted to the new eastern front and the intensity of the blitz in Britain faded. Given these shifting priorities in the wider war, Hull occasionally went months without an attack (such as early 1942, the spring of 1943 and the whole of 1944). Nevertheless, Hull's relative accessibility on England's east coast meant that attacks continued after raids had virtually ceased elsewhere in Britain; isolated raids even lasted into the final months of the war. Hull therefore experienced years of actual attacks, plus years of perpetual alert with the constant fear of raids. This situation posed a clear threat to civilian morale.

The sporadic but deadly nature of the Hull blitz

There were 18 raids on Hull during 1940, which resulted in property damage but relatively few casualties.

- The first bomb was dropped on Hull by an isolated aeroplane on 20 June 1940. It slightly damaged a railway bridge.[12] A second raid, over a month later on 30 July, damaged some flats in the city centre.
- The third raid, almost another month later on 25 August, was far worse as six people died in Rustenburg Street, east Hull (Figure 9.4). The city suffered eight further small raids through August and September 1940, with virtually no damage other than to property.

- Two people were killed in a raid on 13 October, and one person died on 1 November. Otherwise, 1940 ended with five minor raids across 7 and 8 November, and 11, 12 and 17 December: two caused slight damage to houses, but there were no deaths.

These 1940 attacks hit all areas of the city: from the docks and the centre, and along the River Hull corridor, and from to the Avenues and Newland Avenue to the residential streets of east Hull. There were nine casualties, but it was the blitz of 1941 that generated the later infamy. In early 1941 the Germans tried to break the British population by bombing cities across the country. Hull was targeted for the reasons outlined above, and civilian casualties increased sharply.

- February 1941 saw eight raids that killed 19 people across industrial, transportation and residential targets. The number of aircraft involved also rose markedly: 49 bombers attacked Victoria Dock and Albert Dock on 23–24 February, and 25 more struck on 25 and 26 February.[13]

- The situation deteriorated further. March 1941 saw five deadly raids that killed 5, 38 and 16 people (Figures 9.5, 9.6), with a 'heavy raid' on 18–19 March when 378 aircraft dropped 316 tonnes of high explosive (to shatter buildings) and 77,000 incendiary bombs (to set fire to these properties): 91 people were killed, 79 were seriously injured and 116 had lesser injuries.[14] A journalist reported that 12,000 people were left homeless by what the Germans called a 'sharp attack'.[15]

- Another 47 aircraft attacked on 31 March, taking 52 lives; this raid was intended for Liverpool, but it was redirected due to bad weather. The 182 fatalities of March 1941, plus the other casualties and the material damage, were spread right across the city: nowhere was left untouched.

- April 1941 brought seven more raids. Two were fatal: one killed 57 people when the Ellis Terrace shelter was hit by a parachute mine, and nine died

9.4 Bomb damage, Holderness Road, 25 August 1940.
Hull History Centre C TSP/3/310/4

when incendiary bombs fell across east Hull (Figure 9.7). Eight people died when a mine fell on Council Avenue and Rokeby Avenue.

- May 1941 saw the worst of the Hull blitz as seven attacks cost 422 lives. Most fatalities occurred on the nights of 7–8 and 8–9 May when two 'heavy raids' of high explosives, parachute mines and incendiary bombs hit east and north Hull, the docks and the city centre, causing huge damage and subsequent fires (Figures 9.8–9.10).[16] Aside from the human toll, iconic city centre structures were destroyed, including the Prudential Building, with its unsafe tower being demolished soon after. By the end of May 40,000 people were homeless. As a journalist noted: 'They must have got close to the appalling limit in Hull.'[17] This was the most lethal and devastating period of the Hull blitz and it remains the focus of commemoration today.
- There was a lull in attacks in June 1941 as the Germans invaded the Soviet Union, although a notorious incident on 2 June 1941 – the 50th raid on the city – saw 27 killed around the Avenues district after the 'all clear' was sounded erroneously and people returned to the streets.
- July 1941 saw mass casualties again as raids on the 11th and 15th of the month killed 21 and 25 people, and a heavy raid on east Hull and Victoria Dock killed 140 on 18 July.
- Two further raids on central and east Hull on 18 August and 3 September cost 20 and 44 lives.
- After this, the intensity of the raids finally slowed, with just one raid in each of October and November – none causing fatalities. By then the long-standing industrial districts around the River Hull were in ruins, however, and the nearby working-class residential areas to the north-east and east were particularly badly hit.
- There was a longer respite from the bombs until 13 April 1942 when one raid killed four people; two more attacks, on 1 and 19 May, cost seven and ten lives.
- 1942 saw just three more raids – 1 August, 24 October, and 20 December, when three people died.
- Apart from two raids on 4 and 16 January 1943, a hiatus lasted until 24 June and 14 July 1943, when two isolated raids targeted districts across the city – the latter killing 26 citizens.
- 1944 saw no bombing at all.
- The final two raids arrived on 4 and 17 March, 1945 – this final raid, as the war neared conclusion, took 12 lives on Holderness road.

In total, Hull suffered 82 raids between 1940 and 1945, with other attacks on adjacent towns and villages.[18] These raids were staggered in their intensity and there were periods with no attacks at all. While fear might ease during these respites, it would not disappear entirely – especially as occasional raids, or clusters of raids, still materialised after periods of enemy inaction. Neither did location offer residents much protection. Raids hit all areas of the city: the docks and major railway infrastructure (and the residential streets surrounding them) were particularly

9.5 Waterloo Street, North Hull Estate, 14 March 1941.
Hull History Centre TSP/3/357/14

9.6 Prospect Street, 24 March 1941.
Hull History Centre C TSP/3/373/37

9.7 Hedon Road, 16 April 1941.
Hull History Centre C TSP/3/378/32

vulnerable, but housing well away from these prime targets was also bombed. Everyone in Hull was a potential victim, and everyone would know the chill of another air-raid siren.

Finally, according to local lore, Hull's suffering was largely unacknowledged beyond the city at the time or subsequently. Some politicians in London, with access to more accurate reports, appreciated the devastation: Herbert Morrison commented that Hull was the town that 'suffered most'.[19] The wider public were denied this news, however. The official censors decided that reporting the damage would help the enemy, so most reports referred only to attacks on a 'North East coast town'. Eight decades later, this partial silence about Hull's ordeal still rankles with locals.

9.10 Watt Street, 11 May 1941.
Hull History Centre C TSP/3/390/3

Housing and the Move to the Estates

Hull Corporation embarked upon a programme to replace the city's ageing
and insanitary housing stock during the 1919–39 period. The war postponed
progress and brought the added challenge of repairing or rebuilding the 93
per cent of houses damaged by bombing. In response, the 'Abercrombie Plan'
was conceived in an effort to remodel the city and deliver a 'proper healthy and
amenable state of living' for its inhabitants; this included demolishing outdated
inner-city housing and creating new, model suburbs. This plan was never
realised, but the local authority did demolish cramped residential quarters in the
city centre, and overcrowded districts located off the city's main arteries. It also
created new, modern estates of council-owned housing, mainly to the east and
north of the city – Bilton Grange was completed in 1955, Longhill in 1958 and
Greatfield in 1960, with Orchard Park and Ings Road commencing in 1963 and
Bransholme in 1966.[1]

Inevitably, long-established local communities were dispersed, often to
the new outskirts of a rapidly expanding city. These changes disrupted an
established way of life, which was greeted variously with enthusiasm and

Demolition of 24 Eton Street,
Hull, January 1980
Courtesy of Hull History Centre

regret.[2] There was much to celebrate about moving to spacious streets, trees, private gardens and bathrooms. Ivy looked forward to a greener environment when moving to her new house at Bransholme on the northern outskirts of the city, recalling that 'I thought my children's gonna grow up in the country [though] it isn't really the country … but it was for us'. Relocation, however, could mean living some distance from family and friends, which could pose difficulties, especially for older people. Some kept mementoes from their demolished homes and districts; Rose, for instance, rescued and kept a brick from the remnants of her school. People relocating from the tight-knit trawling community of Hessle Road encountered challenges as old friendship networks and a sense of community were fractured. Ron, a former trawler skipper, observed how even a short move from near the fish dock to a new house just north of Hessle Road proved difficult for his mother and father-in-law. 'They lost friends,' he said, 'and the days of standing on your doorstep and talking to your neighbour, as they used to do in the terraced houses … It just became a different way, a different community.' To Jim, another trawler skipper, mixed feelings were unsurprising. Trawling was a dangerous occupation, supported by the neighbourhood bonds and matriarchal networks of Hessle Road. 'Well,' he reflected, 'you don't walk away and ever forget that kind of community.'

Nevertheless, those who were moved out of the inner city reconstructed their social networks and modes of community, and now there are strong senses of local pride on the Hull estates as new communal bonds have developed over the years.

Jo Byrne

Notes
1   David Neave and Susan Neave, *Pevsner Architectural Guides: Hull* (London, 2010), pp. 24–34.
2   Recollections drawn from Jo Byrne, 'After the Trawl: Memory and Afterlife in the Wake of Hull's Distant-Water Trawl Fishery from 1976', unpublished PhD thesis, University of Hull, 2015.

Living beneath the bombs

British civilians proved more robust under aerial attack than gloomy pre-war government predictions had forecast. While post-war narratives of the 'Blitz spirit' suggested that the nation pulled together stoically to survive the bombing, subsequent research suggests that it was never this straightforward.[20] Nevertheless, collective panic was rare:

> In general, the British people responded with fortitude to the aerial assaults of the Second World War, resigning themselves to the dangers while engaging in the war effort. Morale fluctuated, but never broke. Although some individuals lost control during the raids, large scale panic was a rare event.[21]

At the scale of the individual, however, the emotional weight of living with this constant threat often had less visible consequences. Hull's city archives contain several first-hand accounts of life in the bombed city. Most vivid, perhaps, are the voices of children (rarely recorded in more formal histories of the war) that are preserved in a series of essays on the topic: 'What happened to me and what I did in the air raids'.[22] They were written by the 10- and 11-year-old girls of Springburn Street School, near Hessle Road, in February 1942. Their words demonstrate how advancing aircraft technologies posed an immediate, deadly threat and that, for children, air raids had become a regular, but no less terrifying, part of their lives.

Fear and uncertainty were constant themes of the girls' writing. Edna Fewster wrote: 'everytime a bomb came down I screamed and cried. I was very [frightened].'[23] Evelyn Canvass had similar experiences: 'We had just got to sleep [when] we heard incendiaries coming down and one went into [our house] and [burnt] my father's feet, and we felt [frightened].'[24] Likewise, Winifred Stubbins wrote about going to an air-raid shelter: 'We all got on [to] the floor, and a lot of people were [fainting], and we heard screaming and crying. When I was [lying] on the floor I prayed to God to help us.' She concluded her essay with the line: 'And every time the sirens go I am frightened.'[25]

These essays, ranging from half a side of paper to four sheets, and marked for grammar and phrasing by the teacher, Peggy Warren, also hint at individual trauma. Eileen Moote, whose house was bombed, admitted that 'It has made some difference to me because my nerves are [not] so good [as] they [were] before.'[26] Her classmate, Nancy Nunn, wrote plaintively of the night when:

> We went down to the underground shelter ... the people were very frightened indeed. I was terrified ... I thought my time had come, and so did the other people ... it made my nerves terrible and it [has] made a lot of difference to me.[27]

Audrey Ingram recounted another night in a shelter when:

> the [people] in the other part of the shelter woke me up screaming. I thought it was awful. Then all of a sudden [there was] a terrific crash. I thought it was coming for us. I was so frightened I could not keep still.[28]

At the same time, other girls interspersed their accounts with mention of the increasingly routine nature of the raids and the responses of the local people. Sylvia Palmer recounted an episode when: 'My brother was just coming out of the door [when] an incendiary bomb fell right in front of him, [so] he got a bag of sand and [put it out]. We all went to bed.'[29] Others commented on the familiar patterns of inspecting damage, clearing debris, gathering shrapnel pieces and making cups of tea in the aftermath of raids.

Greenhough notes how the girls adopted typical gender roles in response to these dangerous episodes. They wrote about their fathers' duties on fire-watch and air-raid precaution work outside the house, and of their mothers' roles in maintaining the home as safe and secure (although 20 per cent of air-raid wardens in Hull were women).[30] For some children, enacting these expected gender roles lessened their fear. Florence Atkinson wrote that:

> I was glad that I could do something to help, for there was a lady who came into our shelter who was very frightened. She had a little child of one and a half years. The lady was trembling. I took the little baby, and every time a bomb came down I threw a pillow over myself and the little girl, who was called Sheila. She kept crying but at last I hushed her to sleep. I hope we don't have such terrifying nights again.[31]

Several essays also included mention of defiance, collective spirit and the need to 'keep smiling'. Enid Billany wrote:

> It's when I hear the aeroplanes that I am most frightened because we cannot do anything but just sit and wait, even if we sing ... I hope we [do not] have any-more nights like those but if we do we are [keeping] and we will keep up our spirits up [until] we hear the last all clear and our friends and relatives come home again.[32]

A few essays included anti-German sentiments. Edna Fewster wrote: 'I thought about everything we had been through that night. I felt as though I could just go across to Germany and punch Hitler and his Nazi gang in the jaw.'[33] Meanwhile, Mary Oxley earned a comment of 'v. g. indeed' from her teacher for her defiant essay.[34] Other girls made special mention of the particular resilience of Hull. Vera Stephens concluded her essay: 'Hull will never lose her spirit whether there are raids or not'[35] and Sheila Stothard declared: 'although Hull [has] gone through some awful, terrifying raids, we will always keep our spirits up and keep smiling'.[36] We do not know how far the pupils were steered towards these conclusions by their teacher as an exercise in sustaining morale, or how far they were repeating society's wider expectations of fortitude. Nevertheless, their essays offer acute insight into the fear of everyday life in the bombed city, and of the resilience of Hull people in the blitz.

Not everyone found the strength to articulate this kind of resistance. After the first heavy bombing of March and May 1941, a committee of local citizens surveyed the resilience of locals. They were particularly worried about the St Paul's district of Sculcoates where they perceived morale to be worse than elsewhere, and where people displayed 'complete helplessness and resignation [which was] the most disquieting feature. It was not a healthy willingness to accept misfortune without grumbling, but hopeless and indeed helpless incapacity to appreciate the significance of their plight.'[37]

This local committee initially found other districts in Hull to be more stoical, but the heavy raid of 7–8 May 1941 prompted wider anxiety and thousands started to leave the city every night over the following weeks. As noted above, the 'trekking' phenomenon emerged during the Zeppelin raids of the First World War, but during the spring 1941 blitz 7,000–9,000 people evacuated the city nightly – walking or cycling to relative safety in the city's parks or, better, to village halls, barns or other shelter beyond the city.[38] Hull is a relatively concentrated city, with easy access across flat landscape to surrounding countryside, yet this nightly migration concerned the authorities. Although the safety of rural areas underpinned the evacuation policy for urban children, when adults trekked from the city it was seen as a threat to industrial productivity, civil order and the collective mood. Over time Hull's authorities realised that most workers who trekked were disciplined enough to return to work each morning (as many merely sought a decent sleep with a working day to follow). The city council therefore made provisions to help the trekkers. Yet from afar such actions fuelled a 'popular view in Whitehall … that the people of Hull exhibited less moral fibre than other city populations'.[39] These government suspicions helped to prompt a more rigorous survey of local resilience and an attempt to measure trauma to establish just how close Hull was to psychological collapse.

Measuring the fear of bombing and the resilience of Hull

Civilian morale, and its assumed fragility, was a key concern for interwar governments facing aerial warfare. Throughout the 1930s governments and their militaries tried to estimate this breaking point. In 1937 British modelling of wartime scenarios predicted that a 60-day bombing campaign might kill 600,000 and wound 1,200,000 civilians. Given the additional psychological devastation for those who survived such attacks, the British theorised that this might signal the point of civilian collapse.[40] When the actual war started, the British government maintained a bomb survey to record precisely how many enemy bombs fell. Morale, by contrast, was recorded in a more haphazard manner. Through 1940 to early 1941 the government relied on various sources for information on civilian resilience. The Ministry of Home Security gathered reports from the police, civil defence and intelligence officers. The Ministry of Information likewise generated daily reports.[41] At their behest, the 'Mass Observation' initiative (a project that surveyed ordinary, working-class opinions and lifestyles) addressed morale across Britain in December 1940 and January 1941.[42]

Later in 1941, Mass Observation would visit and report on Hull (we encountered a section of their report above), but in early 1941 the government's array of sources on public sentiments was still deemed to be insufficiently systematic. The Ministry of Home Security therefore enlisted more demonstrably robust science by requiring its Security Research and Experiments Branch to establish the exact impact of bombing on British cities.

This new survey sought to apply neutral, dispassionate scientific rigour to quantify the nature and extent of 'fear' in bombed cities. It was run by two leading scientists: Solly Zuckerman, a biologist, and J. D. Bernal, a physicist who had been studying the effects of bomb blasts on humans. It aimed to determine the impact of the blitz on 'productivity, absenteeism, evacuation and even "morale"'.[43] They were also charged with establishing how many bombs, and at what frequency, might 'break a town'.[44] The survey used two cities as case studies: Birmingham (to represent industrial cities) and Hull (to represent port-cities). The government's response to German bombing, and the British bombing of Germany, would rest, in part, on the survey of these two cities.

The business of measuring fear and identifying a city's breaking point scientifically was neither simple nor cheap. Some 40 psychologists travelled to Hull aiming to interview 900 people about their experiences.[45] The survey also demanded essays from all Hull school children aged 10–14 on the theme of 'what happened to me in an air-raid': we have encountered a few of these essays already. Defining and assessing fear and moods is notoriously difficult.[46] Further, the scale of this project and the short time horizons of warfare meant that some of the data remained unprocessed. Zuckerman regretted that many of the children's essays were not examined, especially as he had developed a complex coding mechanism to assess their fear via their choice of words.[47] The survey nevertheless generated results that illuminated Hull's wartime experience.

The research found Hull to be largely resilient with 'no evidence of a breakdown in morale'.[48] Here, as elsewhere, bombed-out families could be rehoused relatively easily: even with significant damage in the city there were usually places for temporary shelter. Transport systems, dock business and industrial productivity were rarely waylaid for long by enemy action. Neither did the survey uncover the mass panic that Zuckerman had initially anticipated (due to the prevalence of trekking in Hull). His 'outline conclusions' found no evidence that trekking undermined production or morale. Instead, he saw it as a 'considered response' to danger, especially when so many had seen family, friends and neighbours killed.[49] We cannot read the official, definitive report until it is released from embargo in 2020, but Zuckerman's autobiography claimed that trekking was also driven by the visible proportion of local buildings damaged (and in Hull this figure was high).[50] Another 1940s study showed that those living in smaller cities, where loss was more concentrated and visible, were more likely to suffer anxiety.[51] Similarly, more recent research suggests that the destruction of familiar landmarks, shops and entertainment venues also fractured spirits by undermining the continuities of working-class lives.[52] Therefore, Hull's scale affected the experience of the blitz. Encounters with bomb damage and death were inevitable within its tight boundaries; equally, mass bicycle ownership made nightly escape feasible. On all three counts therefore, Hull people were more likely to be traumatised by bombing than compatriots elsewhere, and more likely to evacuate the city each night. Indeed, after the worst of the raids were over in 1943, over 1,600 people still left every evening.[53] Collectively, however, this government-commissioned survey reported that Hull remained resilient and did not have a problem of morale.

Beyond the collective scale, though, the impact of bombing was often more marked on individuals. Imagine the incremental strain of preparing to sleep each night while knowing that an air-raid siren might sound. Or of waiting in a shelter (or taking a chance at home), smelling fires burning, and hearing enemy aircraft and the different types of bombs falling (which people could identify with experience), and wondering if you might feel the blast this time. After the war, nationwide medical surveys concluded that although acute fear, anxiety and confusion were immediate responses to bombing, with sufficient rest most people recovered and the number of psychiatric casualties was surprisingly low.[54] Zuckerman and Bernal produced parallel results from their 706 interviewees in Hull. These people were not unduly weak or hysterical collectively, they argued, but some individuals were suffering various nervous conditions from witnessing so much destruction – with moderate neurosis in 53 per cent of women and 20 per cent of men.[55] As Overy points out, the narrative of Hull's collective survival tends to mask the profound trauma of individuals. For example, Hull Survey Case 1, a male worker, lost two members of his family when their house took a direct hit. Case 37, a housewife, was bombed out three times and, having lost her sister with five children, could not sleep and was terrified of the air-raid siren.[56] At this individual, embodied scale, the blitz was horrific for many, despite the resilience of the majority.

The Hull research also had further, and more deadly, consequences elsewhere in the war. The survey had quantified the lethal impacts of the bombing and determined that each ton of bombs dropped on Hull killed four people and left 140 homeless. Moreover, although the intensity of the raids had little impact on collective spirits, those people 'de-housed' were more likely to suffer poor morale subsequently.[57] In March 1942 these figures were used by Frederick Lindemann, the government's Chief Scientific Advisor throughout the war, to persuade Churchill to support the mass 'area bombing' of German cities to 'de-house' civilians and shatter their morale. Subsequent studies have argued that Lindemann misrepresented the Hull data to support destructive area bombing, and as Churchill wanted a reason to carpet-bomb German cities, Lindemann's intervention reinforced saturation bombing as British strategy.[58] The theory behind the thousand-bomber raids and firestorms that would so devastate Germany, with death tolls far higher than those in Britain, were prompted in part by the surveys of Hull. In addition, some of the aeroplanes that formed these raids flew from East Yorkshire – joining formation above the Humber before departing across the North Sea.[59] Such were the geographies of connection between wartime enemies and their modern cities.

The University of Hull

The University of Hull was founded in 1927 with an initial cohort of 16 lecturers, 13 departments and 40 students. Provincial universities were emerging across Britain in the aftermath of the First World War, fuelled by a collective will to build a better society after recent sacrifices. As a successful commercial and industrial port-city of 320,000 people, with a growing middle class who nurtured an emerging civic consciousness, Hull was an obvious candidate for a new university. The local pharmaceuticals industrialist and philanthropist Thomas Ferens gifted the site and £250,000 (equivalent to around £12 million today) to found the institution. Ferens hoped to see technological and commercial training relevant to the city's business community, but Arthur Morgan, the first principal, insisted that a university should also teach the arts and pure sciences. Nevertheless, the published history of the university reports that the first staff cohort were pleased to embed the new institution within the city: they offered additional classes for local people, undertook civic roles and engaged with industry. Despite some rivalry with Leeds University over the Yorkshire market, the university began to grow.

The institution was founded as the University College of Hull, with lecturers teaching the University of London external degree programme from its two original buildings (now the Grade II listed Cohen and Venn buildings). Student numbers increased steadily through the interwar period, as did the research programmes of the academics. The University College suffered during the Second World War, however, when many staff were enlisted, replacements

Archdeacon Lambert delivers his address at the University College of Hull Foundation Stone Laying Ceremony, April 1928, watched by (from the right) Albert Windsor (Duke of York), Thomas Ferens (President of the University College), Elizabeth Bowes-Lyon (Duchess of York), Cosmo Gordon Lang (Archbishop of York), and an unknown person.
Courtesy of the University of Hull

were minimal and student numbers dropped. After 1945, the University College expanded once more. It was granted its university charter and independent degree-awarding powers in 1954, making it England's 14th university.

During the final third of the twentieth century, Hull enjoyed a reputation as a traditional, established city university with good-quality academics and students who made a positive contribution to the north of the city and Cottingham, where many of them lived. In this period, the university was also a pioneering, and sometimes radical, centre of drama, politics, poetry, history and science: the poet Philip Larkin ran the library for three decades, students occupied university buildings in 1968, and Hull appointed Professor Roy Marshall, a Barbadian, as Vice-Chancellor in 1979. Former Hull students from these years have assumed positions of significance across Britain today.

The university faced challenges amid the changing higher education landscape of the 2000s, when the number of universities mushroomed (with the end of the university/polytechnic divide in 1992) and elite university alliances emerged. Student numbers grew from around 5 per cent of school leavers in previous decades to around 35 per cent in a new, mass higher education system increasingly funded by student loans. A Medical School was founded (with the University of York), and a Business School was established. The university also expanded into the adjacent campus of Humberside Polytechnic when this institution left Hull (to eventually become the University of Lincoln). As a medium-sized institution in a shifting higher education environment, Hull has to develop its particular strengths in a competitive sector: it has scaled down its campus in Scarborough and refocused its structures for the years ahead. Nevertheless, as the university approaches its centenary, it is larger than ever, with 16,300 students and 2,500 staff. It retains its international profile and remains one of the largest employers in Hull and an important player in the city and region.

David Atkinson

T. W. Bamford, *The University of Hull: The First Fifty Years* (Oxford, 1978).

'A Poetic Place': The Hull of Philip Larkin

Philip Larkin was born in Coventry in 1922, modern literature's *annus mirabilis*. A grammar school education and parental encouragement to read writers as surprisingly modern as Lawrence and Joyce meant that Larkin's literary sensibilities soon emerged. Some of his earliest poetry was published in the school magazine and, although his headmaster considered him 'not very pleasing except in English', Larkin gained a place at Oxford to read English Literature.[1] Wartime austerity, however, meant that Larkin's Oxford experience was distinctly un-*Brideshead*. Unlike many male contemporaries, he avoided conscription thanks to his poor vision. With time to write, Larkin worked on fiction and poetry, and invented a female-lesbian heteronym, Brunette Coleman, author of stories and poems for schoolgirls. If these writings represented distraction from – or even opposition to – the war, the war nevertheless asserted itself on Larkin's consciousness following the devastating Luftwaffe raid on Coventry in November 1940.

After graduating in 1943, Larkin fell into librarianship and moved to Wellington, Shropshire, to run its public library. Despite being displeased about 'handing out tripey novels to morons' (his comments still offend locals), he again had time for writing; by 1947 Larkin had published two novels (*Jill* and *A Girl in Winter*) and a book of poems (*The North Ship*).[2] He had also been appointed assistant librarian at University College, Leicester, where he met Monica Jones, the English lecturer who became his life partner – albeit one whom he kept at arm's length. In 1950 he moved again, this time to Belfast as sub-librarian at Queen's University.

His life changed in 1955 for two reasons: Larkin moved to Hull to become librarian of the University College, and his second poetry collection, *The Less Deceived*, was published. This book announced the arrival of a new and original talent in British poetry (coincidentally, it was published by the Marvell Press which operated from a garage in the Hull suburb of Hessle). There is no doubt, therefore, that Larkin-the-poet put Hull on the map; but as university librarian he also impacted Hull's actual cityscape. Having inherited 124,000 books and 12 staff on the ground floor of a campus building, Larkin oversaw a massive and complicated two-stage redevelopment of the library that was only completed in 1969. Under his leadership, a seven-floor tower block housing 500,000 books and administered by 100 staff rose above the campus; it was, and remains, one of the best university libraries in the country.[3]

Larkin and puddle, June 1958
Courtesy of the Hull History Centre
(U DLV/3/82/1)

Larkin has come to be seen as Hull's poet, but his statements on this issue are few and do not make for an easy alignment. At times he comes across as unenthusiastic about Hull, but he had something of a knack for seeming unenthusiastic about place. In his foreword to *A Rumoured City*, Larkin writes that 'Poetry, like prose, happens anywhere.'[4] Note the similarity of this phrase to the concluding lines of his poem 'I Remember, I Remember', where, recalling an apparently uneventful childhood, he reflects that 'Nothing, like something, happens anywhere.'[5] Larkin goes on to explain and mitigate this seeming lack of interest. He writes that 'Hull got its clearance on this from Andrew Marvell many years ago', and that 'it is still as good a place to write in as any […] Better, in fact, than some. For a place cannot produce poems: it can only not prevent them, and Hull is good at that. It neither impresses nor insists.'[6]

'Here' is the Larkin poem in which we can most tangibly locate Hull and the East Riding. It takes us to Hull and then beyond into the Holderness plain where 'silence stands/ Like heat' and the 'unfenced existence' of the sea is found.[7] Though not one of Larkin's numerous train poems, 'Here' is nevertheless a poem of transit and arrival, 'swerving east' from 'rich industrial shadows' towards and then beyond the city. From the scrubby pastoral of the first stanza, Hull comes as 'the surprise of a large town'. The specificity of description here is greater than in most located Larkin poems: if 'domes and statues, spires and cranes' might be found in any city, then definition is added to Hull's particularity in the 'barge-crowded water' of the next line, and then further still in the 'pastoral of ships up streets, [and] the slave museum' in the following stanza. Yet it is perhaps the description of the people of Hull that is most interesting. Larkin might seem to denigrate 'residents from raw estates' and their material 'desires' – the cheap clothing and kitchen appliances of department stores in town – but this is not really the case. Their description as 'a cut-price crowd, urban yet simple' is a celebration of stoicism. 'Simple' is not a synonym for stupid; rather it celebrates a lack of pretension. It chimes with Larkin's sense that Hull is 'unpretentious, recent, full of shops and special offers'.[8]

The poem's journey continues east to the 'unfenced existence' of the landscape beyond the city. He describes:

Hidden weeds flower, neglected waters quicken,
Luminously-peopled air ascends;
And past the poppies bluish neutral distance
Ends the land suddenly beyond a beach
Of shapes and shingle. Here is unfenced existence:
Facing the sun, untalkative, out of reach.

This place, in contrast to the foregoing stanzas, is depopulated, but it is nonetheless where 'luminously-peopled air ascends'. This curious and opaque phrase perhaps links the two places; indeed, the atmosphere of the Holderness plain certainly seems to influence and clarify the sense of the Hull in the poem.

Larkin's four poetry collections were slim and published a decade apart from each other. *The Whitsun Weddings* (1964) cemented his immense popularity, but the next, *High Windows* (1974), was also his last – after this, the writing thinned severely. Larkin connected the rise and fall of his muse to his two main homes in Hull: 32 Pearson Park and 105 Newland Park. The first, a Victorian attic flat, he found favourable to writing, but not the starker aesthetic of the modern house he later felt pressured to buy. Larkin died of oesophageal cancer in 1985. He had produced some of the greatest poetry of the century and in British literary history, much of it written in Hull, where the everyday, the 'unpretentious' and the 'recent' are open to 'what lies beyond'.[9]

Daniel Weston and James Underwood

Notes
1   Quoted in Andrew Motion, *Philip Larkin: A Writer's Life* (London, 1994), p. 30.
2   Quoted in James Booth, *Philip Larkin: Life, Art and Love* (London, 2014), p. 82.
3   See Richard Goodman, '"My Particular Talents" – Larkin's 42-year Career as a Librarian', *About Larkin*, 4 (October 1997), pp. 4–11.
4   Philip Larkin, 'Foreword', in Douglas Dunn (ed.), *A Rumoured City: New Poets From Hull* (Newcastle, 1982), p. 9.
5   Philip Larkin, 'I Remember, I Remember', in *Collected Poems* (London: Faber, 2003), p. 69.
6   Larkin, 'Foreword', p. 9.
7   Larkin, 'Here', in *Collected Poems*, pp. 79–80.
8   Larkin, 'Foreword', p. 9.
9   Larkin, 'Foreword', p. 9.

Resilience via utopian planning

The severity of the bombing and its impact on Hull's communities inspired a debate about how best to restore the city. These sentiments were aired at the height of the blitz when the *Hull Daily Mail* carried an article by Max Lock, a prominent planner and Hull resident, who noted that 'There is not a citizen in Hull who is not deeply affected by the devastation of familiar streets and the destruction of well-known buildings … what sort of city are we going to build up after the war?'[60] In 1943 the same newspaper claimed that 'The conflict has made Hull perhaps one of the gloomiest big cities in the country. Because of what we have borne with resignation and courage our reward should [be] generous.'[61] This same connection between destruction and re-planning was articulated directly on the first page of the 1945 plan to rebuild the shattered city. As Leo Schultz, Lord Mayor in 1943 and chair of the Hull Reconstruction Committee, explained in the quotation at the head of this chapter, resilience meant rebuilding a better Hull.[62]

To this end, in November 1942 the city engaged Edwin Lutyens and Patrick

Abercrombie to redesign Hull.[63] These appointments were confident and ambitious. Lutyens was perhaps Britain's leading architect, famous for his design of the Cenotaph in Whitehall to commemorate the First World War dead, and subsequently for planning imperial New Delhi with its neoclassicism, triumphant avenues and vistas. Abercrombie was Britain's leading academic practitioner of the new 'science' of planning: the attempt to improve communities by improving their towns and cities. He had been influenced by Ebenezer Howard's Garden City philosophies, together with the International Modern movement that aimed to produce better urbanism through rational planning. Abercrombie responded to interwar city sprawl with the idea of green belts, later enshrined in the 1947 Town and Country Planning Act. But his reputation also rested on re-planning blitzed cities where he demonstrated his patrician belief that the expert planner knew best how to engineer a better society.[64]

Lutyens and Abercrombie had worked on a series of plans to remake the blitzed cities of interwar Britain as modern, cleaner places for the future. Previous commissions included the plans for London (1943 and 1944) and for other bombed cities, including Plymouth, Southampton, Coventry and Bristol. Abercrombie claimed that their interest in Hull arose when he and Lutyens visited in 1936 and saw the possibilities for reworking the city.[65] When commissioned, they asked for a 'perfectly free hand'.[66] This was granted and they were asked to 'Plan for us a city [as if] you were designing a city for yourselves.'[67] Lutyens would not see the project to completion as he died on 1 January 1944, but Abercrombie finished the plan and released it to the city council in 1944 and to the public in 1945. He considered it 'the best report he had been connected with'.[68]

Justifying 'The Abercrombie Plan'

The published report and proposals, commonly called 'The Abercrombie Plan', ran to 92 pages and included extensive full-colour maps and illustrations. Like Leo Schultz, Abercrombie explicitly connected his vision for a new, modern Hull to its wartime suffering. For these planners, bomb-sites also offered opportunities. In a chapter entitled 'Bomb Damage', Abercrombie outlined Hull's devastation, then asked rhetorically 'What, then, is the scope of the Reconstruction. The resurgence from the destruction of war which should be proposed for Hull?'[69] He had an answer ready. Noting that bombed plots were scattered across the city rather than focused in one or two districts, he admitted that it would be simplest to infill these empty plots and maintain the extant street patterns if 'rebuilding were to be limited to one short term scheme'.[70] But Abercrombie argued for a longer-term regeneration process lasting up to twenty years. This more radical scheme would remove surviving districts that were 'ripe for redevelopment' and instead deliver a 'comprehensive scheme of reconstruction' which meant 'a real improvement to the whole, or parts, of the city'.[71] Only this kind of overhaul, Abercrombie continued, was a suitable response to the devastation and suffering of the city:

It would be the height of folly to miss this opportunity for re-planning in accordance with modern standards of transport, industry and health … The

9.11 'General Development', from Lutyens and Abercrombie, *Plan for Hull*, Map 11, between pp. 78–79.

future of Hull demands these improved conditions: they are the compensation which may go some way to make up for the suffering, loss of trade, inconvenience and squalor of these [war] years; a patched and botched up war-scarred Hull would be a poor object to offer to posterity.[72]

The plan was a remarkable statement of vision and ambition, but it was not a quick solution. Rather, it resonated with the measured and sober rhetoric of the best possible modern planning practice. It also offered a utopian vision of improved urban lives.

Outlining 'The Abercrombie Plan'

The plan opened with extensive discussion of the problems facing Hull. Following contemporary planning theory, it focused heavily upon improving the quality of life in the city centre and redistributing the population to new, healthier suburbs. It prioritised simplified, unified and segregated land-uses for different functions. This would produce a dedicated city centre and shopping zone, and discrete industrial and residential zones separated by green space and connected by a transport infrastructure that allowed easy circulation. It also aimed to curtail the suburban sprawl of interwar Hull, and to separate town and country with a green belt, beyond

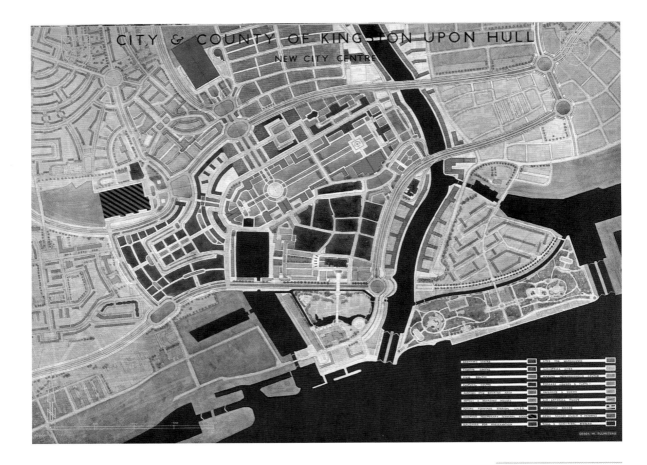

CITY & COUNTY OF KINGSTON UPON HULL

NEW CITY CENTRE

9.12 'New City Centre', from
Lutyens and Abercrombie,
Plan for Hull, Plate XXVI,
between pp. 42–43.

which would be a new satellite town at Burton Constable to the north-east of the
city (Figure 9.11). This kind of coherent, comprehensive planning of a city-region
was the state of the art.[73]

The plan centred upon ambitious schemes for a largely new city centre laid out
on modernist lines with axial routes and vistas (Figure 9.12). When Lutyens and
Abercrombie visited Hull in 1936 they were impressed by Queen's Gardens (the
former Queen's Dock that was reclaimed in the 1930s). Their plan made Queen's
Gardens the central axis of their 'civic centre' which would be flanked by civic
buildings and museums. There would be some preservation of the Old Town, but
much of High Street, the area around Holy Trinity church and Prince Street would
be lost.[74]

To the north of this central axis would be a new, relocated railway terminus,
adjacent to entertainment and leisure facilities including hotels, theatres and cinemas.
To the south-west of the axis would be the Osborne Street quarter: a new pedestri-
anised shopping centre (Figure 9.13) drawing together Hull's central retail functions
and finding sufficient space by demolishing the Dock Offices (now the Maritime
Museum) and the City Hall.[75] This new city centre would be contained within a ring
road that removed non-essential traffic from the area, although as Figure 9.14 shows,

this aspect of the plan impacted on the historic fabric of the Old Town, including Wilberforce House, which we would now protect from such interventions. The ring road would connect with key routes to the suburbs and to other cities and regions. Elsewhere the plan featured high-level railways (to avoid delays at level crossings), landscaped routes into the city and the separation of traffic and pedestrians.[76] Such ideas are familiar today, but in 1945 they were innovative.

Remaking the city centre meant demolishing its slums. According to Abercrombie's figures, the dense terraced housing that enfolded the city centre and adjacent industrial sites and docklands often saw population densities of 100–300 people per acre.[77] Many houses were squeezed around narrow, dark, airless 'courts', and 39.3 per cent of houses lacked bathrooms and hot water in 1939.[78] Intermixed industry and housing was a particular problem in the planner's imagination: such functions were to be separated into industrial zones and distinct residential neighbourhoods, each with healthcare, education and leisure provision, and sufficient open space for 'proper, healthy living'.[79] Hull would have 17 of these self-contained neighbourhoods, with 5,000–10,000 people in each at a density of no more than 50–75 per acre.[80] Each neighbourhood would be separated from others by transport arteries and swathes of greenery. The new housing would be mainly low-rise flats and terraced, family houses with space around them for light, air and recreation. Approximately 54,000 people would be displaced from the central districts to these new neighbourhoods.[81] For Abercrombie, this improved housing, better environment and ease of circulation around the city would mean that lives in these model suburbs would be improved.

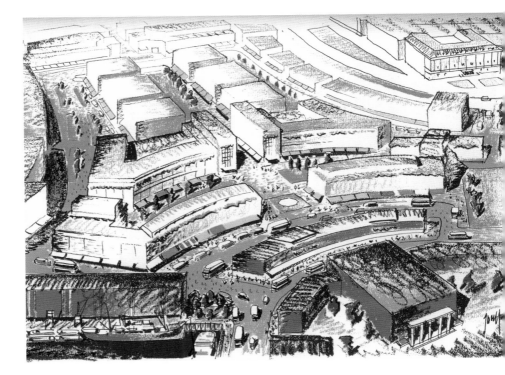

9.13 'Bird's eye view of new Osborne Street Shopping Centre', from Lutyens and Abercrombie, *Plan for Hull*, Plate XXII, between pp. 42–43.

Finally, this ambitious structure extended beyond the city into the wider region. At the edge of the city Abercrombie proposed a green belt to stop Hull's urban sprawl. Although only one or two miles wide, this buffer would separate city and countryside and direct any future growth beyond this protected land. The proposed satellite town at Burton Constable, for example, would house 60,000 people eight miles beyond Hull, and would be connected to the city by the Hull–Hornsea railway. Here again, 'town and country planning' was deemed to improve the urban condition, and residential, retail and industrial functions were separated from each other.

9.14 Wilberforce House framed by a flyover for the proposed new inner ring road that would demolish other parts of the Old Town, from Lutyens and Abercrombie, *Plan for Hull*, p. 4.

This was an encompassing, comprehensive vision to remake blitzed Hull and its region for the late twentieth century. If implemented, it would have destroyed some aspects of the city that we celebrate today, but Abercrombie also anticipated several problems that Hull has been wrestling with ever since, including traffic circulation, a coherent shopping core, a green belt and the creation of functioning communities beyond the city periphery. Despite its visionary promise, however, the plan was not realised in practice.

Implementing 'The Abercrombie Plan'

The plan was released to the council and public in 1944–45. According to the urban geographer Philip Jones, the plan was 'at the forefront of contemporary planning thinking' and 'was strong, coherent and intelligible to the ordinary person'.[82] In 1945 Leo Schultz was more equivocal:

> This is the plan. It is put forward as a guide for the citizens for the future development of our great city. It is theirs to discuss, to consider, to criticise. To amend and to adopt such of it as they consider to be proper.[83]

Unfortunately for Abercrombie's vision, many citizens did criticise. Some had grumbled all along about the transparency of the process, seeking updates and information from the outside 'experts' who were assessing their city.[84] Others complained about the late delivery of the plan, and the chair of the City Reconstruction Committee made this point publicly.[85] Abercrombie acknowledged some of these anxieties, and admitted that the shopping district was a 'controversial' idea.[86]

There was no clear point at which the plan was abandoned, but over the next few years it slipped out of focus steadily due to various intersecting reasons. For one commentator, the opposition of city-centre businesses and traders was a key reason.[87] They resented the prospect of moving from their established locations to the proposed new shopping quarter. Local newspapers printed regular letters complaining about the potential impacts of the plan, and shopkeepers even organised an alternative plan and exhibition in 1949 that celebrated the existing shopping streets. For other commentators, the failure of central government to provide sufficient funding for longer term reconstruction was the primary reason for the plan's failure.[88] Perhaps inevitably, when post-war austerity failed to generate adequate resources for the major rebuilding envisaged, shorter term contingencies resulted. City-centre shops and offices were repaired or rebuilt on their old sites, which re-enshrined the old street pattern. Every business that reopened on its original footprint made the plan's implementation less likely. When large, new, iconic developments like the Hammonds department store of 1950 were constructed, this cemented the old street structure still further and made Abercrombie's wide-scale rebuilding still more untenable. Abercrombie had foreseen and warned against this scenario in his plan.[89] Yet the urban fabric that survived the bombs, and the short-term pressure to reconstruct the city quickly, overwhelmed this longer-term vision.

I have interpreted the plan as a utopian response to the trauma of the blitz and a reward for the citizens' resilience. As Abercrombie feared, events, schedules and a lack of resource prevented its realisation, even though several elements of his vision crept into Hull's post-war planning. In the end, the centre of the city retained much of the street structure of the interwar years, although many of the slums were cleared and their populations were encouraged to move to new, peripheral housing estates such as Bransholme and Orchard Park. That said, these issues do not detract from the overall aspiration and optimism of the plan: this was a proposal to soothe the trauma of the war for a city that had suffered more than most.

Bringing trauma, resilience and utopianism together in Second World War Hull

The destruction of the Hull blitz was appalling and the deaths were numerous. Despite the severity of the bombing in certain periods, and the longevity of the threat of attack, the people of Hull proved to be resilient. Inevitably the citizens suffered some collective trauma, and many individuals were impacted significantly by these events, but despite the ferocity of Hull's blitz, and despite government concerns about its impact, this key wartime city withstood the bombing and emerged battered but undefeated.

Additional evidence of the city's resilience was the plan that the city council commissioned which was a conscious attempt to rebuild Hull as a quintessentially modern city. The Abercrombie plan was undermined by post-war austerity, economic realities and local contingencies, but the ambition to forge a state-of-the-art city from the ruins of the blitz likewise demonstrated Hull's resilience. The devastation, re-planning and reconstruction of Hull since 1940 impacted upon the city, its cultures and its identities for decades afterwards. If the bombs had not fallen, or if the re-planning had been completed to Abercrombie's vision, we might have interpreted Hull in very different ways in recent years, and we might be thinking of it as a different kind of city of culture.

Notes

1 Leo Schultz, 'Foreword', in Edwin Lutyens and Patrick Abercrombie, *A Plan for the City & County of Kingston-upon-Hull* (London and Hull, 1945), p. v.

2 T. Geraghty, *'A North-East Coast Town': Ordeal and Triumph – the story of Kingston-upon-Hull in the 1939–1945 Great War* (Howden, 2002 [1951]). I have used Geraghty for details of the air raids and casualties because this source is used by most other commentators (although some more recent authors have slightly different figures). On Hull's blitz, see also Philip Graystone, *The Blitz on Hull (1940–45)* (York, 1991); James Greenhalgh, '"Till We Hear the Last All Clear": Gender and the Presentation of Self in Young Girls' Writing about the Bombing of Hull during the Second World War', *Gender & History*, 26.1 (2014), pp. 167–83; Derry Jones, 'Hull Blitz, Scientific Surveys and City Bombing Campaigns: 1941–42 Surveys of Morale in much-bombed Hull', *The East Yorkshire Historian*, 9 (2008), pp. 27–36.

3 Geraghty, *North-East Coast Town*.

4 Lutyens and Abercrombie, *Plan for Hull*; see also Philip Jones, '"...a fairer and nobler city" – Lutyens and Abercrombie's Plan for the City of Hull 1945', *Planning Perspectives*, 13.3 (1998), pp. 301–16.

5 Arthur Credland, *The Hull Zeppelin Raids 1915–1918* (Stroud, 2014).

6 Credland, *Hull Zeppelin Raids*.

7 Giulio Douhet, *Il Dominio dell'Aria* (Rome, 1921); Azar Gat, *Fascist and Liberal Visions of War: Fuller, Liddell Hart, Douhet, and Other Modernists* (Oxford, 1998); Thomas Hippler, *Bombing the People: Giulio Douhet and the Foundations of Air-power Strategy, 1884–1939* (Cambridge, 2013); Brett Holman, 'World Police for World Peace: British Internationalism and the Threat of a Knock-out Blow from the Air, 1919–1945', *War in History*, 17.3 (2010), pp. 313–32 (pp. 313–14).

8 Brett Holman, 'The Air Panic of 1935: British Press Opinion between Disarmament and Rearmament', *Journal of Contemporary History*, 46.2 (2011), pp. 288–307.

9 Richard Overy, *The Bombing War, Europe 1939–1945* (London, 2013).

10 Paul Crook, 'Science and War: Radical Scientists and the Tizard-Cherwell Area Bombing Debate in Britain', *War & Society*, 12.2 (1994), pp. 69–101.

11 Juliet Gardiner, *The Blitz: The British under Attack* (London, 2010).

12 The dates and details of the bombing of Hull are taken from Geraghty, *North-East Coast Town*, pp. 109–12.

13 Jones, 'Hull Blitz', p. 32.

14 Geraghty, *North-East Coast Town*.

15 Gardiner, *The Blitz*, p. 318.

16 Powolny's restaurant, a luxury venue in King Edward Street shown in Figure 8.13, was destroyed on the night of 9 May 1941.

17 Gardiner, *The Blitz*, p. 319.

18 Geraghty, *North-East Coast Town*.

19 Tom Harrisson, *Living Through the Blitz* (London, 1976), p. 263.

20 Angus Calder, *The Myth of the Blitz* (London, 1991); Edgar Jones, Robin Woolven, Bill Durodié and Simon Wessley, 'Civilian Morale During the Second World War: Responses to Air Raids Re-examined', *Social History of Medicine*, 17.3 (2004), pp. 463–79.

21 Jones et al., 'Civilian Morale', p. 478.

22 Greenhalgh, 'Till We Hear the Last All Clear'.

23 Edna Fewster, 'What happened to me and what I did in the air raids', Hull History Centre [hereafter HHC], DEX24/12.

24 Evelyn Canvess, 'What happened to me and what I did in the air raids', HHC DEX24/5.

25 Winnifred Stubbins, 'What happened to me and what I did in the air raids', HHC DEX24/28.

26 Eileen Moote, 'What happened to me and what I did in the air raids', HHC DEX24/19.

27 Nancy Nunn, 'What happened to me and what I did in the air raids', HHC DEX24/20.

28 Audrey Ingram, 'What happened to me and what I did in the air raids', HHC DEX24/16.

29 Sylvia Palmer, 'What happened to me and what I did in the air raids', HHC DEX24/22.

30 Greenhalgh, 'Till We Hear the Last All Clear'; Overy, *The Bombing War*.

31 Florence Atkinson, quoted in Greenhalgh, 'Till We Hear the Last All Clear', p. 178.

32 Enid Billany, 'What happened to me and what I did in the air raids', HHC DEX24/3; see also Greenhalgh, 'Till We Hear the Last All Clear', p. 172.

33 Edna Fewster, 'What happened to me and what I did in the air raids', HHC DEX24/12.

34 Mary Oxley, 'What happened to me and what I did in the air raids', HHC DEX24/21.

35 Vera Stephens, 'What happened to me and what I did in the air raids', HHC DEX24/25.

36 Sheila Stothard, 'What happened to me and what I did in the air raids', HHC DEX24/27.

37 Harrisson, *Living through the Blitz*, p. 264.

38 Overy, *The Bombing War*.

39 Overy, *The Bombing War*, 169.

40 Jones et al., 'Civilian Morale', p. 465.

41 Jones et al., 'Civilian Morale', p. 478.

42 Brad Beaven and John Griffiths, 'The Blitz, Civilian Morale and the City: Mass-observation and Working-class Culture in Britain, 1940–41', *Urban History*, 26.1 (1999), pp. 71–88.

43 Ian Burney, 'War on Fear: Solly Zuckerman and Civilian Nerve in the Second World War', *History of the Human Sciences*, 25.2 (2012), pp. 49–72.

44 Solly Zuckerman, *From Apes to Warlords: The Autobiography of Solly Zuckerman, 1904–1946* (London, 1978), p. 141.

45 Crook, 'Science and War'.

46 Beaven and Griffiths, 'The Blitz'.

47 Zuckerman, *From Apes to Warlords*; Burney, 'War on Fear'.

48 Zuckerman, *From Apes to Warlords*, p. 405.

49 Zuckerman, *From Apes to Warlords*.
50 Zuckerman, *From Apes to Warlords*; Crook, 'Science and War'.
51 Jones et al., 'Civilian Morale'.
52 Beaven and Griffiths, 'The Blitz'.
53 Overy, *The Bombing War*.
54 Jones et al., 'Civilian Morale'.
55 Overy, *The Bombing War*.
56 Overy, *The Bombing War*.
57 Zuckerman, *From Apes to Warlords*, p. 405.
58 Burney, 'War on Fear'; Crook, 'Science and War'; Zuckerman, *From Apes to Warlords*.
59 Jones, 'Hull Blitz'.
60 Max Lock and D. A. La Mare, 'What Sort of Hull after the War: Proper Re-planning Can Build a City Beautiful', *Hull Daily Mail*, 18 July 1941.
61 'Post-War Hull', *Hull Daily Mail*, 27 September 1943.
62 Schultz, 'Foreword'.
63 'Hull Town Planning Advisors Appointed', *Hull Daily Mail*, 28 November 1942.
64 See also Peter Larkham and Mark Clapson (eds), *The Blitz and its Legacy: Wartime Destruction to Post-War Reconstruction* (London, 2013).
65 'Experts Take a Peep at Hull of the Future', *Hull Daily Mail*, 24 November 1936. Lutyens and Abercrombie visited Hull on behalf of the Royal Fine Arts Commission.
66 'Re-Planning of Hull', *Hull Daily Mail*, 22 January 1943.
67 'Ministry's Consideration of Hull's Reconstruction', *Hull Daily Mail*, 4 April 1943.
68 Lutyens and Abercrombie, *Plan for Hull*; Jones, '… fairer and nobler city', p. 301.
69 Lutyens and Abercrombie, *Plan for Hull*, p. 18.
70 Lutyens and Abercrombie, *Plan for Hull*, p. 18.
71 Lutyens and Abercrombie, *Plan for Hull*, p. 18.
72 Lutyens and Abercrombie, *Plan for Hull*, p. 18.
73 John Pendlebury, 'Planning the Historic City: Reconstruction Plans in the United Kingdom in the 1940s', *Town Planning Review*, 74.4 (2003), pp. 371–93.
74 Lutyens and Abercrombie, *Plan for Hull*, pp. 41–48.
75 Lutyens and Abercrombie, *Plan for Hull*, pp. 41–48.
76 Lutyens and Abercrombie, *Plan for Hull*, pp.19–30.
77 Lutyens and Abercrombie, *Plan for Hull*, p. 50: an area near Hessle Road had the highest population density in Hull, with over 300 persons per acre.
78 Lutyens and Abercrombie, *Plan for Hull*, p. 13.
79 Lutyens and Abercrombie, *Plan for Hull*, p. 49.
80 Lutyens and Abercrombie, *Plan for Hull*, pp. 49–54.
81 Lutyens and Abercrombie, *Plan for Hull*, p. 3.
82 Jones, '… fairer and nobler city', pp. 313, 314.
83 Schultz, 'Foreword', p. v.
84 'Replanning Hull. A Civic Deputation meets Prof. Abercrombie', *The Yorkshire Post and Leeds Intelligencer*, 14 January 1944.
85 'Not One Step Ahead after Three Years. Ald. Hewitt Condemns "This everlasting procrastination"', *Hull Daily Mail*, 27 March 1945.
86 'Abercrombie Report Reveals Hull's Dream City', *Hull Daily Mail*, 16 October 1946.
87 Jones, '… fairer and nobler city'.
88 Nick Tiratsoo, 'Labour and the Reconstruction of Hull', in Nick Tiratsoo, *The Attlee Years* (London, 1991), pp. 126–46; Nick Tiratsoo, 'The Reconstruction of Blitzed British Cities, 1945–55: Myths and Reality', *Contemporary British History*, 14.1 (2000), pp. 27–44.
89 Lutyens and Abercrombie, *Plan for Hull*, p. 3.

CHAPTER TEN

Memory on the Waterfront in Late Twentieth-century Hull

JO BYRNE and ALEX OMBLER

Coming into port

At the close of the Second World War, as the port-city of Hull faced the challenge of rebuilding an urban fabric shattered by wartime bombing, its maritime industries prepared to return to business as usual. Hull's trawl fishery and commercial docks had both been disrupted by the years of conflict and now, in line with Britain's maritime sector, Hull companies were keen to get things back to normal.[1] In the west of the city, as Britain enjoyed a post-war golden age of rising wages and full employment, Hull's distant-water trawl fishery experienced a boom. Reduced fishing effort during the war years had allowed fish stocks to recover and with the nation still facing food shortages, supplies of non-rationed fish were in demand. Yet by the mid-1950s the boom was proving transitory, as overfishing, changing consumer preferences and, most significantly, shifts in international policy sent ripples into the semblance of calm. Meanwhile, away from the fish quay, cracks were more immediately apparent in the city's extensive commercial docklands. The huge post-war growth of the international economy had increased seaborne trade, stimulating demand for shipping and port services. However, like other large British ports, post-1945 operations at Hull were marred by outdated cargo-handling practices, a dire need of capital investment in new facilities and ongoing industrial unrest.[2] In the decades that followed, waves of legislation, reforming policy and disruptive technologies changed established practices irreversibly. Accordingly, along Hull's expansive waterfront, the late twentieth century saw the breakdown of structures and rhythms that had once seemed immutable. For those caught up in the transition, old certainties would come to an end.

Rhythms of the waterfront

In the wake of the Second World War, men and women along Hull's waterfront returned to patterns of living that had endured for decades. In the nineteenth century the port of Hull had extended along the shores of the Humber, with various activities shaping the docks and the communities that served them. The north–south orientation of the River Hull served to emphasise a dual urban character, giving the compelling, if somewhat imprecise impression of a city divided in two. With commercial docks to the east of the River Hull, and fishing to the west, contrasting rhythms of work, life, environment and culture seemingly moulded Hull into a city of two ports (Figure 10.1).

The duality of the east–west city continued into the post-war years. At the spacious eastern docks increasing quantities of oil arrived from both foreign and domestic refineries, while timber and agricultural produce were imported from Scandinavia and the Commonwealth.[3] In parallel, coal was shipped along the coast and to Europe, alongside machinery and manufactured goods destined for markets across the globe.[4] To the west of the River Hull, fruit, vegetables, meat and other foodstuffs lined the quays of William Wright Dock, Albert Dock and the central Town Docks.[5] Such commercial activity took place downwind from the odour of smokehouse and fishmeal, as at St Andrew's Fish Dock Hull's distant-water trawl

10.1 Dockworkers moving a gangway into position. An unpublished image from a photo shoot by Robert Golden for the 1975 publication *Dockworker*.
Courtesy of Robert Golden

10.2 Vessels from around the globe being discharged and loaded at King George Dock, 1953
Courtesy of Innes
© www.innes.co.uk

fishery continued to thrive. All along the waterfront, commerce and commodity kept pace with supply and demand, and as cargoes arrived, they were unloaded, processed and dispatched by armies of workers from the port-city's shoreside communities.

There were similarities between the neighbourhoods and networks of Hull's commercial dockworkers and those of its fishing community; between the east and the west of the city. With concentrations of people with close social and occupational ties and limited mobility, both shared characteristics with other post-war working-class districts.[6] Both also shared the influence of the sea upon their lives and livelihoods. There are, however, divergences. At the commercial port, ships would arrive and leave, bringing the world to Hull's doorstep and conveying a myriad of British products to all corners of the globe (Figure 10.2). On the dockside, however, the workforce was sedentary and firmly rooted in long-established practices. The seasonal and fluctuating nature of seaborne trade meant that Hull dockers were casually employed, like those at other large British ports. A degree of labour reform had been implemented across the ports following the introduction of the statutory National Dock Labour Scheme in 1947. The scheme was designed to better regulate the supply of dock labour via the national registration of dockworkers. However, it simply built upon and served to formalise existing and long-established organisation within the industry.[7] Dockworkers continued to be hired individually or in gangs by a variety of employers, including stevedores, shipping companies and merchants, with the rate of pay determined by cargo type and method of handling.

The survival of casualism also preserved long-standing working practices on Hull's docks into the 1960s. At liberty to hire and discard dockers as needed, employers had little incentive to invest capital in the new mechanised equipment that had become increasingly available after 1945. As a result, cargo-handling practices remained varied, manual and labour-intensive. Cranes, grabs and hoists were provided by the port authority for bulk cargoes. However, general goods were handled by conventional break-bulk methods, which involved the carriage of man-sized boxes, barrels, sacks and packages from ship to shore. These were then transferred to sheds or to waiting inland rail, river or road transport. The shipment of goods followed the reverse pattern.[8] Docker Mike described the arduous process of timber discharge:

> It all had to be carried off, it had to be slung on to the ship then landed on to these stages and carried off … I used to look down and think they'd 'ave been doing this job 200 years ago. In fact, they wun't let you alter cos you was on piece work and I know one particular ship we could have used long derricks and 'whoa stop the job, – you can't do that, they've got to be lifted and carried' cos we'd have gone through the roof with our wages.[9]

Unchanging organisational and working practices meant that the character of Hull's dock labour force in the early 1960s differed little from a century earlier. Such continuation preserved a distinctive subculture on the waterfront after 1945. The survival of casual employment and strong unionisation was unusual and registration (passed strictly from father to son) encouraged exclusivity, making dock work a closed shop.[10] The long tradition of occupational inheritance was part of a clannish culture, probably derived from the Irish-Catholic origins of the workforce. It has been suggested that comparatively low immigration into Hull during the nineteenth and early twentieth centuries made ethno-religious distinctions on the Hull waterfront negligible.[11] However, oral testimony provides evidence to the contrary. Docker Paul explains:

> You'd go on the dock and there was like Hegarty, Geraghty and Phee – all Irish families all come from Irish people. Probably from centuries ago like eighteen hundred and odd like my family. A lot of the foremen had Irish names like Hegarty and Flannery – them old Irish names or O'Leary.[12]

A strong Irish presence suggests that the origins of Hull dockers compared closely with that of large ports such as Liverpool and London where migrant labour from Ireland stayed on to work the docks that they had dug out, with their children and grandchildren absorbing, embedding and continuing their culture and beliefs.

Narratives also reveal an occupational bond that extended beyond the dock wall, with many Hull docking families, like those in Manchester, continuing to reside in terraced streets close to the dock gates after 1945.[13] Fluctuating wages associated with casual employment and piece work produced a culture of interdependence within tight-knit dockside communities. The child of a dockworker recalled:

The men … used to have to be there before eight o'clock to get a job. The women used to stand at the top of the terrace and watch the men coming home and they'd say: Oh Albert hasn't got a job or Ted hasn't got a job … Then they'd turn to me mother and say: Ooh, Chuck must be working. She said: Oh, that's good, he'll get 12 and six tonight. Well all these women had no money for their dinner, so she lent them all half a crown and she took half a crown and went and got a rabbit and veggies. So she gets this rabbit all ready to put in the oven, and sure enough Chuck come walking down the street. He'd been dawdling. So she gets this rabbit and she says: you can't have it! I thought you were working! Oh, what am I going to do for my rent? She's loaned all her money out so the women in the terrace could get a dinner in![14]

Although some dockworkers and their families continued to live close to the docks, after 1945 most lived a distance from the waterfront. The slum clearance and creation of new housing estates to the north and east of the city during the interwar years and the destruction of much dockside housing by bombing had caused the dispersal of many dockworking families.[15] Nevertheless, a sense of occupational community appears to have endured among those who resided away from the docks, particularly at the Willows Sport and Social Club, established during the 1950s under the National Dock Labour Board. Shirley, whose father and husband were dockworkers, recalled how the Willows had been central to her social life from childhood:

I met a lot of dockworkers' families, that's where I met [my husband] George … In the archery club! … me dad … me and me brother would go as kids and go in the archery club … George had the rowing and the rugby … the Willows it is … was great for the sports because of the social life of the dockers.[16]

Like so many aspects of dock work at Hull, the culture of the wider docking community bore traits that were founded almost a century earlier, and memories of the early post-1945 period probably reflect those of previous generations who had lived or worked on Hull's eastern waterfront.

A similar constancy prevailed in the west of the city, where life for many was tuned to the comings and goings of Hull's substantial distant-water trawling fleet (Figure 10.3). Fishing in Hull was strongly place-centred. Studying the industry in the late 1950s, the sociologist Jeremy Tunstall observed that 'fishermen see themselves in a curious way as working in Hull'.[17] Although trawling predominantly off the coasts of Iceland, Norway and northern Russia, vessels and processing facilities were Hull owned and Hull based. Trawlers steamed from and returned to the city, with 92 per cent of fishermen living within four miles of the fish dock in 1955.[18] Indeed, some 57 per cent of fishermen and 72 per cent of fish landing crew, known as bobbers, lived within a one-mile radius of the dock, and therefore men traditionally sailed or worked predominantly with other men from within a narrow locale.[19]

Within Hull, fishing was synonymous with Hessle Road: a long, thoroughfare running parallel to the fish dock. Dock and district had become entwined from the earliest days of trawling and continued as such into the decades after the Second World War. Not everyone here engaged in fishing, yet the industry pervaded the neighbourhood. Arctic trawling was demanding and dangerous, defined by Tunstall as an 'extreme occupation'.[20] Until the 1970s, the fishery remained largely structured around the 21-day trip of the traditional side trawler, which from the late nineteenth century had shaped not only life at sea, but also that on shore. In the late 1960s side trawlers spent an average of 60–72 hours in port and home life for the fisherman was compressed into three days. It took on a hectic and celebratory nature as Michael describes:

> Well in three days you had to cheer the family up, and the little 'uns and spoil them for a bit cos they don't see their father for three weeks … you'd take your wife shopping up town and spoil her for a couple of hours and sit in shops fed up. And then the kids'd come home from school and you'd've bought them some presents or you'd take them up town … and the next day you relaxed a little bit and then the day after that you was away to sea again.[21]

As fishermen stepped ashore, portside workers swept aboard vessels to unload, process and dispatch fish and to prepare for the next voyage. The practices of

10.3 The 21-day trip: trawlermen working on the deck of a traditional side trawler, 1955.
Courtesy of Innes
© www.innes.co.uk

trawling, not least the limited shoretime and the unsocial working hours required to unload and dispatch a perishable product, encouraged fishermen and ancillary workers alike to live close to the fish dock. Working in the fishery became a neighbourhood tradition and the families of trawlermen and fish dockworkers clustered into a tight-knit community able to support a distinctive way of living.[22] As a result, a recognisable local culture emerged in the streets around Hessle Road, more defined and contained than that of the eastern Hull port (Figure 10.4). For here was 'Trawlertown',[23] a district of fishermen's pubs, clubs and pawnshops, ships' runners, flamboyant spending, loan systems known as backhanding and outfitters 'open to suit all tides'.[24] Former residents of Hessle Road in the 1960s recall it as exceptional; 'a wonderful, wonderful road', where the people were 'a breed of their own'.[25] It was a place of endless bustle. 'Hessle Road was full of people', reported Gill, and amid the everyday activity of a busy working-class district were the movements arising from the fishing fleet (Figure 10.5).[26] Pubs were 'constantly alive with people coming and going and ships coming in and coming out'.[27] Taxis darted about, for fishermen home for just three days did not waste time walking: 'it was a taxi,' said Ivy, 'even though it was only next street'.[28]

A visitor to the area would have recognised a connection with fish. There were filleting factories, rows of slender kipper-house chimneys and women wearing the 'wellies' and 'turban' headscarves of the fish processor. At the hub of the fishery

10.4 Terraced streets off Hessle Road, close to the fish dock, 20 June 1978.
Courtesy of Alec Gill

stood St Andrew's Fish Dock. Just as on the commercial docks, work here was labour-intensive and arrival on the dock met with frenzied activity. Jim describes an efficient disarray:

> It was dangerous walking … You'd have clogs, because there was water and fish slime and ice … you would have the bobbers landing the fish and at the same time they were bringing up the fish room boards … board scrubbers … there would be shore-riggers splicing wires, there'd be electricians, the Marconi man would be going round all the wireless and the electronics … The cod liver oil boat would be alongside, pumping out … organised chaos, everybody knew what they were doing.[29]

Along the western waterfront, St Andrew's Fish Dock, together with the Trawlertown of Hessle Road, forged a landscape of connected activity that was distinct, yet located within the wider city (Figure 10.6). It was the product of the Arctic trawl and hosted a community where everything was 'geared to the rhythm of fishing'.[30]

Disrupted

10.6 Fish being swung
from a trawler using the
traditional basket method.
Maritime Museum: Hull Museums

In the post-war era, even as Hull's waterfront communities returned to their time-served rhythms, fractures were appearing beneath the semblance of 'business as usual'. The years after 1945 were marked by serious problems in Hull and other commercial ports. Gross inefficiency was, in part, attributable to outdated cargo-handling practices and heightened industrial unrest. Strike action at Hull during the period was frequent and often unofficial due to the Transport and General Workers' Union's (TGWU) inability to control its membership.[31] In fact, the TGWU's power and influence was further undermined in 1954 by the arrival of the rival London-based National Amalgamated Stevedores and Dockers' Union, to which many dockers defected.[32] Although poor relations between labour and employers had been a prominent feature in Hull and other ports since the late nineteenth century, industrial unrest increased significantly following the introduction of the National Dock Labour Scheme. Despite the scheme's progressive nature and its adminis-tration by jointly controlled national and local boards composed of labour and employer representatives, it proved highly unpopular with both sides of the industry. It facilitated de-casualisation, which was unpopular among many dockers who cherished their freedom to pick and choose the best-paying work on the docks.[33] The extent to which some Hull dockers were prepared to defend the casual system was evidenced in early 1961 when, following the increase of 'regulars' to 40 per cent of the workforce, a series of unofficial one-day strikes against de-casualisation occurred in the port, a situation that forced employers to cap their permanent staff at 35 per cent of the total workforce.[34] Poor working conditions were also a long-standing source of discontent among the workforce. The casual system had preserved primitive and dangerous working practices, placing little obligation upon employers to provide

10.7 The Klondyke café on Hedon Road, a squalid and ramshackle establishment used by dockers. This sketch is from the *Hull Daily Mail*'s 'Dock Life' supplement.
Courtesy of *Hull Daily Mail*

facilities for employees. The Hull and Goole Dock Labour Board was responsible for the Hull docker's welfare. However, it had done little to improve amenities by the early 1960s (Figure 10.7). One docker recalled:

> There was these two little brick places with the toilets in and I don't know if they ever got cleaned … I mean it was frozen solid [in the winter]. The toilets was atrocious and the coffee shops like the Black Hole of Calcutta it was terrible – filthy, mucky places. They had a little fire in the middle and the auld dockers used to stand gerrin' warm round it.[35]

Conversely, many employers were aggrieved by the scheme's ineffective disciplinary mechanism. A 1952 inquiry found a serious lack of discipline among the dockers in Hull where harmful restrictive practices were particularly widespread.[36] Alongside worsening relations between the labour force and employers, the scheme also exacerbated deep-rooted divisions among the dockers themselves. Grievances within the labour force primarily related to the allocation of work under the casual system. Prior to 1939, the hiring process at Hull, known as the 'tinpot system', had been conducted at the gangway end of a vessel.[37] However, under the new scheme purpose-built hiring halls or 'controls' were erected at each of the docks. Here, dockers were forced to fight each other for the better-paying jobs. Those not hired at the morning 'call' were often transferred or 'shanghai'ed' to another dock or paid a retainer known locally as 'dint' money and expected to return for the lunchtime call. The fight for work could feel degrading and favourites known as 'blue-eyed boys' were widely resented. Dockers Dennis, Barry and Clive describe a typical scene at the controls:

Barry: Yeah it was the pen, what they called 'the pen'.

Clive: Like a cattle pen!

Barry: There was a wall and behind that wall was a stand and the foreman used to come up out the office and on to the stand so they were above you. Way down below in the hall were the dockers fighting for bloody jobs and you'd all have your docker's book in your hand and the foreman comes up. If it's a good job everyone puts their hand up with a book and he picks who 'e wants.

Dennis: I had a right barney with 'em one time cos it was a bad job and all the blue-eyes never used to put their books in.[38]

Like the grievances between labour and employers, internal divisions within the labour force itself were a deep-rooted feature of the casual system, a system that the National Dock Labour Scheme failed to eradicate.

By the early 1960s the need for extensive reform within the British port industry had become alarmingly clear. Conventional break-bulk operations were being increasingly outmoded by the rapid development of unitised and mechanised cargo-handling. While the movement of palletised cargoes by forklift trucks improved efficiency, the introduction of new types of ships, such as container and roll-on-roll-off vessels, enabled the carriage of metal boxes and ready-loaded commercial road vehicles (Figure 10.8).[39] This cargo-handling revolution triggered a major inquiry into British dock labour by a committee chaired by former High Court Judge Lord Devlin. The committee's report was published in 1965 and recognised that the successful operation of new equipment required a stable and reliable labour force. It

10.8 New roll-on/roll-off berths at King George Dock heralded the advent of the cargo handling revolution at Hull.
Courtesy of Innes
© www.innes.co.uk

recommended that dock labour be de-casualised and wage systems reformed.[40] Phase I was implemented on 18 September 1967 (D-Day) and, with all Hull dockworkers being permanently assigned to a single employer, the long-established casual system was ended.[41] After extensive local negotiations and a three-week national dock strike (the first industry-wide stoppage since 1926), Phase II was completed in July 1970, placing Hull dockers on a fixed wage.[42] Within five years the port's dock labour force had been transformed. One docker reflected:

> All this happened in my eight, nine years on the dock from 1964 to 1970 – *everything* happened! That was the period of 3,000 men … years unloading ships … cargo went to a ship and it was loaded and then it was unloaded it *stopped*. The whole world stopped in ten years … I [still] can't believe it.[43]

As this recollection indicates, organisational and working practices that had prevailed on the Hull waterfront for generations had been transformed by 1970 as the labour force was obliged to adapt swiftly to the demands of unitisation and the container age.

To the west of the city, Hull's fishery faced its own challenges. Although the industry had enjoyed a post-war boom, from the mid-1950s overfishing and falling consumer demand increasingly impaired the performance of the industry. From 1960, subsidised by the British government, trawler owners moved towards a revolutionary new technology. The freezer trawler initiated a break with the rhythms of the past. Freed from the bind of bringing perishable wet fish to port, freezer vessels worked further afield and stayed at sea for up to three months. The ships were bigger, safer and carried larger crews. Whereas fish were gutted on the open deck of a side trawler, men worked below in a freezer vessel, sheltered from Arctic winds. Ashore, freezer trawlers precipitated change in the life of the fishing district. Frozen fish needed cold stores, mechanical landing and new sales methods. On the home front, life could relax a little, for although freezer trawlermen spent longer at sea, they also stayed ashore for a week. Into the 1970s, the impact of the freezer ship was yet to disrupt the established rhythms of Hessle Road. A significant number of side trawlers remained and Hull's trawling fleet now assumed a dual form. As trawling reconfigured for the future, however, more significant upheavals were to come.

From the early 1950s, fishing grounds across the globe were becoming increasingly subject to the territorial ambitions of nation states. The Truman Proclamation, which was issued by the United States of America in 1945, pushed the idea of coastal limits on to the international stage. It advocated the extension of territorial rights over sea space, a notion readily embraced by Arctic nations, keen to develop their own fishing industries and alarmed at the expansion of efficient foreign fleets working off their coastline. In 1951 Denmark extended its coastal territory from three miles to four miles, a measure that was followed by Iceland in 1952. In 1958 Iceland moved its limit further to 12 miles. This shift was contested by Britain, leading to the first of three seaborne conflicts between Britain and Iceland known as the 'Cod Wars'. Protest, however, proved futile and Iceland proceeded to extend its Exclusive

Economic Zone to 50 miles in 1972 and 200 miles in 1975. In December 1976, as the third Anglo-Icelandic Cod War came to a close, British trawlers were forced to leave Icelandic waters for good. By the end of 1977, 200-mile exclusion zones had been established by Norway, Russia, Faroe and Canada. For Hull's distant-water trawling fleet, fishing in the North Atlantic ceased to be the uncontested source of income and employment that it had been since the late nineteenth century.

Despite the escalating conflict, there is little evidence that Hull's fishery was prepared for the impact of the final Cod War. Fishing has been described as a 'culture of the moment'.[44] Fishermen could be fatalistic and little inclined to engage in forward planning. While some chose to leave the industry in the uncertain years of the early 1970s, many held on. For those accustomed to the freedom of the high seas, there was a sense of disbelief that nations could claim large expanses of water as their own. John, a trawler deckhand, remembers: 'I don't think we ever dreamt of it declining like it did … with Iceland only being as small as it was and England being as big as it is and then our gunboats going down there, we thought we'd be ok, but … we just wasn't'.[45] Even those less optimistic had at least harboured the hope of a fishing agreement with Iceland and the prospect of a managed process of change. The speed with which fishing opportunities diminished, therefore, came as a blow.

In parallel with the crisis surrounding fishing limits, the British distant-water trawl industry was facing other difficulties. Rising oil prices in the 1970s were straining the economics of fishing off distant shores. A greater challenge, however, lay closer to home. In 1973 Britain had joined the European Common Market, compelling the UK to adhere to a hastily compiled European Common Fisheries Policy. In the ensuing decade, wrangles over revisions to this policy hampered the British distant-water industry as it struggled to adapt to an uncertain future. With seeming duplicity, as Britain had contested the Icelandic 200-mile fishing limit, under its new partnership with Europe it had simultaneously prepared to extend its own 200-mile exclusion zone. The zone declared by Britain in January 1977, however, was to be a 'common pond' shared by the member states of a European community. As Iceland's coast was closed to British distant-water trawlers, Britain's own fish-rich waters were open to the fishing fleets of other nations.

For the Hull trawl fishery, the result of this perfect storm was the rapid decline of its catching sector and the contraction of its fish merchant and processing industry. In a new context, vessel owners and skippers had to contend with the state control and management of fishing grounds, which increasingly took place under a system of allocated fishing quotas. For skipper Peter, quotas ended the freedom of command. Peter loved the thrill of the hunt, using his own judgement to decide where to fish. Quotas took away that liberty and with it the buzz of the chase. Now, he laments, it is the man behind the desk who is the skipper.[46]

Faced with quotas, trawling firms steeped in a cod-based tradition turned towards more flexible fishing. Trawler owner Tom Boyd explained: 'we did everything we could to keep the ships operating … they might go to the North-East Arctic one trip and then be going off herring fishing and going off mackerel fishing at the next trip'.[47] But for trawling firms and trawlermen alike, fishing within limits made it hard to earn a living. Dave eventually found it impossible to make ends meet:

> you didn't catch enough fish to make it worth going … You come and settle up and you get about five pound. That's not good. You felt your life'd ended basically. You think, where do you go from here? Do you carry on going to sea? Or do we just go back ashore, y'know, call it a day?[48]

The struggle to fill large ships with fish from diminishing seas eventually took its toll upon the Hull trawling fleet. In popular memory the sight of trawlers being scrapped at Drapers Yard, at the confluence of the Rivers Hull and Humber, has become an enduring symbol of decline (Figure 10.9). Scrapping ships had been a regular part of fish dock life, as one new technology replaced another. But from the mid-1970s, departures from the fleet were no longer offset by new arrivals. Michael P. witnessed trawlers up for scrap each time he returned from a trip with Hull's shrinking fleet. The sight, said Michael, was 'really demoralising', and others echoed his sentiment.[49] Worse was to come. The adverse economics of trawling were soon forcing the sale and conversion of Hull's advanced and modern stern-freezer fleet. To deckhand Thomas, this was a sure indication of the end: 'We started selling ships to different places and that's when you knew, we won't gonna come back. It was always on a decline … the slide was there and there was no stopping the slide.'[50]

As ships left the dockside, so too did the men who sailed them. Trawlermen in Hull were engaged on a casual basis. Fewer ships meant less chance to sign back

10.9 Hull trawler *Joseph Conrad* being dismantled at Draper's Yard, 31 August 1980.
Courtesy of Alec Gill

on for a trip, forcing hundreds of trawlermen to search for employment elsewhere. The spectre of older redundant fishermen beached on the shores of Hessle Road is embedded in local memory. Yet it was not only trawlermen who were affected by decline. Across the fish dock, from landing gangs to trawler engineers, there was no option but to look for work elsewhere. However, the demands of trawling and the rigours of the fish dock had bred a workforce that was willing and able to work hard and there began a tenacious pursuit of new opportunities. These were not always successful. Margaret tells a story of her brother Harold's futile dash to Fleetwood in the hope of getting a ship. He and two friends followed a tip picked up in a Hessle Road pub. Margaret narrates:

> And off he trotted, they went, the three of 'em. And they said no, we don't want no Yorkies [Yorkshire men] here. So they jumped in a taxi – no money to pay the taxi driver – and when they got to Harold's house, Harold emptied the gas meter in ten pence pieces and paid the taxi driver in a sock.[51]

In other instances, however, the quest to keep working paid off. Long-term unemployment continued to plague the former fishing community. However, for some, the dogged hunt for work brought results, and in the wake of the 1960s and 1970s, as familiar chapters were closing, new episodes were poised to begin.

Hull's Personality: Richard Bean

Born on 11 June 1956, Richard Bean lived first at 1 Corona Drive in the east of the city, before moving to Leads Road. He attended the local Cavendish Primary School, and his academic aptitude was rewarded when he gained entry to Hull Grammar School in his teenage years. The son of a policeman, Bean's natural rebelliousness showed in his indulgence in 'drug and hippy literature' – a covert pastime lest he should face his father's wrath.[1]

On leaving school, Bean worked at Spillers, a mass-production bakery in Wheeler Street, a job that gave him the inspiration for his first full-length professional play, *Toast* (1999), which premiered at London's Royal Court theatre. Having spent a year among the flour and the tins, he went on to study psychology at Loughborough University. Jobs in occupational psychology and communications followed, but in 1989 he began a five-year stint in stand-up comedy that set the 33-year-old on the path to artistic success. However, while the future playwright may have been taken out of the city by his adult life, the city has never been erased from the writer or his work.

Bean's plays do not seek an imaginative redrawing of Hull. Instead they use the post-industrial city as the canvas on which to bring its communities to life. Set predominantly between 1950 and 1970 among the grime of a declining industrial landscape and the grit of its social spaces, Bean's plays deal with the multiplicity of issues that Hull faced during the second half of the twentieth century: social deprivation, diminishing educational standards and increasing crime. They portray the struggles of Hull's working classes at a time when traditional industry was disappearing.

Throughout the generations, Hullensians have divided the city between east and west, using the banks of the River Hull as their guide, and Bean is no different. His plays follow the transport arteries in and out of the city and around Holderness and Hessle Roads; yet despite their opposing geography, both sides remain united in their sense of community and culture, underlined by the robust, relentless River Humber, and their pavements and public houses drip with stories of the sea, the factory and their famous personalities.

Richard Bean acknowledging the acclaim of the audience after accepting an honorary doctorate from the University of Hull at City Hall in July 2014.
Courtesy of the University of Hull

In *Toast* (Royal Court, 1999), which opened to critical acclaim, Bean's talent for strong characterisation and humour shines as a group of men find themselves on the bakery night shift with an increased order. The men struggle with their identities, rebuffing the notion that their work defines them. The most insecure is Dezzie, the 'hero of the cod wars', whose swapping of the deck for the factory floor leaves him wondering whether he is the same man he once was, reflecting the anxiety that thousands of Hull trawlermen must have felt as their former occupation and way of life became a memory. The factory faces imminent closure, so when the ancient oven jams and lives are literally at stake, the antipathies between them are thrown aside in an effort to save the plant and themselves; however, the chronic underinvestment in the site makes their unemployment inevitable.

Under the Whaleback (Royal Court, 2003), originally *Distant Water*, is a dark comedy that takes its audience out into deep, Arctic waters and plumbs the depths of the masculine world of Hull's fishing industry. Each of the play's three acts is a play in its own right, articulating the lives of the deckies on three ships over thirty-seven years: the *Kingston Jet* in 1965, the doomed *James Joyce* in 1972 and the museum ship *Arctic Kestrel* in 2002. Echoes of the city's triple trawler disaster of 1968 ring through the second act as the *James Joyce* lists in a violent storm. The real-life *Arctic Corsair*, the maritime monument to Hull's perished trade and its perished men, is rebranded the *Arctic Kestrel* for Act III, and is lovingly curated by the now 54-year-old Darrel, who faces his past and his maritime heritage at the hands of a troubled Pat, whose father perished on the

Joyce. In *Under the Whaleback*, the plot twists and the myths of the sea smash into the hard reality of the oceanic workplace and a future where its significance becomes a distant memory.

Honeymoon Suite (Royal Court, 2004) was Bean's third Hull play, and while more domestic in tone, it has much to say on the geographical and industrial landscape of the city. Set in 1955, it features the young, newly married Eddie and Irene, who are head-over-heels in love, with a future full of promise. Starting out on Strickland Avenue (actually Strickland Street), Hessle Road, the play's weaving narrative follows the couple's marriage: Irene's aspirations clash with Eddie's ideals, corruption and ignorance meet feminism and a lust for education, and miscarriage and manslaughter put a strain on their once-hopeful union. Against a historical backdrop of slowly increasing opportunities for women, Irene's identity evolves beyond her humble beginnings and the prevailing marital expectations of the 1950s, and the couple's migration through the city to the suburbs reflects this change.

In *Up on Roof* (2004), a commission for Hull Truck, Bean revisited the four-day Hull prison riot of 1976. Through a diverse group of criminal characters, the play tackles issues of social justice, the treatment of prisoners and mental health with humour and tenderness. The local references are detailed, and as they discuss their lives beyond the prison walls in vivid geographical terms, the men comfort themselves and make themselves feel part of Hull's community.

Hull's struggle with economic recession is the framework for *Pub Quiz Is Life* (Hull Truck, 2009), and when Melissa, a regeneration consultant from Hull Advance, brings her misguided suppositions into an east Hull pub, she is soon met with the scepticism of Lee, an unemployed soldier who has completed two tours of Afghanistan. The play questions whether a government quango can ever know what is best for the city and its communities. Murder, drug-dealing, incapacitation and euthanasia, the trouble within the National Health Service and the war in Afghanistan are all themes of a play that melds serious issues, black comedy and melodrama, and questions where Hull is headed in the modern world of regeneration and what will become of the industrial legacy in the city's DNA.

With numerous awards to his name, Richard Bean has become one of the country's premier playwrights. But while he has written many more plays than those about Hull, the city, its history and its communities can be credited with influencing and inspiring his work. Bean writes of his post-industrial home town and its people with an unsentimental generosity, free from infatuation and mawkishness, but with benevolence and a realism that is to the credit of both Hull and the playwright.

Victoria Dawson

Notes
1   'Shelf Life', *The Spectator*, http://blogs.spectator.
     co.uk/2012/07/shelf-life-richard-bean/ (accessed 13
     February 2016).

Alongside the shock of disruption, there emerged novel patterns of working and alternative careers that heralded new lives and broke from the routines and rhythms of the past. Following the Devlin reforms, life and work on the commercial docks was drastically altered. Casual employment and manual cargo-handling had been cornerstones of dock work for generations. Devlin's reorganisation transformed the dockers' occupation. Answerable to a single employer, dockers now spent working days operating machinery. Docker Mike's memories reveal how mechanisation altered the routine of dock work:

> [After Devlin] you went as a tug driver but you got a job for a couple of days, they used to try and vary your jobs – put you on a different ship, you used to do one or two days on roping and you used to drive a little forklift and do all the fork lifting jobs ... And then we had a couple of days in the shed which was like the crane shed and these gantries used to run up and down the shed and the lorries would come in and we'd transfer the container off the lorry on to our own ... tug and trailers.[52]

Although less physical and varied than traditional methods, new practices ensured that dock work was safer and more efficient. Aside from de-casualisation and wage reform, Devlin had also recommended a rigorous branch overhaul of the TGWU, which greatly increased union control within the port.[53] New amenities further improved conditions on the docks. Most notable was the erection of new purpose-built restaurants for dockworkers at each of the docks which included showers and lockers.[54]

Throughout the 1970s and 1980s, traditional working patterns and practices were eroded, giving way to more orthodox contractual terms akin to other modern mechanised industries. Reorganisation and new working patterns at Hull, however, did not bring industrial peace. Increasing mechanisation led to many redundancies and, despite the success in paving the way for containerisation, Devlin's reforms heralded a new era of widespread unrest across the industry. Devlin's Phase II had inflated labour costs, significantly raising operational expenses. The committee also failed to remove or reform the National Dock Labour Scheme. Ongoing registration caused over-manning. Employers could not successfully reduce the size of their workforces in line with increasing mechanisation, and the preservation of an ineffective disciplinary system allowed restrictive practices to continue.[55] Combined, these factors caused shipping customers to divert business from Hull and other scheme ports to emerging 'non-scheme' sites such as Felixstowe, where cheaper unregistered labour was employed to operate new cargo-handling machinery. The loss of trade greatly exacerbated unemployment. On D-Day, September 1967, the number of registered dockworkers at the port stood at 4,057. By 1971 this had fallen to 2,784.[56] Hull dockers engaged in a militant campaign to protect their work, taking a leading role during the national dock strikes of the 1970s and 1980s.[57] However, their protective action served to drive more traffic from the port. Not until August 1989, following the abolition of the National Dock Labour Scheme by Margaret Thatcher, was industrial peace secured.[58] The consequence, however, was further unemployment as hundreds of dockers accepted redundancy and left the industry.

Over on the fish dock, those battling for Hull's beleaguered distant-water industry were also seeking urgent solutions. Spurred by the closure of open seas, trawling firms steeped in a North Atlantic tradition of fishing mainly for cod for a UK market embarked upon a hunt for new opportunities. They pursued possibilities with energy and on each venture they took their Hull crews. Even before the end of the final Cod War, Hull firms were engaging with the booming mackerel fishery off the coast of Cornwall. As opportunities in the Arctic declined, the south-west of England threw a lifeline. Trawlermen accustomed to working icy seas adapted to warmer climes and to handling oily pelagic species (Figure 10.10). In this new fishery, for the first

10.10 A good catch: around 30 tons of mackerel is hauled on to the deck of the stern trawler *Cordella*, 25 November 1980.
Courtesy of Alec Gill

time, fish caught by Hull ships was intended primarily for overseas markets. From 1977, fishing fleets from outside the European Community had been excluded from the British coastline. In response, fish caught by British trawlers was transferred at sea to colossal factory ships, originating mainly from the Eastern Bloc. Known as klondyking, this new way of fishing became a mainstay of the emerging mackerel economy. Bob, a trawler skipper, recalled:

> Russians and Poles was anchored in a bay ... the company used to say, go to so-and-so ship ... then you went alongside him and he just took all the fish off you and then you left that one, went and caught some more fish ... and that's how we carried on.[59]

Mackerel was also carried ashore for transshipment, mainly to Africa. Hull trawling firms invested in facilities at Milford Haven and, in a break with tradition, for the duration of the mackerel season Hull trawlers no longer returned to their home port. Hull crews travelled to join ships by coach or taxi, occasionally accompanied by Hull maintenance engineers, familiar with the vessels. The result was a growing Hull colony in the Welsh port. It was, says radio engineer Ben, 'like little Hull down there sometimes'.[60]

Alongside mackerel, the British distant-water sector experimented with fishing for new species found in very deep water off the UK continental shelf. However, these new species, described by one industry representative as 'bog-eyed monsters from the deep',[61] were difficult to market to the notoriously conservative British consumer. An emerging blue whiting fishery enjoyed a measure of success, but did not progress to become a viable commercial operation. Despite all efforts, experimental fishing was unable to assist the struggling distant-water ports and in the words of fish merchant Chris, the pursuit of species such as monkfish, scabbard and orange roughy proved to be a 'red herring'.[62]

Away from home waters, Hull trawling firms engaged in partnerships or 'joint ventures' with newly emerging fishing nations, which were keen to take advantage of their own 200-mile limits, but which lacked the skills or markets to develop. Joint projects in North Africa and Australia often proved problematic. One Hull company, the Boyd Line, enjoyed better fortune in the south-western Pacific, managing the giant freezer trawlers *Arctic Buccaneer* and *Arctic Galliard*, vessels once owned by the firm but sold to New Zealand owners in the crisis years after the Cod Wars. Ultimately, these new projects were unable to sustain the industry. By the early 1980s, overfishing and quotas had diminished Hull's involvement with the UK mackerel fishery; experimental species had failed to become commercially viable and overseas ventures had proved unpredictable. Amid the struggles, however, there were two notable successes that significantly extended the life of Hull's disappearing trawler fleet.

From the mid-1960s the exploration, discovery and extraction of gas and oil in the North Sea stimulated British maritime activity. The offshore industry developed rapidly throughout the 1970s, bringing an urgent need for ships for platform supply, safety standby work, anchor handling and surveying. Until specialist vessels could be built for these roles, the rugged distant-water trawlers, build to withstand treacherous Arctic seas, fitted the bill. Most Hull trawling firms redirected redundant ships to the new North Sea industry. The Hull-based Marr Group was particularly energetic, progressing into survey and exploration as a new facet to its business. Victor, a former trawler skipper working on supply ships, noted how crews in the offshore sector were often 'refugees from the fishing industry'. For oil companies, trawlermen were a welcome addition, able to endure the challenging environment of the North Sea. In a climate of disruption, the rise of a British offshore industry proved to be a gift, as former skipper Ken reflected: 'Oh, you could sit and think that if [the oil] industry wasn't there, it would've been a complete disaster. We would've had something like four, five thousand men around with nothing to do … so it really was an answer to everybody's problems.'[63]

Another perhaps unexpected new arena for Hull companies lay 8,000 miles away in the South Atlantic. In 1976 an economic survey of the Falkland Islands proposed developing a fishery as a means to boost the islands' economy. However, troubles in the wider British economy, followed by the 1982 Falklands War, served to delay progress. In Hull, by 1985, the continued struggles of the distant-water industry had finally brought long-established fishing firms to an end. Yet two tenacious companies, J. Marr and Son and Boyd Line, remained in operation and when Britain announced a 150-mile limit around the Falklands in 1987, both companies and their crews prepared for business in ever-distant waters. Marr and Boyd Line operated fishing ships, entered into joint ventures, explored new catching opportunities and managed licences. Marr also took a policing role, diverting ships once engaged in the northern trawl to fisheries protection around these southern islands. The protection role continued into the 1990s, even after a change in island policy had brought significant fishing opportunities for Hull firms to a close. For a while, however, the Falkland Islands had provided an opening among closed waters and the skills and knowledge of Hull trawling companies and crews had been instrumental to the development of a new British fishery.

As ships and men dispersed, back on Hull's fish dock foreign-caught fish were arriving at the quay. In 1975 the fish dock had relocated from St Andrew's to the adjacent Albert and William Wright Docks, which had closed to commercial traffic. But the £1 million facilities, intended for the unloading of fish from Hull trawlers, were increasingly engaged in landing and processing a critical supply obtained from overseas. If Hull trawlers could no longer catch sufficient fish, then new suppliers must be attracted to the port. Fish for UK markets was offloaded from foreign trawlers or was imported in containers. The change marked a new and growing independence between Hull's fishing fleet and its fish trades. As a result, although the merchant and processing sector contracted, by forging new relationships it was able to continue successfully. The fish trades survived by breaking old ties and because, in the words of fish merchant Chris, 'there's always somebody, somewhere wanting to send fish'.[64]

By the end of the 1980s the maelstrom of change that had blown into many working lives across Hull's extensive waterfront had given way to a period of relative calm. However, transformations to seafaring and dockside practices had produced ripples that were felt in the networks and rhythms of the portside districts and communities. In the fishery, the struggle for survival had seen Hull's once 'local' industry turn global. As trawlers no longer departed and returned to the city and as foreign-caught fish arrived on its quays, the long-standing bond between industry, workforce and port district was severed. For those still serving at sea, arrival in port no longer meant arriving home. When Gill's husband took a job in the Gulf, travelling to his ship by aeroplane made the distance seem unbearable. She remembers her initial reaction:

> I went [said], oh going all them miles. And he went – well, it's no further than going to, like, Canada, off Newfoundland and all that. But it was, cos I was taking him to a plane. It won't like going away [when] I used to take him to the ship…[65]

Those going to work in other sectors could find that they missed the independence of the trawler skipper, the daily challenge of fishing or the assurance of the familiar. When Ken took a job ashore, he says, 'I missed it. I think it took about four years before I thought to meself, well, it's out your system now…'[66] Working in a local factory, Christine's husband Paul, a deckhand, got 'itchy feet' and secured one of a dwindling number of fishing jobs with Marr. 'He said he'd never go back to sea,' recalled Christine, 'but I knew that he would. I knew he would. It was always there.'[67]

Contemporary Music and Hull

A long-standing British port-city, a hugely successful post-war musical export, a breakthrough moment for British music in America – it's a well-known story, but here it concerns Hull's David Whitfield, the most successful British singer in 1950s America, and the first to earn a gold disc for one million record sales. Whitfield never moved away from East Yorkshire, but later musicians did leave to further their careers. Mick Ronson and Trevor Bolder, with Driffield's Mick Woodmansey, relocated to London in the late 1960s, where they later became David Bowie's band, The Spiders from Mars. Likewise, Roland Gift moved away in the 1980s to become lead singer with the highly successful Birmingham-based trio, Fine Young Cannibals. These Hull musicians influenced music around the world.

Other performers and writers from Hull had significant impacts on a range of musical forms. Britain's first family of folk, the Watersons – siblings Norma, Mike, Lal and their cousin, John Harrison – lived in the Avenues and, like Whitfield,

CULTURE
HISTORY
PLACE

Advertising poster for *London 0 Hull 4*, the Housemartins' debut album, which was released in October 1986 and included the hit singles 'Happy Hour' and 'Think for a Minute'. The album title is understood to mean that the Housemartins considered that Hull had four great bands whereas London had none.
Keith Milburn

remained in the region throughout their long and distinguished career. The group's formative years coincided with a fellow Avenues resident, the poet and Hull University librarian Philip Larkin, becoming one of Britain's most astute jazz critics. Larkin covered jazz for *The Daily Telegraph* from 1961 to 1968 and was a habitué of the jazz clubs of Hull and Beverley.

There is also a strong tradition of musicians moving to Hull. Singer and songwriter Paul Heaton moved from Sheffield in 1983 and formed The Housemartins with Hull's Stan Cullimore. The group readily promoted their Hull allegiance with the title of their debut album, *London 0 Hull 4*. Maintaining the barbed humour, Heaton named his next band The Beautiful South. Like The Housemartins, the band was made up of Hull-based musicians and enjoyed significant commercial and critical success from its inception in 1988 until 2007, when the members disbanded due to 'musical similarities'. Another widely acclaimed group formed by newcomers to Hull was Everything But The Girl. This 1980s duo, named after the slogan of a furniture shop in Beverley Road, consisted of Tracey Thorn and Ben Watt, both former students at Hull University, as were, before them, Throbbing Gristle front man Genesis P-Orridge and, after them, Foals guitarist Jimmy Smith.

Hull's student population, coupled with other music fans in and around the city, has sustained a healthy music scene. This supports well-regarded independent record stores, accessible recording studios, and a boisterous live music scene, exemplified by the New Adelphi Club – a legendary venue for new bands since 1984. Hull also boasts an increasingly influential club scene. This makes use of previously vacant buildings, especially around the Fruit Market (home to the world's only Museum of Club Culture) and, more recently, beside the River Hull where Gate Nº5, for example, attracts DJs and clubbers from across the north.

Hull is also becoming increasingly well known for its festivals, ranging from dedicated folk and jazz festivals to the rock- and dance-orientated Humber Street Sesh, and the Freedom Festival, with its eclectic range of music. Hull's emerging reputation as a place which musicians emerge from, but also somewhere they move to, is likely to be reinforced by the 2017 City of Culture celebrations.

Kevin Milburn

Adjusting to change

There are some commonalities that can be detected in memories of change across Hull's waterfront. East and west, the labour-intensive port industries had given birth to dockside environments that teemed with people and life. In the final decades of the twentieth century, increased mechanisation and restructuring at the commercial docks, and decline, contraction and adaptation in the fishery, saw fewer people engaged in the dockland workforce. An accompanying loss of social connectivity, shared networks, familiar faces, camaraderie and collective encounters is common to narratives both east and west. At the commercial docks, where large numbers of dockers had once worked in gangs to load and discharge a variety of goods, the shrinking workforce was increasingly tied to terminals and berths where machinery rather than muscle was used to handle cargoes. Those who worked on the dockside narrate a growing sense of disenchantment as men were increasingly replaced by machines:

> Me elder brother, 'e was at King George Dock on the containers – a really easy job. You just made sure everything was going smooth. You din't do any physical work cos he was used to real hard physical work and he wasn't keen on it and I said – don't you think it's time Bill? The docks have gone – it's changed. Don't you think it's time you packed it in? And he did. And then all me mates they give it up ... [they missed] the physical side of life.[68]

Similar sentiments were shared by those trawlermen who, transferring to work on oil rig safety vessels, found the work tedious compared with the rigours of fishing.

Reorganisation also affected the social atmosphere of the docks. Although Devlin was responsible for creating unemployment, his reforms brought financial stability and much-improved working conditions, making dockworkers the elite of the working class. New-found affluence, however, came at the expense of the earlier bonds between dockworkers, as one docker recalled:

> You din't have so many men. Say you had six men in a gang, you had 'undred men on a ship [before modernisation] you was all talking to each other – coffee shops, muggers, pubs! Whereas it went down to maybe two or three men ... it just seemed to stop ... You still got a little bit of comradeship in [the new restaurants] ... but the men were gerrin' less and less. Whereas before there was a queue a mile long and you was all packed tight like sardines – all of a sudden there was maybe twenty or thirty people in there ... [it was] completely different.[69]

As the sense of community disappeared on the docks, communal ties beyond the dock wall were also weakened, as regular and vastly improved pay encouraged more dockers to relocate away from the waterfront to more affluent suburban and rural areas.

10.11 Children playing amid the debris of housing clearance, Hessle Road.
Courtesy of *Hull Daily Mail*

During the 1970s and 1980s the physical landscape of the waterside was also transformed. New cargo-handling practices, developments in sea and land transport and the loss of trade to other UK ports contributed to a relocation of activity to the larger, deeper docks further east and the closure of older upstream facilities. Deemed obsolete, the Town Docks and Victoria Dock had already closed to traffic by 1970, while a second wave of contraction during the 1970s and 1980s saw the closure of the Albert, William Wright and Alexandra Docks.[70] Having long formed the nucleus of the port's dock system, the Town and Victoria Docks were left to dereliction and decay before being sold to the local authority. Humber Dock and Railway Dock were remodelled into a marina complex in 1983, Prince's Dock was converted to leisure and retail use during 1991, while Victoria Dock was redeveloped as an 'urban village' from the late 1980s.[71] In the fishery too, the move to the refurbished Albert and William Wright Dock had disrupted the familiar. Although the new facilities delivered much-improved working conditions, some, like deckhand Thomas, lamented the lost character of the bustling old dock:

> there was no atmosphere there. Not like there was ... y' see, everything happened on [St Andrew's] Fish Dock. Everything. Y' know, your trawlers were landed on Fish Dock, you signed on on Fish Dock, you signed off. Everything happened on Fish Dock. So to move it to another dock ... it was all wrong.[72]

For a while, certain functions continued on the old St Andrew's estate, splitting up the collective activity and encounters of the past. But as these gradually ended, decay set in, windows were smashed and wind and tide did its work. For many, the transformation was difficult to witness. Lily, a fish dock secretary, described with emotion her return to the dock after 1981, saying, 'oh, it just looked derelict. It was awful ... it was just so sad to see it ... when I was always used to [there] being so many people about and so many things happening.'[73]

On Hessle Road too, the district that had grown around the rhythms of trawling felt the pace of its decline. From the late 1950s, the area had experienced housing clearances that continued into the 1980s (Figure 10.11). While the new homes provided better living conditions, just as in the eastern port, redevelopment disrupted the close-knit ties of the fish dock community. On top of this, in the 1970s came the contraction of trawling itself. The combined impact took its toll. Many recall the disappearance of familiar faces, as inhabitants moved out to new estates and as fewer came to work in the fishery. Fewer people and less money in pockets was felt in local pubs and shops. 'The shutters were going up,' said Jim, 'shops that you'd used for years ... all of a sudden, one by one, they'd be closing.'[74] It was not only the shops. Michael reported the disappearance of fish houses, fish box suppliers, fish lorries and the fishermen's taxis. The distinctive hustle of Trawlertown came to an end. It was, he said:

> like half of Hull had gone to sleep and just left. Just like, I suppose like California in the gold strike, when it'd gone and you just had towns with all the doors swinging empty … and that's like Hessle Road was. All the factories closed down, cos they didn't need fitters for the trawlers any more. That was it. It was horrible.[75]

Out of the ruins of decline and contraction, however, adjustment to new circumstances brought compensations. Following the abolition of the National Dock Labour Scheme, those dockers returning to work were liberated from the strict union controls and ongoing industrial conflict that had regulated life and work on the docks for decades. Furthermore, once-pervasive restrictive practices that had been designed to protect jobs, but which had also disrupted the natural rhythm of the workforce routine, were eradicated. Andrew recalled a new sense of freedom following the removal of the scheme:

> There was no shop stewards and the men were so happy – it was like a great weight taken off their shoulders. There's nothing worse than driving a forklift truck slowly all day, doing it very carefully, working to rule – it's a nightmare. Men want to get on with the job and those guys took pride in their work but [under the scheme] they were being held down by shop stewards![76]

The merits of labour deregulation and more flexible employment soon became apparent. The rapid recovery and growth of trade after the scheme's abolition was such that Alexandra Dock was re-equipped and re-opened to traffic in 1991.[77] Reversing the pattern of decline, the opening of the refurbished dock heralded a new chapter in the port's history.

In the fishery too, the hard work ethic and the old networks of the fish dock helped many to forge alternative lives. For trawlermen in particular, work ashore or in other maritime careers brought freedom from the pressures of filling large ships with fish. Released from the relentless cycle of the 21-day trip, Michael took up hobbies that he could not manage with just three days at home. John learned to drive. Those who had not seen their own children grow up now enjoyed more time with grandchildren. For some, exciting new careers took them all over the world. Michael illustrates a process of transition:

> I was skipper for over twelve years, so you get used to it – the good and the bad – and you feel happy in yourself at what you're doing. So I was really disappointed when we got thrown out of Iceland … But after a while, it was like a novelty, meeting all these people on the ships who'd been to university, cos I'd never met people like that … so that was interesting. And then when I went to Ghana and saw sunshine and palm trees, I wished I'd been there 50 years before…[78]

At the close of the century, decades of turbulence along Hull's working waterfront were giving way to new routines. During the late 1980s, the commercial docks entered a new phase characterised by industrial peace, the recovery and growth of trade, and diversification of interest. At the same time, people were adapting to the collapse of trawling. The industry had been massively reduced, but there were survivors, in the fish trades and in a much-diminished catching sector, that ensured some continuity. In the years of transition much had been lost, but some things had been gained, and as the waterfront entered a new millennium, there was a real prospect of a more stable future.

A place for the past

The story of change along Hull's waterfront does not end in the past. The focus of this chapter has been on memory and this is something that exists in the present. How the waterfront has been remembered and represented in the modern city is part of its history. Here again, there have been stormy waters. Initially, in the wake of crisis and adjustment, the heritage of Hull's dockland communities was often overlooked, as civic bodies and image-makers, keen to reinvigorate the city, chose to focus upon other elements of Hull's past.[79] In response, grassroots action sought to anchor memory against a torrent of change. Here again there are differences between the commercial docks and the fishery; between east and west. On the commercial docks, remembering could be a complex and at times contentious process. A legacy of strikes and disputes could make the past a difficult terrain to revisit. During times of conflict, the media had often portrayed the dockers as overpaid industrial bully-boys whose selfish actions were responsible for the country's economic ills.[80] As the world of the dockworker was hidden behind the dock wall and largely unknown to outsiders, there was little to alter this negative image. Within the haven of Hull's dockside, however, the docking community forged its own modest private heritage. The Marfleet collection is an assemblage of dockers' tools, photographs and other paraphernalia, which throughout the 1980s and 1990s was displayed on the walls of a barber's shop close to Alexandra Dock (Figure 10.12). Walter Oglesby, barber and curator of the collection, had been disappointed by the lack of reference to dockers at the Town Docks Museum when it first opened in 1976. In response, Walter began gathering and displaying items donated by the many dockers who frequented his shop.[81] Within a short space of time, he had accumulated a vast collection of dockland memorabilia that transformed his shop into a shrine to docking heritage.

As books, plays, community murals and other grassroots projects forged small pockets of remembrance along the waterfront, west Hull witnessed an outpouring of memory that exploded into open protest. From 1988 moves to demolish the redundant and derelict St Andrew's Fish Dock spurred a wave of action aimed at preserving the emotive spaces of the very hub of Trawlertown. Here the surviving networks of the fishing community were mobilised into a sustained campaign to defend and highlight their own heritage. The efforts of local heritage group

STAND saw the basin and buildings at the entrance to the fish dock protected as a conservation area. The designation marked the beginning of a long struggle to find a meaningful new use for the old dock and to secure a permanent memorial to thousands of Hull trawlermen lost at sea. A memorial was finally achieved in February 2017 but the struggle for the dock still continues. A happier outcome was achieved for the *Arctic Corsair*, the last of Hull's sidewinding trawler fleet. Following a partnership between STAND and Hull Museums, the *Arctic Corsair* secured its final berth as a museum ship, moored within the shelter of the Museums Quarter (Figure 10.13). In a similar coming together of civic and community remembering, the tools of the Hull dockers, so carefully collected by Walter Oglesby, also finally found a home in Hull's Maritime Museum. Dockers' tools, the *Arctic Corsair*, books, murals and plays, the concern for the fish dock and the quest for a memorial have all served to keep the past alive and relevant in the present. Collectively, these developments demonstrate the power of community memory in the face of a wider forgetfulness, as well as the continued pull of old rhythms that once shaped life on the waterfront.

10.12 The Marfleet Collection of docking memorabilia housed in Walter Oglesby's barber shop.
Courtesy of Hull Museums

10.13 Home from the sea: the *Arctic Corsair* berthed on the River Hull adjacent to Hull's Museums Quarter.
Courtesy of Hull Museums

Looking forward

Established as a medieval wool port, in its subsequent history Hull has looked seaward. Remote and isolated by land, Hull makes sense from the sea. From the Continent and the Humber, the city is a gateway, while its landward aspect is more of a back door. Yet in the late twentieth century, the city's maritime anchor drifted as modernisation, national strategy and international policy and practice brought turbulence to its quays. As its portside communities struggled with contraction, decline and adjustment, in terms of civic identity and cultural heritage it can be argued that the city turned its back on the water. By the early 1990s the storm was beginning to pass. Hull's commercial port – privatised, mechanised and de-casualised – looked forward to a new era of stability and growth. In the much-depleted fishery, those who had weathered the years of crisis faced, for the time being anyway, a period of modest recovery. The port historian Gordon Jackson has shown how the fortunes of ports and their cities can rise and fall, buffeted by the vagaries of supply and demand.[82] In Hull, wool's commercial primacy was supplanted by cloth, which gave way sequentially to lead, timber, manufactures, coal and so on; likewise whaling was superseded by fishing. This ability to adapt to the ebb and flow of trade and resources is testament to the port's striking resilience over the long term. Today there are new portside opportunities on the horizon. In the early twenty-first century and with the Green Port development in the offing, it is perhaps time for the city to turn back to the water with confidence and to embrace its maritime past as an inspiring exemplar of what might be achieved in the future.

Notes

1. Alan Jamieson, 'An Inevitable Decline? Britain's Shipping and Shipbuilding Industries since 1930', in David J. Starkey and Alan Jamieson (eds), *Exploiting the Sea, Aspects of Britain's Maritime Economy since 1980* (Exeter, 1998), pp. 83–84.

2. Alan Jamieson, '"Not More Ports, But Better Ports": The Development of British Ports since 1945', *The Northern Mariner*, VI (1996), p. 29.

3. Henry Rees, *British Ports and Shipping* (London, 1958), pp. 76–79.

4. Rees, *British Ports*, pp. 76–79.

5. Rees, *British Ports*, pp. 76–79.

6. Josephine Klein, *Samples from English Cultures* (London, 1965), p. 130.

7. David F. Wilson, *Dockers: The Impact of Industrial Change* (Woodbridge, 1972), p. 96.

8. Gordon Jackson, *The History and Archaeology of Ports* (London, 1983) pp. 151–52.

9. Interview with Mike by Alex Ombler, 13 May 2013.

10. Sarah Palmer, 'Ports 1840–1970', in M. J. Daunton (ed.), *The Cambridge Urban History of Britain, Vol. III* (Cambridge, 2000), p. 149.

11. Sam Davies, 'The History of the Hull Dockers, c. 1870–1960', in Sam Davies, Colin J. Davis, David de Vries, Lex Heerna Van Voss, Lidewij Hesselink and Klaus Weinhauer (eds), *Dock Workers: International Explorations in Comparative Labour History, 1790–1970* (Aldershot, 2000), p. 185.

12. Interview with Paul by Alex Ombler, 7 April 2014.

13. T. S. Simey (ed.), *The Dock Worker: An Analysis of Conditions of Employment in the Port of Manchester* (Liverpool, 1956), p. 43.

14. 'Docklife', *Hull Daily Mail*, 3 August 1996, p. 4.

15. Davies, 'History of the Hull Dockers', pp. 193–94.

16. Interview with Shirley and June by Alex Ombler, 7 May 2013.

17. Jeremy Tunstall, *The Fishermen: The Sociology of an Extreme Occupation* (London, 1969), p. 171.

18. G. W. Horobin, 'Community and Occupation in the Hull Fishing Industry', *The British Journal of Sociology*, 8 (1957), pp. 343–56.

19. Horobin, 'Community and Occupation', pp. 348, 354.

20. Tunstall, *The Fishermen*.

21. Interview with Michael P. by Jo Byrne, 21 November 2012.

22. Horobin, 'Community and Occupation'.

23. The term Trawlertown is widely associated with the folk album by John Conolly and Pete Sumner, *Trawlertown: The Singing of the Fishing* (Fellside, 2000). Predating this is the local history video, *Trawlertowns – Hull and Grimsby* (Forest Edge, 1993).

24. Alec Gill, *Hessle Road: A Photographer's View of Hull's Trawling Days* (Beverley, 1987), p. 29.

25. Interviews with Victor and Pauline by Jo Byrne, 31 August 2013, and with Billy by Jo Byrne, 24 April 2013.

26. Interview with Gill by Jo Byrne, 10 September 2013.

27. Interview with Alan H. by Jo Byrne, 29 November 2012.

28. Interview with Ivy by Jo Byrne, 22 April 2013.

29. Interview with Jim by Jo Byrne, 9 November 2012.

30. Horobin, 'Community and Occupation', p. 348.

31. Bill Hunter, *They Knew Why They Fought: Unofficial Struggles and Leadership on the Docks, 1945–1989* (London, 1994).

32. Keith Sinclair, *How the Blue Union Came to the Hull Docks* (Hull, 1995).

33. Wilson, *Dockers*, p. 113.

34. Wilson, *Dockers*, p. 113.

35. Interview with X (name omitted) by Alex Ombler, 2 April 2014.

36. UK National Archives, MT 63/496, Ports Efficiency Committee – Effect of Inland Transport Difficulties on Turnaround of Ships, 1952.

37. *Report Concerning Transport Workers' Wages* (HMSO, 1920), p. 165.

38. Interview with Dennis, Barry and Clive by Alex Ombler, 2 April 2013.

39. Jackson, *History and Archaeology of Ports*, pp. 151–56.

40. *Final Report of the Committee of Inquiry into certain matters concerning the Port Transport Industry* (HMSO, 1965), p. 88

41. *Hull Daily Mail*, 18 September 1967.

42. *Hull Daily Mail*, 16 July 1970.

43. Interview with X (name omitted) by Alex Ombler, 2 April 2014.

44. Roger Mumby-Croft and Michaela Barnard, 'An Antiquated Relationship? Trawler Owners and Trawlermen, 1880–1980', in D. J. Starkey, C. Reid and N. Ashcroft (eds), *England's Sea Fisheries: The Commercial Sea Fisheries of England and Wales since 1300* (London, 2000), p. 126.

45. Interview with John K. by Jo Byrne, 12 July 2013.

46. Group discussion with former skippers and White Fish Authority professionals, 8 November 2012.

47. Interview with Tom Boyd by Jo Byrne, 19 November 2013.

48. Interview with Dave B. by Jo Byrne, 29 October 2013.

49. Interview with Michael P.

50. Interview with Thomas N. by Jo Byrne, 23 September 2013

51. Interview with Margaret by Jo Byrne, 25 September 2013.

52. Interview with Mike by Alex Ombler, 13 May 2013.

53. Wilson, *Dockers*, pp. 192–93.

54. National Dock Labour Board, *Amenities Report*, 1966.

55. Wilson, *Dockers*, pp. 296–307.

56. Terry Turner, *Diary of the Docks Dispute 1972–1973* (Hull, 1980), p. v.

57. Turner, *Diary of the Docks Dispute*; *Hull Daily Mail*, 10 July 1984; *Hull Daily Mail*, 31 August 1984.

58. *Hull Daily Mail*, 11 July 1989.

59. Interview with Bob by Jo Byrne, 12 July 2013.

60. Interview with X (name omitted) by Jo Byrne, 21 April 2013.

61. Interview with Tom Boyd.

62. Interview with Chris by Jo Byrne, 6 February 2013.

63. Interview with Ken.

64. Interview with Chris.

65. Interview with Gill.

66 Interview with Ken.

67 Interview with Christine by Jo Byrne, 24 September 2013.

68 Interview with X (named omitted) by Alex Ombler, 2 April 2014.

69 Interview with X (named omitted) by Alex Ombler, 2 April 2014.

70 Phillip Jones and John North, 'Ports and Wharves', in David Symes (ed.), *Humberside in the Eighties: A Spatial View of the Economy* (Hull, 1987), pp. 104–05.

71 Colin McNicol, *Hull's Victoria Dock Village* (Beverley, 2002).

72 Interview with Thomas N.

73 Interview with Lily by Jo Byrne, 10 September 2013.

74 Interview with Jim.

75 Interview with Michael P.

76 Interview with Andrew by Alex Ombler, 22 May 2013.

77 Associated British Ports, *Annual Reports & Accounts 1991*, p. 12.

78 Interview with Michael P.

79 Craig Lazenby and David J. Starkey, 'Altered Images: Representing Trawling in the Late Twentieth Century', in David J. Starkey, Chris Reid and Neil Ashcroft (eds), *England's Sea Fisheries: The Commercial Sea Fisheries of England and Wales since 1300* (London, 2000), pp. 166–72; David Atkinson, Steven Cooke and Derek Spooner, 'Tales from the Riverbank: Place-Marketing and Maritime Heritages', *International Journal of Heritage Studies*, 8.1 (2002), pp. 25–40.

80 *The Sun* (London), 11 August 1972.

81 *Hull Daily Mail*, 29 April 1983.

82 Jackson, *History and Archaeology of Ports*.

Timeline

c. 4900–4000 BC	Hunter-gatherers present in Sutton (north Hull) during Late Mesolithic period (Middle Stone Age); evidence consists of a pebble macehead. Thick layer of peat forming in area that is now central Hull
c. 4000–2400 BC	Neolithic (New Stone Age) activity on the slopes of the Hull valley on the north-western edges of Hull; evidence consists of flint arrowheads and polished stone axes found in Kirk Ella, Anlaby and Willerby. On the valley floor alongside the River Hull, peat begins to form at around c. 3290 cal BC; this process continued for the next thousand years in other parts of the future city. Growth of forests on the edges of the peat
c. 900–750 BC	A central European bronze axe and the remains of a boat found at Alexandra Dock, and pottery found in north Hull, indicate Bronze Age settlement
c. 750–500 BC	Settlement at Castle Hill, Swine (on the north-eastern edges of Hull), demonstrated by finds of Early Iron Age pottery
c. 300–100 BC	Middle Iron Age activity shown by the find of a sword in Hymers Avenue. Pottery of similar date now known from several sites in north, east and west Hull
c. 50 BC–AD 100	At least two enclosures, five roundhouses, pottery and animal bone indicate settlement at Saltshouse Road, east Hull. Salt-working was being practised near Preston Road (east Hull)
c. AD 71–200	Romano-British settlements established alongside the bends in the River Hull, from Stoneferry northwards into Kingswood and beyond. Excavated settlements at Malmo Road, Gibraltar Farm, and at the Foredyke
AD 300–335	Roman coin hoard from this period found in Sutton
c. 870–1066	Place-name evidence suggests colonisation of slightly higher ground in north and east Hull had begun
1086	Settlements at Sutton, Drypool, Marfleet, Myton and Southcoates recorded in Domesday Book, as well as Anlaby, Bilton, Kirk Ella, Wolfreton and others on the outskirts of the modern city
c. 1160–1182	The port of Wyke mentioned in the Camin Charter, and in documents of the 1190s

1203–05	'Hull' was sixth largest port on England's eastern and southern coasts by amount of customs duties collected
1253–56	The course of the River Hull shifts, and its outlet to the Humber moves almost 1 km east to flow through Sayer's Creek to its modern mouth
1275	Wyke designated customs head port for the north of England
1280	Wyke granted weekly markets and an annual fair
1282	A freshwater supply created for the town, bringing water from Anlaby
1285	First mention of a chapel in Wyke
1289	First Carmelite (or White Friars) friary founded in the town
1290	Wyke collects the third largest total of customs revenue of any port on the east and south coasts of England
1293	Edward I purchases Wyke, and makes Crown Survey of the town. He subsequently founded Kingston upon Hull, expanding the settlement. The new town was granted two weekly markets and a six-week long annual fair
1299	Town Charter granted and Kingston upon Hull established as a royal borough

1300–1499

1300	Hull has its own mint; this was very short-lived, but some of the coins struck here still survive
1302–20	Present east end and transepts of Holy Trinity church built; Holy Trinity was under construction during the fourteenth and fifteenth centuries; Holy Trinity tower completed in the late fifteenth century
1316–17	Foundation of the Augustinian (or Black Friars) friary on the site of present-day Magistrates' Courts, the A63, and parts of two car parks
1320	Crown Rental of the town
1321–24	Hull's first town defences constructed. These originally consisted of a great ditch, enclosing a bank topped by a timber palisade. From the later 1330s the timber defences were gradually replaced by massive brick walls, which took over 70 years to complete
1320s	Scale Lane constructed
c. 1320	St Mary's church completed
c. 1330	de la Pole family acquire the manor of Myton
1331	Burgesses of the town granted freedom from the authority of the royal keeper for the one-off sum of £166 13s 4d [plus £70 per annum]
1331–34	Meat market (or shambles) established in The Butchery (now Queen Street)

1333	Guildhall mentioned for first time in documentary records
1347	Crown Rental of the town. Street names make it clear that a school already existed somewhere to the south of Holy Trinity
1357	Guild of the Virgin Mary founded
1358	Corpus Christi Guild (for Merchants) founded
1364	Guild House of Corpus Christ Guild (Beverley Street) first mentioned in documentary records
1369	Holy Trinity Guild (for Shipmen) founded
1377	Poll tax records a population of 1,557 adult taxpayers in Hull
1378	Carthusian Priory (or Charterhouse) founded. Part of it now underlies Charterhouse School, off Wincolmlee
1380s	de la Pole Manor, now called 'Courthall', rebuilt
1401	Freshwater supply greatly improved by the construction of Julian's Dyke
1402	Riots against the Mayoralty
1412–13	Crafts guilds in existence
1420s–1430s	Hull merchants and seafarers engaged in Iceland fisheries. Rivalry with merchants of Iceland, Norway and Denmark over commercial rights
1440	Hull given corporate status, and made a county in its own right
1442	Hull's aldermen listed by name in documentary records
1447	New county of Hull extended over 5 miles to the west. Hull Corporation given authority to appoint an Admiral for the county of Hull, the township of Drypool and the whole of the Humber
1449–61	Hull briefly has its own piped water supply, making it one of the most advanced towns in northern England, but crippling financial problems, made worse by the Wars of the Roses, force the corporation to dig up the lead pipes and sell them to pay off its debts
1460s–1470s	Conflict between Hull and Hanse merchants over commercial rights
1460s	Holy Trinity Guild constructs hall, chapel and almshouses
1468	The *Valentine* of Hull seized by Denmark
1474	Hanse Peace Treaty signed
1490	Ordinances for the Guild of Weavers established
1498	Ordinances for the Guilds of Fullers and Shearmen established
1499	Ordinances for the Guild of Glovers and Guild of Merchants established

1500–1699

1515	Fish market established in what would become Fish Street
1518	St Mary's tower collapsed

1536	Pilgrimage of Grace spreads from Lincolnshire to Yorkshire in early October. On 20 October the Pilgrim Army seize Hull and hold it until the peace of early December
1537	Second rebellion of the Pilgrimage of Grace fails at Hull in January. Leaders of the first rebellion tried in May and executed in summer
1537	Outbreaks of plague reported; further outbreaks occur in 1575–76, 1602–04 and 1637
1538–39	First detailed maps of the town made (probably surveyed by John Rogers) in preparation for the construction of new town defences
1538–41	Ferry across the River Hull to Drypool replaced by a bridge. This is the origin of North Bridge
1541–43	Three new blockhouses, connected by a massive curtain wall, constructed on the east bank of the Hull. Other parts of the town walls and gates strengthened
1539	The Suppression of Religious Houses Act 1539 closes the remaining monastic houses, including the two friaries in Hull
1540s	Protestant minister John Rough preaches in the town. He fled when Mary I came to the throne and was burnt at the stake in London in 1557
1541	Henry VIII twice visits the town and inspects the defences
1548	Hull Grammar School given a royal warrant
1572	The Corporation of Hull bans mummers and masked players, having previously forbidden excessive drinking, lewd conduct and blasphemy
1583	New and larger schoolroom constructed in the building now called The Old Grammar School in South Churchside. Upper floor used by a guild of merchants as the Merchants' Hall
1588	Town walls repaired in response to fears about the Spanish Armada. Further defensive works built in 1620s and 1630s, with new South Battery constructed in 1637
1594	Charity Hall established on the north side of Whitefriargate
c. 1600	Hull Castle used as a gaol for recusant clergymen, at least 12 of whom died there
1626	Growing tensions over 'Ship Money' demanded of Hull by the Crown
1642	Charles I turned away from the town gates by Sir John Hotham
1642	First siege of Hull in July
1643	Second siege of Hull in September
1659	Andrew Marvell first returned as MP for Hull
1661	Holy Trinity church becomes a parish church, independent of the chapel of Hessle
1672	Presbyterian meeting house built in Blackfriargate
1673	Hearth Tax records 1,373 households in Hull and a population of at least 6,500

1674	Greenland House, for processing whale products, built above North Bridge
1681–90	Citadel built on east side of River Hull
1688	Catholic governor overthrown on 'Town Taking Day' (4 December)
1692	Presbyterian chapel built in Bowlalley Lane
1697	Celia Fiennes visits the town, noting 'the buildings of Hull are very neat, good streets'
1698	Independent chapel built in Dagger Lane

1700–1899

1725	William Mason, poet, born at Holy Trinity vicarage, Vicar Lane
1730	Vicar's School, Vicar Lane established, Hull's first public elementary school
1732	Sugar House (refinery) built
1734	King William III statue erected in Market Place
1735	Publication of Thomas Gent's *History of the Royal and Beautiful Town of Kingston upon Hull*
1739	*Hull Courant*, Hull's first newspaper, published. Ceased in 1750, revived 1755–59
1743	Destruction of Maister House, High Street, by fire
1744–46	Turnpike Trusts established for Hull–Beverley, Hull–Anlaby–Kirk Ella and Hull–Preston–Hedon roads
1752	John Wesley visits Hull for the first time
1752	Assembly Rooms, Dagger Lane, built
1753	Trinity House almshouse rebuilt
1757	Baptist chapel built in Salthouse Lane
1759	William Wilberforce born in what is now Wilberforce House on High Street
1766	Hull's whaling industry revived
1768	Theatre Royal built in Finkle Street
1771	Methodist chapel built in Manor Alley
1773	Steam engine introduced at water works
1774	Hull Dock Company established by Act of Parliament, Britain's first private dock company
1775	Hull Subscription Library founded
1778	The Dock, later Old Dock and (from 1854) Queen's Dock, opened on Tuesday 22 September. Construction had begun on 19 October 1775. It closed in 1930 and was filled in and landscaped to form Queen's Gardens
1801	Hull's population in the first decennial census is 22,161

1809	Humber Dock opened. Construction had begun in 1807. Closed to shipping in 1967, and reopened as Hull Marina in 1983
1813	Hull Cricket Club plays its first match
1829	Junction Dock opened. Renamed Prince's Dock in 1854. Closed to shipping in 1968. Redeveloped to accommodate Prince's Quay Shopping Centre in 1991
1840	Hull–Selby Railway opened
1845	First public baths opened at Stoneferry
1846	Railway Dock opened on Friday 18 June. Closed to shipping in 1968. Now part of Hull Marina
1850	Victoria Dock opened on Wednesday 3 July. Construction had begun in 1846. Closed to shipping on 1 February 1970. Filled in and developed into a housing estate in 1988
1851	Hull's population in the decennial census is 84,690
1861	Thomas Wilson Sons and Company – the Wilson Line – formally established as partnership between Thomas Wilson and his two youngest sons, Charles H. Wilson and Arthur Wilson, through an indenture signed on 12 July
1865	Hull Football Club (Hull FC) founded
1869	Albert Dock opened in July
1873	William Wright Dock opened on Monday 24 May. Joined with Albert Dock in 1910
1878	Hull & District XI play the Australians at Argyle Street cricket ground
1879	Hull Athletic Club founded
1882	Hull Kingston Rovers founded by apprentice boilermakers on Hessle Road
1883	St Andrew's Dock opened on Monday 24 September. Home of the fishing industry. Closed to shipping on 3 November 1985. Filled in and now a retail park
1885	Alexandra Dock opened on 16 July. Built by the Hull & Barnsley Railway Company, primarily to export coal extracted from the south Yorkshire coalfield
1887	First women's rugby match staged near the Elephant and Castle, Holderness Road
1891	Thos Wilson Sons & Co. Ltd formally established as private limited company owned by Charles H. Wilson and Arthur Wilson and five other members of the Wilson family
1893	Hull Dock Company, which built, owned and operated all of Hull's docks excepting Alexandra Dock, taken over by North East Railway Company
1898	The Circle opened on Anlaby Road. Yorkshire CCC played its first match there in 1899

1901	Hull's population in the decennial census is 236,772
1901	Hull & East Riding rugby union club founded
1904	Hull Golf Club founded
1904	Hull City Association Football Club founded
1905	Hull City AFC accepted into Division 2 of the Football League
1907	Riverside Quay opened
1911	Hull's population in the decennial census is 277,991
1914	King George Dock opened on 26 June
1916	Saltend Oil Jetties opened
1916	Thos Wilson Sons & Co. Ltd sold in October to John Reeves Ellerman, who had been born in Hull, for £4.3m. The firm, dubbed the 'largest privately owned shipping firm in the world' in 1912, became Ellerman's Wilson Line and operated out of Hull until the late 1970s
1921	Hull's population in the decennial census is 295,017
1921	First women's soccer match played in Hull
1927	Ferens Art Gallery opened on 29 November. The opening exhibition included many works bought by Thomas Robinson Ferens himself
1931	Hull's population in the decennial census is 309,198
1935	Municipal golf course opened at Sutton Park
1938	Hull baseball club win the British Championship
1946	Hull City's Boothferry Park opened
1946	The Dock Workers (Regulation of Employment) Act, 1946 creates the National Dock Labour Scheme, which in turn establishes the Hull and Goole Dock Labour Board
1950	Hull's Jack Hale wins swimming gold medal at British Empire Games
1951	Hull's population in the decennial census is 295,172
1952	Iceland declares a four-mile fishing limit, measured from straight baselines, stretching from coastal features
1955	Philip Larkin moves to Hull as University Librarian; publishes *The Less Deceived* with Hessle-based 'The Marvell Press'
1956	Barbara Buttrick wins the first official women's boxing world championship
1958	Iceland declares a 12-mile fishing limit, precipitating the first Cod War with Britain
1960	Kay Ibbetson becomes first-ever women's rugby league coach
1960	The Queen Mother officially opens the new Library at the University of Hull
1961	Hull's population in the decennial census is 289,716

1962	Britain's first whole fish stern freezer trawler, *Junella*, arrives at St Andrew's Fish Dock
1964	Philip Larkin publishes *The Whitsun Weddings*, containing poems inspired by experiences and places in Hull, such as 'Here', 'Broadcast', 'Toads Revisited' and 'The Large Cool Store'
1965–69	'Unit-load revolution': new roll-on/roll-off berths and container terminal constructed at King George Dock and newly opened Queen Elizabeth Dock
1965–71	Following the Devlin Committee's *Inquiry into Certain Matters Concerning the Port Transport Industry*, Hull's dockers are de-casualised and piece-work wage structure reformed in line with modern, mechanised cargo-handling methods
1966	Roger Tighe wins light-heavyweight boxing gold at the Commonwealth Games
1967	Douglas Dunn publishes debut collection, *Terry Street*, drawing on his experiences living off Beverley Road
1968	Triple Trawler Disaster: three Hull trawlers lost within a month: *Kingston Peridot* and *St Romanus* (11 January), *Ross Cleveland* (4 February)
1970	The Port of Hull comes to a standstill during the first national dock strike since 1926
1970	The tower block and second stage of the University's Brynmor Jones Library, overseen by Librarian Philip Larkin, officially opened
1970–73; 1975–76	'The Spiders from Mars' play with Ziggy Stardust, David Bowie's *alter ego*. Many of the Spiders, notably Mick Ronson, Trevor Bolder and Mick Woodmansey, were from Hull and district
1971	Hull's population in the decennial census is 285,965
1971	Hull Vikings bring speedway to the Boulevard
1972–73	Second Cod War between Britain and Iceland triggered by Icelandic government's declaration of a 50-mile fishing limit
1974	*Gaul*, a Hull freezer trawler with a crew of 36, lost without trace, triggering decades of speculation about the circumstances leading to the tragedy
1974	Philip Larkin publishes *High Windows*, containing poems inspired by experiences and places in Hull, such as 'Friday Night in the Royal Station Hotel' and 'The Building'
1975	Hull's fishing fleet moves to refurbished Albert and William Wright Dock
1975	Iceland extends fishing limits to 200 miles, precipitating third Cod War
1976	Britain agrees 200-mile Icelandic fishing limit; Hull trawlers withdraw from Icelandic waters on 1 December
1977	Britain declares 200-mile fishing exclusion zone, managed as part

	of European 'common pond'. Canada, Norway and Russia extend limits to 200 miles in a new global era of managed fisheries
1979	Spiders nightclub opened on Cleveland Street. The music venue quickly became the 'alternative home' of rock, punk, Motown, indie and metal music in Hull
1980	Hull KR defeat Hull FC 10–5 at Wembley in Rugby League Challenge Cup Final
1981	Hull's population in the decennial census is 266,751
1981	Humber Bridge opened. 'Bridge for the Living', a cantata composed by Anthony Hedges with words by Philip Larkin, first performed at Hull City Hall in April
1982	Douglas Dunn publishes *A Rumoured City*, an anthology of new poets from Hull, with a foreword by Philip Larkin
1982	Peter Didsbury publishes debut poetry collection, *The Butchers of Hull*
1983	Sean O'Brien publishes debut poetry collection, *The Indoor Park*
1983–91	Hull's derelict Town and Victoria Docks regenerated into Hull Marina, Prince's Quay shopping centre and Victoria Dock Village
1985	Philip Larkin dies in Hull on 2 December, aged 63
1989	National Dock Labour Scheme abolished
1991	Hull's population in the decennial census is 266,180
1992	Sharon Rendle wins judo bronze medal at the Olympic Games
1993	Mick Ronson, session musician, guitarist, multi-instrumentalist, song-writer, arranger, and producer dies on 29 April, aged 46. Ronson achieved great success with the Spiders from Mars

2000–

2000	Hull Trains commences direct rail services to and from London King's Cross on 25 September
2001	Hull's population in the decennial census is 243,589
2002	KC Stadium opened on the site of the Circle
2002	The Deep opened in March. Situated at Sammy's Point, at the confluence of the rivers Hull and Humber, this remains 'the world's only submarium'
2007	Hull experiences severe flooding on 15 June and again, more severely, on 25 June. The city council reported that 7,800 houses and 1,300 business premises were flooded, and an estimated 35,000 people suffered damage and loss as a result of water inundation
2007	John Prescott, MP for Hull East, resigns as Deputy Prime Minister on 27 June, a post he had held since 2 May 1997

2007	Paragon Interchange, a facility in which Hull's rail and bus termini are integrated under the canopy of a railshed built in 1900, opened in September, together with the adjacent St Stephen's shopping centre
2008	Hull's first Freedom Festival of music and performing arts held in Queen's Gardens. Named in recognition of William Wilberforce's struggle against the slave trade, the Freedom Festival has since become a major annual cultural event
2008	Hull City defeat Bristol City 1–0 on 24 May at Wembley Stadium to win promotion to the English Premier League for the first time in club's 104-year history
2010	Hull History Centre opened on 25 January. This archive and education centre was the outcome of a collaboration between Hull City Council and the University of Hull, the first such partnership in the UK
2010	John Prescott resigns as MP for Hull East on 12 April to take his place as The Lord Prescott in the House of Lords. He had been one of Hull's three MPs since 19 June 1970
2010	*Old City, New Rumours: A Hull Anthology*, edited by Ian Gregson and Carol Rumens, published
2010	On 25th anniversary of his death, a bronze statue of Philip Larkin, sculpted by Martin Jennings, is unveiled on Paragon Station concourse
2011	Boothferry Park, home of Hull City from 1946 to 2002, demolished
2012	Luke Campbell wins bantamweight boxing gold at the Olympic Games
2013	Hull named UK City of Culture for 2017 on 20 November
2014	Hull City contest the FA Cup Final for the first time, losing 3–2 to Arsenal in extra time despite leading 2–0 after 10 minutes (17 May)
2015	The Dean of Westminster, the Very Reverend Dr John Hall, visits Brynmor Jones Library and announces the dedication of a memorial stone to Philip Larkin in Westminster Abbey; Carol Ann Duffy, Poet Laureate, officially opens the Brynmor Jones Library following a £28 million redevelopment, describing it as 'the best university library I have ever seen'
2016	Hull FC win the Rugby League Challenge Cup at Wembley for the first time, defeating Warrington Wolves 12–10 (27 August)
2016	Memorial to Philip Larkin unveiled in Poets' Corner, Westminster Abbey, on 2 December

Notes on Contributors

David Atkinson is a Professor of Cultural and Historical Geography who has worked at the University of Hull since 1998. His research encompasses the histories of geographical knowledge, science, imaginations and understandings; the landscapes and memories of twentieth-century Italy; and the experience, representations and legacies of Italian colonialism. He has also researched the history, heritage and cultural geographies of Hull and he has supervised a series of PhD students on Hull-based themes. His books include *Cultural Geography* (Tauris, 2005) and *Geopolitical Traditions* (Routledge, 2000).

Jo Byrne was born and raised in Hull and, after living in South Yorkshire and the Midlands, she returned home in 1997. She has over twenty years' experience as a heritage and built environment practitioner. The daughter of a trawlerman, Jo has a longstanding interest in the fishing industries and in 2015 she completed a PhD at the University of Hull's Maritime Historical Studies Centre on Hull's distant-water fishery in the aftermath of the Cod Wars. This research spanned history, cultural geography and heritage curatorship; it also linked themes of time and place, and Jo advocates the importance of cultural heritage in building senses of place and social well-being.

Susan Capes is Assistant Curator at Hull Museums, part of Hull Culture and Leisure Ltd, where she has worked since 2005. She studied for a BA and MA in History at the University of Hull and an MA in Museum Studies at the University of Leicester. She has lived in Hull for most of her life and, along with her colleagues, is committed to promoting Hull Museums as a major visitor destination. She is currently working on the Humber Museums Partnership project (funded by Arts Council England) which links museums across Hull, the East Riding of Yorkshire and North Lincolnshire. Her most recent publication was an entry on Madame Clapham for the 2016 edition of the *Oxford Dictionary of National Biography*.

Katharine Cockin, Professor of English at the University of Hull, is interested in northern English literary production and cultures. She is editor of *The Literary North* (Palgrave, 2012), a collection of essays from the Literary North conference (2006) with additional contributions by Sean O'Brien and Josephine Guy. She also developed a postgraduate module on the Literary North and curated a series of public talks as the 'North and South Culture Café' at University of Hull (2014–16). Forthcoming publications include 'Writing Back from the "Strange Country": Literature from the North of England', in *Accelerated Times: British Literature in Transition, Vol. 5: 1980–2000* (Cambridge, 2018) and 'Re-reading *Edge of Darkness* (1985): The Power of Northernness and the "Man of Feeling"', in *Heading North: The North of England in Film and Television* (Palgrave, 2018). In 2016 she gave a public lecture for the Hull branch of Amnesty International on Dr Mary Murdoch at Hull History Centre.

Tony Collins is Professor of History at De Montfort University in Leicester. He is the author of a number of books on the social history of sport, including *Rugby's Great Split: Class, Culture and the Origins of Rugby League Football* (Cass, 1998), *The Oval World: A Global History of Rugby* (Bloomsbury, 2015) and *Sport in Capitalist Society* (Routledge, 2013). He was editor of the academic journal *Sport in History* from 2001 to 2009 and also works on British social history and British imperial history. Born and bred in Hull, he attended South Holderness School and is today a director of the Hull KR Community Trust.

A scholar of literature and history, Victoria Samantha Dawson is completing a PhD in history at De Montfort University, Leicester. She previously gained a BA in English at the University of Hull and an MA in English Literary Studies at the University of York. Her research interests include issues of class, gender, community, science, and social and cultural identity, and she has written chapters in *Bram Stoker and the Gothic: Formations to Transformations* (Palgrave, 2016) and *13 Inspirations: The Guiding Lights of Rugby League* (Scratching Shed, 2014). Victoria moved to Hull as a child, attended Thoresby and Sydney Smith Schools, and despite being a mild Hull FC fan she is a proud member of the Hull Kingston Rovers Heritage Committee.

D. H. Evans was the last County Archaeologist for Humberside, and subsequently served as the Archaeology Manager for the City of Hull and the East Riding of Yorkshire councils for two decades. During a 43-year career as a professional archaeologist, he covered both field archaeology and curatorial roles in almost equal measure. He has worked extensively on both rural and urban archaeology projects in the region, and has published widely on these themes. His research interests are diverse, but he specialises in the archaeology of medieval and post-medieval northern European towns.

Nicholas Evans is Lecturer in Diaspora History at the University of Hull. His PhD was based at the University of Hull's Maritime Historical Studies Centre and explored the forgotten story of European transmigration to North America via the UK between 1836 and 1914. Alongside his scholarly work he has worked as a historical advisor to the BBC, the National Archives and numerous heritage organisations. He is presently a member of the university's Wilberforce Institute for the Study of Slavery and Emancipation, where he has played a key role in raising awareness of the city's migrant heritage.

Janine Hatter is an Early Career Researcher in the University of Hull's Centre for Nineteenth-Century Studies. Her research interests centre on nineteenth-century literature, art and culture, with particular emphasis on popular fiction. She has published on Mary Braddon, Bram Stoker, the theatre and identity, short stories as a genre, and Victorian women's life writing, as well as nineteenth- to twenty-first-century science fiction and the Gothic. She is co-editor of two series, *New Paths in Victorian Fiction and Culture* and *Key Popular Women Writers* (both Edward Everett Root Publishers); co-organiser for the Victorian Popular Fiction Association; and co-founder of the Mary Elizabeth Braddon Association.

Brian Lavery is a Scottish writer, journalist and creative writing tutor based in Hull. His book, *The Headscarf Revolutionaries: Lillian Bilocca and the Hull Triple Trawler Disaster*, was published by Barbican Press in 2015, and he also contributed the entry for 'Mrs Lillian Bilocca' in the *Oxford Dictionary of National Biography* (2013). He is an Honorary Research Fellow of the University of Hull.

Briony McDonagh is a historical and cultural geographer at the University of Hull. She is the author of *Elite Women and the Agricultural Landscape* (Routledge, 2017), and has published widely on the geographies of riot and rebellion, on women's histories and on the history of the English landscape. Her particular interest in Hull and the East Riding stretches back to her PhD research on the late medieval and early modern Yorkshire landscape. She is also chair of the Historical Geography Research Group of the Royal Geographical Society (with the Institute of British Geographers) and co-director of the University of Hull's 'Gender, Place and Memory' research cluster.

Sarah McKeon is Academic Coordinator of the Heritage Consortium in the Faculty of Arts, Cultures and Education at the University of Hull. She was awarded a PhD by the University of Aberystwyth in 2014 for her thesis on '"The Blake Cloude of Errour": poetry, philosophy, and the Boethian aesthetic in the late fourteenth century'. She has research interests in the history of ideas and specialises in late medieval and early modern literary studies. McKeon's book on cultural assimilation in the English vernacular, *c.* 1380–1500, will be published by Brepols. She also contributes to the 'Lay Literacy in England *c.* 1350–1550' project, and is a collaborator in the 'New Communities of Interpretation' research network.

Kevin Milburn is a Teaching Fellow in the Department of Culture, Media and Creative Industries at King's College London, and formerly Teaching Fellow in Human Geography at the University of Hull. He gained his PhD, 'Songs of the City: Geographies of Metropolitanism and Mobility in the Music of Frank Sinatra and The Blue Nile', from the University of Nottingham, and holds an MA in Japanese Cultural Studies from Birkbeck, University of London and an MLitt in Media Culture from Strathclyde University. His research examines culture and identity in music, film and painting, and how notions of place, memory and belonging are shaped by, and in turn shape, different forms of creative practice.

Stewart Mottram is Lecturer in Late Medieval and Early Modern Literature at the University of Hull. His research explores the role of English literature in shaping regional, national and religious identities across the course of the long Reformation in England and Wales (1520–1688). He has a particular interest in how Hull helped shape the life and literature of the poet and politician, Andrew Marvell (1621–78). He organised an exhibition on Marvell and Hull at Hull History Centre in autumn 2015, gives regular public talks on this theme, and has discussed Marvell's poetry on BBC Radio 4. He is author or editor of several books.

David Neave was Senior Lecturer in Regional and Local History at the University of Hull, where he is now a Life Fellow. He is the author of over 60 books and articles on aspects of the social, landscape and architectural history of east Yorkshire. These include a revision of the Pevsner volume on the buildings of York and the East Riding, and co-authorship (with Dr Susan Neave) of the *Pevsner Architectural Guide to Hull* (Yale, 2010). An active conservationist, in 2008 he was awarded an honorary degree from the University of York for the promotion of the history and heritage of the region.

Susan Neave is Honorary Research Fellow in History at Hull University, and worked for a number of years for the *Victoria County History*. She has written extensively on the buildings and landscape of the region, and is currently researching pre-eighteenth-century houses in Beverley as part of Historic England's 'Early Fabric in Historic Towns' project. She is joint author of the *Pevsner Architectural Guide to Hull* (Yale, 2010).

Alex Ombler has research interests in the history and geography of ports and their communities. He was awarded a PhD in human geography at the University of Hull for his thesis on 'The Port of Hull, 1945–2000: Change, Adaptation and Memory', which explored how the economic, technological and political developments of the post-1945 period impacted the working population and landscape of Hull's waterfront. He previously completed an MA at Hull on the social implications of naval impressment during the eighteenth and early nineteenth centuries, and contributed to a study of the drainage history of the River Hull valley. He works as an Archives Assistant at the East Riding Council's Archives and Local Studies Service.

Robb Robinson is based at the Maritime Historical Studies Centre, University of Hull. He is from Hull, and both sides of his family engaged in seafaring for generations. His research interests include international fisheries history, whaling, the maritime history of Yorkshire and the North Sea, the role of coastal communities in the First World War and the historic impact of people from Hull across the globe. The author of four books and a wide range of articles, he was an academic advisor to the BBC *World War One at Home* series, and has contributed to a number of TV and radio programmes. Between 1988 and 1991 he was Honorary General Secretary of the City of Hull Athletic Club.

Elisabeth Salter is Professor of Medieval Studies and Cultural Creativity at the University of Hull. She uses archival evidence, including last wills and testaments, to reconstruct the lives and lived experiences of women and men in town and country *c.* 1350–1600. She has a particular interest in popular literacy and religious experience. She is a member of the management committee for a European network that explores new communities of interpretation in medieval and early modern Europe. Her most recent book is *Popular Reading in English c. 1400–1600* (Manchester University Press, 2012) and she is currently working on her fourth book, *The Poetics of Popular Religious Reading c. 1350–1550* for Amsterdam University Press.

David J. Starkey is editor-in-chief of the *International Journal of Maritime History*. Some time ago, when Britain still had shipping and shipbuilding industries, he was awarded a PhD by the University of Exeter for his thesis on 'British Privateering, 1702–1783'. He was Europe's first Lecturer in Maritime History when he joined the University of Hull in 1994. Now Professor of Maritime History at Hull, Starkey's research interests embrace all aspects of humankind's relationship with the sea, particularly shipping, seafaring, piracy, privateering and the fisheries in the North Atlantic region since the late seventeenth century. He was once Head of the History Department at Hull (2011–16), but will always be the father of four fine children – Frankie, Michael, Ellen and Lois – to whom his contribution to this book is dedicated.

Jane Thomas teaches and researches the literature of the nineteenth and early twentieth centuries, British women's writing and the 'literature of place'. She has worked at the University of Hull since 1995 and regards the city as her adopted home having arrived in 1973 as an undergraduate and worked for some years at Hull Truck Theatre while completing her PhD. A specialist in the work of Thomas Hardy, her research also encompasses other regional writers including Winifred Holtby and Hubert Nicholson. She has written two monographs and several articles and book chapters on Hardy as well as editing critical editions of his novels. She has also published on the interaction between the visual arts and literature, in particular sculpture and ekphrasis, and is currently working on the novels and paintings of Beryl Bainbridge. She was a Research Fellow of the Henry Moore Institute (2013–14) and has been the Academic Director of the International Thomas Hardy Society since 2010.

James Underwood is Research Fellow in Modern and Contemporary Literature at the University of Huddersfield, where he works on the Ted Hughes Network. His research interests are in twentieth- and twenty-first-century poetry, literary biography, and poets and letter-writing. His PhD on the work of Philip Larkin was awarded by the University of Hull in 2015, and he is currently working on a monograph entitled *Early Larkin*.

Daniel Weston is Lecturer in English Literature at the University of Greenwich. His monograph, *Contemporary Literary Landscapes: The Poetics of Experience*, was published by Ashgate in January 2016. He has published work on modern and contemporary poetry, prose fiction and non-fiction, with particular emphasis on literary geographies and place writing. He was a lecturer in the Department of English at the University of Hull between 2012 and 2015.

Martin Wilcox is a Lecturer in History at the University of Hull. He gained his MA and PhD at Hull before moving to the University of Greenwich as a postdoctoral fellow to work on the 'Sustaining the Empire' project where he was co-author (with Roger Knight) of *Sustaining the Fleet 1793–1815: War, the British Navy and the Contractor State* (Boydell & Brewer, 2010). He returned to the University of Hull in 2014 and his current research encompasses various aspects of modern British and international maritime history.

Index

Page numbers in *italics* indicate illustrations.